*Working in the Service Society*

IN THE SERIES

# Labor and Social Change

*edited by Paula Rayman and
Carmen Sirianni*

# Working in the Service Society

EDITED BY

Cameron Lynne Macdonald
and Carmen Sirianni

TEMPLE UNIVERSITY PRESS    Philadelphia

Temple University Press, Philadelphia 19122
Copyright © 1996 by Temple University
All rights reserved
Published 1996
Printed in the United States of America

⊛ The paper used in this publication meets the requirements of the American National Standard
for Information Sciences — Permanence of Paper for Printed Library Materials,
ANSI Z39.48–1984

Text design by Kate Nichols

Library of Congress Cataloging-in-Publication Data

Working in the service society / edited by Cameron Lynne Macdonald and
   Carmen Sirianni.
      p.   cm. — (Labor and social change)
   Includes bibliographical references.
   ISBN 1–56639–479–1 (cloth : alk. paper). —
ISBN 1–56639–480–5 (pbk. : alk. paper)
   1. Service industries workers — United States.   2. Service
industries — United States.   I. Macdonald, Cameron Lynne.
II. Sirianni, Carmen.   III. Series.
HD8039.S452U688   1996
331.7′93′0973 — dc20                                     96–23091

# Contents

# Preface

Recently, this tidbit of service-sector lore crossed our computer screens via the Internet:[1]

A single gate agent was rebooking a long line of inconvenienced travelers after the cancellation of a crowded flight. Suddenly an angry passenger pushed his way to the desk. He slapped his ticket down on the counter and said, "I HAVE to be on this flight and it HAS to be FIRST CLASS."

The agent replied, "I'm sorry, sir, I'll be happy to help you, but I've got to help these folks first, and I'm sure we'll be able to work something out."

The passenger was unimpressed. He asked loudly, so that passengers behind him could hear, "Do you have any idea who I am?"

Without hesitating, the gate agent smiled and reached for her public address microphone.

"May I have your attention please?" she began, her voice bellowing throughout the terminal. "We have a passenger here at the gate *who does not know who he is*. If anyone can help him find his identity, please come to gate 17."

With the passengers behind him in line laughing hysterically, the man glared at the gate agent, gritted his teeth, and swore, "(Expletive) you."

Without flinching, she smiled and said, "I'm sorry, sir, but you'll have to stand in line for that, too."

The man retreated as the people in the terminal applauded loudly.

Although the flight was canceled and passengers were late, they were no longer angry at the airline.

This volume is dedicated to service-sector workers everywhere who serve the public with dignity and good humor.

## NOTE

1. Thanks to Marty Gaetjens for forwarding this story to us.

*Working in the Service Society*

## Chapter 1

# The Service Society and the Changing Experience of Work

• Cameron Lynne Macdonald and Carmen Sirianni

> McDonald's has more employees than U.S. Steel. Golden Arches, not blast furnaces, symbolize the American economy.
> — George Will[1]

> When you see them receiving passengers with that big smile, I don't think it means anything. They have to do that. It's part of their job. But now you get into a conversation with a flight attendant . . . well . . . no . . . I guess they have to do that too.
> — Airline passenger[2]

> Bellboy! I got to get running now.
> Bellboy! Keep my lip buttoned down.
> Bellboy! Carry this baggage out.
> Bellboy! Always running at someone's bleedin' heel.
> — "Bellboy" by Pete Townshend[3]

We live and work in a service society. Employment in the service sector currently accounts for 79 percent of nonagricultural jobs in the United States (U.S. Department of Labor 1994: 83). More important, 90 percent of the new jobs projected to be created by the year 2000 will be in service occupations, while the number of goods-producing jobs is projected to decline (Kutscher 1987: 5). Since the mid-nineteenth century the U.S. economy has been gradually transformed from an agriculture-based economy to a manufacturing-based economy to a service-based economy. Near the turn of the century, employment distribution among the three major economic sectors was equally divided at roughly one-third each. Since then, agriculture's

**U.S. Employment Trends by Sector**

**1850–1990**

Legend
— — —  Service Producing
— – – –  Goods Producing
· · · · · ·  Agriculture

Sources: Michael Urquhart, "The Employment Shift to Services: Where Did It Come From?" *Monthly Labor Review* (April 1984): 15–21; and U.S. Department of Commerce, Bureau of the Census, *Statistical Abstract of the United States* (Washington, DC: U.S. Government Printing Office, 1994), p. 402.

labor market share has declined rapidly, now accounting for only about 3 percent of U.S. jobs, while the service sector provides over 70 percent and the goods-producing sector about 25 percent (see the accompanying graph).

The decrease in proportion of manufacturing jobs occurred not because U.S. corporations manufacture fewer goods, but primarily because they use fewer workers to make the goods they produce (Albrecht and Zemke 1990). They use fewer workers due to increasing levels of automation and the exportation of manufacturing functions to low-wage job markets overseas. In addition, the feminization of the work force has created a self-fulfilling cycle in which the entrance of more women into the work force has led to increased demand for those consumer services once provided gratis by housewives (cleaning, cooking, child care, etc.), which in turn has produced more service jobs that are predominantly filled by women.

Still, these trends fail to account fully for the dominance of service work in the U.S. economy, since companies outside of the service sector also contain service occupations. For example, 13.2 percent of the employees in the manufacturing sector work in service occupations such as clerical work, customer service, telemarketing, and transportation (Kutscher 1987). Further, manufacturing and technical occupations are comprised increasingly of service components as U.S. firms adopt Total Quality Management (TQM) and other customer-focused strategies to generate a competitive edge in the global economy. When production efficiency and quality are maximized, the critical variable in the struggle for economic dominance is the quality of interactions with customers. As one business school professor remarks, "Sooner or later, new technology becomes available to everyone. Customer-oriented employees are a lot harder to copy or buy" (Schlesinger and Heskett 1991: 81). So whether one believes that U.S. manufacturing is going to Mexico, to automation, or to the dogs, it is clear that the United States is increasingly becoming a service society and that service work is here to stay.

What do we mean when we speak of "service work"? By definition, a service is intangible; it is produced and consumed simultaneously, and the customer generally participates in its production (Packham 1992). For the purposes of this volume, service work includes jobs in which face-to-face or voice-to-voice interaction is a fundamental element of the work. "Interactive service work" (Leidner 1993; Chapter 2) generally requires some form of what Arlie Hochschild (1983) has termed "emotional labor," meaning the conscious manipulation of the workers' self-presentation either to display feeling states and/or to create feeling states in others. In addition, the guidelines, or "feeling rules," for this emotional labor are created by management and conveyed to the worker as a critical aspect of the job. The essays in this collection focus on the relational rather than the task-based aspects of service jobs, and examine how relational work shapes workers' experiences on the job.

This book also focuses primarily on the work and experiences of the "emotional proletariat" — the front-line service workers and paraprofessionals engaged in interactive work — even though much managerial and professional work also entails emotional labor. For example, doctors are expected to display an appropriate "bedside manner," lawyers are expert actors in and out of the courtroom, and managers, at the most fundamental level, try to instill feeling states and thus promote action in others. However, there remains a critical distinction between white-collar work and work in the emotional proletariat: in management and in the professions, guidelines for emotional labor are generated collegially and, to a great extent, are self-supervised. In front-line service jobs, workers are given very explicit instructions concerning what to say and how to act, and both consumers and managers watch to ensure that these instructions are carried out. However, one could argue that even those in higher ranking positions increasingly experience the kinds of monitoring of their interactive labor encountered by those lower on the occupational ladder, be it by customers, supervisors, or employees. In this sense, the trends discussed in this book have important implications for a broader spectrum of the work force.

Given the rising dominance of service occupations in the labor force, what are the special difficulties and opportunities that workers encounter in a service society? A key problem seems to be how to inhabit the job. In the past there was a clear distinction between *careers*, which required a level of personalization, emotion management, authenticity in interaction, and general integration of personal and workplace identities, and *jobs*, which required the active engagement of the body and parts of the mind while the spirit and soul of the worker might be elsewhere. Workers in service occupations are asked to inhabit jobs in ways that were formerly limited to managers and professionals alone. They are required to bring some level of personal identity and self-expression into their work, even if it is only at the level of basic interactions, and even if the job itself is only temporary. The assembly-line worker could openly hate his job, despise his supervisor, and even dislike his co-workers, and while this might be an unpleasant state of affairs, if he completed his assigned tasks efficiently, his attitude was his own problem. For the service worker, inhabiting the job means, at the very least, pretending to like it, and, at most, actually bringing his whole self into the job, liking it, and genuinely caring about the people with whom he interacts.

This demand has several implications: who will be asked to fill what jobs, how they are expected to perform, and how they will respond to those demands. Because personal interaction is a primary component of all service occupations, managers continually strive to find ways to oversee and control those interactions, and worker responses to these attempts vary along a continuum from enthusiastic compliance to outright refusal. Hiring, control of the work process, and the stresses of bringing one's emotions to work are all shaped by the characteristics of the worker and the nature of the work. The self-presentation and other personal characteristics of the worker make up the work process and the work product, and are increasingly the domain of management-worker struggles (see Chapter 2 and Leidner 1993). In addition, because much of the labor itself is invisible, contests over control of the labor process are often more implicit than explicit.

This collection will focus on the implications of three trends emanating from the rising dominance of service work. First, the need to supervise the production of an intangible, good service, has given rise to particularly invasive forms of workplace control and has led managers to attempt to oversee areas of workers' personal and psychic lives that have heretofore been considered off-limits. Second, the fact that workers' personal characteristics are so firmly linked to their "suitability" for certain service occupations continues to lead to increasing levels of stratification within the service labor force. Finally, the essays in this volume will consider how workers can respond to these and other aspects of working in the service society, and how they might build autonomy and dignity into their work, ensuring that service work does not equal servitude.

## Management Control of the New Labor Process

As service work has become the leading form of labor in the American economy, sociological perspectives on the nature of the labor process have failed to keep pace. Most industrial sociologists continue to focus on the factory setting (Burawoy 1985; Edwards 1979, 1994), and those who do study service workers often focus on the task-based elements of their work (for example, document production in the office, burger production at the fast-food chain), rather than its relational elements.[4] In addition, as Robin Leidner (Chapter 2) and Steven H. Lopez (Chapter 3) point out, theorists of the manufacturing labor process limit their studies to the management-worker dyad and ignore the role of the customer, a key determinant in shaping the labor process in service jobs. The essays in Part I of this volume attempt to fill this gap by analyzing how managerial attempts to control and supervise the labor process must change when the work under supervision no longer entails the assembly of a product but the creation and maintenance of a relationship.

What happens when we turn our focus to management control of the relational processes of service work? Since the central binary of worker versus manager becomes destabilized by the addition of a third party, the customer, the labor process relationship becomes a triangular interaction that complicates attempts to theorize management control strategies. Ultimately, managers aim to influence customers, using workers as a means to that end; however, the customer's influence on the labor process depends on what Leidner (Chapter 2) terms the "dominant pattern of alliance." Manager and worker may join in league to manipulate or coerce the customer, as seen in Nicole Biggart's discussion of direct sales (Chapter 7); or, as Linda Fuller and Vicki Smith (Chapter 4) point out, manager and customer may jointly supervise the worker. In some cases, workers may even use their hands-on understanding of the needs of the customer to influence management. In addition, as Lopez (Chapter 3) indicates, depending on the importance of a given customer to the economic health of a business, the customer may oversee or override management. In other cases, customer feedback may replace some layers of management altogether.

The management of relationships in the service labor process also requires new forms of control and supervision. The new emphasis on customer service dictates that managers be both more dependent upon and more interested in workers' "demeanor, expression, mood and thought" (Leidner 1993: 9). A primary problem for management in this context becomes how to direct, control, and monitor customer service interactions without disrupting them. Constant personal supervision in these cases would not only frequently be inefficient, but would present the risk of "spoiling" the product: the service relationship. Managers therefore attempt to determine these interactions in advance, combining methods of both technical and bureaucratic control[5] with varying degrees of routinization and indoctrination.

Depending on the nature of the service and customer expectations, managers will tend toward using a "production-line" approach or an "empowerment" approach to direct the work process (Bowen and Lawler 1992). Production-line management of service workers includes strategies such as managing workers via technology. For example, computerized programs prompt telemarketers what to say next. Or, management may adopt techniques of routinization and scripting, as in Disneyland's scripted patter, for example. Managers even routinize the behavior of customers, as Leidner (Chapter 2) shows in her discussion of how McDonald's trains customers to place an order properly. As described by an early advocate of this approach,

> through painstaking attention to total design and facilities planning, everything is built into the machine itself, into the technology of the system. The only choice available to the attendant is to operate it exactly as the designers intended it. (Levitt 1972: 46)

This management approach advocates the "substitution of technology for motivation," replacing spontaneous interaction with predetermined scripts, and supplanting worker decision-making with management design. Proponents of this model argue that it provides both managers and customers with a modicum of consistency and few surprises.

From the standpoint of most labor process theorists, the production-line approach to service management mirrors the deskilling and speed-up trends that are well documented in studies of manufacturing. Decision-making is appropriated in advance by management and coded in tightly scripted routines or bundled into the technical design of the service "plant." As one researcher notes, machines are a "complex bundle of rules that are built into the machine itself. Successful interaction with the machine necessitates compliance with the

rules of the organization" (Sperow, quoted in Rosen and Baroudi 1993: 220).
The result, for workers, is generally low skill, low pay, low security employment that offers little or no autonomy or opportunity for advancement. This
management approach is designed to maximize flexibility while minimizing
costs, often at workers' expense.

When the nature of the customer service interaction requires more flexibility and spontaneity from workers, management will tend to adopt a second
strategy, the "empowerment approach" (Bowen and Lawler 1992), or what
Leidner terms "routinization by transformation." Through careful selection,
training, and motivation, employers create the "kinds of people who would
make decisions that management will approve" (Leidner 1993: 18). Rather
than presenting employees with scripted patter, for example, managers will
seek individuals whose personal characteristics make them likely to interact
spontaneously and perform in the manner management intends. On this approach, the president of one large restaurant chain writes that "the goal is to
remove the spiel and inject the personality . . . to bring it down to an intensely personal experience" (president of Red Lobster USA, quoted in
Heskett 1990: 201).

To implement this approach, managers must first select the right kinds of
people for the job, often using gender, class, age, and other status markers to
serve as a proxy for required personality types. In the case of insurance sales,
for example, managers seek young, uneducated (and therefore more malle-
able) men with new families whose needs drive them to strive continuously
for high commissions. As David Knights and Glenn Morgan (1991) point
out, women are seen as lacking the stamina to withstand the "soul-destroying"
(p. 223) aspects of the work. Once they have found the right candidates,
managers train workers for empowerment by arming them with information
rather than instructions. As one consultant urges, "A person who has information cannot avoid taking responsibility" (Heskett 1990: 228). Finally, the
empowerment approach advocates giving employees the power to make decisions based on their own judgment:

> You've got to let people take appropriate risks to serve customers . . .
> even if it means making a mistake or two once in a while. Well-
> intentioned efforts are just as important as successes. And if you hang
> your sales and customer support people for trying to do something
> that doesn't quite work, you'll just get people who won't try anything.
> (President of Federal Express, quoted in Flood 1993: 517)

Advocates of the empowerment approach argue that job enrichment, enhanced autonomy, and input in decision-making are key benefits to workers.

Its benefits to the firm range from cost-saving resulting from the reduced need for middle management and supervisory staff, to the increased productivity and reduced union activity generated by similar participatory and TQM plans in manufacturing settings. In addition, advocates believe that creating an organization based on the premise that "those nearest to the work are in the best position to solve the problems" enhances customer service (Albrecht and Zemke 1990: 135–36). Based on this belief, such large conglomerates as Scandinavian Airlines and Federal Express have inverted their organizational structures to ensure that it becomes "everyone else's responsibility to serve those who serve the customer," putting the front-line employees first (Scandinavian Airlines chairman, quoted in Heskett 1990: 223).

While industry leaders refer to this approach as "servant leadership" (Flood 1993) or the "employee-centered approach" (Albrecht and Zemke 1990), critics call this type of management control "self-regulation," "ideational control," and "subjectification" (Edwards 1994; Grenier 1988; Knights and Morgan 1991; Knights and Wilmott 1989). Of course, the empowerment approach can go well beyond selecting the right people, arming them with enough information, and turning them loose. Critics point out that like Quality of Work Life and Total Quality Management plans in manufacturing, the real goal of such an approach is to get workers to "think and act like managers, without, at the same time sharing managerial power" (Fischer 1994: 191). Certainly, if managers subscribe in theory but not in practice to the concept of empowering workers, the result can be demands to work extra hours without compensation, intense job insecurity, and union busting. At Nordstrom's, the retail chain that has been celebrated, condemned, and sued for its customer-focused, employee-centered policies, salespeople were routinely expected to spend off hours delivering merchandise and writing thank-you notes to customers. The company hired customer-oriented workers, paid them on an incentive basis, inculcated them into the "Nordstrom Way," and threatened them with dismissal if they failed to meet the excessively high sales quotas or called in sick. One employee remarked, "It reminds me of a cult the way they program you to devote your life to Nordstrom. . . . Granted, the customer gets treated like a hundred bucks. And Nordstrom gets rich off it. So nobody loses — except the employee" (Faludi 1990: A1). In cases such as these, employee empowerment is merely a veil designed to mask the absence of basic worker rights and protections.

Given that the service labor process involves the manufacture of relationships and the production of feeling states in workers and customers, attempts to ensure consistent and reliable performances in workers can result in intrusive methods of indoctrination and surveillance, even when management interventions are well intentioned. Since the "empowered" service worker must custom-craft spontaneous responses to customers' individualized needs, maintaining quality control is a matter of "transforming workers' characters, personalities, and thought processes so that their reactions to variable work situations will be predictable" (Leidner 1993: 37). Therefore, under the empowerment method, management control frequently invades more areas of employees' personal and psychic lives than do other modes of supervision. As Biggart (Chapter 7) notes, direct selling organizations use workers' families as mechanisms of control to motivate, assist, and supervise the performance of each salesperson. Other organizations pit workers against one another, using them both to motivate through competition and to supervise through "peer reporting" (Faludi 1990; Grenier 1988; Knights and Morgan 1991).

In addition, for many service workers, "the emotional style of offering the service is part of the service itself" (Hochschild 1983: 6). The demand to perform what Hochschild terms "emotional labor" at work can take several forms, including "personalizing an impersonal relation" (p. 109), refraining from reacting to abusive behavior, and maintaining a perpetual, sincere smile. The costs to workers of performing this type of work can be great, and can include emotional burnout, confusion about emotional authenticity, and an inability to "turn off" emotional production at the end of the day. In short, workers can experience alienation from that part of themselves controlled by management: their emotions.

As competition between service firms intensifies, the emotional display of the front-line service worker becomes the most important weapon in the corporate arsenal. Hochschild (1983: 89) cites the PSA Airlines jingle, "our smiles aren't just painted on." As competition escalates, a simple smile becomes insufficient; the smile must be *sincerely* offered. Hochschild argues that in some service industries, deep acting, that is, convincing oneself of the sincerity of one's emotional display, replaces surface acting, or merely pretending, in the job requirements of interactive service workers. Deep acting exacts the greatest toll from workers' psyches; Hochschild argues that workers burn out rapidly whether they "identify too wholeheartedly with the job" (p. 187) or engage in self-defense by "going into robot" (p. 135). The result in either case, according to Hochschild, is an "emotional numbness" that invades the worker's personal life and hampers her capacity for authenticity.

While no one argues that emotional labor is not a real component of the job requirements of many service workers, some researchers take issue with Hochschild's description of its dire consequences. For example, Amy S. Wharton (Chapter 5) compared the experiences of hospital and bank workers who perform emotional labor with workers in the same industries who do not. She finds that it is not the emotion work that creates job stress but other factors such as the level of autonomy on the job and personal characteristics. Hochschild (1983), however, sees potential dangers for workers in the increasing personalization of work and the blurring of personal and work personas:

> A woman may apply for a job as flight attendant because she is "genu-inely" friendly and outgoing. She may experience little gap between her "natural" self and her on-the-job self. But should that gap emerge, she is required to be friendly and outgoing anyway because, in some important way, feelings are the job. (p. 443)

Overlooking this gap, she argues, blurs the distinction between the worker's "natural" and "on-the-job" selves. This blurring robs emotions of their au-thenticity and, more importantly, of their important signaling function. If, in the course of her job, the worker becomes numb to her own feeling states, how will she ever know what she feels? In Hochschild's view, the costs of emotional labor far outweigh the benefits.

Finally, concerns arise over the effects of new forms of surveillance on workers' rights and autonomy. In their efforts to monitor the quality of service delivery unobtrusively, managers use such tools as "secret shoppers," customer surveys and comment cards, wiretapping, video surveillance, and computer-ized performance evaluation.[6] Often these measures are implemented under the rubric of improving security, but they present the added advantage of allowing managers to monitor workers' activities continuously, or at least to give workers the impression that they could be observed at any time. In some cases, surveillance techniques monitor the quality of interactions; in others, they measure the quantity (for example, see Lopez on computer monitoring in Chapter 3).

In all instances, these specially tailored forms of management observation centralize power to the extent that one manager can track the activities of workers in many locations while at the same time maintaining an illusion of worker autonomy. For example, Mrs. Field's Cookies rid itself of layers of mid-dle management by using a computer system to measure against quotas the daily and hourly performance of each salesperson at every outlet. While the branch managers and counter workers at these outlets seem to work autono-mously and exercise independent control over their store, each member of the staff knows that he or she is under continuous surveillance by the computer. As Michael Rosen and Jack Baroudi (1993) note, "A fundamental aspect of this is the knowledge on the part of the employee that such detailed information on their performance is collected as a matter of course" (p. 226). This knowledge alone disciplines the employee to monitor his or her own performance contin-uously, regardless of whether management acts on, or even reads, the information gathered. In this sense, the technologies of unobtrusive surveillance designed to monitor the service labor process become an "information panopticon" (Zuboff 1988: 315), continuously reminding workers that although no manager may be physically present, every aspect of their performance may be, and in that sense, might as well be, constantly monitored. As Michel Foucault (1979) remarked concerning Bentham's panoptic prison design, "the perfection of power should render its actual exercise unnecessary. . . . Inmates should be caught up in a power situation of which they are themselves the bearers" (p. 201). As a result of this new form of pseudoautonomy, workers often become burned out, anxious, even paranoid.

The paradox of empowerment in the service labor process is that while seeming unobtrusive, these forms of control are actually more invasive than more direct means, penetrating into more aspects of workers' psychic and personal lives. They are omnipresent, and as Fuller and Smith (Chapter 4) point out, these customer-focused worker empowerment forms of control are more insidious than other management strategies because they obscure the exercise of managerial power. The "upside down" organization presents the front-line worker with the ideology that management works to serve them and that everyone works together to serve the customer. It further obscures management power by enabling them to present themselves as "agents for the customer" rather than as authority figures. Ultimately, as Lopez (Chapter 3) and others point out, this system presents empowered workers with not fewer but more supervisors from whom they can never escape.

## Gender, Race, and Stratification in the Service Sector

Service industries tend to produce two kinds of jobs: large numbers of low-skill, low-pay jobs and a smaller number of high-skill, high-income jobs, with very few jobs that could be classified in the middle. As Joel Nelson (1994) notes, "Service workers are more likely than manufacturing workers to have lower incomes, fewer opportunities for full-time employment, and greater inequality in earnings" (p. 240). A typical example of this kind of highly stratified work force can be found in fast food industries. These firms tend to operate with a small core of managers and administrators and a large, predominantly part-time work force who possess few skills and therefore are considered expendable (Woody 1989).

As a result, service jobs fall into two broad categories: those likely to be production-line jobs and those likely to be empowered jobs. This distinction not only refers to the level of responsibility and autonomy expected of workers, but also to wages, benefits, job security, and potential for advancement. While empowered service jobs are associated with full-time work, decent wages and benefits, and internal job ladders, production-line jobs offer none of these. Some researchers have described the distinction between empowered and production-line service jobs as one between "core" and "periphery" jobs in the service economy (Hirschhorn 1988; Walsh 1990; Wood 1989). For example, Larry Hirschhorn describes the postindustrial economy as composed of firms seeking to adapt to ever-changing market demands by restructuring their labor force and creating two distinct sets of workers: core functions are performed by retrained workers with upgraded skills and responsibilities, while peripheral functions are subcontracted to other firms or performed by part-time, temporary, or other contingent workers.

Terming this new arrangement the "post-industrial firm's new dualism," Hirschhorn (1988: 27) points out that "while in the industrial economy people typically work for core or peripheral firms, in the post-industrial economy, the same firm creates both long-term and contingent relationships with different groups of workers." Thus, in service industries, in which workers represent both the producers and the inventory, managers attempt to respond to changing market needs by upgrading certain occupations and deskilling or outsourcing others.

The core/periphery distinction may be a misleading characterization of functions in service industries, however. In many firms contingent workers perform functions essential to the operation of the firm and can comprise up to two-thirds of a firm's labor force while "core" workers perform nonessential functions (Walsh 1990). For example, a majority of key functions in industries such as hospitality, food service, and retail sales are performed by workers who, based on their level of benefits, pay, and job security, would be considered periphery workers. In low-skill service positions, job tenure has no relation to output or productivity. Therefore, employers can rely on contingent workers to provide high-quality service at low costs. As T. J. Walsh (1990: 527) points out, it is therefore likely that the poor compensation afforded these workers is due not to their productivity level but to the perceptions of their needs, level of commitment, and availability.

Given the proliferation of service jobs in the United States, key questions for labor analysts are what kinds of jobs are service industries producing, and who is likely to fill them? At the high end, service industries demand educated workers who can rapidly adapt to changing economic conditions. This means that employers may demand a college degree or better for occupations that formerly required only a high school diploma, even though many of the job-holders' activities have not changed, or appear relatively simple, because they want workers to be more responsive to the general situation in which they are working and the broader purposes of their work. (Hirschhorn 1988: 35)

In addition, core workers are frequently expected to take on more responsibilities, work longer hours, and intensify their output.

At the low end of the spectrum of service occupations are periphery workers who are frequently classified as part-time, temporary, contract, or contingent. These flexible-use workers act as a safety valve for service firms, allowing managers to redeploy labor costs in response to market conditions. In addition, they allow managers to minimize overhead because they rarely qualify for benefits and generally receive low wages. In 1988, 86 percent of all part-time workers worked in service sector industries, and this trend has continued since (Tilly 1992: 230). Labor analysts argue that the bulk of the expansion in part-time and contingent work is due to the expansion of the service sector, which has always used shift and part-time workers as cost-control mechanisms. In fact, some argue, "had the industrial distribution of jobs remained as it was in 1950, all other things being equal, today's economy would include at least three million fewer part-time jobs" (Leviatan and Conway 1992: 52).

Service sector expansion has also sparked the rapid growth of the temporary help industry. Over the past decade, the number of temporary workers has tripled (Kilborn 1995). As the chairman of Manpower, Inc., the largest single employer in the United States, remarked, "The U.S. is going from just-in-time manufacturing to just-in-time employment. The employer tells us, 'I want them delivered exactly when I want them, as many as I need, and when I don't need them, I don't want them here'" (quoted in Castro 1993: 44). Like part-time workers, temporary workers carry no "overhead" costs in terms of taxes and benefits, and they are on call as needed. Since they experience little workplace continuity, they are less likely than full-time, continuous employees to organize or advocate changes in working conditions.

Women, youth, and minorities comprise the bulk of the part-time and contingent work force in the service sector. For example, Karen Brodkin Sacks (1990) has noted that the health care industry is "so stratified by race and gender that the uniforms worn to distinguish the jobs and statuses of health care workers are largely redundant" (p. 188). Patients respond to the signals implicitly transmitted via gender and race and act accordingly, offering deference to some workers and expecting it from others. Likewise in domestic service, race and gender determine who gets which jobs. White American and European women are most likely to be hired for domestic jobs defined primarily as child care, while women of color predominate in those defined as house cleaning (Rollins 1985), regardless of what the actual allocation of work might be. The same kinds of stratification can be found in secretarial work, food service, hotels, and sales occupations (Hochschild 1985; Leidner 1991; Pierce, Chapter 8). In all of these occupational groups, demographic characteristics of the worker determine the job title and thus other factors such as status, pay, benefits, and degree of autonomy on the job.

As a result, the shift to services has had a differential impact on various sectors of the labor market, increasing stratification between the well employed and the underemployed. The service sector work force is highly feminized, especially at the bottom. Within personal and business services, for example, Bette Woody (1989) found that "men are concentrated in high-ticket, high commission sales jobs, and women in retail and food service" (p. 57). And although the decline in manufacturing forced male workers to move into service industries, Jon Lorence (1992: 150) notes that within the service sector, occupations are highly stratified by gender. From 1950 to 1990, 60 percent of all new service sector employment and 74 percent of all new low-skill jobs were filled by women. In evaluating changes in the service sector labor force during this period, Thomas Steiger and Mark Wardell (1995) found that "the employment pattern in the service sector remained largely segregated by gender; and skill degradation rather than skill upgrading tended to be the rule in industries where women held the numerical majority or came close to equalling the number of men" (p. 105).

Service sector employment is equally stratified by race. For example, Woody (1989) finds that the shift to services has affected black women in two important ways. First, it has meant higher rates of unemployment and under-employment for black men, which increased pressure on black women to be the primary breadwinners for their families and contributed to the overall reduction in black family income. Second, although the increase in service sector jobs has meant greater opportunity for black women and has allowed them to move out of domestic service into the formal economy, as Evelyn Nakano Glenn (Chapter 6) also notes, they have remained at the lowest rung of the service employment ladder. Unlike some white women who "moved up" to male-intensive occupations with the shift to services, black women "moved over" to sectors traditionally employing white women (Woody 1989: 54). These traditionally male occupations are not only low-security, low-pay jobs, but they lack internal career ladders. As Ruth Needleman and Anne Nelson (1988) note, "There is no progression from nurse to physician, from secretary to manager" (p. 297).

Service work differs most radically from manufacturing, construction, or agricultural work in the relationship between worker characteristics and the job. Even though discrimination in hiring, differential treatment, differential pay, and other forms of stratification exist in all labor markets, service occupations are the only ones in which the producer in some sense equals the product. In no other area of wage labor are the personal characteristics of the workers so strongly associated with the nature of work. Because at least part of the job in all service occupations is to "manufacture social relations" (Filby 1992: 37), traits such as gender, race, age, and sexuality serve a signaling function, indicating to the customer / employer important cues about the tone of the interaction. Women are expected to be more nurturing and empathetic than men and to tolerate more offensive behavior from customers (Hochschild 1985; Leidner 1991; Pierce 1996 and Chapter 8; Sutton and Rafaeli 1989). Similarly, both women and men of color are expected to be deferential and to take on more demeaning tasks (Rollins 1985; Woody 1989). In addition, a given task may be viewed as more or less demeaning depending on who is doing it.

These occupations are so stratified that worker characteristics such as race and gender determine not only who is considered desirable or even eligible to fill certain jobs, but also who will want to fill certain jobs and how the job itself is performed. Worker characteristics shape what is expected of a worker by management and customers, how that worker adapts to the job, and what aspects of the job he or she will resist or embrace. The strategies workers use to adapt to the demands of service jobs are likely to differ according to gender and other characteristics. Women are more likely to embrace the emotional demands (e.g., nurturing, care giving) of certain types of service jobs because these demands generally fit their notion of gender-appropriate behavior. As Pierce (Chapter 8) notes, heterosexual men tend to resist these demands because they find "feminine" emotional labor demeaning; in response they either reframe the nature of the job to emphasize traditional masculine qualities or distance themselves by providing service by rote, making it clear that they are acting under duress.

All of these interconnections between worker, work, and product result in tendencies toward very specific types of labor market stratification. A long and heated debate has raged concerning the ultimate impact of deindustrialization on the structure of the labor market. On one side are those who argue that a shift to a service-based economy will produce skill upgrading and a leveling of job hierarchies as information and communications technologies reshape the labor market (see, for example, Bell 1973). Others take a more pessimistic view, arguing that the shift to services will give rise to two trends: "towards polarization and towards the proliferation of low-wage jobs" (Bluestone and Harrison 1988: 126). In a sense, both positions are correct but for different segments of the labor market.

Overall, the transition to a service-based economy will likely mean a more stratified work force in which more part-time and contingent jobs are filled predominantly by women, minorities, and workers without college degrees. In jobs lacking internal career ladders, these workers have little chance for upward mobility. Contingent workers are also less likely to organize successfully due to their tenuous attachment to specific employers and to the labor force in general. At the opposite end of the service sector occupational spectrum are highly educated managerial, professional, and paraprofessional workers, who will have equally weak attachments to employers, but who, due to their highly marketable skills, will move with relative ease from one well-paying job to another. Given this divided and economically segregated work force, what are the opportunities for workers to advocate, collectively or individually, for greater security, better working conditions, and a voice in shaping their work?

## Worker Resistance, Organizing, and Participation

Workers have a long history of resisting many forms of managerial control in the name of dignity and participation (Cronin and Sirianni 1983; Sirianni 1987). Indeed, the demand for dignity and respect is perhaps the single most consistent theme in workplace struggles, from the coal miners and machinists in early twentieth-century Pittsburgh and Petrograd to the flight attendants and clerical workers of today's Pan Am and Harvard. Some of the issues are the same: surveillance, speed-up, and supervisors exercising arbitrary power. But others can only be understood in the context of service work and its distinctive forms of control. And because service and its idioms have become so central to our public life, the everyday struggles for recognition in the service workplace have become integral to the meaning of democratic citizenship. How can we serve and still be recognized as equal citizens? Can we develop a civic culture that is up to the challenges of a postindustrial world without transforming the culture of the service workplace?

As the essays in Part III demonstrate, the idiom of servant and master is alive and well in many kinds of service workplaces. This holds that the customer is always right and that the role of the server is to be deferent in serving, even if the customer's demands are unreasonable and demeanor abusive. Dress and speech codes, as well as formal training, drive this point home again and again. The domestic servant is called by her first name and even referred to as "my girl," but her female employer is called "Mrs." The waitress has her first name on her tag, and can be threatened and embarrassed by a public display of withholding her tip. A legendary training session at Harvard counseled clerical workers upset at angry students' rebukes to "think of yourself as a trash can. Take everyone's little bits of anger all day, put it inside you, and at the end of the day, just pour it in the dumpster on your way out the door."

The asymmetry in the exchange of respect is often built into structural features of service work. Flight attendants have important safety and rescue skills, and manage emotions in such a way so as to create an atmosphere of reassurance, as Hochschild (1983) shows. But they are discouraged from displaying these in more than a routine fashion, lest passengers come to feel that they are at risk in flying. Thus, flight attendants are vulnerable to being perceived primarily as hostesses and waitresses commanding much less respect and authority. Service workers performing "Everyman's" or "Everywoman's" skills are vulnerable to the embarrassment of everyday failures but have few opportunities to display skill of a higher order, even if they often use such skills to accomplish their tasks. Thus, their daily work experience is often one of a series of minor complaints assuming major proportions for the customer, or of empty "thank you's" for doing something well that virtually anyone could have done — including the customers themselves, had they apparently not had better things to do with their time. Indeed, the relatively greater value placed on the time of the customer in the "fast" service industries makes the worker more vulnerable to these kinds of failures.

The politics of skill in interactive service work is thus much more than objective deskilling and upgrading, but is about the conditions for controlling the public display of skills in ways that elicit respect and recognition. And since much of our public life occurs in service settings in which we are actors and witnesses in this asymmetrical exchange of respect, the fabric of our civic culture — indeed, ordinary civility — is vulnerable.

Resistance, of course, is pervasive and diverse. Often it simply takes the form of sabotage and cynicism: screw it up, slow it down, return the abuse, and complain endlessly that the public is inherently rude and thoughtless. The public returns these sentiments in full, and talk shows assemble employees and customers to rub the sores further. A more thoroughly debased view of service work in the public culture, for instance, would be hard to find than the "Oprah" show that featured disgruntled people from both sides of the service divide shouting about all the ways that the other is abusive and incompetent.

Yet everyday resistance is often thoughtfully educative and reconstructive. A nice example: a male undergraduate approaches the reserve desk at a university library and simply says three words: "Cyril Roth Venice." His economy of words is met with the following response by the middle-aged woman behind the desk, articulated slowly and addressed as well to the surrounding group of students and professors waiting their turn: "Would you like a book?" ("Yes.")

"And who is the author of that book?" ("Cyril Roth.") "And what is the title of that book?" ("*Venice.*") In a simple and dignified way, and with a gentle irony, the woman takes control of the interaction and uses the economy of time in the service interaction as a public lesson in respect.

Specific strategies and cultures of resistance tend to form in specific service settings. Greta Foff Paules's (Chapter 11) essay analyzes the dynamics of resistance among waitresses in a family-style restaurant. Far from internalizing the inferior position in the master/servant idiom, waitresses develop several counteridioms. One is the "waitress as soldier," who goes into battle with potentially hostile—or simply too many—customers who threaten her lines of defense. Another is the "waitress as private entrepreneur," who is separate from the company and develops her own strategies to use the relationship with the customer to her own financial advantage. The domestic servants in Judith Rollins's (Chapter 9) study do not internalize the inferiority implicit in the deference and invisibility of their work relationships. They maintain their sense of self-worth, deflect assaults on their dignity and adulthood, and utilize their greater "consciousness of the Other" to reverse the scales of judgment.

Some of these resistance strategies are available to nannies and *au pairs* as well. They come to view their own mothering skills as superior to those of the child's mother, or see the mother as undermining in the evening the good work they have done during the day. But as Cameron Macdonald's (Chapter 10) essay shows, loyalty to the children and a different relationship to the market limit their use of resistance strategies available to other service workers. They seek to make visible the value of their care and their affective ties with the children. Many mothers experience this as a threat of usurpation, although some come to recognize the legitimacy of these claims and the need to make concessions to a nanny or *au pair* whose leverage has been enhanced by the children's attachment to her. Nannies and *au pairs*, for their part, seem to learn how to do the complex emotion work involved in not preempting the mother in especially valued areas of child rearing. Resistance, in this case, can trigger important developmental work from each party within a context of increasing mutual trust and respect.

An alternative set of themes has begun to redefine service work in recent years, and these have emerged at both management and union initiative. On the management side, these have stressed the empowerment of service workers, usually within the context of broader approaches such as the learning organization, Total Quality Management, or reengineering (Bowen and Lawler 1992, 1995; Schlesinger and Heskett 1991). Empowered employees are seen as enabling the organization to reduce and recover from service failures, thus enhancing its capacity to develop and sustain competitive advantages, improve the quality of the interaction for the employee as well as the customer, and increase opportunities for individual learning. There are many interesting cases where these claims seem to have been borne out, although there are also many where empowerment has proved to be a thin and temporary veneer for management practices that tighten control and further routinize interaction. We still lack the kind of in-depth case studies of management-initiated empowerment programs in services that would permit us to evaluate their dynamics at the level of workers' experiences of power and participation. Nothing yet exists that is comparable to the critical ethnographic work of Hochschild (1983) on flight attendants, Leidner (1993) on fast-food workers and insurance salesmen, or Gideon Kunda (1992) on corporate culture in a high-tech firm.

One of the most interesting cases of a union-initiated attempt to develop an alternative language of service as well as practices that enhance worker participation and mutual respect is the work of the Harvard Union of Clerical and Technical Workers (HUCTW). As Susan Eaton's (Chapter 12) essay shows, workers' rights to participation and respect have been the central organizing themes of HUCTW in the 1980s and 1990s, and the union built upon relational organizing and an "ethic of care" in its attempt to weave these into the fabric of the union and larger workplace culture (see also Hoerr 1993; Hurd 1993). The approach is one of "public service" that attempts to enhance the quality of service without assuming that the customer is always right and that solidifies workplace citizenship without assuming that the worker is always right. Indeed, the union utilizes the relational strategy of organizing to enhance workers' capacities to manage complex relationships between managers, faculty, students, and others in such a way that the diverse and legitimate interests of each party are recognized. The ultimate goal of this approach is to strengthen further mutual respect and trust as the best foundation for common problem-solving.

There are no detailed work rules and no broad management rights clause in the HUCTW contract — a choice that extends some of the more innovative union strategies in industry (Bluestone and Bluestone 1992; Heckscher 1988; Kochan, Katz, and McKersie 1987; Kochan and Osterman 1994), while building upon the nonadversarial everyday work culture of women clericals at a university such as Harvard. The union provides training to make this work. Eaton's case studies of three Joint Councils in different parts of the university reveal the promise of this approach, but also delineate the obstacles workers have met in the face of larger questions of gender and power.

Dorothy Sue Cobble's (Chapter 13) concluding essay takes up the broad challenge of the prospects of unionism in a service society. Potential worker support for unions is still substantial, according to survey data, and unions have become increasingly feminized in membership and issue focus. But as the myth that women workers are unorganizable has been shattered, a new myth has grown up that certain kinds of jobs, especially those held by women and in private-sector service industries, are unorganizable. As Cobble notes, this argument tends to be circular and tells us more about who has *not* been organized than who *can*.

But new models of unionism will have to be developed to respond to some fundamental changes in the world of work for this potential to be realized. The rise of interactive service work means that worker satisfaction and control often depend much more on relations with clients and customers, and unions must assume greater responsibility for this. The Harvard union represents one form of response to the needs of interactive service workers. Teachers' unions also show signs of moving beyond the previous two stages of professional association and traditional collective bargaining to a third model, in which teachers assume greater responsibility for the overall functioning of the educational system. Unions are challenged to cooperate in educational reforms, such as site-based management, multidisciplinary teams, and the development of innovative schools within controlled choice systems (Fliegel with MacGuire 1993; Kerchner and Mitchell 1988; Rosow and Zager 1989). Nurses' unions are challenged to maintain a strong ethic of care and self-regulation of professional conduct without abandoning collective bargaining strategies to improve pay and working conditions. Flight attendants' unions internalize the basic requirements of emotion work, where passengers value an atmosphere of assurance and hospitality, and yet renegotiate their own individual and collective responses to rude and unruly behavior, and to management's standards for appearance.

Unions will also have to come to grips with the rise of nonstandard work, which now covers some one-quarter of the work force and is steadily increasing. This includes part-time, part-year, temporary, leased, on-call, subcontracted, and off-site workers. Much of this is driven by employer interests in flexibility, lower costs, and fewer long-term commitments to employees. But workers themselves, especially women, have likewise shown significant interest in flexible arrangements, programs that adjust workplace demands to family needs, and mobility between employers and work experiences. Destandardization raises many challenges for unions (Hinrichs, Roche, and Sirianni 1991), although various components of a model of the self-management of time in postindustrial society (Sirianni 1991) and of "equitable flexibility" (Olmsted and Smith 1989) have emerged, sometimes with union support.

Drawing upon a long tradition of occupational unionism among waitresses, Cobble (1991) argues that this model has become more relevant as a result of the growth of service work and nonstandard work, the proliferation of smaller work sites, and the decentralization of production. Occupational unions devise entrance standards for their trade, oversee training, develop guidelines for acceptable work performance, and enforce these norms on the job. Unlike the model of industrial unionism that became predominant in the 1930s and 1940s, occupational unionism is not oriented to the single work site, but to building ties among workers within an occupation who work across many sites and for various employers. It aims at achieving broad employment security, with portable rights and benefits, rather than at ensuring job rights at a particular work site. Home health care workers, janitorial and cleaning workers, and others have begun to organize in this way, and some nurses' unions have organized their own registries for placing temporary and short-term nursing help.

Occupational unionism, the Harvard model, equitable flexibility in scheduling, and other developments represent innovative forms developing in the service workplace. They also suggest, however, that the full potential of organizing and empowerment in the service sector is unlikely to be realized without an expansive conception of organizing as civic innovation. The market power of service workers cannot check or reverse the trends toward a more stratified and contingent work force. Old forms of solidarity and collective action have real limits in the face of new forms of employer leverage in a postindustrial global economy.

Organizing as civic innovation can take many forms. But several dimensions seem critical. First, a wide-ranging public conversion needs to occur concerning the role of service cultures and interactions in constituting our civic culture and our everyday experience of mutual recognition as citizens. What kinds of "servants" do we want and might we want ourselves to be: ones who act with full dignity and collaboration, or ones who are deferent and demeaned? Ones who can support a family and have the time for community involvements, or ones who always work at the margins and are forever running to their next part-time job? If we are determined to form a civic culture on foundations of racial and gender equity, can we afford to pursue service employment strategies that build upon and reinforce gendered and racialized idioms of service and recruitment? Service unions and civic associations need to take much greater responsibility for raising the many discourses of workplace resistance and complaint to the level of a common, public conversation about the nature of civic culture in a postindustrial society and the role of service workers in our common destiny. It is this conversation that can serve as the cultural resource in the struggle for genuine empowerment and public policies that can check and even reverse trends toward greater stratification and vulnerability for those in the lower tiers of employment.

Second, organizing as civic innovation must fully take on the challenges of diverse temporal commitments to paid work, and the relation between paid work in the labor market and unpaid work in the family and community.

Flexible working time options, as well as parental and community service leaves, represent important innovations, but they can only begin to do what will be needed to create the civic capacities for managing diversity with equity and integrating social spheres that have fundamentally different dynamics. There are no magic policy bullets here and many deceptively simple solutions. Civic innovation, be it in unionized or nonunionized settings, will have to build upon a broader discourse about work, family, and community, and will need to address the many legitimate and often competing interests of workers and managers, and among employees themselves. Broader and more effective public policies on working time and the relation between paid and unpaid work are unlikely to emerge without much greater local innovation that builds learning capacities adequate to specific organizations, markets, and communities.

Finally, organizing as civic innovation must address how to generate lifelong learning and career opportunity structures that are not fully dependent on the capacities of all service workplaces to upgrade skills. Many services, even in the best of worlds, will inevitably remain routine and suitable to a modified production-line approach that represents some form of "democratic Taylorism" (Adler and Cole 1993; Sirianni 1981) or "family-oriented Taylorism" (Bowen and Lawler 1995). But this need not entail a cap on individual development or a service dead end, if employers, unions, and other civic and public actors develop opportunities for further learning. This, again, will require a broader public conversation about the importance of lifelong learning to civic life and the meaning of equity in a dynamic and differentiated labor market.

## NOTES

1. Quoted in Albrecht and Zemke (1990: 1).
2. Quoted in Hochschild (1983: 89).
3. From the song "Bellboy," lyrics by Pete Townshend, performed by The Who on the album *Quadrophenia*, 1973, MCA Records.
4. For example, in the foundational work in labor process theory, *Labor and Monopoly Capital*, Braverman (1974) examined clerical work and concluded that it, like work in manufacturing, was undergoing a process of speeding up and deskilling whereby autonomy, decision-making, and skill were being appropriated from workers by management, leaving workers with pared down, monotonous tasks requiring little or no discretion.
5. Edwards (1979) coined the terms "technical control" and "bureaucratic control" in *Contested Terrain*. Technical control refers to production processes "based on a technology which paces and directs the labor process," while bureaucratic control refers to processes governed by institutional hierarchies and documented "work criteria" (Edwards 1994: 99, 107).
6. Customers also find these management techniques offensive. See the recent furor over Dunkin Donuts' "bugging" of Boston area restaurants in Murphy and Coakley (1994).

# REFERENCES

Abel, Emily K., and Margaret Nelson, eds. 1990. *Circles of Care*. Albany: State University of New York Press.

Adler, Paul, and Robert Cole. 1993. "Designed for Learning: A Tale of Two Auto Plants," *Sloan Management Review* (Spring): 85–94.

Albrecht, Karl, and Ron Zemke. 1990. *Service America!: Doing Business in the New Economy*. New York: Warner Books.

Applebaum, Eileen. 1992. "Structural Change and the Growth of Part-Time and Temporary Employment." In Virginia L. Du Rivage, ed., *New Policies for the Part-Time and Contingent Work-Force* (pp. 1–14). Armonk, NY: M. E. Sharpe, Economic Policy Institute Series.

Bell, Daniel. 1973. *The Coming of Post-Industrial Society: A Venture in Social Forecasting*. New York: Basic Books.

Biggart, Nicole Woolsey. 1989. *Charismatic Capitalism*. Chicago: University of Chicago Press.

Bluestone, Barry, and Irving Bluestone. 1992. *Negotiating the Future: A Labor Perspective on American Business*. New York: Basic Books.

Bluestone, Barry, and Bennett Harrison. 1988. *The Great U-Turn: Corporate Restructuring and the Polarizing of America*. New York: Basic Books.

Bowen, David E., and Edward E. Lawler, III. 1995. "Empowering Service Employees." *Sloan Management Review* (Summer): 73–84.

——. 1992. "The Empowerment of Service Workers: What, Why, How, and When." *Sloan Management Review* (Spring): 31–39.

Braverman, Harry. 1974. *Labor and Monopoly Capital: The Degradation of Work in the Twentieth Century*. New York: Monthly Review Press.

Burawoy, Michael. 1985. *The Politics of Production*. London: New Left Books.

Castro, Janice. 1993. "Disposable Workers." *Time Magazine*, March 29, pp. 43–57.

Cobble, Dorothy Sue. 1991. "Organizing the Postindustrial Work Force: Lessons from the History of Waitress Unionism." *Industrial and Labor Relations Review* 44(3): 419–36.

Craypo, Charles. 1991. "Industrial Restructuring and the Working Poor in a Midwestern U.S. Factory Town." *Labour and Society* 16: 153–74.

Cronin, James E., and Carmen Sirianni, eds. 1983. *Work, Community, and Power: The Experience of Labor in Europe and America, 1900–1925*. Philadelphia: Temple University Press.

Czepiel, John A., Michael R. Solomon, and Carol F. Surprenant, eds. 1985. *The Service Encounter: Managing Employee/Customer Interaction in Service Business*. Lexington, MA: Lexington Books.

Du Rivage, Virginia L., ed. 1992. *New Policies for the Part-Time and Contingent Work-Force*. Armonk, NY: M. E. Sharpe, Economic Policy Institute Series.

Edwards, Richard. 1994. "Forms of Control in the Labor Process: An Historical Analysis." In Frank Fischer and Carmen Sirianni, eds., *Critical Studies in Organization and Bureaucracy*, rev. ed. (pp. 86–119). Philadelphia: Temple University Press.

——. 1979. *Contested Terrain: The Transformation of the Workplace in the Twentieth Century*. New York: Basic Books.

Faludi, Susan. 1990. "At Nordstrom Stores, Service Comes First—But at a Big Price." *Wall Street Journal*, February 20, sec. A, p. 1.

Filby, M. P. 1992. "'The Figures, the Personality, and the Bums': Service Work and Sexuality." *Work, Employment, and Society* 6(March): 23–42.

Fischer, Frank. 1994. "Organizational Expertise and Bureaucratic Control: Behavioral Science as Managerial Ideology." In Frank Fischer and Carmen Sirianni, eds., *Critical Studies in Organization and Bureaucracy,* rev. ed. (pp. 174–95). Philadelphia: Temple University Press.

Fischer, Frank, and Carmen Sirianni, eds. 1994. *Critical Studies in Organization and Bureaucracy,* rev. ed. Philadelphia: Temple University Press.

Fishman, Pamela M. 1978. "Interaction: The Work Women Do." *Social Problems* 75: 397–406.

Fliegel, Seymour, with James MacGuire. 1993. *Miracle in East Harlem: The Fight for Choice in Public Education.* New York: Times Books.

Flood, Robert L. 1993. *Beyond TQM.* New York: Wiley.

Foucault, Michel. 1979. *Discipline and Punish: The Birth of the Prison.* Trans. Alan Sheridan. New York: Vintage Books.

Grenier, Guillermo J. 1988. *Inhuman Relations: Quality Circles and Anti-Unionism in American Industry.* Philadelphia: Temple University Press.

Hall, Elaine J. 1993. "Smiling, Deferring, and Flirting: Doing Gender by Giving 'Good Service.'" *Work and Occupations* 20: 452–71.

Heckscher, Charles. 1988. *The New Unionism: Employee Involvement in the Changing Corporation.* New York: Basic Books.

Heskett, James L. 1990. *Service Breakthroughs: Changing the Rules of the Game.* New York: Free Press.

———. 1986. *Managing in the Service Economy.* Boston: Harvard Business School Press.

Hinrichs, Karl, William Roche, and Carmen Sirianni, eds. 1991. *Working Time in Transition: The Political Economy of Working Hours in Industrial Nations.* Philadelphia: Temple University Press.

Hirschhorn, Larry. 1988. "The Post-Industrial Economy: Labour, Skills, and the New Mode of Production." *The Service Industries Journal* 8: 19–38.

Hochschild, Arlie Russell. 1983. *The Managed Heart: Commercialization of Human Feeling.* Berkeley: University of California Press.

Hoerr, John. 1993. "Solidaritas at Harvard." *The American Prospect* 14(Summer): 67–82.

Hurd, Richard. 1993. "Organizing and Representing Clerical Workers: The Harvard Model." In Dorothy Sue Cobble, ed., *Women and Unions: Forging a Partnership* (pp. 316–36). Ithaca: Cornell University ILR Press.

Kerchner, Charles Taylor, and Douglas E. Mitchell. 1988. *The Changing Idea of a Teachers' Union.* New York: Falmer Press.

Kilborn, Peter T. 1995. "In New Work World, Employers Call All the Shots: Job Insecurity, a Special Report." *New York Times,* July 3, p. A1.

Knights, David, and Glenn Morgan. 1991. "Selling Oneself: Subjectivity and the Labour Process in Selling Life Insurance." In Charles Smith, David Knights, and Hugh Wilmott, eds., *White-Collar Work: The Non-Manual Labour Process* (pp. 217–40). London: Macmillan.

Knights, David, and Hugh Wilmott. 1989. "Power and Subjectivity at Work: From Degradation to Subjugation in Social Relations." *Sociology* 23: 535–58.

Kochan, Thomas, Harry Katz, and John McKersie. 1987. *The Transformation of American Industrial Relations.* New York: Basic Books.

Kochan, Thomas, and Paul Osterman. 1994. *The Mutual Gains Enterprise.* Boston: Harvard Business School Press.

Kunda, Gideon. 1992. *Engineering Culture: Control and Commitment in a High-Tech Corporation*. Philadelphia: Temple University Press.

Kutscher, Ronald E. 1987. "Projections 2000: Overview and Implications of the Projections to 2000." *Monthly Labor Review* (September): 3–9.

Leidner, Robin. 1993. *Fast Food, Fast Talk: Service Work and the Routinization of Everyday Life*. Berkeley: University of California Press.

———. 1991. "Serving Hamburgers and Selling Insurance: Gender, Work, and Identity in Interactive Service Jobs." *Gender and Society* 5: 154–77.

Leviatan, Sar A., and Elizabeth A. Conway. 1992. "Part-Timers: Living on Half Rations." In Barbara Warme, Katherina Lundy, and Larry Lundy, eds. *Working Part-Time: Risks and Opportunities* (pp. 45–60). New York: Praeger.

Levitt, Theodore. 1972. "Production-Line Approach to Service." *Harvard Business Review* (September–October): 41–52.

Lorence, Jon. 1992. "Service Sector Growth and Metropolitan Occupational Sex Segregation." *Work and Occupations* 19: 128–56.

Murphy, Sean P., and Tom Coakley. 1994. "Sssh! Your Cruller Might Be Listening." *Boston Globe*, May 28, p. 1.

Needleman, Ruth, and Anne Nelson. 1988. "Policy Implications: The Worth of Women's Work." In Anne Statham, Eleanor M. Miller, and Hans O. Mauksch, eds., *The Worth of Women's Work: A Qualitative Synthesis* (pp. 293–308). Albany: SUNY Press.

Nelson, Joel I. 1994. "Work and Benefits: The Multiple Problems of Service Sector Employment." *Social Problems* 41: 240–55.

Noyelle, Thierry J., ed. 1990. *Skills, Wages, and Productivity in the Service Sector*. Boulder, CO: Westview Press.

———. 1987. *Beyond Industrial Dualism: Market and Job Segmentation in the New Economy*. Boulder, CO: Westview Press.

Olmsted, Barney, and Susanne Smith. 1989. *Creating a Flexible Workplace*. New York: American Management Associations.

Packham, John. 1992. "The Organization of Work on the Service-Sector Shop Floor." Unpublished paper.

Pierce, Jennifer L. 1996. *Gender Trials: Emotional Lives in Contemporary Law Firms*. Berkeley: University of California Press.

Rollins, Judith. 1985. *Between Women: Domestics and Their Employers*. Philadelphia: Temple University Press.

Rosen, Michael, and Jack Baroudi. 1993. "Computer-Based Technology and the Emergence of New Forms of Managerial Control." In Andrew Sturdy, David Knights, and Hugh Wilmott, eds., *Skill and Consent: Contemporary Studies in the Labour Process* (pp. 213–34). London: Routledge.

Rosow, Jerome, and Robert Zager. 1989. *Allies in Educational Reform*. San Francisco: Jossey-Bass.

Sacks, Karen Brodkin. 1990. "Does It Pay to Care?" In Emily K. Abel and Margaret K. Nelson, eds., *Circles of Care: Work and Identity in Women's Lives* (pp. 188–206). Albany: SUNY Press.

Sakolsky, Ron. 1993. "'Disciplinary Power' and the Labour Process." In Andrew Sturdy, David Knights, and Hugh Wilmott, eds., *Skill and Consent: Contemporary Studies in the Labour Process* (pp. 235–54). London: Routledge.

Schlesinger, Leonard, and James Heskett. 1991. "The Service-Driven Service Company." *Harvard Business Review* (September–October): 71–81.

Sirianni, Carmen. 1981. "Class, Production, and Power: A Critical Analysis of the Utopian Dimensions of Marxist Theory." *Socialist Review* 59 (September–October): 33–82.

Sirianni, Carmen, ed. 1991. "The Self-Management of Time in Postindustrial Society." In Karl Hinrichs, William Roche, and Carmen Sirianni, eds., *Working Time in Transition* (pp. 231–74). Philadelphia: Temple University Press.

———, ed. 1987. *Worker Participation and the Politics of Reform.* Philadelphia: Temple University Press.

Smith, Charles, David Knights, and Hugh Wilmott, eds. 1991. *White-Collar Work: The Non-Manual Labour Process.* London: Macmillan.

Smith, Vicki. 1993. "Institutional Flexibility in a Service Firm: Paradoxes and Consequences." Paper presented at the annual meeting of the American Sociological Association.

Steiger, Thomas L., and Mark Wardell. 1995. "Gender and Employment in the Service Sector." *Social Problems* 42: 91–123.

Sturdy, Andrew, David Knights, and Hugh Wilmott, eds. 1993. *Skill and Consent: Contemporary Studies in the Labour Process.* London: Routledge.

Sutton, Robert I., and Anat Rafaeli. 1989. "The Expression of Emotion in Organizational Life." *Research in Organizational Behavior* 11: 1–42.

Sweeney, John J., and Karen Nussbaum. 1989. *Solutions for the New Work Force.* Washington, DC: Seven Locks Press.

Tilly, Chris. 1992. "Short Hours, Short Shrift: The Causes and Consequences of Part-Time Employment." In Virginia L. Du Rivage, ed., *New Policies for the Part-Time and Contingent Work-Force* (pp. 15–43). Armonk, NY: M. E. Sharpe, Economic Policy Institute Series.

U.S. Department of Labor, Bureau of Labor Statistics. 1994. *Monthly Labor Review* (July): 74–83.

Walsh, T. J. 1990. "Flexible Labour Utilisation in the Private Service Sector." *Work, Employment, and Society* 4: 517–30.

Warme, Barbara D., Katherine L. P. Lundy, and Larry A. Lundy, eds. 1992. *Working Part-Time: Risks and Opportunities.* New York: Praeger.

Wood, Stephen, ed. 1989. *The Transformation of Work? Skill, Flexibility, and the Labour Process.* London: Unwin Hyman.

Woody, Bette. 1989. "Black Women in the Emerging Services Economy." *Sex Roles* 21: 45–67.

Zemke, Ron. 1989. *The Service Edge: 101 Companies That Profit from Customer Care.* New York: New American Library.

Zuboff, Shoshana. 1988. *In the Age of the Smart Machine: The Future of Work and Power.* New York: Basic Books.

# Part I

## Management Control of the New Labor Process

*Chapter 2*

# Rethinking Questions of Control: Lessons from McDonald's

- Robin Leidner

O ne consequence of the ongoing shift in employment from manufacturing to services (Mills 1986; Noyelle 1987; Smith 1984) is that hamburgers have taken their place alongside guns and butter as the staples of political discourse about economics, with politicians and commentators questioning whether the United States is becoming "a nation of hamburger-flippers" (Kirkland 1985; also see Wildavsky 1989). Somewhat surprisingly, service work has not assumed an equally important place in sociological theorizing about work. Although scholars have acknowledged the growing importance of service jobs, they have failed to recast models of work that were derived from manufacturing. This failure is especially striking with regard to workplace control, since several excellent studies have demonstrated that service work raises distinctive problems of control (e.g., Benson 1986; Biggart 1989; Hochschild 1983). Examination of the case of McDonald's shows why we must reconceptualize workplace control in order to illuminate the dynamics of service work. Because the greatest challenge to accepted understandings of work comes from what I call "interactive service work" — work that involves direct interaction between workers and service recipients — I will focus not on hamburger-flippers, but on hamburger-servers.

Like many factory and office jobs, McDonald's jobs have been "routinized." Management has specified in advance almost all aspects of the work, so workers repeat a set of relatively simple tasks over and over again, with little opportunity for decision-making. In Braverman's (1974) term, the jobs have been "deskilled." Historians and sociologists of work have devoted considerable attention to struggles over control of the workplace. Studies of manufacturing and clerical work have focused on employers' and workers' ongoing attempts to take or maintain as much control as possible over the work, which puts the interests of these two groups directly at odds. Since routinization limits the control that workers have over many aspects of their jobs, writers on the subject have typically assumed that workers will make every effort to resist it. How do the distinctive aspects of interactive service work affect how routinization is imposed and how workers respond to it?

In important ways, routinization affects service jobs much as it affects other kinds of jobs: it makes workers relatively easy to replace, it minimizes their autonomy, and it lowers their wages. In other ways, though, working behind the counter at McDonald's puts different demands on workers than, say, assembly-line work does. Instead of having just one boss issuing instructions, McDonald's workers literally take orders from anyone who comes into the restaurant. Instead of being held accountable only for their physical exertions, workers' moods, facial expressions, and words are subject to supervision.

McDonald's is hardly a "typical" service sector organization: its size, success, and visibility are all extraordinary. However, all interactive service work, ranging from sales to teaching to psychotherapy, shares certain characteristics. By definition, nonemployees are a part of the work process of interactive services. Their presence decisively changes the dynamics of workplace control, since service recipients may both try to exert control themselves and be the target of workers' and managers' control efforts. Also, because the quality of the interaction is frequently part of the service being delivered, there are no clear boundaries between the worker, the work process, and the product in interactive service work. For this reason, employers often feel entitled to extend their control efforts to more and more aspects of workers' selves. Workers' looks, words, personalities, feelings, thoughts, and attitudes may all be treated by employers as legitimate targets of intervention. Controlling interactive service work can therefore require techniques and induce responses that are not typical in other kinds of workplaces.[2]

While opinions differ on whether McDonald's jobs are worth having, they are well worth analyzing. Given the growing dominance of service sector employment, social scientists should take even low-level service work as seriously as they have taken manufacturing, managerial, and professional work. Since McDonald's has the virtue of almost universal familiarity, it provides a convenient starting place for a discussion of how our understanding of workplace control needs to be expanded if it is to accommodate the range of experiences of interactive service workers. It is important to keep in mind, however, that although McDonald's approach to controlling service work — strict standardization — has been emulated by many businesses, strategies for resolving the dilemmas of control peculiar to service work vary considerably.

I collected data at McDonald's through participant observation and interviewing during the spring through fall of 1986. I attended classes at McDonald's main management training facility, Hamburger University, in Oakbrook, Illinois. At a local franchise, I was trained to serve customers (to "work window" in McDonald's phrasing) and worked half a dozen shifts. I conducted twenty-seven interviews with crew people and interviewed or spoke informally with management trainers, the managers of the franchise and its owner, and a former McDonald's executive who had been in charge of employee research. I also spent a great deal of time hanging around the franchise's crew room, listening to and talking with workers. Because my research was part of a larger project on the routinization of service interactions, my worker interview sample was limited to the window crew, the people who deal with customers most directly. While I did not investigate the experiences of grill workers and other crew people as systematically, I got to know some of these workers and heard about their reactions to their jobs through informal conversations and observation. All of my informants were aware that I was conducting research on McDonald's, although customers were not.

In the sections that follow I show how McDonald's instituted control mechanisms that allowed the company to overcome difficulties inherent in the application of the principles of routinization to interactive service work. It has extended organizational control in several ways: in scope, by subjecting customers to standardization; in depth, by subjecting more aspects of workers' selves to regulation; and in intensity, by using multiple forms of constraint and supervision to standardize every detail of the work. Next, I turn to the outcomes of McDonald's control efforts, showing that we can understand these outcomes only by applying a more complex model of workplace dynamics than the literature provides. The interests and resources of workers and management remain crucial determinants of workplace practices, but the interests of service recipients must also be taken into account. The involvement of nonemployees in the work process means that a three-way struggle for control, with sometimes shifting alliances, replaces the familiar tug of war between workers and management. To understand the responses of workers and customers to managerial control strategies, we must therefore examine their effects on relations between workers and customers.

## McDonald's: Routinizing Interactive Service Work

McDonald's has tried to control almost every aspect of its business by using the classic principles of routinization — make as many decisions as possible in advance and make sure that the work is carried out according to managerial dicta. In doing so, however, the company has had to go beyond the practices used to routinize manufacturing work by subjecting more aspects of people to control, by making nonemployees targets of control, and by using additional techniques of control.

Routinization is only one managerial approach to controlling work, and one that seems, on the face of it, to be ill-suited to interactive service work. In fact, many discussions of service companies stress that adding value through customization is increasingly central to competitiveness (e.g., Noyelle 1987). Moreover, it seems self-evident that the possibilities for routinizing service work are limited by the intrinsic fluidity and negotiability of human interactions. Whereas routinization is intended in part to insure that outputs of uniform quality are produced, the goal of uniformity is itself problematic in interactive work. Since good service is often equated with "personal service," standardization may necessarily undercut quality in human interactions.

Aside from the desirability of routinizing service interactions, the distinctive features of interactive service work would seem to make the process extremely difficult. First, the involvement of nonemployees in the work process complicates routinization considerably, since routines are only useful if the conditions and specifications of work are relatively predictable (Stinchcombe 1990). Service recipients' presence introduces an element of unpredictability (Mills 1986), so their behavior must somehow be standardized if the routines are to be workable. Second, the indivisibility of workers' selves from the work process and work product motivates some employers to extend their control efforts to aspects of workers' lives usually considered matters of individual personality or choice. Such intervention might well be resented and resisted.

McDonald's amply illustrates, however, that customization is only one route to success in a service business. Not only is routinization of service interactions quite possible, it can also be extremely profitable. With over 11,800 outlets worldwide, McDonald's is by far the world's largest fast-food company (*McDonald's Annual Report for 1990:* 1). It is also a major employer: in the United States alone, McDonald's restaurants employ about half a million people (Bertagnoli 1989: 33), including one out of fifteen first-time job seekers (Wildavsky 1989: 30). Ray Kroc, McDonald's founder, aimed to achieve the kind of tight control over work routines and product quality that centralized production in factories makes possible, in a business that is necessarily highly decentralized. He succeeded on a massive scale. Kroc instituted strict standardization of every element of the business. Although there are some matters that the company is legally obliged to leave to the discretion of its franchise owners, McDonald's has created centrally promulgated standards for how to perform every task associated with running its restaurants, as well as programs to teach these practices, equipment designed to implement the standards, and systems for monitoring the compliance of workers in both company-owned and franchise outlets.

Some service organizations grant front-line workers discretion to vary their work in response to the uncertainties and irregularities introduced into the work process by service recipients, but McDonald's has found ways to overcome the obstacles to routinization noted above. To deal with the tension between quality service and customization, it has minimized customers' expectations of individualized treatment while also trying to provide some semblance of personal service through the routinization of emotion work. It has greatly curtailed the unpredictability customers might bring to the work process by making sure they know how to fit into McDonald's routines. It has tried to make the standardization of personal characteristics palatable to workers and has also curtailed their ability to resist organizational dictates.

McDonald's has carried routinization so far that workers' decision-making power is almost eliminated. As one window worker told me, "They've tried to break it down so that it's almost idiot-proof." Most of the workers agreed that there was little call for them to use their own judgment on the job, since there were rules about virtually everything. If unusual problems arose, the workers were supposed to turn them over to a manager.

The interactive part of the job was standardized as the "Six Steps of Window Service," an unvarying routine for taking orders, assembling meals, and accepting payment. Greeting and thanking customers and asking for their return business were required, but workers were allowed some leeway to vary their phrases to avoid sounding like robots. Smiles, eye contact, and friendliness were monitored by managers (although workers who were speedy but minimally civil were tolerated).[3]

Many of the noninteractive parts of the window workers' job (as well as the grill workers') had been made idiot-proof through automation. At the franchise I studied, not only did the computerized cash registers make it unnecessary for the window workers to remember prices, calculate taxes, or make change, they also helped regulate some of the crew's interactive work by reminding them to try to increase the size of each sale through "suggestive selling." For example, when a customer ordered a Big Mac, large fries, and a regular Coke, the cash register buttons for cookies, hot apple pies, ice cream cones, and ice cream sundaes would light up, prompting the worker to suggest dessert.

To ensure that the detailed routines were carried out as intended, McDonald's management had to face two problems of control characteristic of interactive service work: how to standardize the self-presentation of workers and how to standardize the behavior of service recipients. Workers' self-presentation was subject to managerial control because McDonald's was selling customers a particular kind of experience as well as a meal. To create that experience, workers were asked not only to carry out physical tasks as specified but also to assume the cheerful, wholesome, agreeable persona McDonald's advertises. That is, they were asked to cede considerable control of their self-presentation to management.

The crew workers' appearance was standardized with uniforms and with rules detailing acceptable haircuts, jewelry, make-up, and fingernail length and color.[4] Window workers' words and manners were closely regulated, too. Their scripts, while not completely rigid, allowed quite limited variation in the service interaction. On some occasions workers were required to use specific sentences, such as, "Would you like to try our Bacon Double Cheeseburger?," in every encounter. There were also rules about what workers could *not* say. No matter how rude or insulting a customer was, crew members could not talk back, but were expected to remain polite and accommodating. To ensure that they conveyed cheerfulness and eagerness to serve, window workers' demeanor and body language were subject to regulation. Managers reprimanded those who did not follow through on their instructions to smile and make eye contact.

So that workers would be more likely to follow through on these requirements of their own accord, McDonald's taught "emotion rules" (Hochschild 1983) and ways of thinking that justified them. Managers acknowledged that some customers could be obnoxious, but guided workers to swallow their pride and suppress any annoyance they might feel. Several kinds of practices conveyed that message with varying degrees of subtlety. The "Ten Commandments of Service" studied by window workers preached, "The customer is not someone to argue with or match wits with," and "The customer does us an honor when he calls; we are not doing him a favor by serving him." Customers were usually called "guests," a term that made it somewhat easier for workers to accept the requirement that they remain politely deferential by invoking a familiar situation in which such behavior does not imply subservience. In encouraging workers not to take ill-treatment personally, McDonald's managers asked that they distance themselves from their jobs. However, the managers did want workers to identify with their jobs at least strongly enough to regard job performance as reflective of their discipline and capability. One low-level manager invoked the ideal of "professionalism," out of place as it might seem, to urge workers to take pride in doing their work well. "Don't let me catch you balling up the top of the bags," she cautioned the window workers. "You should fold it neatly twice so you look like a professional."

Through uniforms, rules about self-presentation, scripts, and emotion rules, McDonald's tried to control many aspects of its workers' selves. They required window workers to suppress some emotional reactions and simulate others, allowing them relatively little scope for self-expression. McDonald's window workers did not experience an extreme version of managerial manipulation, however. Although the inseparability of the worker, the work process, and the product meant that more aspects of the window workers' selves were subject to managerial control than is true in most manufacturing jobs, for example, for the most part the demands on them were limited to "surface acting" (see Hochschild 1983).

Many interactive service workers are subject to considerably more intensive manipulation of their thoughts and attitudes that McDonald's exerts. McDonald's did not find it necessary to attempt a thoroughgoing transformation of workers' personalities because it relied so little on workers' discretion. Organizations that depend on the decision-making of employees are likely to pay more attention to their hearts and minds. For example, insurance agents and direct sales distributors, who work without direct supervision and who must try to overcome the resistance of unwilling prospects, are subjected to quite sweeping attempts to change their characters (see Chapter 7; Biggart 1989; Butterfield 1985; Leidner 1993). In such cases, the effects of standardization are intended to extend beyond working hours, creating people who are, depending on the job, more optimistic, determined, assertive, materialistic, ruthless, or understanding.

Some elements of this more transformative approach to routinization were apparent in McDonald's management training. The company could not have removed decision-making authority from its crew workers' jobs so thoroughly were it not for the constant presence of managers whose capacity for decision-making it could trust. McDonald's went as far as it could in guiding that decision-making, issuing reams of directives and creating computer programs that standardized managerial techniques (see Garson 1988). But since it had to rely on managers to act in the company's interests in resolving unpredictable or difficult problems, it also worked on their selves in a variety of ways.

McDonald's encouraged management trainees to take Ray Kroc as a model, requiring Hamburger University students to read his autobiography (Kroc with Anderson 1977) and frequently quoting him in lectures and printed materials.[5] Since the managers worked within an organization that minimized flexibility, it was Kroc's determination and commitment to excellence that they were asked to emulate, not his entrepreneurial creativity. The training continually emphasized the tremendous success of the company, both to encourage managers to identify with that success and to drive home the message that managers and owners could rely on corporate directives. Managers' personal identities and styles of interaction were addressed most directly

at Hamburger University through training in transactional analysis, as popu-
larized in *I'm OK, You're OK* (Harris 1969). This training was intended to
alter managers' style in dealing with workers, customers, and fellow managers,
dissuading them from using tyrannical or belittling "parent-child" approaches
and urging them to deal with others on an "adult-adult" level.

For both window workers and managers, then, McDonald's found ways to
bring the selves of employees — whether merely self-presentations or personal
identities — into line with organizational requirements. Persuading employees
to accommodate themselves to the desired persona was an important element
of the control of this interactive service work because of the difficulty of distinguishing between workers and their work processes. Employees were thus
likely to experience at least some sense of disjuncture between their McDonald's persona and their self-identity, a disjuncture to which they could respond
in a variety of ways: they might judge the McDonald's model of the self
positively and embrace it (more common for managers than workers); try to
maintain role distance (Goffman 1961b); focus on agreeable aspects of the role
and resist others; or try to personalize the standardized role.

Extending the range of controls over employees' selves is one challenge for
interactive service organizations, but employers must also concern themselves
with the behavior of nonemployees. Service recipients partly determine the
content of the work as the interactions are in progress, often by direct orders,
and almost always by their attitudes and by their willingness and ability to
cooperate in the service routine. Sometimes, as at McDonald's, they also perform part of the work that might otherwise be done by paid employees.[6]
Concerted efforts to shape the personal identities of service recipients are not
usually necessary, but organizational routines can proceed as planned only if
service recipients' behavior can be made relatively predictable. An analysis of
the control of interactive service work is thus incomplete without attention to
the means by which customers' cooperation is marshaled.

It was obvious that the great majority of the customers at the McDonald's
franchise I studied knew what they were supposed to do and were willing and
able to play their parts in the service routines. They stood in line to order their
food rather than waiting to be served at a table; they delivered their meal orders
in the conventional sequence (hamburgers or other entrees, fries, drinks, des-
serts); they cleaned up after themselves. The customers had been trained in
several ways. First, McDonald's advertising familiarized people with the service
system and products. Second, the design of the restaurants provided cues to
customers, guiding them toward the service line, for example, and making clear
that they were supposed to use the well-marked trash cans (see Wener 1985).
Moreover, most customers had been socialized through long experience with

McDonald's and similar fast-food restaurants, and newcomers could take their cues from more experienced customers.

Not only were McDonald's customers able to play their roles properly, but they were generally willing to cooperate, since, of course, they had already made the decision to do business with McDonald's. It was the relative predictability of customer behavior that made it possible for McDonald's to create such inflexible routines for the window crew. When service recipients are less compliant or well informed, workers are likely to need more discretion to respond to contingencies.

The example of McDonald's demonstrates that basic assumptions about managerial strategies of workplace control need to be revised to make sense of interactive service work. Compared with manufacturing, *what* managers of service workers try to control is different. Not only are workers' physical tasks brought under managerial authority, but many more aspects of workers' selves are manipulated. Another major difference is in *whom* managers are trying to control: service recipients as well as workers are targeted. Meanwhile, the selves of managers may themselves be subject to standardization. In solving the problem of *how* to routinize interactive service work, McDonald's and other service organizations have employed control techniques uncommon in other kinds of work.

We should not assume, however, that the particular strategies McDonald's used to control the work process are available to all interactive service work organizations. Factors such as the complexity of the service transactions, the degree of supervision possible, and the stakes of service recipients and workers in the outcomes of interactions determine what strategies are appropriate for various organizations. The features of McDonald's window crew's routine—the extreme constriction of decision-making authority and the relative superficiality of standardization of workers' identities—reflect the brevity and simplicity of the service interaction, the presence of managers on the scene to handle difficulties, and the motivation of customers to cooperate. In service organizations where the service provided is complex and context-dependent or where only customized service will do, employers will be more dependent on workers' discretion, and workers' power relative to management will be accordingly enhanced. In cases where service recipients are not motivated to cooperate or where they are not sure how to do so, the service workers' routines may themselves be designed to channel the nonemployees' behavior, enhancing workers' control in a different way.

At McDonald's, however, workers' capacity to exercise control over their work was sharply limited. Richard Edwards (1979) has described three main types of control used by employers to direct, evaluate, and reward or punish workers: direct (or simple) control, technical control, and bureaucratic control. McDonald's crew workers were subject to all three of these forms. The ratio of supervisors to workers was quite high, so direct control was exercised by ever-present managers and trainers. Technical control was built into the computerized cash registers, which both dictated how window workers did their jobs and monitored their performance. Bureaucratic control of both the crew workers and the managerial staff was embodied in the detailed sets of regulations that described McDonald's standards for each task and prescribed criteria for evaluation. In addition, McDonald's window workers were further constrained by the direct supervision of customers, who could observe their work, make demands, and register complaints. The combination of these control methods left workers exceptionally little autonomy.

## The Three-Way Dynamic of Control in Interactive Service Work

McDonald's efforts to manipulate the selves of workers and channel the behavior of customers illustrate that interactive service work organizations differ from other employers in what and whom they try to control. To understand the outcomes of these efforts, we must also reopen the questions of who tries to exercise control and how they define their interests.

A basic criticism of Harry Braverman's (1974) formulation of labor process theory was that it overstated management's success in achieving control (Edwards 1979; Littler and Salaman 1982). Numerous sociologists and labor historians have demonstrated that, although managers might try to achieve total control over the work process, their efforts are often met by workers' resistance (see Benson 1986; Edwards 1979; Halle 1984; Montgomery 1979). Even when workers do not fully succeed in withstanding these efforts, they may hold on to control over some matters, and their resistance can affect workplace outcomes in others.[7] We should not assume, therefore, that just because managers of interactive service workers have found ways to deal with the novel problems of regulating the behavior of nonemployees and of standardizing the self-presentations, ideas, and attitudes of workers, the outcomes of their control efforts are obvious. Workers and service recipients have their own preferences about how the interactions are to be carried out and their own resources for trying to act on those preferences.

To make sense of service work, we need to revise the model of workers and employers inevitably working to resist the other's control efforts. While the dynamic of conflict between workers and managers certainly does not disappear, the presence of service recipients greatly complicates the picture. Not only can workers resist employers' efforts to control the work, so too can service recipients. Moreover, customers can themselves try to exert control over workers, management, or both. Still, it is not enough to expand the resistance model of control by simply including service recipients as actors. The participation of three parties means that we can no longer take for granted that the interests of each are in conflict — that is, we cannot assume that workers or customers will resist managerial control efforts. In fact, the alignment of interests of these three parties varies in different kinds of work and even for different features of the same job (see Benson 1986; Wouters 1989).

Service recipients play varied roles in service encounters. They may give orders (restaurant customers) or follow them (doctors' patients) or both (airline passengers); they may have no choice but to participate (citizens dealing with government bureaucracies), or they may try to evade the interaction (fund-raising targets) or seek it out (prostitutes' customers); they may serve simultaneously as raw material and judge of the service (hair salon customers); they may contribute labor, willingly or not (fast-food customers). This variability means that how the interests of service recipients, workers, and management are balanced must be an empirical question. In some circumstances, workers' routines are designed to further their control over customers, in which case their motive to resist them is undermined but customers may try to resist. In others, routines can constrain workers, aligning the interests of managers and customers in controlling the workers. When customers and managers have different interests, workers are often put in the middle. Consequently, not only is the ability of workers and customers to evade managerial controls variable, so too is the interest of each group in doing so.

In interactive service work, we find not a stable pattern of workers and managers acting on interests that are directly opposed to each other, but a complex dynamic in which each of three groups of participants has interests that bring them sometimes into alliance, sometimes into opposition with each of the other two. The three-way play of interests can result in workers having less room to maneuver than they would if customers were not present, but it can also motivate managers to give workers leverage to control the interactions. Workers therefore might have reason either to resent routinization or to appreciate it. In some cases, customers and workers share an interest in avoiding the constraints of the employer-designed routine, but in others one party tries to enforce it on the other. The pattern at McDonald's is thus not generalizable to all interactive service work, but gives some sense of the complexity of the struggle over control in this type of work.

The routines of McDonald's window workers were designed primarily to give customers what they wanted, so long as they limited their wishes to the speedy delivery of a limited range of foods. For the most part, then, customers and managers shared an interest in having workers comply with their prescribed routines. Peter Mills (1986: 121) sees customers as subordinates of service providers, but at McDonald's they functioned more as supervisors. Since customers were generally quite familiar with the routine and since window work was done in full view of customers, service recipients joined management in pressuring workers to perform speedily, politely, and accurately. In other circumstances, such as commission sales jobs, managers and workers share an interest in persuading prospective customers to participate in service interactions they might wish to avoid. In such cases, workers' routines can be designed to enhance workers' control over service recipients, making customers rather than workers more likely to resist organizational control efforts (see Leidner 1993 on insurance sales).

Although particular service organizations generally have a dominant pattern of alliance, the interests of any two parties are unlikely to coincide precisely, creating cross-pressures and incentives for resistance. For example, while most elements of the McDonald's window workers' routine encouraged workers to behave deferentially to customers and to comply with their wishes rather than to manipulate them, there was one element of the routine that was intended to increase sales rather than to please customers: suggestive selling. In every interaction, window workers were required to suggest that the customer buy either another item ("Would you like a hot apple pie with that?") or a more expensive version of an item already ordered ("Will that be a large fries?"). Suggestive selling tended to irritate customers, bringing to the surface the organization's interest in manipulating customers and making the scripted nature of the interaction completely transparent. Most customers simply declined the proffered item, but some snapped, "If I'd wanted it, I'd have ordered it." When customers' and management's preferences differed, as in this matter, workers were put in the difficult position of having to please one party at the expense of the other. Since workers did not benefit directly from higher sales but did feel the effects of customers' annoyance, they usually resolved this dilemma in the customers' favor, omitting suggestive selling whenever they could get away with it.

To the extent that customers shared management's criteria for good work, they could reinforce management's control efforts, reprimanding workers for dawdling or behaving rudely, responding with gratitude and thanks to good work, complaining to workers' superiors when service did not meet their expectations (see Fuller and Smith, Chapter 4). When customers' preferences differed from those of management, workers were put in a still more difficult position.

Elsewhere, service recipients do not necessarily feel free to express their preferences and opinions so directly. If the service is understood to require special expertise, if the worker holds a higher status than the service recipient, or if the service recipient cannot easily take his or her business elsewhere, customer complaints are less commonly voiced than they are at McDonald's (see Goffman 1961a). McDonald's customers had clear expectations and were thus easily dissatisfied, but the window workers had no "status shield" (Hochschild 1983) to protect them from customers' expressions of dissatisfaction.

The workers were quite conscious that they bore the brunt of customers' irritation even when they were not directly to blame for a problem. Some McDonald's customers seemed to be angry for no particular reason and felt free to unleash their bad moods on workers. But others were irritated by the mistakes of backstage McDonald's workers who did not keep up a steady supply of food or who got an order wrong, and customer dissatisfaction often resulted directly from managerial choices. Rigid rules about which items could be served at which hours of the day disappointed some people, for example, and skimping on labor costs resulted in slower service. Since window workers were the most readily available targets, they were frequently blamed for things that were beyond their control. Evelyn Nakano Glenn and Roslyn L. Feldberg (1979) point out that interactive service workers, who often do not have the authority to change routines to meet customer requests, can serve as useful buffers who protect management from customer dissatisfaction.

In contrast, workers had relatively few resources for exercising control over customers or even for defending their dignity in the face of insult. Workers did try to guide customer behavior in some minor ways. For example, they sometimes conveyed by their manner that the customer should make decisions quickly, prompted customers with questions, or tried to preempt a display of impatience or anger by being especially cordial. But the workers' routines were not designed to empower them to control customers, except in the matter of suggestive selling, since most customers came to McDonald's willing and able to fit into the company's routine. Moreover, the rules about proper treatment of customers expressly ruled out most countermeasures by which workers might respond to obnoxious service recipients. Forbidden to talk back and unable to withdraw from unpleasant encounters by leaving their posts, workers could do little to counter rude or hostile customers or display their resentment other than scowl, for which they might be reprimanded, or project an icy distance. As one worker summed up the relation between crew and customers, "We're sort of at their mercy."

The balance of power between customers and workers varies considerably in different kinds of interactive service work. Some workers, who have the means to subject unpleasant service recipients to inconvenience or other trouble, may even feel that service recipients are at *their* mercy. Employers may contribute to workers' power over service recipients through the design of the service routines. The insurance agents I studied memorized scripts and practiced body language that made it as difficult as possible for prospective customers to interrupt them or turn down their sales pitch (Leidner 1993). In such cases, the interests of workers and employers are more closely aligned than those of service recipients and employers.

Whatever the dominant pattern of alliance in a given service organization, there are likely to be elements of the work process that set up different incentives, just as suggestive selling runs counter to the alliance of interest between McDonald's management and customers. For example, although the insurance agents and the company generally shared an interest in getting prospects to buy as much life insurance as possible, there were times when the prospect and the agent shared an interest that was contrary to the company's: an agent might be eager to get the commission on a sale to a willing customer who did not quite meet the guidelines for acceptable underwriting risk. Sometimes, of course, the worker's interests might be contrary to those of both the service recipient and the company, as when a greedy agent cheats customers and threatens the reputation of the company.

Furthermore, there can also be considerable individual variation in how much workers and customers value autonomy, custom service, and emotional investment, so members of these groups vary in the extent to which they try to evade organizational controls. At McDonald's, some window workers who resented the requirement that they be smiling and personable withheld all expression of involvement in interactions with customers (until rebuked for not smiling), protecting their own interests at the expense of management and customers. Some workers, in contrast, enjoyed chatting with customers or took pride in being able to provide a pleasant moment in someone's day. By following the scripted routine with enthusiasm or going a bit beyond it, they usually served both management's and customers' interests as well as their own. Still others focused their efforts on performing speedily rather than courteously, since that allowed them to challenge themselves without accepting a subservient stance. Their strategy satisfied certain customers and furthered some of management's interests, but their no-nonsense attitude and undisguised impatience with indecisive people made other customers feel rushed and pressured.

Customers as well as workers varied in their preferences, with some trying to engage the worker in conversation while others refused even to meet the worker's eye or otherwise acknowledge that they were dealing with a human being. Treatment that offended some workers was appreciated by others, who were grateful for undemanding and efficient interactions. Unlike salespeople's or fundraisers' prospects, McDonald's customers rarely made significant efforts to evade the routine imposed by management. Customer dissatisfaction was more often a response to what they felt was improper functioning of the routine, such as a long wait or a nondeferential worker.

Managerial success in instituting controls therefore depends in part on the balance of interests among the three parties. Do service recipients benefit when workers follow their prescribed procedures closely? Do workers' routines circumscribe customer behavior in ways that workers appreciate? Are employers' preferences about the conduct of service interactions closest to workers' or to service recipients'? How can workers and service recipients exercise control over each other in the course of the service interaction (see, e.g., Prottas 1979; Whyte 1946)? Because the answers to these questions vary, workers and customers may or may not try to resist the control efforts of management.

An appreciation of the triangular pattern of relations in interactive service work makes clear the limitations of the resistance model that has characterized studies of workplace control. Virtually all sociological and historical writing on this topic has taken for granted that managerial efforts to extend their control over the work process, especially through routinization, are contrary to the interests of workers. The literature therefore suggests a limited range of possible worker responses. They can try, individually or collectively, to resist managerial control; they can be dissatisfied with work they experience as alienating, unchallenging, and unconnected to themselves; or, suffering from false consciousness, they can fail to grasp that they should be unhappy or resistant. Attention to the three-way play of control reveals a wider range of worker responses and provides a framework for understanding them.

At McDonald's, some workers did dislike the stringent controls of routinization, and they expressed their resentment either directly or through behavior that demonstrated their determination to maintain an autonomous stance. Some seemed to be neutral rather than hostile toward their routinized work, however, and still others enthusiastically embraced either routinization in general or the content of their own work routines. The involvement of service recipients in the work process means that employers' control efforts can serve some of the interests of interactive service workers, so there is no reason for analysts to dismiss positive and neutral responses.

In the case of insurance sales, it was easy to understand why the agents showed little resistance to an extreme version of routinization. Because both they and management benefited when agents maintained the upper hand in interactions with potential customers, the agents' routines had been designed to maximize their control over prospects. While routinization might have lessened the workers' autonomy vis-à-vis management, it gave them more control over their work. At McDonald's, even without the compensation of greater leverage over customers, workers did not consistently object to management's tight control over the work.[8]

There were several factors that muted McDonald's workers' resistance to routinization. First, the routine provided workers with some benefits. It gave them a clear sense of what was required of them, thus limiting the demands that could be placed on them and making them feel confident that they could do their jobs. Furthermore, while the literature on work tends to assume that workers prefer jobs that engage and challenge them, some McDonald's workers appreciated the way the routine allowed them to disengage from the work. Quite a few of the workers preferred interactions that did not require that they give their full attention to or make personal contact with a service recipient. When the work role is a subordinate one, role distance can be valuable, and a repetitious routine makes such distance easier to maintain. For that reason, the routine also provided psychic protection from the rudeness or inconsiderateness of customers, since workers could avoid interpreting such behavior as an assault on the self. If the strict routines, by exasperating some customers, made poor treatment of workers more likely, it also made it easier for workers not to take it personally. Another factor that dampened workers' resentment of managerial control was the tendency of interactive service routines to refocus conflict between workers and service recipients. Not only did customers tend to direct their irritation at workers, but workers tended to focus on the unreasonableness of customers' behavior and demands, not of managements'. For example, rather than deploring managerial pressure to hurry, they resented indecisive customers who held things up.

The literature does not provide a clear prediction of how service recipients will react to organizational controls. In most writing on work, nonemployees are simply absent. Among writers on service work there is little agreement, with some assuming that routinization makes it more difficult for customers to have their wishes met and others that customers would be better served if workers followed their routines more faithfully (Garson 1988; Koepp 1987; Roman 1979). In fact, whether service recipients' interests are furthered by routinization varies by organizational context and by individual circumstances and preferences. Standardization may benefit service recipients by defining their prerogatives clearly, mandating equal treatment, and providing a floor of competent service. However, some service routines are explicitly designed to constrain service recipients' behavior, and most limit the possibilities for delivering customized service to meet individual preferences or needs.

Thus the dynamics of control in interactive service work are not as easily predictable as the standard model of resistance would suggest. Both workers and service recipients can derive some benefits from employers' control strategies. How closely the interests of workers and service recipients are aligned with those of management varies, so the degree of acquiescence and resistance of both workers and customers varies as well. Furthermore, since participants have an assortment of interests and there is individual variation in how much workers and customers value autonomy, custom service, and emotional investment, members of these groups vary in the extent to which they choose to evade organizational controls. It is a mistake to believe, then, that the only reason that workers (or service recipients) would embrace routinization is that they misperceive their own interests.

## *Conclusion*

This examination of workplace control at McDonald's calls into question some basic premises of theories of the labor process. The scope of employers' control efforts, the responses of workers to those efforts, the centrality of skill as a determinant of control, and the societal effects of regimes of workplace control each need to be reconsidered in light of the distinctive attributes of interactive service work.

The involvement of nonemployees in service interactions fundamentally alters the dynamics of the contest over control of the work process. Instead of a struggle between two parties whose interests are assumed to be directly contradictory, interactive service work presents a more variable three-way pattern. Employers must find ways to control service recipients if their operations are to run smoothly, and in some circumstances these service recipients try to resist that control. If customers share many interests with management and have the means to reinforce managerial control, workers will find that the presence of service recipients further weakens their position. However, in other circumstances, management's interests are served by enhancing workers' control over service recipients, in which case customers rather than workers look for ways to elude organizational control. The alignment of interests of the three parties to service interactions thus varies across types of services, depending largely on the degree to which workers are empowered to manage the behavior of service recipients. The assumptions of the "resistance model" of workplace control do not predict the behavior of interactive service workers well, because such workers have a stake in complying with those employer controls that enhance their capacity to control service recipients or to protect themselves psychologically from treatment they consider demeaning.

The inseparability of the worker, the work process, and the product of interactive service work means that employers extend their control efforts to workers' internal lives. To be sure, interactive service organizations are not the only employers to take an interest in their workers' thoughts and feelings. Managers of all sorts concern themselves with workers' motivation, willingness to cede authority to management, dedication, and loyalty to the organization. But interactive service organizations have reason to attempt more open and systematic control of workers' selves than other employers. Edwards (1979: 148–51) argues explicitly that employers take an interest in workers' attitudes to ensure the proper functioning of the control and reward system, not to direct the work process itself. In interactive service work, however, workers' attitudes, emotions, and ideas are clearly closely related to the accomplishment of their jobs. Employers may therefore make unusually invasive interventions without the legitimacy of those efforts being challenged.

Sociologists often make a distinction between workers' skill and their attitudes (see, e.g., Finlay and Martin 1991). Here, however, that distinction is hard to sustain, since the willingness and capacity of workers to manipulate and project their attitudes in the organization's interest are central to their competence on the job. The accounts of routinization provided by Braverman (1974) and subsequent analyses have treated deskilling as the crux of employer control, but skill is a misleading label for the attitudes, personal attributes, character traits, and interactional styles that interactive service employers try to standardize. Workers' subjectivity is at the heart of service employer efforts to control the labor process, and our theories must be reconsidered to give subjectivity a more central place. The self of the worker is the ground of workplace struggles for control in interactive service work, not just the worker's capacity and right to exercise skill.

Finally, the study of control in interactive service work provides a bridge between the sociology of work and broader studies of culture and society. Most studies of work assume that the struggle for control affects the society at large through its effects on workers' consciousness and on their degree of economic power. If, however, the Marxist argument that consciousness is determined at the point of production is valid, then the control efforts of interactive service organizations have a more direct impact on the culture at large. As service recipients, people find themselves at numerous points of production on their own time, forced to respond to organizational efforts to shape their interactions with other people. Understanding the effects of such manipulations on the cultural milieu and on social relations in general challenges sociologists of work to broaden their vision.

## NOTES

*Acknowledgments:* Thanks to Sam Kaplan and Annette Lareau for their help with this chapter.
1. Simpson (1985) does note the relevance of relations with clients to determining the extent of worker control.

2. The recent boom in business literature on managing services supports the contention that controlling such work presents novel challenges. Some early work argued that service productivity could be maximized by applying the principles of the assembly line, and simply extending industrial methods of production and assessment to new settings (e.g., Levitt 1972). The trend in advice to managers, however, has been to focus on the distinctive challenges of service provision: How can the quality of services be measured? How can managers inspire their front-line workers? Can the expectations and behavior of customers be managed? (See, e.g., Albrecht 1988; Albrecht and Zemke 1985; Cziepel, Solomon, and Surprenant 1985; Heskett, Sasser, and Hart 1990; Lovelock 1988; Mills 1986; Normann 1984; Zemke with Schaaf 1989.) The intangibility of the product and the real-time involvement of customers in service work complicate the control issues that are the heart of management.

3. Hochschild's (1983) work on flight attendants and bill collectors provides a detailed account of methods of standardizing the emotion work demanded of interactive service workers.

4. These rules sometimes impinged on workers' dignity as well as their self-expression. Many found their polyester tunic outfits degrading and were pleased when those uniforms were replaced by ones that more closely resembled street clothes. Some felt aggrieved at having to wear large Styrofoam Chinese peasant hats during a special promotion of "Shanghai McNuggets," which they believed made them ridiculous.

5. Biggart (1989) shows that direct sales workers are also frequently encouraged to model themselves on a charismatic leader.

6. Glazer (1984) has analyzed this trend, and many business writers (e.g., Lovelock and Young 1979; Normann 1984) strongly support it.

7. Furthermore, others have pointed out that it can be in employers' interests to allow workers some degree of autonomy to build their commitment or to add flexibility (see Burawoy 1979; Friedman 1977; Fuller and Smith, Chapter 4).

8. Given McDonald's high rates of employee turnover, however, it is reasonable to assume that my sample of current workers understated the level of dissatisfaction with these jobs.

## REFERENCES

Albrecht, Karl. 1988. *At America's Service: How Corporations Can Revolutionize the Way They Treat Their Customers.* Homewood, IL: Dow Jones–Irwin.

Albrecht, Karl, and Ron Zemke. 1985. *Service America! Doing Business in the New Economy.* Homewood, IL: Dow Jones–Irwin.

Benson, Susan Porter. 1986. *Counter Cultures: Saleswomen, Managers, and Customers in American Department Stores, 1890–1940.* Urbana: University of Illinois Press.

Bertagnoli, Lisa. 1989. "McDonald's: Company of the Quarter Century." *Restaurants & Institutions,* July 10, pp. 32–60.

Biggart, Nicole Woolsey. 1989. *Charismatic Capitalism: Direct Selling Organizations in America.* Chicago: University of Chicago Press.

Braverman, Harry. 1974. *Labor and Monopoly Capital: The Degradation of Work in the Twentieth Century.* New York: Monthly Review Press.

Burawoy, Michael. 1979. *Manufacturing Consent: Changes in the Labor Process under Monopoly Capitalism.* Chicago: University of Chicago Press.

Butterfield, Steve. 1985. *Amway: The Cult of Free Enterprise.* Boston: South End Press.

Cziepel, John A., Michael R. Solomon, and Carol F. Surprenant. 1985. *The Service Encoun-*

*ter: Managing Employee/Customer Interaction in Service Businesses.* Lexington, MA: Lexington Books.

Edwards, Richard. 1979. *Contested Terrain: The Transformation of the Workplace in the Twentieth Century.* New York: Basic Books.

Finlay, William, and Jack K. Martin. 1991. "Attitudes vs. Skill: Technology and Hiring Decisions in Electrical and Textile Plants." Paper presented at the annual meeting of the American Sociological Association, Cincinnati.

Friedman, Andrew. 1977. *Industry and Labour.* London: Macmillan.

Garson, Barbara. 1988. *The Electronic Sweatshop: How Computers Are Transforming the Office of the Future into the Factory of the Past.* New York: Simon and Schuster.

——. 1975. *All the Livelong Day: The Meaning and Demeaning of Routine Work.* New York: Doubleday.

Glazer, Nona Y. 1984. "Servants to Capital: Unpaid Domestic Labor and Paid Work." *Review of Radical Political Economics* 16: 61–87.

Glenn, Evelyn Nakano, and Roslyn L. Feldberg. 1979. "Women as Mediators in the Labor Process." Paper presented at the annual meeting of the American Sociological Association, Boston.

Goffman, Erving. 1961a. "The Medical Model and Mental Hospitalization: Some Notes on the Vicissitudes of the Tinkering Trades." In *Asylums: Essays on the Social Situation of Mental Patients and Other Inmates* (pp. 321–86). Garden City, NY: Anchor Books.

——. 1961b. "Role Distance." In *Encounters: Two Studies in the Sociology of Interaction* (pp. 83–152). Indianapolis, IN: Bobbs-Merrill.

Halle, David. 1984. *America's Working Man: Work, Home, and Politics among Blue Collar Property Owners.* Chicago: University of Chicago Press.

Harris, Thomas A. 1969. *I'm OK, You're OK: A Practical Introduction to Transactional Analysis.* New York: Harper & Row.

Heskett, James L., W. Earl Sasser, Jr., and Christopher W. L. Hart. 1990. *Service Breakthroughs: Changing the Rules of the Game.* New York: Free Press.

Hochschild, Arlie Russell. 1983. *The Managed Heart: Commercialization of Human Feeling.* Berkeley: University of California Press.

Kirkland, Richard I. 1985. "Are Service Jobs Good Jobs?" *Fortune*, June 10, pp. 38–43.

Knights, David, and Hugh Wilmott. 1990. *Labour Process Theory.* London: Macmillan.

Koepp, Stephen. 1987. "Pul-eeze! Will Somebody Help Me?" *Time*, February 2, pp. 48–55.

Kroc, Ray, with Robert Anderson. 1977. *Grinding It Out: The Making of McDonald's.* Chicago: Contemporary Books.

Leidner, Robin. 1993. *Fast Food, Fast Talk: Service Work and the Routinization of Everyday Life.* Berkeley: University of California Press.

Levitt, Theodore. 1972. "Production-Line Approach to Service." *Harvard Business Review* 50: 41–52.

Littler, Craig, and Graham Salaman. 1982. "Bravermania and Beyond: Recent Theories of the Labour Process." *Sociology* 16: 251–69.

Lovelock, Christopher H., ed. 1988. *Managing Services: Marketing, Operations, and Human Resources.* Englewood Cliffs, NJ: Prentice Hall.

Lovelock, Christopher H., and Robert F. Young. 1979. "Look to Consumers to Increase Productivity." *Harvard Business Review* 57(May–June): 168–78.

*McDonald's Annual Report.* 1990. Oak Brook, IL.

Mills, Peter K. 1986. *Managing Service Industries: Organizational Practices in a Postindustrial Economy.* Cambridge, MA: Ballinger Publishing Co.

Montgomery, David. 1979. *Workers' Control in America: Studies in the History of Work, Technology, and Labor Struggles.* Cambridge: Cambridge University Press.

Normann, Richard. 1984. *Service Management: Strategy and Leadership in Service Businesses.* Chichester: John Wiley and Sons, Ltd.

Noyelle, Thierry J. 1987. *Beyond Industrial Dualism: Market and Job Segmentation in the New Economy.* Boulder, CO: Westview Press.

Prottas, Jeffrey. 1979. *People Processing.* Lexington, MA: Lexington Books.

Roman, Murray. 1979. *Telephone Marketing Techniques.* New York: AMACOM (American Management Association).

Silvestri, George T., and John M. Lukasiewic. 1987. "A Look at Occupational Employment Trends to the Year 2000." *Monthly Labor Review* 10(September): 46–63.

Simpson, Richard L. 1985. "Social Control of Occupations and Work." *Annual Review of Sociology* 11: 415–36.

Smith, Joan. 1984. "The Paradox of Women's Poverty: Wage-Earning Women and Economic Transformation." *Signs* 10: 291–310.

Stinchcombe, Arthur L. 1990. *Information and Organizations.* Berkeley: University of California Press.

Thompson, Paul. 1989. *The Nature of Work: An Introduction to Debates on the Labour Process.* 2nd ed. London: Macmillan.

Wener, Richard E. 1985. "The Environmental Psychology of Service Encounters." In John A. Czepiel, Michael R. Solomon, and Carol F. Suprenant, eds. *The Service Encounter: Managing Employee/Customer Interaction in Service Businesses* (pp. 101–12). Lexington, MA: Lexington Books.

Whyte, William F. 1946. "When Workers and Customers Meet." In William F. Whyte, ed., *Industry and Society* (pp. 123–47). New York: McGraw-Hill.

Wildavsky, Ben. 1989. "McJobs: Inside America's Largest Youth Training Program." *Policy Review* 49: 30–37.

Wouters, Cas. 1989. "The Sociology of Emotions and Flight Attendants: Hochschild's *Managed Heart.*" *Theory, Culture, & Society* 6: 95–123.

Zemke, Ron, with Dick Schaaf. 1989. *The Service Edge: 101 Companies That Profit from Customer Care.* New York: NAL Books.

## Chapter 3

# The Politics of Service Production: Route Sales Work in the Potato-Chip Industry

- Steven H. Lopez

M any evenings, Rudy spends several hours at the warehouse getting ready for the next day, even though he's always the last driver in from his potato-chip route for the Granddad's snack-food company. Rudy's route is the hardest, and most dangerous, of the thirty or so in the midwestern city of Springfield; most of his stops are small liquor stores, beer drive-throughs, and bars in the poorest and most violent neighborhoods in the city.

Rudy may be the fastest route person I've ever seen. He flies through his route at an incredible physical pace, starting at 6:30 in the morning and working nonstop until 4:30 or 5:00 in the afternoon. He can pack small bags of chips into boxes and onto shelves a dozen at a time — six in each hand. He can pull into a stop, make out a $150 small-bag order, fill it, stock the shelves, get paid, bullshit with the owner, and be on his way in about twenty minutes.

By the time he gets back to the warehouse, Rudy is always wired from the adrenaline and is usually seething with more than a day's worth of frustration. The first thing he does when he gets in is to check the board to see what items they're out of; the second thing he does is to yell at the warehouse manager for being out of the products he needs for the next day. If the route sales supervisor is around, Rudy will yell at him, too, but the supervisor usually just leaves Rudy alone and lets him vent. Most drivers spend only about an hour at the warehouse (to straighten up their trucks, make out their orders for the next day, pull the orders from the warehouse, load their trucks, and turn in their money and paperwork), but Rudy, exhausted, often goes slowly, sometimes taking two hours to get out of there, around 6:30 or 7:00 in the evening.

Rudy worries that his life is slipping by and that he's missing it because he's spending so much time out on his route. He's still eighteen in his mind, he says, but he's actually almost forty, and his body feels old. He's slowing down; he can't go as fast as he used to. He's usually so tired when he gets home that all he can do is eat something and go to bed, and he hates the fact that his job has dominated his waking hours to such an extent for so many years.

Rudy's route is slowly becoming less lucrative, but it's not getting any easier. Recent changes in the structure of the retail grocery business in Springfield—most notably, the arrival of the new warehouselike "superstores"—have hurt the few real grocery stores Rudy did have on his route, driving several of them out of business. At the same time, Granddad's chips are no longer "king of the hill" in Springfield; Granddad's faces more and more competition from Frito-Lay, Eagle Snacks, and other large snack-food companies. Across the country, local and regional snack companies like Granddad's are giving way to snack-food subsidiaries of global corporations; the neighborhood supermarket, having long ago supplanted the corner grocer, is now giving way to the chain of superstores.

Route sales work in the potato-chip business is an ideal site to investigate changes in authority relations over time because workers' relations with customers are nearly as enduring as, and often more significant than, their relations with their own managers. Because the most important customers are large retail stores rather than private individuals or individually run small businesses, route sales workers must try to successfully negotiate the boundaries among multiple, powerful organizations as well as manage personal relationships with the individuals who represent them. As customer organizations become larger, they gain the ability to reshape authority relations affecting the route sales workers who serve them. On the other hand, workers like Rudy, who are left behind on routes without the biggest chain stores, retain some of their autonomy only at the cost of a declining income.

Contact between workers and customers makes service work different from traditional manufacturing, since customers as well as managers can attempt to control the labor process. Recent studies of service work have explored some dimensions of this difference. Managers may use customers as part of their own managerial strategies for controling the labor process; customer feedback techniques make organizational power and the capacity for surveillance more diffuse and insidious, allowing managers to present their own control initiatives as requirements of the customer (Fuller and Smith, Chapter 4; Rafaeli 1989). The decentralized and intermittent nature of much service work has accentuated the role of the customer as management surrogate at sites of service production from which the employer may in fact be physically absent (Gottfried 1992). In many forms of interactive service work in which attitudes and emotions are part of the service, employers are encouraged by the intertwining of labor process and labor product to attempt to control workers' personalities as well as their behavior (Hochschild 1983; Leidner 1993). Robin Leidner (Chapter 2) also shows that authority relations in service work can be complex and situational; alliances between parties to the labor process are formed and broken in different contexts and settings.

All of these studies call attention to the rising importance of service occupations and emphasize important features of service work organization. However, they suffer from several weaknesses. First, unlike the classic studies of the labor process pioneered by Harry Braverman (1974), the new service work studies generally fail to study changes in work organization and its regulation. They argue persuasively that the labor process in service work is different from that in traditional forms of industrial production, but they do not systematically analyze changes within service occupations themselves, nor do they attempt to show the significance of these changes for capitalism as a whole. Second, studies of service work have tended to focus exclusively on the provision of services to individuals, ignoring the extensive and growing networks of interfirm services. This chapter attempts to partially rectify both of these problems by focusing precisely on changes in patterns of control affecting route sales workers in the snack-food industry.

## Production Politics

Leidner (1993; see also Chapter 2) has persuasively argued that existing models of the labor process derived from studies of industrial work are inapplicable to service work. Such models consider only relations between workers and managers, treating customers as external to the labor process. But the nontransferability of these kinds of models does not mean that studies of service work must reject all of the concepts developed by studies of manufacturing. In particular, Michael Burawoy's (1979; 1985) notion of *production regimes* is an idea that transcends the limitations of his traditional-manufacturing model. Burawoy argues that production has a politics of its own; production regimes are modes of regulating labor and of organizing force and consent in the labor process. At any given time, different regimes can be found in different sectoral or geographic locations, but capitalism itself can be seen as a succession of dominant regimes of labor regulation whose trajectories are connected to political struggles both inside and outside of production. Such a conception allows a much better understanding of changes in capitalism than relying, as Leidner does, on the unilinear concept of routinization (or, as Braverman does, on deskilling). Conceptualizing the labor process and its regulation in such a one-dimensional way fails to capture the qualitative differences among modes of labor regulation; it forces the observer to reduce qualitative changes to issues of more or less.

Burawoy (1985) argues that the dominant modes of labor regulation in the nineteenth and early twentieth centuries were *despotic* regimes of production. Pure market despotism obtained where workers' separation from the means of subsistence was complete rather than incomplete, where capitalists' control over the labor process was real rather than formal (i.e., where capitalists were able to separate conception from execution and reduce the labor process to tasks devised by capitalists), where there was a large pool of surplus labor, and where interfirm competition was anarchic rather than limited. Under these conditions, workers were dependent on particular capitalists, and the labor market acted as a whip: the fear of being sacked ensured workers' compliance with the demands of their employers.

Competitive capitalism and its despotic regimes of production were ultimately not viable in the long run. The very success of despotism in subordinating labor to capital tended to destabilize the entire system of accumulation; the meager purchasing power of the working class resulted in ever more severe crises of overproduction. Centralization and concentration gave rise to large oligopolistic corporations that carried the expropriation of skill to new levels (Braverman 1974), while in every industrialized country, workers' political struggles forced new forms of state intervention (e.g., social insurance legislation, compulsory trade union recognition).

These social and political rights outside the firm laid the foundation for *hegemonic* production regimes (Burawoy 1985). Labor's new rights meant that workers had to be persuaded to cooperate; the regulation of labor could no longer be achieved through coercion alone. Under hegemonic regimes, workers consented to the conditions of labor through collective bargaining agreements. Coercion, when applied, was done so only under conditions agreed to by workers. Institutions like grievance procedures and internal labor markets effectively coordinated the interests of workers with those of firms, secured workers' consent, reduced the ability of managers to exercise arbitrary authority, and pushed coercion out to the margins, while the steady gains in the purchasing power of the working class they made possible helped to provide a new basis for system stability.

Finally, Burawoy (1985) argues that core manufacturing sectors in advanced nations are currently undergoing another fundamental shift, as global competition and the mobility of capital have undermined hegemonic regimes of production. The threat of disinvestment and capital flight marks the rise of a new despotism against the "collective worker." The increasing frequency of job loss, concession bargaining, and declining wages in manufacturing sectors signals the formation of a new regime Burawoy terms "hegemonic despotism."

In this essay, I apply Burawoy's notion of production regimes to service work. I borrow his concepts of despotic and hegemonic regimes of production in analyzing contemporary changes in the regulation of route sales workers at a medium-sized firm in the snack-food industry. I argue that service workers are subjected to multiple, overlapping production regimes involving both managers and customers. I analyze how concentration and competition in the snack-food and grocery industries have brought about changes in these separate but overlapping regimes, and hence in the organization of conflict and consent in the labor process. Finally, I tentatively suggest that the idea of multiple axes of control may have parallels in manufacturing after all: the rise of *networked* production systems (Harrison 1994), which entail a proliferation of close supplier-customer relationships across firms, may require new models of production politics in manufacturing that also take customers into account.

## *Route Sales in the Snack-Food Industry*

During the summers of 1988, 1989, and 1990, as well as in January through August 1991, I worked as a route sales worker at Granddad's, in the city of Springfield. In the summer of 1987, I was a route sales worker for a national snack-food company in Springfield, and in the summer of 1992, I worked for a regional snack-food company in California. This study focuses only on changes at Granddad's in the late 1980s, and is based on my experiences as a worker as well as on telephone interviews conducted in the spring of 1992 with twelve (about one-third) of my former co-workers.

At all three companies, I was an "extra" salesperson, which meant that I ran a different route every week, filling in for vacationing workers. Each worker had a schedule of stores to service each day. Some stores, such as the larger supermarkets, required service every day; smaller stores were served less frequently. Routes with more small stops (7-11s, neighborhood groceries, and bars) required more time and were less lucrative, since small bags of chips were less valuable but more time-consuming to handle. Routes with good supermarkets and few small stops were considered "gravy." At Granddad's in 1988, most workers' workdays averaged between eight and ten hours in length, although several "small-bag" routes required eleven or twelve hours to complete.

At each stop, workers followed roughly the same procedure. The first step was to enter the store, straighten up the rack, and make out the order. Then they returned to their delivery trucks and "pulled" the order. At larger stores, they tried to save time by ordering only whole cases of chips (or half-cases if really necessary), but at the smaller shops, they ordered in small quantities —

three bags of this, six of that, and so on. Once the order was all together, the worker reentered the store and checked-in the order. Most customers checked the order against the invoice, making workers open boxes and count bags of chips. After the order was checked-in, the worker filled the shelf, collected the empty boxes, accepted payment, and proceeded to the next stop. At the end of the day, he or she returned to the warehouse, loaded the truck for the following day, and turned in the day's money and paperwork.

An average route at Granddad's, when I started working there in 1988, sold about $4,000 a week. Workers were paid on commission, with most workers' pay averaging around $600 a week.[1] While routes' weekly sales were only partially dependent on the skills of the salesperson, "taking care of the route" was also important. Keeping the product rotated to minimize the number of stale chips (which had to be bought back from the customer), making sure shelves didn't sit empty, and cultivating good relations with store managers in order to maintain shelf space and receive permission to put up extra displays during sales were all important elements of success.

## Concentration and Competition
## in the Production and Retail of Snack Foods

Historically, the U.S. snack-food industry has been composed of small, regional companies facing little competition in their home cities. In the 1960s, Frito-Lay became the first snack-food company large and powerful enough to compete with regional companies in their home territories; it eventually became part of PepsiCo. Frito-Lay first entered the Springfield market on a small scale in the late 1960s, but its share of the market grew rapidly. In the 1980s, three more national brands emerged nearly all at once. Eagle Snacks is a division of Anheuser-Busch, the multinational beer manufacturer; Keebler is part of the RJR-Nabisco empire; and Borden, the multinational food conglomerate, bought a number of smaller, regional companies and has attempted to forge them into a national line. The penetration of local markets by the large corporations put pressure on small companies, forcing them expand into each others' home cities in an attempt to become large enough to compete with the national brands. Where expansion failed, buyouts and mergers resulted; during the time I worked at Granddad's, three of the five or six small snack-food companies operating in Springfield were bought either by larger regional competitors or by the national corporations.

Granddad's was begun as a family business in 1913. It enjoyed a virtual monopoly on potato chips in Springfield until Frito-Lay arrived. With the appearance of the other three national brands in Springfield in the late 1980s, the situation for Granddad's was radically transformed. Not only were there now four powerful national brands competing in Springfield, but the city was also being encroached upon by other regional companies struggling to survive against national competition.

In the context of this heightened competition, the practice of "buying space" — bribing supermarket managers to get more shelf space — became commonplace. According to one Granddad's company worker,

> Buying space is being done so boldly now. Not too long ago, a store manager at my Kroger[2] walked up to me and said, "You're going to be losing this end-cap[3] unless you can get your people in here to make me an offer." My sales supervisor went out there to talk to him, but I ended up losing the end-cap anyway. We had to make a deal with him just to get a smaller end-cap in the back. A few days later, while I was serving the store, the Kroger manager came up to me and told me I was lucky to have the small end-cap since Keebler had also made him an offer on it. . . . There's not a store in town [in which] Frito does not have the *primary* space. They've *bought* it. It's no secret. (A. C.)

In addition to buying shelf space, the big companies could "deep-discount" to a level that companies of Granddad's size could not easily match. One Granddad's worker expressed an oft-repeated sentiment: "[The national brands'] chips taste like shit. But when they're selling them 'buy one, get one free,' people are going to buy them — I don't care how bad they taste" (T. H.).

As a result of this heightened competition, Granddad's found itself struggling to compete in its home city. Workers were only too aware that the aggressive behavior of the large companies posed a long-term threat to the continued existence of Granddad's as an independent entity. Their biggest fear was that Granddad's would be bought by a big company, which could declare a nonunion shop and set wages at a substantially lower level (Granddad's workers were very conscious that this had happened to a local beer distributor in 1989). Many workers, contemplating the uncertainties of the future, were quite pessimistic about their prospects:

> I have a feeling that my days of making big money are over. It was good while it lasted, but I'm going to have to get used to making less. (D. A.)

> To tell you the truth, I just won't be able to take it if my income goes much lower. There's a certain minimum amount necessary to run a

household, and I'm almost at that minimum now. We have already had to scale back our lifestyle considerably. (A. C.)

The route man, his days are numbered. Eventually it's going to be drop-shipment except for the little stops. I hate to see a young guy start in there in this business; there's just no future in it. (P. J.)

When I started here in 1981, I honestly thought I would retire here. But not now, I don't. (B. R.)

In addition to the increased concentration and competition in the snack-food industry, another relevant change affecting Granddad's was an increase in the concentration of retail outlets. The market for snack foods has long been divided between small "Mom and Pop" operations and supermarkets. Since the 1930s, there has been a succession of dominant supermarket chains in Springfield, each of whose stores have been larger than the last. The first of these chains, Liberal's, was locally based; the chain and its stores would have been considered quite small by today's standards. Liberal's failed when the region was invaded by the midwestern chain Kroger. The most recent invasion (in 1988 and 1991) came from two chains of so-called superstores. Both of the new chains boast stores of 60,000 square feet each (two or three times that of a regular supermarket); one of the chains also houses a 90,000 square-foot department store under the same roof.

During the five years in which I worked as a route salesperson, virtually every independently owned supermarket in Springfield was forced to close its doors because of the invasion of the superstores. Even the Kroger chain, previously dominant, was having trouble dealing with the situation. The superstores were able to use low prices to lure people away from the older supermarkets; many Granddad's routes without superstores had suffered losses in sales of 25 percent or more since their arrival.[4] By 1992, while a handful of drivers with superstores on their routes were earning as much as $60,000 a year, others were making as little as $20,000 while working between fifty and sixty hours a week.

## The Constellation of Hegemonic and Despotic Regimes in the Mid-1980s

Authority relations between Granddad's management and its workers before the mid-1980s approximated Burawoy's (1985) concept of a hegemonic regime of production. Workers at Granddad's enjoyed the protection of all three kinds of arrangements Burawoy describes as necessary to a hegemonic regime of production. First, they bargained collectively as members of the Teamsters union. Second, they had an elaborate machinery for the resolution of grievances. And, finally, they were part of a highly developed internal labor market — a set of regularized procedures, based on seniority, for filling openings from within the firm.

These arrangements functioned at Granddad's to regulate relations between labor and management much as they did at Allied, the Chicago machine shop studied by Burawoy (1979). Granddad's collective bargaining arrangements, grievance machinery, and internal labor market all reduced the ability of management to exercise arbitrary authority by specifying employees' rights and the rules of the contract. The internal labor market coordinated the interests of labor and management at Granddad's in two ways. First, the system almost entirely eliminated conflict over the allocation of desirable routes by distributing the more desirable routes to the more senior workers.[5] Instead of resenting time spent on less desirable routes, workers tended to see these routes as temporary stepping-stones to a "gravy" route — the reward of seniority. Second, as workers' seniority increased, they had more to lose from leaving Granddad's, and so their individual interests were tied ever more closely to the fortunes of the firm.[6]

Until the mid-1980s, these arrangements clearly formed the underpinnings of a hegemonic production regime. Workers were *persuaded* to cooperate with management through the operation of these political apparatuses. Management strategy, too, seemed to explicitly incorporate the assumption that Granddad's workers were to be persuaded, not forced, to cooperate. Management fostered a benign relationship with its workers:

> When I came here, any time we had a problem — with the product, with a customer, anything — we could call somebody and get results fast. (P. J.)

> They really tried to be fair. They would not let a guy suffer. If a route was doing poorly, they would try to even the routes out. (B. R.)

> Back then, when management wanted to do something new, like come out with a new product or whatever, they would get together with us and ask us if we thought it was a good idea. If we told them no, then they didn't do it. (M. D.)

Granddad's workers were also granted a number of perks that were not available to workers at other companies. Until the end of 1988, although Granddad's workers worked six days a week, Wednesdays and Saturdays were always "short" days of four or five hours. In return for spreading their work out over six days (which enabled more consistent customer service), the workers received eighteen paid days off a year, which they could take three days at a time, in addition to their regular paid vacations. (In 1989 the company eliminated the eighteen days off and went to a five-day week with Wednesdays and Sundays off; all workdays were now to be long days.)

In a hegemonic regime, liberal management practices and the presence of perks could be coupled with a great deal of worker autonomy. Until the mid-1980s, there was no formal inventory control; everything was on the honor system. Workers ordered what they needed from the warehouse, and auxiliary workers brought them the product, with no accounting whatsoever. Also, workers were allowed complete control over how they ran their routes, from the way they merchandised the product, to the way they organized their routes (how many times each stop was serviced each week, for example), to the size and number of discounts given to customers who wanted to run sales.

It appears that this hegemonic regime was fairly successful in mobilizing worker effort and commitment. Granddad's grew very rapidly during the 1970s based on workers' own efforts to build their routes up. Workers' statements such as these are typical descriptions of the effects of the hegemonic regime as it existed before the mid-1980s:

> Granddad's didn't want their people working anywhere else. The little perks we had were designed to keep us happy and keep us there. At one time, I would bend over backward to help make the company look good — not because I was afraid of being disciplined, but because I felt the company *cared* about me. (A. C.)

> Back then, I used to go out of my way to get new stops, extra displays, and sales. It really meant something to be a Granddad's man in those days. (T. H.)

While it may be tempting to discount these comments as examples of looking at the "good old days" through rose-colored glasses, profound changes actually did take place at Granddad's in the late 1980s: As will become clear below, the condition of these workers' labor was transformed from nearly complete autonomy with respect to management into a situation in which almost every aspect of the job was being dictated to them.

The preceding discussion of the hegemonic regime at Granddad's delineates one axis of the production politics affecting its workers before the mid-1980s; the second axis involves customers. Even before the invasion of the superstores, the division between small and large customers was significant in terms of authority relations. Dealing with the manager of an $800-a-week Kroger store and dealing with the proprietor of a $20-a-week neighborhood bar were always entirely different things.

Small customers, such as the owner of a $20-a-week tavern or a $40-a-week corner grocery, were never able to establish control over Granddad's workers. They could (sometimes) demand that workers follow Granddad's policies, but they could not influence those policies. Attempts to apply despotic control, to make the route worker do "extra" things that Granddad's policy did not require, invariably ended in failure; route workers who were really harassed by a small customer would usually give that person an ultimatum, based on company policy, saying that the job was going to be done the worker's way or not at all. If the customer decided to quit, it was not a big loss, and company management would usually support route workers as long as they could make a convincing case that a customer's demands were unreasonable. To be sure, workers used this tactic sparingly, and some were more willing than others to do so. But the point is that there was room on the worker's side to avoid attempts at despotic control by small customers.

On the other hand, route workers were much more constrained when dealing with the manager of an $800-a-week Kroger store, because they could not afford to jeopardize such a large weekly sale. Route workers needed to stay in supermarket managers' good graces in order to ensure permission to put up special displays, run sales, etc. Supermarket managers, of course, knew this, and realized that they had a large amount of leeway in terms of how to treat the route salesperson. Hence, even before the mid-1980s, it was extremely rare for a route worker to insist on following the letter of Granddad's policy in the face of a Kroger manager's demand to do more (i.e., to mark the product a certain way, or to give credit for stale or damaged product when perhaps it was the fault of the store and not the route person). When it came to such a customer, Granddad's management could not be expected to stand behind the salesperson and was more likely instead to apply pressure on the worker to acquiesce to the demands of the large customer.

Still, before the arrival of the superstores and the new national brands, there were relatively well-defined limits on the kinds of demands even a Kroger manager could make. A supermarket manager could not easily dictate the level of service or demand multiple appearances of the route worker in a single day when the product was on sale, nor could he or she make the salesperson conform to onerous and time-consuming check-in procedures. Route workers had to acquiesce to certain kinds of procedural demands that might be made, but they could legitimately put limits on the amount of time they would allot to one particular store. Workers had some power vis-à-vis supermarket managers because managers recognized that: (1) the route salesperson had to balance the amount of service their store received with several other stores whose sales volumes gave them roughly equivalent claims to service; and (2) since Granddad's faced limited competition in its home market from other chip companies, the supermarkets' own customers were likely to be quite upset if the supermarket stopped carrying a good selection of Granddad's products. Hence, at this stage, the regime of labor control between super-markets and Granddad's workers could be described perhaps as *limited* despo-tism; the boundaries inside which supermarket managers could impose arbi-trary authority on route workers were fairly narrow and well defined.

## *The Rise of New Forms of Despotism in the Late 1980s*

As the industry changed in the 1980s, a general tightening of control occurred along both the worker-management and the worker–large customer axes of authority; by 1992, the arrangement of authority relations was considerably altered. The regime of labor control within Granddad's underwent a transfor-mation from hegemonic to despotic. Top Granddad's management, assessing the situation in the mid-1980s, decided that it had to change the way the company was run or Granddad's would lose the competition with the national brands. During the last half of the 1980s, a number of changes were initiated that, while ostensibly oriented toward increasing Granddad's overall competi-tiveness, had the effect of transforming the regime of labor control within the firm from a hegemonic regime into a despotic one. From 1986 to 1992, management at Granddad's steadily increased the amount of control it exerted over how the work was done, forcing change after change on the workers. Many of the new areas of management control proved to be fruitful sites for the exercise of arbitrary authority against individual workers.

Three changes underlie the turn toward despotism at Granddad's. First, a new general sales manager was hired from Frito-Lay. Second, the company ini-tiated a computerized inventory control and sales system. And third, the com-pany managed to get a management rights clause into the workers' contract.

The first step toward despotism was the 1986 hiring of a new general sales manager (Bill) from Frito-Lay; many Granddad's workers felt that he was brought over specifically to undermine the hegemonic regime and to assert more control over the route sales workers. I asked workers whether the change in atmosphere since the new manager's arrival merely reflected his personality or the intentions of the company's owner. A typical response was, "Bill is just being Bill, but he was brought in to do just what he's doing" (A. C.). In general, according to workers, not only was the current sales manager not interested in their input or point of view, but he also took a more confrontational and contemptuous attitude toward the route sales force: "Bill doesn't want to hear anything from us. We're just dumb route men, so I guess we don't know anything. He wants to tell us exactly how to do our jobs, and he wants us to be out there doing them his way" (M. D.).

Many workers were convinced that the new sales manager's ultimate goal was to reduce their pay drastically and to increase the number of things they were required to do. They respected him as a tactician, but they feared what he might ultimately be able to do to their jobs:

> The way he sees it, we're overpaid and we've got it too easy. He came right out at a sales meeting and said, "There's not a route man alive worth more than $20,000 a year." He'd like to see us all working twelve hours a day at $5 or $6 an hour. (D. C.)

> Bill wants all the bonuses, which is fine, but anyone under him, he wants at $4 an hour. He says he can run this job just as good with $4-an-hour men as with us — and maybe he can, I don't know. I just hope I'm not around to see it. (P. J.)

> Bill is a master of divide and conquer. He plays the branch warehouses off against each other and against us. He tries to get the branches to start doing something, and often they will go along because they're not as unified as we are here. Then, when he's got the branches doing it, he comes back to us and says we've got to start doing it too. We can't win a grievance on it because the company can claim it's "past practice." (B. R.)

The second change underlying the increased ability of management to assert control was the introduction of the NORAND computer system. Starting in 1987, each route truck was equipped with a computer system consisting of a printer mounted in the truck and a hand-held unit that plugged into the printer. Instead of filling out invoices by hand, the worker simply punched in orders on the computer, then walked back to the truck to print out the sales ticket. The computer kept track of the truck's inventory, and at day's end, spit out detailed reports on paper as well as directly to a central computer overnight. Management now had access to extensive, detailed information about the activities of the route workers. Before the computers were introduced, management was limited to spot-checking stores to see how they looked. According to workers, this was not done often. Now, however, management could see at the touch of a button exactly which stores a worker served, how long it took, and what was sold. Stores' sales of particular items could be tracked over time, and the time it took workers to complete their routes could be measured.

The new system had some beneficial effects for the route workers, including the elimination of tedious handwritten and manually calculated invoices, and daily and weekly paperwork. The information provided by the computers was useful in convincing large customers to buy more of certain items or to authorize new items. However, the increase in information available to management about what was going on in the field facilitated new forms of control and intrusive harassment techniques, particularly when combined with the third change, the increase in contractual freedom of management.

In 1988, the company slipped a management rights clause into the workers' contract. Workers say their union official "sold them down the river." The workers had agreed on the contract, but after the union official signed it, they discovered that the management rights clause had been added without their knowledge. Some workers speculated that the union representative had been paid off by the company. Previously, workers had discretion over any aspect of the job not covered by the contract. The management rights clause reversed this; now, anything not spelled out in the contract reverted to management.

Management used its new prerogatives under the contract in various ways. First of all, by expanding the number of issues over which management has the right to assert control, the new clause made the harassment of individual workers easier for the aggressive new head sales manager. One worker asserted that

> if you say something wrong, then they'll try to fuck you. That's what happened to Craig. He and Bill [the manager] had an argument, so Bill came down on him. He made him run extra stops, made him stay out longer, redo his racks—anything to fuck with him. Dennis [the route salespeople's immediate supervisor] doesn't want to do that, but he's got to enforce what they tell him. (M. D.)

Another management control initiative that was made possible by the management rights clause was the "plan-o-gram." This was a diagram that specified to the workers exactly how the various items were to be arranged on the shelf. Its purpose was ostensibly to ensure that all racks were set in the same attractive pattern. This was supposed to boost sales. However, Granddad's manipulated the plan-o-gram to its advantage; since it was designed with large quantities of puff corn on every eye-level shelf (the best-selling spot on a rack). Workers' commission on items the company purchased from a distributor was only 12 percent—three-quarters of the commission on potato chips. Soon after introducing the plan-o-gram, the company began to manufacture its own puff corn (thus raising the profit margin), but the commission remained at 12 percent. This incensed many of the sales workers, who wanted to sell potato chips, at 16 percent commission, from their eye-level shelves. One worker put the overall effect of the plan-o-gram this way: "You've got to put out what they want you to put out, and you've got to do it just the way they say. Hell, I know what sells in my stores better than they do. The end result is that you lose control as a salesman" (P. J.).

A third initiative made possible by the management rights clause was the way new customers were assigned; management now reserved the right to assign new customers to anyone they chose. This gave management another opportunity to exercise arbitrary authority. When the new superstores opened, management could reward specific workers by manipulating how the routes were rearranged.[7] The rearrangement was necessary because the routes that gained superstores had to give up some other customers. But it also presented an opportunity for arbitrariness: the union steward's route, which gained a superstore in 1991, now averaged $8,000 a week, because he was allowed to keep all of his other lucrative supermarkets and give away most of his time-consuming small stops. In retrospect, I believe it was a conscious management decision not to take good stops away from the union steward. As one worker told me: "The union steward always has a good route. That's no coincidence; it's all politics. He was in the right place at the right time, and they took care of him" (F. L.).

The fourth and most intrusive new management policy from the workers' point of view was that management began dictating the number of times stops must be served a week:

> In the old days, basically all you had to do was keep the customer happy. If no one called in on you [to complain], then they left you alone. Hell, out in Brownville [a branch warehouse 45 miles away from the plant] we went for months at a time without ever *seeing* Roger [the sales manager]. Then they came out with all of this harassment. They've got me serving a gas station three times a week for a total of $12! (P. J.)

> I used to go to Greentown [about 25 miles further out in the country from the rest of the route] once a week. I'd put in about $350 in the IGA [a supermarket]. Remember when the price of gas was so high, during the [Gulf] war? They had me going all the way out there three times a week, and the second two times, I wouldn't even need to put anything in! (V. O.)

This new level of control was made "legitimate" by the management rights clause, but before the introduction of the new computers, thorough enforcement would have been impractical: management could not physically check on everyone to see if they were actually serving their smaller stops as many times a week as they had been ordered. Now, workers who attempted to resist the new policies were called into management offices and confronted with the computer printouts proving that they had skipped a stop they had been ordered to serve. Steadily, the space in which workers could exercise autonomy or hide from management surveillance was being eliminated.

Turning to the relations between route workers and small customers, the only major change since the mid-1980s was the incorporation of the small customers into a network of fairly complete surveillance. This surveillance, however, really emanated from Granddad's management, not from the small customers themselves. In many cases, small customers actually expressed annoyance at the increased number of times a week they had to deal with their route salesperson as a result of Granddad's new management policies. That these complaints had no effect, however, demonstrates that small customers were unable to exercise any control over management. They could not, for example, force the company to give them special deals on sale prices; they could not successfully demand more (or less) service, or different products, than Granddad's management wanted to provide. Against the small customer, just as in the earlier period, the official policies of the firm could be applied. In sum, management was able to subordinate the interests of the small customer to its own interests, and Granddad's workers were able to use company routines as a defense against excessive demands from small customers. The small customer only entered into the picture of authority relations as a point from which Granddad's management could obtain information about and apply control over its workers. In other words, small customers were not powerful enough to penetrate the firm, at the level of either managers or workers.

However, the largest customers could and did penetrate the firm. There were few limitations on their ability to create and sustain despotic relationships over Granddad's route workers. If the manager of an $800-a-week Kroger had considerably more power over the route salesperson than did the small customer, the manager of the $2,000- to $3,000-a-week superstore operated with an entirely new level of domination. We can see this in the qualitatively different demands the superstores began making and enforcing upon their arrival in Springfield. The managers of a superstore whose sales represented perhaps two-thirds of a salesperson's entire route, and therefore two-thirds of the salesperson's income, could demand practically anything they wanted. If they wanted the route person there at 5:00 in the morning or 9:00 at night, the worker complied. If, during a sale, they wanted to buy several hundred extra cases at a discount and then let them go stale in their back room so that the route person had to take them all back and give them credit at the regular price, the worker complied. If they wanted to make the route person wait an hour to get checked in, the route person waited. The boundaries of what the superstores could require the salesperson to do were much wider than those applying to ordinary supermarkets.

One evening, at 9:00 on a Saturday night, I telephoned a worker, whose route included a superstore, to set up an interview. He wasn't home because his superstore was running a sale that week; despite the fact that his union contract said he didn't have to work evenings or days off, he was out at the store keeping his shelf full. When we did speak a few days later, he evaluated the impact of the big stores like this:

> For a long time, we didn't work on Wednesdays, Sundays, or Satur-
> day afternoons. Now I go out on Saturday afternoons to fill the shelf
> at Meijer [a superstore]. When they're on sale, I'm there at 9:00 P.M.
> a lot of times. If there's money out there, you'll do what you have to
> do to make it. The [union] contract is one thing, but if I've got kids to
> feed, I'm gonna go out and get the money. These big accounts, if
> you've got one, you're going to go out and do what you have to
> do. . . . The guy that hustles is going to be the one to get the sales, the
> displays. If you're not willing to hustle and take care of them like I do,
> they'll give the displays to someone else. (D. C.)

The "fear of being fired" (Burawoy 1985), which was now the fear of losing space, or, in extreme circumstances, of being thrown out of the store, had intensified.

An important aspect of this new market despotic regime of control is the fact that the large customers did not employ the workers over whom they exercised control. But as many workers pointed out to me, the relation between Granddad's worker and large customer increasingly took on the contours of a worker-employer relationship:

> The manager of the store is not only my boss, but also my boss's
> boss. . . . I am basically just a figurehead, and I'm at the whim of what
> that store manager says. My relationship with him doesn't amount to
> anything except my doing whatever he wants me to do. And the
> accounts that operate this way are getting more numerous. All of
> the big stores are now subject to making these kinds of demands.
> (A. C.)

As in the analysis of customer control by Linda Fuller and Vicki Smith (Chapter 4), the worker now had not one but many bosses. Granddad's workers were more and more caught up in a triangular web of authority relations: they experienced market despotism not only from within the firm but also from without. The institutions that once underpinned a hegemonic production regime were now doubly inadequate; collective bargaining, grievance machinery, and the internal labor market could no longer guarantee a "benign" hegemony within the firm, and they were useless to prevent the spread of market despotism outside it. The despotism within the firm put ever sharper pressure on the worker to conform to the goals of management; the despotism outside it put ever sharper pressure on the worker to conform to the goals of the large customer.

Unlike the situation Fuller and Smith describe, however, managers within the firm were not in a position to subordinate their largest customers' demands to serve their own interests. The large stores often made tyrannical demands that conflicted with the interests of both route workers and Granddad's management, neither of whom had the power to resist. The worker had multiple bosses, to be sure, but the boss within the firm, whose interests did not exactly correspond to those of the bosses outside it, was often the weaker of the two.

The interplay of interests and control relationships where large customers were involved decoordinated the interests of management and workers at Granddad's. This was true in cases where the interests of management and the large customers coincided in opposition to those of workers, as well as where the interests of Granddad's management and workers coincided in opposition to those of the large customers. For example, it was in the interests of customers to make Granddad's route workers go out at night or on their days off to fill shelves during sales. This practice allowed customers to obtain labor ordinarily performed by their own employers without having to pay for it. Granddad's management's interests were not in conflict with this new demand, so they were only too glad to cooperate in forcing their workers to provide the extra service. Workers could feel the oppressive weight of both management and the customers bearing down on them; they could see that their interests differed sharply from those of management and of their customers.

In other cases, the interests of management actually did coincide with those of workers against the large customers, but the large customers were powerful enough to force management to enforce the customers' interests at the expense of those of the firm. An example of this situation was the common demand by large customers to buy (at a discount) more chips than they needed during a sale. Then, when the sale was over, the customer obtained a higher profit margin by selling these chips at the regular price. If the chips went stale before they could be sold, the customer still made money on them by getting credit from Granddad's at the regular price. Both Granddad's management and its route workers lost money by selling product at a discount that really ought to have been sold later at full price. However, the permeability of the firm to despotism by large customers meant that it was not strong enough to resist these kinds of demands; as a result, Granddad's management could not stand behind its workers or enforce its own routines; it had to enforce the demands of the customer. In this case, too, there was a breakdown in the ability of Granddad's management to coordinate its interests with those of its workers; the workers could clearly see that their interests differed from those of management and of their customers.

The new constellation of authority relations combined to produce vertical tensions within the firm and quiescence at the point of service. Workers were forced to comply with the demands of the despotic large customers; therefore, they focused their anger on Granddad's management. Even when the largest customers were clearly behind management actions, workers' only recourse was to pressure management. In cases I observed, however, the workers, despite exhibiting a great deal of hostility and anger toward Granddad's management, were unable to exert any effective pressure on management to defy the largest customers.

During the summer of 1991, for example, Granddad's experienced a severe potato shortage. For about five or six weeks, there were so few potatoes coming in that production had to be cut to one or two days a week. When we arrived in the mornings, we would groan and grumble if there was no smoke coming from the stacks over at the plant, because it meant that we'd have no chips to load again that afternoon.

In the context of this situation, the workers were extremely surprised to learn that one of the superstore chains, Meijer's, was advertising a sale on our twin-pack potato chips (our best-selling item) for the following week. We jokingly asked each other what was going to happen when there weren't any chips to put on their shelves. But that same afternoon in the warehouse, skids of chips marked "Do Not Use" began to appear. For the next five days, the row of skids we weren't allowed to touch grew longer and longer, while we went out every day with no chips. Obviously, these twin-packs were being hoarded for Meijer's. There were only four workers with Meijer stores on their routes, and the rest of us could see that they would make a great deal of money the following week when they got to sell all of those twin-packs, and we had to continue going without. Moreover, the other large chain stores were bound to find out about the sale, and we knew their managers would be very interested to know why we were telling them we had no chips while the Meijer stores were having a sale with full shelves.

As the week went on, the grumbling grew louder and louder. On Saturday, when the four Meijer workers began loading their trucks with twin-packs for the sale, the tension on the dock was palpable. Several loud arguments erupted between angry workers and the two sales supervisors, with most of the volume being supplied by the workers. Workers suggested to each other that the four Meijer workers really ought to refuse to take more than their fair share of chips, and others declared that they were going to file a grievance over the unfair rationing of product. The voices, however, were muted within the hearing range of the union steward, who happened to be one of the four Meijer workers — a huge, powerfully built man, weighing at least 250 pounds, with a reputation for being easily provoked. He was unconcernedly wheeling skid after skid of chips out to his truck, speaking to no one, and no one dared suggest to him that he do otherwise.

In the end, the workers, as livid as they were, were unable to do anything except verbally abuse the lowest rung of management, whose hands, the workers recognized, were tied anyway. Without the support of the union steward, there was no possibility of unified resistance to the company's decision to cater to Meijer's demands at the expense of all other customers. Had the union steward not been a Meijer worker, or had he possessed a greater sense of responsibility toward the other workers, it is likely that a major conflict would have erupted. But as it turned out, Meijer's had its sale, and the rest of the workers suffered losses in pay as well as the acute displeasure of managers on their routes.

This example illustrates the kinds of tensions produced by the constellation of interests associated with multiple, overlapping production regimes. By the time I left Granddad's in August of 1991, the workers were in a more or less constant state of hostility toward management, which had not been the case when I started there in the spring of 1988. By 1991, their frustrations seemed ready to boil over at any moment. Workers were constantly asking each other when they were going to "stop taking this shit." Indeed, in the fall of 1991, just after I left the company, the workers very nearly went out on strike. According to those I interviewed, a majority of workers were strongly in favor of striking until a lawyer from the Teamsters got up and told them that if they went on strike, they would probably lose their jobs to permanent "replacement workers." He advised them to take whatever was being offered rather than strike, because, he said, since the issue was not unfair labor practices, there was nothing to prevent the company from firing strikers and hiring permanent nonunion replacements. Even after this advice, the strike motion was defeated by only a handful of votes.

The narrowness by which the motion was defeated demonstrates how close to the wall Granddad's workers felt by the end of the period of study. Every worker I interviewed in the spring of 1992 expressed anger and bitterness toward the company. Workers repeatedly expressed the belief that at some point they would be forced to strike; if autonomy, good wages, benefits, and reasonable hours were all going to be taken away, they said, eventually they would have little to lose by striking, even if it did mean risking their jobs. In the spring and summer of 1988, most workers still talked proudly about Granddad's as a great place to work; by the spring of 1992, Granddad's management and workers seemed to be on a collision course of mutual hostility.

## Conclusion: A New Labor Process Paradigm?

Unlike previous studies of service work, this study has examined the effects of changes in the structures of an industry on the regulation of labor. I have proceeded from the assumption that the labor process in service work is structurally different from that in manufacturing, but I have made use of relevant insights of the manufacturing-centered labor process literature to explore changes in service production politics.

One implication of the emerging complex of relations among workers, managers, and customers illustrated in this study is that traditional labor union strategies and contracts may be unable to provide workers with adequate protection from the demands of large customers in interfirm service occupations. Labor unions, like labor process theorists, still largely rely on a factory model of the labor process, but a resurgence of the labor movement will depend in large part on its ability to organize service occupations. As the division of labor continues to widen and deepen, the expansion of interfirm services of all kinds is likely to continue (Sayer and Walker 1992). Unions, therefore, should explore new strategies for organizing and representing workers in these kinds of occupations. One possibility is to pursue three-way collective bargaining agreements among workers, managers, and large customers. Such a strategy would represent a radical break with the past for most U.S. labor unions, but there is some evidence already that these kinds of agreements are possible and can be successfully implemented against seemingly insurmountable odds.[8]

Insights developed in this study may also have relevance not just for other service occupations but for manufacturing itself. The bipolar view of the labor process developed in the factory has long been seen as prototypical of the capitalist labor process in general, but labor process theorists and analysts of the service sector alike have failed to perceive how the complexity of authority relations in service work may in fact have its parallels in industrial production. Recent changes in the organization of manufacturing on a global scale may mean that a new labor process paradigm, based on complex, shifting authority relations that include customers, may have increasing salience to manufacturing.

In the context of global economic integration, single-firm production systems are increasingly seen as insufficiently flexible for success in rapidly changing global markets; as a result, firms are building what Bennett Harrison (1994) calls "flexible networked production systems" — cooperative interfirm arrangements that create dense networks of close supplier-customer relationships. Harrison describes several different kinds of production networks. In "craft-type industries," production networks are created for specific projects and then dismantled when the project is complete. Examples of this type include film, construction, and garment industries. In "small-firm led industrial districts," of which the most-discussed example is probably the industrial districts of northern Italy, small firms simultaneously compete and cooperate, sharing information and working together on projects that no single firm could complete alone.

A third type of networked production is the core-ring network involving big customer firms and smaller supplier firms; the Japanese "supply *keiretsu*" system is the prototypical example. In this system, large core firms manage dense networks of first-tier suppliers. Suppliers are organized into cooperative associations, and core firms offer financial and technical assistance to members of the association (often numbering in the hundreds). Core-firm customers make long-term commitments to their suppliers, sharing the costs of modernizing equipment or training at the supplier level (Harrison 1994).

Finally, Harrison points out that competing large firms (many of which are operating as part of core-ring production systems already) are forming "strategic alliances" with each other as central elements of their competitive strategies. Such alliances provide firms with competencies in new areas or expand their abilities to manage a wide variety of activities flexibly. Prominent examples include the IBM-Motorola-Apple partnership that produces PowerPC microprocessors, the European Airbus project, and numerous cooperative arrangements between U.S. and Japanese auto firms producing small cars for the U.S. market. These alliances often overlap; Mitsubishi Heavy Industries is not only involved in the European Airbus project, but has also become an important supplier to Boeing — Airbus's largest competitor (Harrison 1994).

In sum, cooperative networking strategies are becoming central to the competitive strategies of manufacturing firms. Customer firms in these production systems tend to be intimately involved in the production processes of suppliers or partners, since these systems often require close coordination among firms at the level of the shop floor. However, there has as yet been no serious inquiry into the effects of interfirm coordination on shop-floor production regimes.

But examples hinting at important changes are not difficult to find. A recent television documentary on the economy, hosted by Robert Reich, shows a Boeing executive interrogating workers at Mitsubishi Heavy Industries, which makes body panels for 747s, on the shop floor in Japan. The executive wants to know how the workers are planning to modify their production process to ensure that Boeing's specifications will be met. According to the documentary, Boeing executives are intimately involved with planning every aspect of the production process and are consulted by production workers at every stage. Boeing plays a key role in deciding not just product specifications but exactly how work is to be performed on the shop floor. Customer or boss? Increasingly the lines are blurred. Perhaps it is not premature to speculate that the service sector, with its multiple actors and its complex and shifting authority relations, contains within it the seeds of a new production paradigm.

## NOTES

*Acknowledgments:* I would like to thank Michael Burawoy, Harley Shaiken, Eddy U, Kim Voss, and two anonymous reviewers for their valuable comments and suggestions on this chapter.
1. Granddad's workers received a commission of 16 percent on potato chips and 12 percent on products the company purchased from a distributor (corn chips, pretzels, and various other items like meat snacks). At the national company and the regional company in California, workers received a guaranteed base pay plus commission on sales over a certain amount. At both of the other companies, workers had to sell substantially more product to earn as much as Granddad's workers.
2. A midwestern supermarket chain.
3. An "end-cap" is a permanent rack on the end of an aisle. End-caps at the front of the store near the check-out counters are particularly lucrative since they are seen by everyone who enters the store.
4. A good nonsuperstore route might have three or four Krogers and forty or so other customers of varying sizes. Total weekly sales might be in the vicinity of $4,000, about half of which comes from the combined sales of the Krogers. By way of contrast, each of the new superstores by itself can give Granddad's from $2,000 to $4,000 in weekly sales. Just one of the new stores, in other words, can bring as much in sales as an entire route.
5. Workers rank routes on a number of dimensions, such as the amount of driving (which is unpaid time), the proportion of small accounts (which reduces the rate at which money can be earned), the character of the neighborhoods (which often involves a racist desire on the part of white workers to avoid routes in predominantly minority communities), the overall route average, and the hours required to run the route.
6. There is one difference between the functioning of the internal labor markets at Granddad's and at Allied. Granddad's system does not really increase "possessive individualism" in the manner described by Burawoy for two reasons: first, openings are relatively infrequent, and second, workers who take new routes lose their bidding rights for a year.

Granddad's workers, therefore, cannot solve job problems by bidding off their jobs as easily as workers at Allied could.

7. For instance, a new superstore that opened in a branch city, right in the middle of one worker's route, was given to another worker whose route was actually some distance away.

8. One example is the Farm Labor Organizing Committee (FLOC) of Toledo, Ohio, a migrant farm workers union. FLOC fought and won a long, innovative campaign for three-way contracts among farm workers, small growers, and large processors such as Heinz and Campbell during the 1980s. The union argued that by dictating prices and acreage to the growers, large processors effectively set the terms of workers' employment even though the workers were actually employed by the growers. Growers were initially very hostile to the idea of forming an association that would bargain collectively with the workers and the large processors, but FLOC eventually persuaded them that such an arrangement would be in growers' as well as workers' interests. The large processors were barraged with a negative publicity campaign about conditions in the fields and eventually submitted (Lopez 1990). The three-way negotiating system has been working well for half a decade; growers have achieved a new degree of stability in their income, and workers' wages have risen.

## REFERENCES

Braverman, Harry. 1974. *Labor and Monopoly Capital: The Degradation of Work in the Twentieth Century*. New York: Monthly Review Press.

Burawoy, Michael. 1985. *The Politics of Production*. London: Verso.

———. 1979. *Manufacturing Consent*. Chicago: University of Chicago Press.

Gottfried, Heidi. 1992. "In the Margins: Flexibility as a Mode of Regulation in the Temporary Help Service Industry." *Work, Employment, and Society* 6(3): 1–18.

Harrison, Bennett. 1994. *Lean and Mean: The Changing Landscape of Corporate Power in the Age of Flexibility*. New York: Basic Books.

Hochschild, Arlie Russell. 1983. *The Managed Heart: Commercialization of Human Feeling*. Berkeley: University of California Press.

Leidner, Robin. 1993. *Fast Food, Fast Talk: Service Work and the Routinization of Everyday Life*. Berkeley: University of California Press.

Lopez, Steven. 1990. "After the Victory: The Farm Labor Organizing Committee and the Institutionalization of Social Movement Success." Unpublished paper.

Rafaeli, Anat. 1989. "When Cashiers Meet Customers: An Analysis of the Role of Supermarket Cashiers." *Academy of Management Journal* 32: 245–73.

Ritzer, George. 1989. "The Permanently New Economy: The Case for Reviving Economic Sociology." *Work and Occupations* 16(3): 243–72.

Sayer, Andrew, and Richard Walker. 1992. *The New Social Economy: Reworking the Division of Labor*. Cambridge, MA: B. Blackwell.

*Chapter 4*

# Consumers' Reports: Management by Customers in a Changing Economy

• Linda Fuller and Vicki Smith

## Introduction

There is growing consensus among sociologists and industrial relations experts that macro-economic changes of the 1980s have led employers to change the organization of the American workplace in fundamental ways. Researchers use various conceptualizations to describe these broad economic changes, ranging from "the permanently new economy" (Ritzer 1989) to "postindustrial capitalism" (Heydebrand 1989) and "the new rules of competition" (Hage 1988). Referring to a core set of phenomena, such as increased competition from foreign industry, a more quality-conscious consumer population, rapidly changing product markets, deregulation and new technologies, these changes have prompted U.S. industrial and service sector firms to seek new ways to increase their productivity and competitiveness (Hage 1988; Heydebrand 1989; Schoenberger 1989; Wood 1989).

In this paper we explore how competitive pressures resulting from such factors have affected strategies of control in the workplaces of "interactive service employees" (Leidner 1988) whose primary job task is directly serving customers. The category of interactive service work encompasses a large group of workers, in many different industries, whose jobs display wide variation in terms of routinization and amount of customer interaction. At one extreme are fast food workers and telephone operators, at the other are workers in the child care, automobile sales and service, and financial industries.

We argue that the strategies managers use to control interactive service

Reprinted by permission from *Work, Employment & Society* 5 (March 1991): 1–16.

workers are linked to their objective of eliciting *quality service work*. To encourage quality service work, service employers must look for management methods that deemphasize obtrusive managerial or bureaucratic control and give greater leeway to employees when working with customers. One such method is the utilization of consumer feedback to manage employees. Consumer feedback has been used by companies in the past but, we argue, may become more important as managers increasingly perceive the customer/worker interaction to be a source of profitability.

## Quality of Service and Theories of Control

As pressures for profitability in the service sector have increased service firms have been forced to search for new ways to compete for customers. One of these has been to stress not only the content of services but also their quality (Hochschild 1983; Noyelle 1987; Albrecht 1988; Hirschhorn 1988). A corporate ideology of quality has emerged, reflected in managerial assertions that customers' loyalty depends on the treatment they receive from service workers, as well as in corporate reorganization policies, trade journals and advertising. In employers' eyes quality of service has become an importance source of value (Hirschhorn 1988) and a prime determinant of service firms' competitive success or failure (Koepp 1987).[1]

At one level management's definition of quality service is simple: quality service is being delivered when customers keep coming back and when they recommend a particular company to their friends. On the other hand exactly what prompts a customer to return and to recommend a company's service varies tremendously from individual to individual. As a consequence interactive service workers are required to make on-the-spot, subtle judgments about what would please individual customers hundreds of thousands of times daily in the American workplace. In other words, workers must continually utilize their "tacit knowledge" (Manwaring and Wood 1984) to determine what constitutes quality service. For one customer this might be friendliness, for another (or the same one at a different time) it might be speed, for yet another it might mean taking the time to share information and knowledge or just to chat, for still others quality service might mean service delivered by an employee who is flirtatious, solicitous or deferent. In other words, to perform quality service labor an employee must tailor delivery to the idiosyncratic and changeable needs of individual customers.

Since what is considered quality service varies so greatly by individual customer, how can managers and employers ever make sure that their employees are delivering it? How can they be certain that such an intangible product as service meets consumers' subjective needs and preferences? Here, previously identified methods of control have proven insufficient, if not counter-productive. For example, continuous simple or direct control by managers (Edwards 1984), a potentially abrasive type of management that can engender hostility among employees, may be untenable for ensuring the delivery of quality service. One of the main things quality-service workers must "produce" over and over again every workday is a good-natured, helpful and friendly attitude toward customers, a productive task they are likely to perform poorly when relations with their superiors are intrusive or overtly antagonistic.

Similarly, bureaucratic control, which prespecifies the "rules, procedures, and expectations governing particular jobs" (Edwards 1984: 130), may be insufficient for ensuring that workers interact satisfactorily with customers. Quality service requires that workers rely on inner arsenals of affective and interpersonal skills, capabilities which cannot be successfully codified, standardized or dissected into discrete components and set forth in a company handbook. Indeed, to the extent that managers succeed in perfecting bureaucratic control over quality-service labor, they may extinguish exactly those sparks of worker self-direction and spontaneity that they are becoming ever more dependent upon.

Claiming that simple or bureaucratic control methods are insufficient and possibly counterproductive is not to say that they are not utilized in interactive service workplaces. Many fast food restaurants make regular use of a quintessential combination of technical and simple control — automatic cameras mounted in the ceiling which continuously photograph employees. Furthermore, as we discuss later, customer management can be used to bolster systems of bureaucratic control. Different forms of control are often used together, but we maintain that reliance on simple, bureaucratic and even technical forms of control to manage interactive service workers is particularly problematic given the dynamics of the work itself in the new competitive environment.

In an effort to deal with the control dilemma before them, many firms have turned to what we call consumer control or management by customers. We wished to discern whether customer control allowed management to execute the three principal functions of control systems underscored by Edwards (1984) — direction, evaluation and discipline — yet simultaneously allow interactive service workers, even those in comparatively routinized jobs, to make the skilled judgments necessary to provide quality service under fluctuating circumstances.[2]

In addition to analyzing control over workers, we studied how customer feedback was used to manage supervisors and middle managers. The service firms we studied were mostly large and structurally complex and consisted of a multitude of widely dispersed delivery sites.[3] The hallmark of these corporations was a large category of mid-level employees who, while responsible for managing workers within decentralized quality-service delivery sites, themselves had to be managed. As with workers, middle managerial employees' labor in service firms is frequently customer-focused. In many of the businesses where we interviewed middle managers regularly engaged in customer interactions, either to help lower-level service workers on the "front lines" of customer contact, or to mediate when customers had complaints or questions concerning business transactions. In addition, whether a business delivers consistently high quality service can depend on whether the manager of the work site successfully elicits high-quality performance from lower-level employees. Thus, another focal point in our research was the degree to which customer feedback supplemented or even preempted on-site, middle managerial control.

In sum, we understand customer control as a management response to an old, but somewhat altered, imperative: to simultaneously exclude workers from exerting genuine control yet secure their participation in the process of production (Cardan n.d.: 123). Profitable production under capitalism has always required that managers convince or coerce workers to do what they want them to, when they want them to and how they want them to. In other words, the expenditure of labor power must occur under the employer's command. At the same time, employers cannot control workers too completely. Profits invariably suffer when workers are prohibited from exercising some degree of autonomy on the job.

Employers of interactive service labor continue to face the traditional dilemma of achieving a balance between managerial control and worker self-direction. What is distinctive about interactive service labor, however, is that the most profitable resolution of this dilemma obligates that employers expand, to a greater or lesser degree, workers' control over their own labor. This, of course, does not mean managers of interactive service workers now turn a blind eye to the direction, evaluation and discipline of employees. Rather, it means that they must continue their search for new management techniques which simultaneously maintain their own control prerogatives but interfere as little as possible with employees' ability to exercise the amount of self-direction necessary to delivery quality service.

## Methods

We interviewed managers and owners in fifteen firms located in three large metropolitan areas. The industries we studied included automobile, supermarket, hospital, child care, banking, hotel, restaurant, insurance and liquor; thus our data cover service jobs that range from the fairly routinized (cashiers in the supermarket and retail liquor industries) to the comparatively non-standardized, requiring greater degrees of employee discretion (automobile sales, nurses, insurance agents). In addition, we interviewed a union official and the president of a firm that collected consumer data for auto dealerships around the country. The names and identifying features of the companies in which we interviewed have been changed. In slightly under half of them we knew in advance that they employed at least one mechanism for collecting customer feedback. Over half the companies were selected blindly. That is, we did not know ahead of time whether they gathered feedback from their customers, but we hypothesized they would, given the nature of their business activities. We also examined survey data provided us by managers in five companies and read relevant articles in trade journals.

With the exception of one interview conducted in 1987, the interviews were conducted between July and November 1988. They were semistructured, lasting between one and a half and two hours. We asked a series of questions about how consumer feedback was collected, how and why it was used in firm operations, the company's history of gathering these data and finally, the difficulties with and limitations of management by customers. We encouraged interviewees to talk extensively about various management practices and to explore issues about this method of control which we had not included in our survey.

Since we wished to analyze the control of service delivery from the viewpoint of employers, middle and top managers, we have data from these groups only. A logical and important companion research project should not only interview workers about consumer feedback, but should present participant observation material demonstrating how worker/customer interactions are shaped by the use of this feedback (cf. Rafaeli 1989).

## Customer Control Mechanisms: How They Work and Why They Are Used

As expected, the collection, analysis and utilization of customer feedback was an important aspect of management in the fifteen companies we surveyed. Every company employed not one but multiple mechanisms for gathering this information; indeed, the *average* number of distinct feedback mechanisms used in the companies we contacted was five. We identified three categories of mechanisms for gathering customer feedback: company-instigated, company-encouraged and customer-instigated.

In the company-instigated category companies actively recruited customer feedback, through printed and telephone surveys and face-to-face meetings arranged with customers, such as focus groups (Langer 1987). Eighty percent of the firms we studied recruited feedback from customers using these techniques. Company-encouraged feedback mechanisms, which we found in 86% of our sample, included comment cards and toll-free 800 telephone numbers provided by firms at the site of worker-customer interactions. Finally, a company employed a customer-initiated mechanism whenever it had a systematic procedure for dealing with unsolicited phone calls or letters from customers. Every company in our sample had an established channel through which to process such calls and letters.

One company-instigated method of soliciting customer feedback warrants separate discussion: the use of "shoppers," individuals employed by management to pose anonymously as patrons, clients, policy holders, guests, passengers, etc. The only two businesses in our sample that did not use shoppers were hospitals, though one reported having considered hiring people to pose as patients after an outside consultant specializing in "guest relations" proposed it. While pretending to be customers, shoppers monitored and reported on workers and middle managers, as well as on product quality and other matters often covered in the customer surveys. Two companies used shoppers in an extreme way: they wired the shoppers so that all interactions were picked up by microphone. Companies sometimes arranged and supervised "shopping" visits themselves, but they also utilized outside "shopping businesses" which existed solely to provide shoppers for other companies.

## Managing Workers with Customer Feedback

We expected that a principal reason employers and managers would use customer management would be to monitor workers to evaluate whether they were delivering quality services to consumers. Furthermore, we expected that they would use these data to reward workers who succeeded in this task and discipline those who did not. What evidence is there that companies utilize customer input to carry out these objectives?

First, in every business in which we conducted interviews it was possible to identify individual workers through company-instigated or company-encouraged feedback mechanisms. Thus, approximately one-third of the comment cards available at the point of the service transaction included a line on

which customers were invited to write employees' names. On the remaining
two-thirds of the cards employees' names were not solicited specifically but
easily could be discerned from other information already known or requested
from the customer, such as the time and date of customer interaction, or the
department, floor and/or store to which the customer's comments pertained.
Importantly, employees in the companies we studied frequently wore name
tags. Five of our respondents showed us examples of customer-supplied information, demonstrating how easily and regularly they were able to identify
individual employees by name even when names were not overtly solicited.
Comments such as "Pam was great" and "Susan stunk" appeared on one hospital's monthly summary of its discharge survey. The comment: "The blonde
lady in the produce department doesn't like management" (store and date
identified), was offered by one supermarket patron whose phone complaint
was received by the chain's president. As one middle manager stated, the
customer survey is important for monitoring workers because: "It's like a
report card on individual employees."

Second, surveys and shoppers relayed detailed information about individual employee's behavior and attitudes. The following questions from printed
surveys indicate the specificity, and often the subjectivity, of the information
customers were asked to provide about employee behavior:

- Were your nurses *concerned*?
- How was the *temperature* of your food?
- Was our employee *knowledgeable*?
- Was our employee *quick* and *efficient* at the cash register?
- Were you greeted *graciously*?
- How was your salesperson's *appearance*?
- Was our employee *cheerful*?
- Approximately how many minutes did you wait to receive ser-
  vice? (no wait; 1–2; 3–4; 5–9; 10+).

Third, such detailed feedback about specific employees derived from customers was funneled into employees' personnel files and often used in bureaucratic systems of evaluation and discipline. A brief sketch of one firm illustrates
the dynamics that can lead a company to implement customer management
and subsequently to link this with its overall and thoroughly bureaucratized
system of monitoring and evaluating employees. With the objective of maintaining current and attracting new customers "Amer-Insure," a large insurance
company, turned an aggressive eye to improving customer service in the early
1980s. The company manager we interviewed claimed that:

Customer service is one of the top important factors in our competitive position. The survivors in the insurance industry are determined more by their service than by their product. The products are the same, with a few exceptions. Once there's a product innovation by one company, it's not long before everyone has it. People will pay more for good service; it's the cutting edge. It will determine who makes the cut and who does not.

This company implemented an extensive and rigorously-monitored system for securing customer feedback, including written surveys that were mailed to customers and unannounced visits by anonymous shoppers in selected regions. "Amer-Insure's" shoppers were retired claims adjusters who would "buy" insurance, a dummy file would be opened on them and eventually (after a dummy accident or theft) they might "make claims."

Once "Amer-Insure" began to gather this feedback, it revised its employee performance evaluation form to include a customer service section, putting customer service on an: "equal level with other job responsibilities here at Amer-Insure." Customer feedback was routed into workers' personnel files, on the basis of which periodic quantitative performance reviews used to determine raises, promotions and the like were prepared. Acceptable customer service ratings are now a condition of employment at this firm.

In a similar vein, one large supermarket chain transferred information about individual employees from comment cards and customer-initiated letters to computerized files used by supervisors to complete yearly employee evaluations. A manager in an automobile dealership used customer feedback in two different ways. First, he leafed through customer comment cards, throwing away all with positive and saving all those with negative comments "for later." Second, he reviewed the summary statistics from the monthly customer surveys, conducted by an outside firm hired by the dealer, in order to pinpoint employees whose numbers deviated substantially from the norm. Whenever this occurred, the manager called the employee into his office to discuss his/her performance.

A union official representing grocery workers provided further evidence of management use of customers' reports to control employees, as well as insight into the increasingly complex relations between workers and customers that this establishes. According to him, not only was customer feedback used to initiate the first stages of disciplinary action against supermarket employees (warnings and written conduct reports), but such information also provided the grounds for temporary suspensions and on-the-spot terminations. Moreover, should an employee file a grievance in response customers nearly always became involved in the arbitration proceedings that followed. The union, usually in management's presence, interviewed the complaining customer and sometimes customers were subpoenaed to arbitration hearings where they were, as in an ordinary trial proceeding, sworn to testify under oath and examined and cross-examined by union and company counsel.

## Using Customer Feedback to Manage Managers

Consumers' reports provided data for managing individual service workers, but they were also a source of data about the *overall* quality of each separate service delivery site. Such data thus gave upper levels of company management evidence about how well middle-level managers were doing their jobs. Middle managers were expected to use detailed data about customer/worker interactions as a basis for promoting quality service; how well they succeeded was reflected in the feedback that was channelled to the higher reaches of corporate management. Indeed in 80% of the diverse businesses in which we conducted interviews top-level managers and employers suggested that managing middle-level managers was as important a reason for gathering customer feedback as managing workers.

To begin with, like workers, middle-level managers could often be individually identified in consumers' reports, either by name or indirectly through customers' identification of particular work shifts, store locations, or dates. Additionally, in every company we studied ultimate control over some of this customer information was held, not by middle managers, but at the highest management levels. For example, in all firms at least one of the mechanisms employed to gather customer feedback was initiated by corporate management, which then gathered and analyzed the ensuing data itself; furthermore, a great deal of the customer information collected was regularly reviewed by top officers in the organization. The president of a supermarket chain claimed personally to read forty to fifty customer comment cards daily; in two hospitals summaries of all patient feedback were reviewed monthly by their presidents, vice presidents and boards of directors.

Third, customer data were often aggregated and analyzed by service delivery unit, allowing top management to control middle managers through comparison. The owners of a restaurant chain broke down the information they collected from patrons by restaurant and by management shift and posted it in their eating establishments, thereby setting up an explicit comparison amongst middle managers. Similarly, an auto manufacturer summarized its customer data by dealership, the main purpose of which was to facilitate inter-dealer comparisons. Corporate-level management, furthermore, used this information to discipline and control middle managers. Middle managers were clearly expected to demonstrate to top managers an awareness of the weak spots highlighted by customer feedback, to provide explanations for these and eventually to rectify their performance.

A pair of examples illustrate how middle managers were held accountable and were disciplined on the basis of consumer feedback. A customer relations manager in a hotel chain reported that when top management received the results of customer surveys they wrote to middle managers, informing them of problems and complaints; middle managers had to respond within 30 days, notifying upper-level management of the ways in which they had rectified any faulty conditions. If no response was made by 30 days corporate management instigated formal proceedings against the manager via his or her superior. Poor customer satisfaction ratings sometimes sparked even more elaborate top management efforts to bring middle managers into line. The example of an auto manufacturer and its dealers provides a case in point. To monitor the quality of service delivered by its dealerships this manufacturer conducted extensive and ongoing surveys of customers. Very poor dealer ratings on these surveys sparked corporate branch management to organize on-site, up-to-one-week long, "quality service improvement" sessions in which the dealership's owner, general manager and employees, selected customers and representatives of the manufacturer participated. Consistently poor ratings were also used to deny dealers new franchises, financing, access to particular company products and the privilege of placing special orders. While the position of a dealer, who holds a company franchise, is structurally different from a middle manager who lacks ownership privileges, the core function of consumer management remains. That is, consumer data are used by upper levels of corporate management to control the behavior of middle levels of employees, insofar as their behavior shapes, encourages or fails to elicit, quality service from front-line service workers.

In sum, our data indicate that middle- and upper-level managers were using devices such as customer surveys, shoppers and comment cards to provide data on how well services were being sold. In all the firms we studied, diverse mechanisms were used to obtain information about service workers' and middle managers' attitudes and overall presentation of self, as well as the latter's success in eliciting high-quality service from workers. At a time when all these firms saw quality service as integral to their profitability, consumer feedback was an increasingly important foundation for monitoring, evaluating and disciplining workers precisely at the point where they understood profits to be created: the customer/worker interaction. As one bank manager noted: "Without the responses from our customers, we will be unable to improve the quality of our workers in order to compete with other financial institutions." Moreover, approximately three-quarters of our respondents indicated that they were in the process of refining and strengthening the mechanisms through which they collected and used customer feedback or that they would soon do so.

## *Discussion*

We have discussed the ways in which service companies collected customer feedback and used it to manage both individual employees and the work of middle managers, the latter often measured by the totalistic picture of the workplace that customer feedback provides. We begin this section by highlighting four implications that may follow from systems of customer management. Although only suggestive, they nevertheless point to important foci of study for workplace sociologists concerned with power, hierarchy and control in a changing economy.

First, customer management may increase the complexity of authority and power arrangements at the workplace. Because the customer/worker interaction is used as the primary measure of workplace performance, the power to control workers and mid-level managers may appear to be removed from upper management's hands and redistributed to a company's clients, customers, passengers, patients, etc. In fact, however, feedback from consumers strengthens employers' hold over the workplace by providing them with an additional source of data they can use for control, evaluation and discipline.

As management continually impresses the importance of the customer/worker interaction on its employees, consumer feedback may appear to be a more legitimate basis on which to reward and discipline service workers than information provided by managers. Experientially it is the customer who knows how a worker delivers service, not the manager. Positioned as agents in the management circuit, customers, rather than managers, are set up as the ones who must be pleased, whose orders must be followed, whose ideas, whims and desires appear to dictate how work is performed. Workers are judged on their interactions with customers *by* customers themselves. It would then appear that managers, in using customer data to control employees, were acting more as customers' agents or intermediaries, and less out of the managerial privilege accorded by their superordinate positions in the social relations of production.

Yet, while customer management techniques appear to dilute management responsibility for how employees are directed, disciplined and evaluated, in essence workers gain an additional boss. Managers now have formally designated accomplices in controlling workers, insofar as they exploit customers for their observations about how service is delivered. In sum, consumers' reports broaden *managerial* power, augmenting it with *customer* power; conflicts between employers and employees may thus be reconstituted as conflicts between employees and customers.

A second implication of our research is that customer management may make organizational power a constant yet elusive presence. The fact that customers potentially can evaluate the service interaction at any time may serve as a continuous, though invisible, check on service workers' interactions with the public. The knowledge that any interaction could flair into an antagonistic encounter, if the worker fails to provide service that satisfies the customer, may shape and reshape a worker's behavior. Organizational power is a constant in the sense that workers may always feel someone is looking over their shoulder.

Paid shoppers may represent the perfected form of this particular sort of control over workers. Much like the anonymous surveillance of the Panopticon (Foucault 1979), when the technique works as it should, service workers have no idea when an anonymous shopper will do business with them. But the knowledge that shoppers may be there at any time may continuously constrain workers' actions.

Third, customer management may mystify power by enveloping managerial practice in a mantle of objective, rigorously accumulated and analyzed data. A comparatively small number of people in the firms we studied monopolized the power to direct, demote and promote, discipline and lay off employees, but their power was at least partially shielded behind a veil of quantification and the science of survey research. For example, the owners of a restaurant chain calculated a "P/N ratio" (the ratio of positive to negative marks customers gave on comment cards) for each of their employees. All employees were rank ordered according to their "P/N ratios" and the owners circulated a letter to each manager (also posted in each work site), drawing attention to their employees' positions in the ranking.

Yet even by "soft" social science criteria, the data which underpin such customer control practices hardly warrant the scientific label. Samples tend not to be representative (Lewis 1983), survey responses tend to be biased toward negative evaluations because of the self-selection problem (Trice and Layman 1984) and response rates are generally poor—20–65% in the companies we studied. Furthermore, though survey and industry specialists have collaborated to devise reliable and valid instruments for gathering information on customer satisfaction, their measures, much like the "P/N ratio," are often crude, yielding results that: "defy meaningful interpretation" (Lewis and Pizam 1981: 38).

As a consequence, data that claim to capture the reality of workers' and middle managers' performance may, in fact, severely distort it. The murkiness of much customer feedback data was revealed in the comments of a union official representing supermarket workers. To begin with, he argued, such information was very subjective. "You're often dealing," he explained, "with how a customer interprets something — a mannerism, a tone of voice or something like that. 'She just threw the change back at me!' 'He didn't smile at me!' 'She was carrying on a conversation with the counter clerk instead of paying attention to me!' There are very gray areas." In addition, this official was familiar with cases in which customers had registered phony complaints against workers, occasionally in response to material incentives businesses offered customers who provided feedback. As a result he was adamant that any disciplinary action inspired by customer feedback had to be scrutinized especially closely by the union.

Finally, customer control may prompt various contradictions and resistances, ruptures in the organization of work that sociologists may want to investigate. First, insofar as it positions customers to assume antagonistic, adversarial roles in relation to employees it may spawn resentment, perhaps overt resistance, amongst workers and middle managers.[4] We uncovered limited evidence of worker resentment of and resistance to customer control practices. One-quarter of our interviewees stated that employees had become sensitive about customers providing negative reports on their work. Because of its deceptive character, shopping in particular may engender misgivings on the part of workers.[5] Indeed, a manager in a large hotel reported that her desk clerks had been so angry about the prospect of being anonymously observed by shoppers that one shift staged a "smile strike," treating each and every customer that day in a rapid, affect-less fashion. In certain circumstances, customer control practices may thus produce precisely the opposite kind of service delivery from what management is trying to encourage and this in turn might force the curtailment or tempering of such methods. Our understanding of this possibility would be greatly enhanced by research on workers' responses to customer control, specifically how they negotiate or comply with, or resist consumers as managers (Rafaeli 1989).

Alternatively, workers and mid-level employees may attempt to appropriate, interpret or collect customer feedback data to protect themselves from the customer data collected by their superiors. The interpretation of data can also be the object of intense contestation, tacking significant organizational costs onto top management's attempt to use them to control employees. Thus, in a bank we studied, it was virtually impossible to rely exclusively on consumer feedback as a basic for serious disciplinary action because, at most, the use of these data would prompt a series of prolonged discussions and mediations between the criticized worker and various personnel and grievance groups in the corporation. Finally, we learned that auto dealers' efforts to protect themselves from reprisals based on the consumer feedback gathered by manufacturers has not only prompted many to collect their own data but has also spawned independent businesses that collect customer feedback solely for dealers.

We note one final issue of interest to sociologists studying changes in the contemporary workplace. Our research found evidence of increased managerial enthusiasm for employee *self-control* used in conjunction with, and, perhaps, in response to the failures of, customer management.[6] According to certain managers and employers we interviewed, employees must come to internalize the appropriate "values." They must become aware of their central role in adding value to products and services through quality labor and to be able automatically, as if by second nature, to balance competing demands for highly individualized quality service delivery and bottom line financial considerations, variously described as efficiency, profitability, productivity, growth, and so forth.

We uncovered a number of attempts to operationalize employee self control in the companies we studied, including an employee self-evaluation procedure in one supermarket chain. But the seriousness with which some firms have come to regard employee self-control was clearest in a discussion of structural changes in the company that had proceeded the furthest with its implementation. For many years every regional office in this corporation had had its own customer affairs department. Rather than expanding these departments as part of their effort to improve customer service, however, top corporate managers abolished them all. In their place they created very small customer relations units on a temporary basis. This action only makes sense if understood as part of a corporation-wide effort to institute employee self-control. Explained a man who headed one of these newly created units:

> My customer relations unit should never become permanent, or it will become a corporate dumping ground, as the customer affairs departments had turned into. Employees dumped all the responsibility for customer service with the customer affairs department. That would defeat our whole purpose. We want every employee to internalize responsibility for customer service. My unit's job is to disseminate this philosophy to every individual. Once we've done that we (the unit) disappear.

Such corporate attempts to convince workers to manage themselves, used in conjunction with customer management, can form the twin pillars of continuous, unobtrusive control systems, whereby managers attempt to insure the delivery of quality service by enlarging the arena of employee self-direction.

## Conclusion

Some observers have argued that new approaches to the organization of work in manufacturing and production, such as "flexibly specialized" (Piore and Sabel 1984), "post industrial" (Hirschhorn 1984) or "neo-Fordist" (Sabel 1982) arrangements, signal an increase in discretion and authority for workers. Others are less optimistic, pointing to the way that allegedly autonomous worker participation schemes simply mask rigid forms of management control and conceal the extent of concessions made by workers (Wells 1987; Parker and Slaughter 1988; Burawoy and Lukacs 1989).

Our analysis indicates that the issues raised in this debate are of equal relevance in the service sector where profits depend on employee autonomy. At the same time, it suggests that the conclusions of the latter, less optimistic, group best portray the situation in interactive service work. Employers have continued to seek ways to circumscribe or limit the autonomy of interactive service workers that borrow heavily from and extend traditional management paradigms, paradigms based on "low trust" relations (Fox 1974). Customer control, a continuous yet unobtrusive management form, allows employers access to very direct observations about work performance, while tending to obscure the real locus of power over production. Customer management techniques, in short, have helped employers perfect the direction, evaluation and discipline of their subordinates. The three longstanding functions of control systems appear to be inseparable features of social relations at the capitalist workplace.

### NOTES

*Acknowledgments:* This article is a revised version of a paper presented at the American Sociological Association meeting, August, 1989, San Francisco. We'd like to thank David Ellison, Paul Goldman, Larry Hirschhorn and the students in Linda Fuller's "Work and Workplace" class, fall 1985, University of Southern California, for their contributions to this paper.

1. We are not able, in this brief article, to investigate whether, in fact, the delivery of quality service actually increases profitability. Although corporate employers express this belief (Sutton and Rafaeli 1988), little conclusive data exist to confirm their claims. Instead, we propose to investigate how employers articulate this position and how it shapes their strategies of labor control.
2. Consumer feedback is initially a means for *evaluating* employees. It is then used in the service of two other components of management: to *direct* workers and middle managers (feedback is circulated upwards to personnel management and back down to individual work units in the form of new guidelines for performing tasks or revised job descriptions) and to *discipline* workers (managers use the feedback to determine promotions and raises, and implement sanctions).
3. Their mean number of employees was 8,538, with a median of a little over 9,000.

4. Anecdotal evidence suggests some resentment of consumer commentary amongst other types of workers. Trucks have been spotted with bumper stickers reading "How am I driving? Call 1-800-WHO-CARES" and "How am I driving? Call 1-800-EAT SHIT."

5. According to an official of the Association of Flight Attendants, the equivalent of shoppers in the airline industry — "ghost riders" or "sky spies" — has produced much anger and fear among flight attendants (Dallos 1987).

6. The idea of employee self-control, currently undergoing a revival in industrial production sectors (Heckscher 1988), parallels self-management philosophies that have been periodically advocated by students of management.

## REFERENCES

Albrecht, K. (1988) *At America's Service: How Corporations Can Revolutionize the Way They Treat Their Customers*, Homewood, IL: Dow Jones-Irwin.

Burawoy, M. (1979) *Manufacturing Consent: Changes in the Labor Process under Monopoly Capitalism*, Chicago: University of Chicago Press.

Burawoy, M., & Lukacs, J. (1989) "What Is Socialist about Socialist Production?" in S. Wood (ed.), *The Transformation of Work? Skill, Flexibility and the Labour Process*, London: Unwin Hyman, 295–316.

Cardan, P. n.d. *Redefining Revolution*, London: Solidarity.

Dallos, R. (1987) "Airlines Spy on Selves in Service War," *Los Angeles Times*, July 21, 1 & 16.

Edwards, R. (1984) "Forms of Control in the Labor Process: An Historical Analysis," in Frank Fischer and Carmen Sirianni (eds.), *Critical Studies in Organization and Bureaucracy*, Philadelphia: Temple University Press.

Foucault, M. (1979) *Discipline and Punish*, New York: Vintage Books.

Fox, A. (1974) *Beyond Contract: Work, Power and Trust Relations*, London: Faber and Faber.

Hage, J. (1988) *Futures of Organizations: Innovating to Adapt Strategy and Human Resources to Rapid Technological Change*, Lexington, MA: Lexington Books.

Heckscher, C. (1988) *The New Unionism: Employee Involvement in the Changing Corporation*, New York: Basic Books.

Heydebrand, W. (1989) "New Organizational Forms," *Work and Occupations*, 16: 323–357.

Hirschhorn, L. (1984) *Beyond Mechanization*, Cambridge: MIT Press.

Hirschhorn, L. (1988) "The Post-Industrial Economy: Labor, Skills and the New Mode of Production," *Service Industries*, January.

Hochschild, A. (1983) *The Managed Heart*, Berkeley: University of California Press.

Koepp, S. (1987) "Whatever Happened to Good Service," *Time*, February 2, 48–57.

Langer, J. (1987) "Getting to Know the Customer through Qualitative Research," *Management Review*, April 75: 42–46.

Leidner, R. (1988) *Working on People: The Routinization of Interactive Service Work*, Ph.D. Department of Sociology, Northwestern University.

Lewis, R. (1983) "When Guests Complain," *The Cornell H.R.A. Quarterly*, August: 23–32.

Lewis, R., & Pizam, A. (1981) "Guest Surveys: A Missed Opportunity," *The Cornell H.R.A. Quarterly*, November: 37–44.

Manwaring, T., & Wood, S. (1984) "The Ghost in the Machine: Tacit Skills in the Labor Process," *Socialist Review*, 74: 57–86.

Noyelle, T. (1987) *Beyond Industrial Dualism*, Boulder and London: Westview Press.

Parker, M., & Slaughter, J. (1988) *Choosing Sides: Unions and the Team Concept*, Boston: South End Press.

Piore, M., & Sabel, C. (1984) *The Second Industrial Divide*, New York: Basic Books.

Rafaeli, A. (1989) "When Cashiers Meet Customers: An Analysis of the Role of Supermarket Cashiers," *Academy of Management Journal* 32: 245–273.

Ritzer, G. (1989) "The Permanently New Economy: The Case for Reviving Economic Sociology," *Work and Occupations* 16: 243–272.

Sabel, C. (1982) *Work and Politics*, Cambridge: Cambridge University Press.

Schoenberger, E. (1989) "Multinational Corporations and the New International Division of Labor: A Critical Appraisal," in S. Wood (ed.), *The Transformation of Work? Skill, Flexibility and the Labour Process*, London: Unwin Hyman, 91–101.

Sutton, R., & Rafaeli, A. (1988). "Untangling the Relationship between Displayed Emotions and Organizational Sales: The Case of Convenience Stores," *Academy of Management Journal*, 31: 461–487.

Trice, A., & Layman, W. (1984) "Improving Guest Surveys," *The Cornell H.R.A. Quarterly*, November: 10–13.

*Wall Street Journal* (1900) "Chain Finds Incentives a Hard Sell," July 5, B1 & B4.

Wells, D. (1987) *Empty Promises: Quality of Working Life Programs and the Labor Movement*, New York: Monthly Review Press.

Wood, S. (ed.) (1989) *The Transformation of Work? Skill, Flexibility and the Labour Process*, London: Unwin Hyman.

## Chapter 5

# Service with a Smile: Understanding the Consequences of Emotional Labor

• Amy S. Wharton

*A*rlie R. Hochschild's (1983) analysis of emotional labor in the airline industry has inspired numerous case studies of particular interactive service jobs (e.g., Leidner 1993; Rafaeli and Sutton 1987; Sutton 1991; Van Maanen and Kunda 1989). Although these qualitative studies have yielded important insights, they have raised analytical issues that are best resolved by quantitative research. In particular, little attention has been devoted to systematic study of issues Hochschild and others raise concerning the social-psychological and affective effects of emotional labor on incumbents of these service jobs. In light of these considerations, this chapter explores the social-psychological consequences of emotional labor for a sample of male and female workers in two organizations. An additional objective is to identify the individual and job conditions under which performance of emotional labor will have negative social-psychological consequences for interactive service workers, as well as the conditions under which it may enhance these workers' psychological well-being.

## Emotional Labor and Its Consequences

### Hochschild's Conception of Emotional Labor

According to Hochschild (1983), jobs involving emotional labor possess three characteristics: they require the worker to make voice or facial contact

This chapter is a revised version of an article published in *Work and Occupations* (July 1993).

with the public, they require the worker to produce an emotional state in the client or customer, and they provide the employer with an opportunity to exert some control over the emotional activities of workers. Applying these criteria, Hochschild (1983: Appendix C) identified a set of forty-four census occupations that involve significant amounts of emotional labor. Consistent with Hochschild's views on the relations between jobs requiring emotional labor and the growth of services, these occupations are all interactive service positions, meaning that they involve either face-to-face or phone contact with the public. This categorization, which Hochschild (1983) characterizes as "no more than a sketch, a suggestion of a pattern that deserves to be examined more closely" (p. 234), has not been used in empirical research on emotional labor, nor has it been superseded by a more systematic attempt to classify jobs involving emotional labor. Instead, emotional labor research has focused exclusively on particular interactive service occupations, including flight attendant, bill collector, fast-food worker, grocery check-out clerk, amusement park employee, and child-care worker (Hochschild 1983; Leidner 1993; Rafaeli and Sutton 1987; Sutton 1991; Van Maanen and Kunda 1989).

The central emotion management task for these workers is to display publicly an emotion that they may not necessarily feel privately. Workers performing emotional labor thus must learn to manage what Hochschild (1983) calls the "emotive dissonance" (p. 90) engendered when there is a disjuncture between what one feels and what one is required to display. As Karl Albrecht and Ron Zemke (1985) observe: "The service person must deliberately involve his or her feelings in the situation. He or she may not particularly feel like being cordial and becoming a one-minute friend to the next customer who approaches, but that is indeed what interactive work entails" (p. 114). While some interactive service workers are required to display less positive emotions, such as anger or disappointment (see, e.g., Sutton 1991), even these workers must manage their own emotions so as to produce a particular emotional state in the customer or client.

## The Psychological Consequences of Emotional Labor

While the occupational focus of previous studies varies, many share Hochschild's (1983) approach to understanding the consequences of emotional labor. Central to this approach is the view that the performance of emotional labor is potentially psychologically damaging, although Hochschild does acknowledge that the negative effects of emotional labor may be more severe for some workers than others. As she (1979) observes, "Surely the flight attendant's sense that 'she should feel cheery' does more to promote profit for United than to enhance her own well-being" (p. 573).

In this view, the underlying problem with employer-regulated emotion management is that it eliminates or substantially limits individuals' control over their emotion management efforts. Workers have little flexibility in negotiating their interactions with customers and hence lack autonomy in a key aspect of their jobs. In the same way that physical and mental labor can be deskilled through the transfer of decision-making from workers to managers, the regulation of emotion work by employers diminishes workers' opportunities for self-direction and initiative. Hence, when the management of feeling shifts from being a strictly private act, performed almost unconsciously, to a public act, performed according to others' guidelines, negative consequences follow. As Hochschild (1983) states, "When the transmutation of the private use of feeling is successfully accomplished — when we succeed in lending our feelings to the organizational engineers of worker-customer relations — we may pay a cost in how we hear our feelings and a cost in what, for better or worse, they tell us about ourselves" (p. 21).

While a lack of control over working conditions poses psychological problems for all types of workers (Karasek and Theorell 1990), those performing emotional labor are believed to be vulnerable to a particular set of outcomes related to their lack of control over the emotion management requirements of their jobs. The negative psychological consequences associated with emotional labor thus primarily pertain to workers' orientations to feeling. Specifically, sustained performance of emotional labor is believed to engender an inability to feel emotion, or a sense that one is being insincere and inauthentic in the feelings displayed. The former situation occurs when workers too thoroughly embrace employer-imposed guidelines for emotion management, while the latter reflects an inability to feel other than superficial in the work role.

An inability to feel emotion is associated with the condition of burnout. Burnout is a form of job stress involving feelings of "emotional exhaustion, depersonalization, and reduced personal accomplishment" (Maslach and Jackson 1985: 837). It may also be experienced as a sense of "emotional numbness" or a loss of access to one's feelings (Hochschild 1983: 188). Burnout is a potential occupational hazard for all performers of emotional labor, but may be most likely to occur among workers strongly identified with their jobs (Hochschild 1983). These workers' ongoing attentiveness to employer-imposed guidelines for emotion management makes them especially vulnerable to a depletion of their emotional resources and the loss of their ability to respond emotionally to others.

Performance of emotional labor may also result in feelings of inauthenticity or a sense of estrangement from one's emotions and self. Workers whose jobs require them to monitor their emotions constantly thus may pay a price in terms of their capacity to distinguish their "real" selves from their "on-stage" selves (Hochschild 1983: 184). In Hochschild's (1983) words, "The self we define as 'real' is pushed further and further into a corner as more and more of its expressions are sensed as artifice" (p. 183). In contrast to burnout, which reflects the emotional drain on workers who are unable to separate themselves from their work role, inauthenticity reflects a chronic inability to feel whole. As Hochschild (1983) explains, "When display is required by the job, it is usually feeling that has to change; and when conditions estrange us from our face, they sometimes estrange us from feeling as well" (p. 90).

These themes regarding the psychological effects of emotional labor have been elaborated by others with both academic and applied concerns. For instance, Albrecht and Zemke (1985) caution that "contact overload is a recognizable syndrome in interactive work," whose symptoms include becoming "robotic, detached, and unempathetic" (p. 114). Similarly, John Van Maanen and Gideon Kunda (1989) suggest that "the more emotional labor involved in a particular work role, the more troublesome work identity becomes to the role holder" (p. 54). In sum, because the effective performance of emotional labor may require that workers display emotions they may not necessarily feel, workers must learn to manage potential disjunctures between work role requirements for emotion and their own feelings.

Despite these assertions, there is scant empirical research evaluating the consequences of emotional labor. In fact, these arguments have come under increasing criticism from several sources. These critiques call for more attention to issues unexplored in Hochschild's work, including her suggestion that the costs of emotional labor will fall more heavily on some workers than others. For instance, while their arguments differ in certain respects, Steven L. Gordon (1989) and Cas Wouters (1989) both reject claims that institutionally regulated emotion management is necessarily experienced as an assault upon workers' private selves. For example, Gordon (1989) suggests that "the effect of commoditization of emotion is interactive; it differs depending on one's cultural orientation to emotion" (p. 131). Similarly, Wouters (1989) argues that "Hochschild's preoccupation with the 'costs' of emotion work not only leads to a one-sided and moralistic interpretation of the working conditions of flight attendants, it also hampers understanding of the joy the job may bring" (p. 116). Consequently, both Gordon and Wouters call for greater attention to factors that may mediate the effects of emotional labor.

The literature on organization boundary roles has similar implications for understanding the psychological effects of emotional labor and is thus another source of alternative hypotheses. "Organization boundary roles" are positions whose function is to represent an organization to groups outside the organization's boundary (Miles 1980). While the emotion management component of these roles has not received attention, "boundary-spanning" positions share much in common with the jobs highlighted in discussions of emotional labor. Both definitions emphasize public contact, which in turn requires that incumbents of these positions be skilled in managing interpersonal contacts. In addition, both definitions acknowledge that incumbents of these jobs play important roles as representatives of the organization.

Studies of organization boundary roles reveal that these positions are "not uniformly aversive" to their occupants (Miles 1980: 71). In particular, Robert H. Miles (1980) argues that whether the boundary-spanning is active or passive, routine or nonroutine, and voluntary or mandatory will influence its effects on job stress and satisfaction. Hence, this literature implies that emotional labor, too, may be psychologically damaging only under certain conditions.

Greta Foff Paules's (1991; see also Chapter 11) study of waitresses offers some support for those claiming that performance of emotional labor is not always psychologically damaging. As she notes: "Like all social actors, the waitress monitors her projected personality and manipulates her feelings in the course of social interaction, but she does so knowingly and in her own interests. This manipulation of self does not induce self-alienation or emotional disorientation" (Paules 1991: 162). The waitresses in her study derived satisfaction from their emotion management skills, viewing their expression as an assertion of autonomy and a source of material reward. Paules (1991) traced waitresses' ability to resist the negative consequences of emotional labor in part to the organizational structure of the restaurant. The tipping system, along with a chaotic and chronically understaffed work environment, enhanced waitresses' ability to control their working conditions and defy management efforts to take charge. This argument implies that the context within which emotional labor is performed may play an important role in conditioning its effects on people.

## Hypotheses: Under What Conditions Should Emotional Labor Have Negative Psychological Consequences?

The literature inspires several hypotheses regarding the psychological effects of emotional labor. Most importantly, previous analyses of emotional labor imply that workers employed in jobs involving significant degrees of emotional labor should experience less psychological well-being than other workers. Alternatively, others argue that performance of emotional labor will be psychologically damaging only under certain conditions. Hence, specific hypotheses must be developed concerning those factors that should condition the effects of emotional labor on psychological well-being.

Several characteristics, some of which Hochschild (1983) alludes to, are expected to mediate the effects of emotional labor on psychological well-being. Most significantly, workers whose performance of emotional labor occurs under relatively autonomous conditions should be less negatively affected than workers with less control over job conditions. If emotion management becomes problematic for individuals when it is no longer private and is instead guided by employers, as Hochschild (1983) assumes, it follows that workers whose paid emotional labor is performed relatively autonomously should fare better than those who perform this labor under more restricted conditions. This is also consistent with Miles's (1980) claim that organization boundary roles are less aversive for workers when they are voluntarily performed and with Paules's (1991) analysis of waitressing.

In addition, the effects of emotional labor are also expected to depend upon workers' job involvement and their self-presentation skills. Workers expressing higher levels of job involvement are expected to suffer more negative consequences from performing emotional labor than those less involved in their jobs. This follows from Hochschild's (1983) finding that flight attendants who psychologically distanced themselves from their jobs, and thus were less closely identified with their work, were better able than others to avoid some of the negative psychological costs of emotional labor. Finally, the potentially negative consequences of emotional labor may be offset by workers' skills in "self-monitoring," the means by which people observe and control the self they present in social interaction (Snyder 1987). High self-monitors are highly sensitive to what is expected of them in any particular situation, whereas low self-monitors are less attentive to their social environments. David R. Caldwell and Charles O'Reilly III (1982) found that self-monitoring ability was positively related to the job performance of workers employed in boundary-spanning roles. This implies that these skills may also enhance the performance and lower the psychological distress of workers who perform emotional labor.

Other individual characteristics, such as gender and marital status, are also expected to mediate the effects of emotional labor. All else being equal, women and those involved in intimate relationships should suffer more negative effects of emotional labor than men or those with partners. As Hochschild (1983) notes, women (and members of other low-status categories) are less protected than men from poor treatment of their feelings on the job, implying that public-contact work may be more stressful for women than their male counterparts. Also, both men and women with partners at home should be more vulnerable to the negative effects of emotional labor than single workers. Those with nonwork responsibilities for others' emotional well-being may find it more difficult to perform emotional labor on the job than those without a "second shift" of emotion work at home (Hochschild 1989). Although evidence suggests that married women provide more emotional support to their male partners at home than vice versa (Belle 1982; 1987), married men also perform this activity to some degree (Van Fossen 1981). Hence, to the extent that providing emotional support at home interferes with one's ability or inclination to perform emotional labor on the job, married women *and* married men should experience more negative consequences of emotional labor than their single counterparts.

In sum, initial studies of emotional labor stressed its negative psychological consequences for workers, while more recent accounts emphasize factors that may condition the effects of this type of work. In general, those reporting less job autonomy and higher job involvement are expected to suffer more negative consequences from performing emotional labor, as are female workers, those married or cohabiting, and low self-monitors, compared to others who hold these jobs.

## The Research: Data and Measures

### Data

The data analyzed in this study consist of responses to a questionnaire distributed to employees of two Pacific Northwest companies during the spring and summer of 1989. The questionnaire included items measuring work and family situations, a variety of social-psychological dimensions, and demographic characteristics. The first company was an eighteen-branch bank and the second was a large, Catholic, teaching hospital. Hence, both companies are in service sector industries (e.g., banking and health) and should therefore contain interactive service jobs involving emotional labor. It cannot be claimed, of course, that the sample is representative of all interactive service workers or service sector industries. However, given the paucity of research on the effects of emotional labor and the inattention these particular industries have received from researchers interested in these issues, these data represent a useful testing ground for ideas developed in previous studies (e.g., Hochschild 1983; Sutton 1991; Sutton and Rafaeli 1988).

Due to the small number of bank employees ($n = 135$), all were included in the sample; 117 surveys were returned, for an overall response rate of 87 percent. The hospital was much larger, with approximately 5,100 employees. I surveyed every third name listed on an employee roster ($n = 1,706$); 555 surveys were returned, for a response rate of 33 percent.

## Sample

The sample for this research ($n = 622$) consists of male and female workers from both companies with complete data on the measure of emotional labor. Given the size difference between the two companies, 83 percent of the sample are hospital employees and 17 percent are employed by the bank. Ninety-six percent of the respondents are white, which reflects the racial homogeneity of this particular city. Therefore, race is not a variable in the analysis. Women comprise 83 percent of the respondents.

## Dependent Variables: Psychological Consequences of Emotional Labor

Two dependent variables are examined. The first measures one dimension of respondents' work-related emotional well-being, while the second measures their overall job satisfaction. *Emotional exhaustion* is measured by a six-item scale, which taps respondents' feelings of being "used-up" at the end of the workday. While emotional exhaustion is not the only psychological outcome that may be associated with emotional labor, it has been linked to this type of work (e.g., Albrecht and Zemke 1985; Hochschild 1983; Maslach 1976). The second dependent variable, *job satisfaction*, is a more global measure of respondents' assessment of their job. This variable measures their answer to the question: "Overall, how satisfied are you with your present job?"

## Measuring Emotional Labor

Emotional labor is the key independent variable in the analysis, and I rely on Hochschild's (1983) effort to designate such work. Hence, *emotional labor* is constructed as a dichotomous variable differentiating between those occupations Hochschild identified as involving significant amounts of emotional labor and other occupations in the sample. Twenty out of the forty-four occupations on Hochschild's list are included in the sample. These occupations, along with the full list identified by Hochschild, appear in Table 5.1. Approximately 64 percent of the sample hold jobs involving emotional labor, according to the

TABLE 5.1
**Occupations Requiring Emotional Labor**

| Occupation | Present in Sample |
|---|---|
| Lawyers and judges | |
| Librarians | X |
| Personnel and labor relations | X |
| Registered nurses | X |
| Therapists | X |
| Dental hygienists | |
| Therapy assistants | X |
| Clergymen and religious workers | X |
| Social and recreation workers | X |
| College and university teachers | |
| Teachers, except college and university | X |
| Vocational and educational counselors | |
| Public relations and publicity writers | X |
| Radio and television announcers | |
| Physicians, dentists, and related personnel | X |
| | |
| Bank tellers | X |
| Cashiers | X |
| Clerical supervisors | X |
| Bill collectors | |
| Counter clerks, excluding food | X |
| Enumerators and interviewers | |
| Insurance adjustors and examiners | |
| Library attendants | |
| Postal clerks | |
| Receptionists | X |
| Secretaries | X |
| Stenographers | |
| Teachers aides | |
| Telegraph operators | |
| Telephone operators | X |
| Ticket agents | |
| | |
| Bartenders | |
| Food counter and fountain workers | X |
| Waiters | |

TABLE 5.1 *Continued*
## Occupations Requiring Emotional Labor

| *Occupation* | *Present in Sample* |
| --- | :---: |
| Health service workers | X |
| Personal service workers | |
| Child care operators | |
| Elevator operators | |
| Hairdressers and cosmetologists | |
| Housekeepers (excluding private household) | X |
| School monitors | |
| Ushers, recreation and amusement | |
| Welfare service aides | |
| Protective service workers | |

Source: Arlie Russell Hochschild, *The Managed Heart: Commercialization of Human Feeling* (Berkeley: University of California Press, 1983), Appendix C, pp. 234–41.

measure used in this study. As Table 5.1 shows, these workers are employed in jobs such as nurse, bank teller, and receptionist, among others. The kinds of jobs in the sample that involve little emotional labor are numerous, and include such positions as health technician, records clerk, bookkeeper, mechanic, and kitchen worker.

## Other Independent Variables

To test the hypotheses outlined earlier, several other variables are also included in the model. *Control at work* asks respondents to indicate how much control they have over how their work is done. *Job involvement* measures respondents' answer to a question regarding how involved they are in their job. *Self-monitoring* is measured by Mark Snyder's (1987) eighteen-item Self-Monitoring Scale. Additional variables needed to test the hypotheses include *gender* and *marital status*.

Finally, the model also includes several control variables that past research suggests may be associated with the dependent variables. *Professional* and *clerical* are variables designating the two largest major occupational groups of workers who perform emotional labor. (Seventy-three percent of workers who perform emotional labor fall into one of these two groups.) Other control variables include: respondent's *income*, *hours worked per week*, *job tenure*, *age*, and *education*.

## Results: The Consequences of Emotional Labor

### Who Performs Emotional Labor?
### Characteristics of the Sample

The first step in this analysis is to examine the differences between those employed in jobs requiring emotional labor and other workers in the sample. This reveals only a few significant differences between these two groups. First, as Hochschild (1983) notes, women are significantly more likely to be employed in jobs requiring emotional labor than men. This difference is statistically significant, even for the predominantly female sample used in this study. In addition, workers performing emotional labor are more likely than others to hold professional and clerical jobs, and are more highly educated than other workers in the sample. Nonperformers of emotional labor receive higher incomes, work more hours per week, and have been in their jobs longer than workers who perform emotional labor.

### Emotional Labor, Emotional Exhaustion, and Job Satisfaction

Are workers who perform emotional labor more likely than other workers to report emotional exhaustion? The results of this research suggest a negative answer to this question. Contrary to assumptions, workers who perform emotional labor are no more likely than other workers to suffer from emotional exhaustion. Instead, workers' levels of emotional exhaustion are better predicted by their degree of job autonomy, the number of hours they work per week, and their job tenure. On average, workers with low job autonomy, those who work more hours per week, and those who have spent fewer years in their jobs report more emotional exhaustion than other workers. No additional worker or job characteristics, such as gender, marital status, and education, are related to emotional exhaustion.

Slightly different results are found for job satisfaction. This dependent variable offers a way to examine the effects of emotional labor on workers' overall assessment of their job, rather than its more specific effects on one facet of their emotional well-being. Contrary to predictions, however, emotional labor is positively related to job satisfaction. In other words, workers whose jobs require emotional labor are more satisfied than other workers, other factors being equal. Consistent with prior research (e.g., Hodson 1989; Wharton and Baron 1987, 1991), women express significantly higher levels of job satisfaction than other workers. Job satisfaction is also higher among workers who report high involvement with their jobs. In addition, workers who report having high levels of job autonomy report greater job satisfaction than other workers in the sample.

## Making Sense of These Results

Two important ways this analysis differs from the case studies that inform previous work are the inclusion of a broader range of jobs that involve emotional labor and statistical controls for other job and individual characteristics that may be associated with the dependent variables. These differences may help explain why these results fail to support the hypothesized negative effects of emotional labor suggested in previous accounts. Most importantly, since no research prior to this analysis compares jobs involving emotional labor with other types of work, it may be that previous researchers have overstated the psychological costs and understated the psychological rewards of emotional labor, relative to other types of work. While previous research on emotional labor has identified emotional exhaustion as one consequence of this type of work, the factors that produce emotional exhaustion may simply be more prevalent in other kinds of jobs, a finding that requires a comparison between jobs involving emotional labor and those not involving this activity. At the same time, emotional exhaustion represents only one of many potential psychological costs of emotional labor. Perhaps these costs are expressed in other forms besides emotional exhaustion, such as feelings of inauthenticity, that are unique to jobs involving emotional labor. Research that examines other dependent variables is necessary to explore this possibility.

The results for job satisfaction also challenge existing literature on emotional labor, as they show a positive effect of emotional labor on this outcome. Although no prior research has explicitly examined relations between emotional labor and job satisfaction, previous research implies a negative relationship between these two variables. However, as noted above, earlier studies, such as Hochschild's (1983) analysis of flight attendants, focus on a specific occupational context, where workers' reactions to emotional labor would be undoubtedly influenced by the particular conditions under which it is performed (e.g., degree of autonomy, income, etc.). If these conditions are unfavorable, workers are likely to evaluate their job negatively. The proceeding analyses examine these conditions in more detail, but they are controlled in the analysis described above. Hence, the preceding results refer to the relations between emotional labor and job satisfaction, net of other job and individual characteristics, suggesting that when all else is equal, workers find jobs involving emotional labor more satisfying than comparable jobs that do not involve this activity.

Why would workers find jobs involving emotional labor more satisfying than comparable types of work not involving this activity? One possibility is that jobs involving emotional labor attract workers whose personal qualities are especially suited to working with the public (e.g., friendliness, empathy, patience, etc.). These qualities may also include the ability to engage in "deep acting," Hochschild's (1983) term for techniques people rely on in order to feel desired or required emotions. If employers select applicants for interactive service positions on the basis of their interpersonal skills and if workers seek jobs compatible with their personality, the "fit" between job demands and personal qualities may be high in these positions, leading to increased satisfaction (Diener, Larsen, and Emmons 1984). Evidence suggests that employers do attempt to distinguish between "people people" and "things people," and are sensitive of the need to employ the former in high-contact service roles (Tansik 1990: 158; Zemke and Schaaf 1989).

This argument implies that self-selection operates more strongly in jobs involving emotional labor than in comparable types of work not involving this activity. While there is no direct evidence that this is true, it is plausible. Jobs that involve extensive contact with the public are highly visible (e.g., flight attendant) and hence offer prospective applicants more information about job demands than comparable but less visible types of employment. This implies that those who hold jobs requiring emotional labor may have had more opportunity than others in comparable positions not involving this activity to obtain a job perceived as compatible with their personal characteristics. This congruence between job and personal characteristics should lead to higher satisfaction among workers in jobs involving emotional labor, all else being equal (Chatman 1989).

A more straightforward explanation for the positive association between emotional labor and job satisfaction is that this type of work provides important rewards that are unavailable in comparable jobs that do not require emotional labor. For instance, Wouters (1989) argues that flight attendants develop what he calls "playful flexibility" (p. 117), referring to an ability to use one's skills in dealing with people to create a pleasurable experience for others. Paules (1991) suggests that waitresses derive satisfaction from emotional labor in part because they experience it as an expression of control. In general, however, little is known about the possible sources of satisfaction deriving from emotional labor, an issue that the above results suggest requires further study.

While these results are informative, one limitation of the results described earlier is their assumption that the job and individual characteristics measured by the independent variables have similar effects on workers who perform emotional labor and those not performing this work activity. However, if jobs requiring emotional labor are distinctive, as sociologists of emotion presume, different factors may explain the work-related well-being of these workers compared to those not engaged in emotional labor. Exploring these issues requires further examination of the data.

## Do the Same Factors Explain the Results for Performers and Nonperformers of Emotional Labor?

In general, the answer to this question is "no." The results suggest that the surveyed workers who perform emotional labor are a distinct population who differ in some important ways from other banking and hospital workers in the sample. Specifically, several independent variables related to the two measures of work-related well-being operate differently among workers who perform emotional labor than among those whose jobs do not involve this activity. Hence, clear support was found for hypotheses pertaining to factors expected to mediate the effects of emotional labor.

**Emotional Exhaustion:** First, the analysis reveals that negative impact of emotional labor on workers' levels of emotional exhaustion is lessened for those with some job autonomy. In other words, emotional labor is significantly less aversive among workers who have greater job autonomy. This finding is consistent with Hochschild's (1983) claim that emotion *management* becomes problematic when it becomes emotional *labor*; that is, when it is directed by the employer rather than the worker. In addition, the results show that while job autonomy decreases the likelihood of emotional exhaustion for all workers in the sample, this effect is greater among those who perform emotional labor (although this difference fails to achieve statistical significance). Control at work is the *only* job condition with a significant effect on emotional exhaustion for this group of workers.

The finding for self-monitoring is also consistent with predictions. This independent variable has opposite effects on performers and nonperformers of emotional labor. High self-monitors are less adversely affected by performance of emotional labor than those scoring low on self-monitoring. Among nonperformers of emotional labor, however, self-monitoring is positively related to emotional exhaustion. This lends support to the claim that workers with the inclination and skill to monitor their social environments may fare better in jobs requiring emotional labor than those not so inclined. Given that attentiveness to others is a key component of emotional labor, high self-monitoring abilities may reduce emotional exhaustion by enhancing the effectiveness of and lowering the effort required from workers engaged in this activity. This also implies that among those performing emotional labor, low self-monitors are most at risk for the negative emotional consequences associated with this type of work.

A similar pattern is found for job involvement. High job involvement increases emotional exhaustion among workers performing emotional labor (although this effect is not statistically significant), while it significantly lowers emotional exhaustion among other banking and hospital workers. Hence, workers performing emotional labor differ from other workers in the sample in that absorption in their job fails to offset emotional distress. Contrary to hypotheses, gender and marital status do not mediate the effects of emotional labor on emotional exhaustion. Neither variable is associated with emotional exhaustion at work, and this holds true regardless of whether the respondent performs emotional labor.

Overall, these results lend support to those claiming that performance of emotional labor has some negative consequences for workers. At the same time, they also suggest that the relationship between emotional labor and emotional exhaustion is conditioned by several factors. Workers who perform emotional labor under conditions of low job autonomy or high job involvement are more at risk of emotional exhaustion than others who perform this activity. Both results are consistent with aspects of Hochschild's research showing that the negative effects of emotional labor fall more heavily on some types of workers than others.

Low self-monitors who perform emotional labor are also more likely to experience emotional exhaustion than those scoring higher on this characteristic. This finding extends previous research on emotional labor, as it suggests that the psychological effects of this type of work depend upon individual personality characteristics, such as self-monitoring ability. High self-monitors may be more likely than those scoring lower on this characteristic to seek out jobs requiring emotional labor and may experience fewer negative consequences than others in these jobs. Hence, while jobs requiring emotional labor do not place workers at any greater risk of emotional exhaustion than other jobs, all else being equal, emotional labor does result in negative consequences under some conditions.

Finally, these results show that neither women nor those with partners at home are more likely than others performing emotional labor to experience emotional exhaustion. The results for gender are surprising, given Hochschild's (1983) suggestion that women are less protected than men on the job from poor treatment of their feelings. Failure to uncover gender differences may reflect the relatively small number of men in the sample, especially among performers of emotional labor. At the same time, these results concur with those of Christina Maslach and Susan E. Jackson (1985), who found no gender differences in their study of burnout among public-contact workers in a federal service agency. The results for marital status seem to imply that workers' family-based emotional obligations do not undermine their ability to derive social-psychological rewards from jobs involving emotional labor. Married workers, assumed to be providers of emotional support to partners at home, are no more likely than single workers to report negative effects of emotional labor. Marital status may not be a good proxy for "provider of emotional support," however, indicating a need for more direct measures of this form of family-based emotion work. Overall, these results suggest that relations between gender, family, and emotional labor are more complicated than previous research assumed.

**Job Satisfaction:** The results for job satisfaction are equally illuminating. For instance, as hypothesized, job autonomy positively affects satisfaction among both performers and nonperformers of emotional labor, although this effect is significantly greater among the former group. Also consistent with predictions is the effect for job involvement. While job involvement is positively associated with job satisfaction among both performers and nonperformers of emotional labor, this effect is greater among nonperformers. Job involvement does not have a similar positive effect among those whose jobs require emotional labor, because it places these workers at greater risk of emotional exhaustion. Self-monitoring is also associated with higher levels of job satisfaction, lending support to the earlier suggestion that self-monitoring abilities may enhance the effectiveness of workers who perform emotional labor.

These results thus indicate some important differences between those who perform emotional labor and those not involved in this type of work. While job autonomy and job involvement are positively associated with job satisfaction for both performers and nonperformers of emotional labor, the effects differ for each group. These results support Hochschild's (1983) claims regarding the conditions under which emotional labor has negative consequences. Although the relations between self-monitoring and job satisfaction are slightly weaker than those for emotional exhaustion, they are consistent with the argument developed in that context.

Of particular significance is the finding that women who perform emotional labor are significantly more satisfied than their male counterparts engaged in this type of work. These results are directly contrary to predictions that women's greater vulnerability to others' negative emotions at work would lead them to view their jobs less favorably than men. While women may be more vulnerable than male workers to others' negative emotions, this is not expressed in lower levels of job satisfaction. Because women's job satisfaction reflects women's evaluations of their jobs relative to those of other *women*

(Hodson 1989; Wharton and Baron 1991), the findings may imply that interactive service work involving emotional labor is preferable to other jobs available to these women workers. However, the effect for gender is also consistent with arguments that women's socialization prepares them better than men for and instills in them a greater propensity to seek out roles construed as requiring empathy and attentiveness to others (e.g., Chodorow 1978; Gilligan 1982). Moreover, if women are more likely than men to value "working with people," as some evidence reveals (e.g., Marini and Brinton 1984: 206), this may also explain their higher levels of satisfaction in jobs requiring emotional labor.

Although there have been no direct attempts to determine whether women are, on average, more effective performers of emotional labor than men, some evidence supports this view. For example, the social support literature contains studies suggesting that women are more effective providers of informal social support than men (House, Umberson, and Landis 1989). Further, Hochschild's (1983) argument that women do more emotion-managing than men in nonwork roles implies that women may be better prepared for the demands of some jobs requiring emotional labor. If women are better equipped than men for the interpersonal demands of interactive service work, they may experience these jobs more positively than their male counterparts.

Robin Leidner's (1993) study of interactive service work suggests that these claims may be overstated, however. She argues that whether women are seen as more effective than men in service jobs requiring emotional labor depends more upon the gender composition of the job than its objective demands or skill requirements, or the worker's own characteristics. This implies that gender differences in workers' skills or effectiveness explain little about gender differences in job satisfaction. In fact, further exploration of the data used in this study revealed no evidence of gender differences in self-monitoring ability, one indicator of skill in performing emotional labor. These results suggest that the higher job satisfaction of female as compared to male performers of emotional labor may stem from factors other than women's superior "people skills." For instance, one possibility is that women who perform emotional labor are more likely than other women to be employed in predominantly female jobs, which Leidner (1993) suggests offers the opportunity to enact gender in a socially appropriate and therefore satisfying way. Exploratory analyses of this argument confirmed that women in the sample who performed emotional labor were significantly more likely than other women to be employed in jobs dominated by women. However, I did not find evidence that women employed in predominantly female jobs who performed emotional labor were more satisfied than other female emotional-labor performers.

In sum, unraveling the relations between gender, job satisfaction, and emotional labor is a difficult task that requires attention both to workers' willingness and capacity to confront the demands of jobs requiring emotional labor, and to the social construction of these jobs as appropriate for a particular gender. These two aspects are not unrelated, yet have often been cast as competing explanations. Leidner's (1993) work reveals some of the ways that interactive service jobs become gendered; A worthy topic for future research would be to examine the links between gender identity and satisfaction among women and men who perform emotional labor in "gender-appropriate" domains.

These results, in conjunction with those for emotional exhaustion, thus reaffirm the earlier suggestion that the relations between gender and emotional labor are more complicated than Hochschild and others assume. The results for the two dependent variables examined here indicate that women who perform emotional labor do not suffer more negative consequences than men in these roles and may even derive certain psychological rewards from these jobs. More research is needed regarding the relations between gender and other costs and rewards associated with emotional labor.

## Discussion:
## Assessing Emotional Labor's Costs for Workers

While sociologists of emotion have called attention to emotional labor in interactive service jobs as an arena for investigation, exclusive concentration on these jobs may have exaggerated their uniqueness. In addition, by failing to control for other job and individual characteristics, previous studies have been unable to disentangle the effects of emotional labor from other factors. By examining a range of jobs and including controls for other factors expected to be associated with the dependent variables, this study overcomes these limitations and extends earlier analyses. The results indicate mixed support for previous studies, as they show that the effects of employment in a job requiring emotional labor are not uniformly negative. However, performance of emotional labor is psychologically distressing for some individuals under some conditions.

As predicted, the impacts of job autonomy, job involvement, and self-monitoring on emotional exhaustion differ depending upon whether the respondent performs emotional labor. The findings for the latter two variables are particularly important, as they indicate that conditions enhancing emotional well-being for those not performing emotional labor have precisely the opposite effects among those whose jobs require this activity. Consistent with Hochschild (1983), who implies that workers who find it difficult to distance themselves from the job may be more at risk of negative consequences than those with a greater ability to disengage, this study shows that high job involvement does not have the same positive effects on the emotional well-being of those who perform emotional labor as on those who do not. Consistent with the literature on self-monitoring and boundary-spanning roles (e.g., Caldwell and O'Reilly 1982), self-monitoring abilities significantly reduce emotional exhaustion among workers who perform emotional labor. This suggests that jobs requiring emotional labor are similar in certain respects to boundary-spanning roles, as these have been explored by organizational researchers. The literature on boundary-spanning may be a fruitful source of additional hypotheses regarding the consequences of emotional labor.

Not all of the hypothesized conditions expected to mediate the effects of emotional labor were supported. Most important was the finding that women are no more likely than men to suffer negative consequences from performance of emotional labor and even report higher levels of job satisfaction than their male counterparts. While women may lack the "status shield" against poor treatment of their feelings that protects men, as Hochschild (1983: 174) argues, women apparently derive other rewards from these jobs.

In sum, the results of this study suggest that interactive service jobs requiring interactions with the public are experienced as emotionally exhausting for certain workers but not others and are even a source of satisfaction for some. Emotional labor leads to increased emotional exhaustion among workers with low job autonomy, longer job tenure, and longer working hours. Low self-monitors are also at greater risk of emotional exhaustion than other workers who perform emotional labor. While high job involvement reduces emotional exhaustion among nonperformers of emotional labor, it fails to have this effect among emotional-labor performers. By contrast, women and those with high job autonomy report significantly higher levels of satisfaction than others who perform emotional labor. Job involvement also increases satisfaction among emotional-labor performers, but this effect is significantly greater among nonperformers of emotional labor.

These findings suggest the need for research on the rewards as well as the costs of emotional labor. Also useful would be studies exploring the mechanisms through which individual characteristics, such as gender and self-monitoring ability, enhance the psychological well-being of emotional-labor performers. Understanding why women and high self-monitors are more likely than others to find emotional labor rewarding may become especially important if services continue to expand. As more and more workers of all kinds find themselves with few opportunities other than service employment, achieving a "fit" between worker characteristics and job requirements may become more difficult. Creating the conditions for satisfying work thus may require more concerted efforts by employers than reliance upon selection of those with "people skills."

Finally, it should be remembered that the findings reported here pertain only to emotional exhaustion and job satisfaction. Research on other outcomes, such as job-related self-esteem or feelings of inauthenticity, may yield different results. Hence, not only should we inquire about the conditions under which emotional labor is distressful or emotionally enhancing, we should also identify the particular consequences and rewards associated with it. This should bring us closer to treating emotional labor as a multidimensional concept with diverse consequences for workers in different work situations.

In conclusion, this study offers some support for those claiming that interactive service jobs, because they require emotional labor, constitute a distinctly new form of work, with unique consequences for workers. Interactive service workers are not homogeneous, however, with differences among them being at least as significant as differences between themselves and other workers. Future research on interactive service work should begin to uncover these sources of differentiation and their implications for workers.

## NOTE

*Acknowledgment:* This research was supported by a grant from the National Science Foundation (SES-89-08787).

## REFERENCES

Abel, Emily K., and Margaret K. Nelson, eds. 1990. *Circles of Care*. Albany: State University of New York Press.

Albrecht, Karl, and Ron Zemke. 1985. *Service America! Doing Business in the New Economy*. Homewood, IL: Dow Jones–Irwin.

Belle, Deborah. 1987. "Gender Differences in the Social Moderators of Stress." In Rosalind C. Barnett, Lois Beiner, and Grace C. Baruch, eds., *Gender and Stress* (pp. 257–77). New York: Macmillan, Inc.

———. 1982. "The Stress of Caring: Women as Providers of Social Support." In Leo Goldberger and Sholmo Breznitz, eds., *Handbook of Stress: Theoretical and Clinical Aspects* (pp. 496–505). New York: The Free Press.

Caldwell, David R., and Charles A. O'Reilly III. 1982. "Boundary-Spanning and Individual Performance: The Impact of Self-Monitoring." *Journal of Applied Psychology* 67: 124–27.

Chatman, Jennifer A. 1989. "Improving Interactional Organizational Research: A Model of Person-Organization Fit." *Academy of Management Review* 14: 333–349.

Chodorow, Nancy. 1978. *The Reproduction of Mothering*. Berkeley: University of California Press.

Diener, E. R. Larsen, and R. Emmons. 1984. "Person X Situation Interactions: Choice of Situations and Congruence Response Models." *Journal of Personality and Social Psychology* 47: 580–92.

Gilligan, Carol. 1982. *In a Different Voice: Psychological Theory and Women's Development.* Cambridge: Harvard University Press.

Gordon, Steven L. 1989. "Institutional and Impulsive Orientations in Selectively Appropriating Emotions to Self." In David D. Franks and Doyle McCarthy, eds., *The Sociology of Emotions: Original Essays and Research Papers* (pp. 115–36). Greenwich, CT: JAI Press.

Hochschild, Arlie R. 1979. "Emotion Work, Feeling Rules, and Social Structure." *American Journal of Sociology* 85: 551–75.

——. 1983. *The Managed Heart: Commercialization of Human Feeling.* Berkeley: University of California Press.

Hodson, Randy. 1989. "Gender Differences in Job Satisfaction: Why Aren't Women More Dissatisfied?" *Sociological Quarterly* 30: 385–99.

House, J. S., D. Umberson, and K. R. Landis. 1989. "Structures and Processes of Social Support." *Annual Review of Sociology* 14: 293–318.

Karasek, Robert, and Tores Theorell. 1990. *Healthy Work: Stress, Productivity, and the Reconstruction of Working Life.* New York: Basic Books.

Keller, Robert T., and Winford E. Holland. 1975. "Boundary-Spanning Roles in a Research and Development Organization: An Empirical Investigation." *Academy of Management Journal* 18: 388–93.

Leidner, Robin. 1993. *Fast Food, Fast Talk: Service Work and the Routinization of Everyday Life.* Berkeley: University of California Press.

Marini, Margaret Mooney, and Mary C. Brinton. 1984. "Sex-Typing in Occupational Socialization." In Barbara F. Reskin, ed., *Sex Segregation in the Workplace* (pp. 192–232). Washington, DC: National Academy Press.

Maslach, Christina. 1976. "The Burn-Out Syndrome in the Day Care Setting." *Child Care Quarterly* 6: 100–113.

Maslach, Christina, and Susan E. Jackson. 1985. "The Role of Sex and Family Variables in Burnout." *Sex Roles* 12: 837–51.

Mattingly, Martha A. 1977. "Sources of Stress and Burn-Out in Professional Child-Care Work." *Child Care Quarterly* 6: 127–37.

Miles, Robert H. 1980. "Organization Boundary-Roles." In C. L. Cooper and R. Payne, eds., *Current Concerns in Occupational Stress* (pp. 61–96). New York: John Wiley & Sons, Ltd.

Oakes, Guy. 1990. *The Soul of the Salesman.* Atlantic Highlands, NJ: Humanities Press International, Inc.

Paules, Greta Foff. 1991. *Dishing It Out: Power and Resistance among Waitresses in a New Jersey Restaurant.* Philadelphia: Temple University Press.

Rafaeli, Anat, and Robert I. Sutton. 1989. "The Expression of Emotion in Organizational Life." *Research in Organizational Behavior* 11: 1–42.

——. 1987. "Expression of Emotion as Part of the Work Role." *Academy of Management Review* 12: 23–37.

Rosenberg, Morris. 1990. "Reflexivity and Emotion." *Social Psychology Quarterly* 53: 3–12.

Snyder, Mark. 1987. *Public Appearances, Private Realities: The Psychology of Self-Monitoring.* New York: W. H. Freeman and Company.

Sutton, Robert I. 1991. "Maintaining Norms about Expressed Emotions: The Case of Bill Collectors." *Administrative Science Quarterly* 36: 245–68.

Sutton, Robert I., and Anat Rafaeli. 1988. "Untangling the Relationship between Displayed Emotions and Organizational Sales: The Case of Convenience Stores." *Academy of Management Journal* 31: 461–87.

Tansik, David A. 1990. "Managing Human Resource Issues for High-Contact Service Personnel." In David E. Bowen, Richard B. Chase, Thomas G. Cummings, and Associates, eds., *Service Management Effectiveness* (pp. 152–75). San Francisco: Jossey-Bass Publishers.

Van Fossen, Beth E. 1981. "Sex Differences in the Mental Health Effects of Spouse Support and Equity." *Journal of Health and Social Behavior* 22: 130–43.

Van Maanen, John, and Gideon Kunda. 1989. "'Real Feelings': Emotional Expression and Organizational Culture." *Research in Organizational Behavior* 11: 43–103.

Wharton, Amy S., and James N. Baron. 1991. "Satisfaction? The Psychological Impact of Gender Segregation on Women at Work." *Sociological Quarterly* 32: 365–88.

———. 1987. "So Happy Together? The Impact of Gender Segregation on Men at Work." *American Sociological Review* 52: 574–87.

Wouters, Cas. 1989. "Response to Hochschild's Reply." *Theory, Culture, & Society* 6: 447–50.

Zemke, Ron, and Dick Schaaf. 1989. *The Service Edge*. New York: New American Library.

# Part II

## Gender, Race, and Stratification in the Service Sector

*Chapter 6*

# From Servitude to Service Work: Historical Continuities in the Racial Division of Paid Reproductive Labor

- Evelyn Nakano Glenn

Recent scholarship on African American, Latina, Asian American, and Native American women reveals the complex interaction of race and gender oppression in their lives. These studies expose the inadequacy of additive models that treat gender and race as separate and discrete systems of hierarchy (Collins 1986; King 1988; Brown 1989). In an additive model, white women are viewed solely in terms of gender, while women of color are thought to be "doubly" subordinated by the cumulative effects of gender plus race. Yet achieving a more adequate framework, one that captures the interlocking, interactive nature of these systems, has been extraordinarily difficult. Historically, race and gender have developed as separate topics of inquiry, each with its own literature and concepts. Thus features of social life considered central in understanding one system have been overlooked in analyses of the other.

One domain that has been explored extensively in analyses of gender but ignored in studies of race is social reproduction. The term *social reproduction* is used by feminist scholars to refer to the array of activities and relationships involved in maintaining people both on a daily basis and intergenerationally. Reproductive labor includes activities such as purchasing household goods, preparing and serving food, laundering and repairing clothing, maintaining furnishings and appliances, socializing children, providing care and emotional support for adults, and maintaining kin and community ties.

Marxist feminists place the gendered construction of reproductive labor at the center of women's oppression. They point out that this labor is performed

Reprinted by permission from *Signs: Journal of Women in Culture and Society* 18 (Autumn 1992): 1–43, published by the University of Chicago Press. © 1992 by The University of Chicago.

disproportionately by women and is essential to the industrial economy. Yet because it takes place mostly outside the market, it is invisible, not recognized as real work. Men benefit directly and indirectly from this arrangement — directly in that they contribute less labor in the home while enjoying the services women provide as wives and mothers and indirectly in that, freed of domestic labor, they can concentrate their efforts in paid employment and attain primacy in that area. Thus the sexual division of reproductive labor in the home interacts with and reinforces sexual division in the labor market.[1] These analyses draw attention to the dialectics of production and reproduction and male privilege in both realms. When they represent gender as the sole basis for assigning reproductive labor, however, they imply that all women have the same relationship to it and that it is therefore a universal female experience.[2]

In the meantime, theories of racial hierarchy do not include any analysis of reproductive labor. Perhaps because, consciously or unconsciously, they are male centered, they focus exclusively on the paid labor market and especially on male-dominated areas of production.[3] In the 1970s several writers seeking to explain the historic subordination of peoples of color pointed to dualism in the labor market — its division into distinct markets for white workers and for racial-ethnic workers — as a major vehicle for maintaining white domination (Blauner 1972; Barrera 1979).[4] According to these formulations, the labor system has been organized to ensure that racial-ethnic workers are relegated to a lower tier of low-wage, dead-end, marginal jobs; institutional barriers, including restrictions on legal and political rights, prevent their moving out of that tier and competing with Euro-American workers for better jobs. These theories draw attention to the material advantages whites gain from the racial division of labor. However, they either take for granted or ignore women's unpaid household labor and fail to consider whether this work might also be "racially divided."

In short, the racial division of reproductive labor has been a missing piece of the picture in both literatures. This piece, I would contend, is key to the distinct exploitation of women of color and is a source of both hierarchy and interdependence among white women and women of color. It is thus essential to the development of an integrated model of race and gender, one that treats them as interlocking, rather than additive, systems.

In this article I present a historical analysis of the simultaneous race and gender construction of reproductive labor in the United States, based on comparative study of women's work in the South, the Southwest, and the Far West. I argue that reproductive labor has divided along racial as well as gender lines and that the specific characteristics of the division have varied regionally and changed over time as capitalism has reorganized reproductive labor, shifting parts of it from the household to the market. In the first half of the century racial-ethnic women were employed as servants to perform reproductive labor in white households, relieving white middle-class women of onerous aspects of that work; in the second half of the century, with the expansion of commodified services (services turned into commercial products or activities), racial-ethnic women are disproportionately employed as service workers in institutional settings to carry out lower-level "public" reproductive labor, while cleaner white collar supervisory and lower professional positions are filled by white women.

I will examine the ways race and gender were constructed around the division of labor by sketching changes in the organization of reproductive labor since the early nineteenth century, presenting a case study of domestic service among African American women in the South, Mexican American women in the Southwest, and Japanese American women in California and Hawaii, and finally examining the shift to institutional service work, focusing on race and gender stratification in health care and the racial division of labor within the nursing labor force. Race and gender emerge as socially constructed, interlocking systems that shape the material conditions, identities, and consciousnesses of all women.

## Historical Changes in the Organization of Reproduction

The concept of reproductive labor originated in Karl Marx's remark that every system of production involves both the production of the necessities of life and the reproduction of the tools and labor power necessary for production (Marx and Engels 1969, 31). Recent elaborations of the concept grow out of Engels's dictum that the "determining force in history is, in the last resort, the production and reproduction of immediate life." This has, he noted, "a twofold character, on the one hand the production of subsistence and on the other the production of human beings themselves" (Engels 1972, 71). Although often equated with domestic labor or defined narrowly as referring to the renewal of labor power, the term *social reproduction* has come to be more broadly conceived, particularly by social historians, to refer to the creation and recreation of people as cultural and social, as well as physical, beings (Ryan 1981, 15). Thus, it involves mental, emotional, and manual labor (Brenner and Laslett 1986, 117). This labor can be organized in myriad ways—in and out of the household, as paid or unpaid work, creating exchange value or only use value—and these ways are not mutually exclusive. An example is the preparation of food, which can be done by a family member as unwaged work in the household, by a servant as waged work in the household, or by a short-order cook in a fast-food restaurant as waged work that generates profit for the employer. These forms exist contemporaneously.

Prior to industrialization, however, both production and reproduction were organized almost exclusively at the household level. Women were responsible for most of what might be designated as reproduction, but they were simultaneously engaged in the production of foodstuffs, clothing, shoes, candles, soap, and other goods consumed by the household. With industrialization, production of these basic goods gradually was taken over by capitalist industry. Reproduction, however, remained largely the responsibility of individual households. The ideological separation between men's "productive" labor and women's non-market-based activity that had evolved at the end of the eighteenth century was elaborated in the early decades of the nineteenth. An idealized division of labor arose in which men's work was to follow production outside the home, while women's work was to remain centered in the household (Boydston 1990, esp. 46–48). Household work continued to include the production of many goods consumed by members (Smuts 1959, 11–13; Kessler-Harris 1981), but as an expanding range of outside-manufactured goods became available, household work became increasingly focused on re-production.[5] This idealized division of labor was largely illusory for working-class households, including immigrant and racial-ethnic families, in which men seldom earned a family wage; in these households women and children were forced into income-earning activities in and out of the home (Kessler-Harris 1982).

In the second half of the twentieth century, with goods production almost completely incorporated into the market, reproduction has become the next major target for commodification. Aside from the tendency of capital to expand into new areas for profit making, the very conditions of life brought about by large-scale commodity production have increased the need for commercial services. As household members spend more of their waking hours employed outside the home, they have less time and inclination to provide for one another's social and emotional needs. With the growth of a more geographically mobile and urbanized society, individuals and households have become increasingly cut off from larger kinship circles, neighbors, and traditional communities. Thus, as Harry Braverman notes, "The population no longer relies upon social organization in the form of family, friends, neighbors, community, elders, children, but with few exceptions must go to the market and only to the market, not only for food, clothing, and shelter, but also for recreation, amusement, security, for the care of the young, the old, the sick, the handicapped. In time not only the material and service needs but even the emotional patterns of life are channeled through the market" (Braverman 1974, 276). Conditions of capitalist urbanism also have enlarged the population of those requiring daily care and support: elderly and very young people, mentally and physically disabled people, criminals, and other people incapable of fending for themselves. Because the care of such dependents becomes difficult for the "stripped-down" nuclear family or the atomized community to bear, more of it becomes relegated to institutions outside the family.[6]

The final phase in this process is what Braverman calls the "product cycle," which "invents new products and services, some of which become indispensable as the conditions of modern life change and destroy alternatives" (Braverman 1974, 281). In many areas (e.g., health care), we no longer have choices outside the market. New services and products also alter the definition of an acceptable standard of living. Dependence on the market is further reinforced by what happened earlier with goods production, namely, an "atrophy of competence," so that individuals no longer know how to do what they formerly did for themselves.

As a result of these tendencies, an increasing range of services has been removed wholly or partially from the household and converted into paid services yielding profits. Today, activities such as preparing and serving food (in restaurants and fast-food establishments), caring for handicapped and elderly people (in nursing homes), caring for children (in child-care centers), and providing emotional support, amusement, and companionship (in counseling offices, recreation centers, and health clubs) have become part of the cash nexus. In addition, whether impelled by a need to maintain social control or in response to pressure exerted by worker and community organizations, the state has stepped in to assume minimal responsibility for some reproductive tasks, such as child protection and welfare programs.[7] Whether supplied by corporations or the state, these services are labor-intensive. Thus, a large army of low-wage workers, mostly women and disproportionately women of color, must be recruited to supply the labor.

Still, despite vastly expanded commodification and institutionalization, much reproduction remains organized at the household level. Sometimes an activity is too labor-intensive to be very profitable. Sometimes households or individuals in them have resisted commodification. The limited commodification of child care, for example, involves both elements. The extent of commercialization in different areas of life is uneven, and the variation in its extent is the outcome of political and economic struggles (Brenner and Laslett 1986, 121; Laslett and Brenner 1989, 384). What is consistent across forms, whether commodified or not, is that reproductive labor is constructed as "female." The gendered organization of reproduction is widely recognized. Less obvious, but equally characteristic, is its racial construction: historically, racial-ethnic women have been assigned a distinct place in the organization of reproductive labor.

Elsewhere I have talked about the reproductive labor racial-ethnic women have carried out for their own families; this labor was intensified as the women struggled to maintain family life and indigenous cultures in the face of cultural assaults, ghettoization, and a labor system that relegated men and women to low-wage, seasonal, and hazardous employment (Glenn 1985; 1986, 86–108; Dill 1988). Here I want to talk about two forms of waged reproductive work that racial-ethnic women have performed disproportionately: domestic service in private households and institutional service work.

## Domestic Service as the Racial Division of Reproductive Labor

Both the demand for household help and the number of women employed as servants expanded rapidly in the latter half of the nineteenth century (Chaplin 1978). This expansion paralleled the rise of industrial capital and the elaboration of middle-class women's reproductive responsibilities. Rising standards of cleanliness, larger and more ornately furnished homes, the sentimentalization of the home as a "haven in a heartless world" (Lasch 1977), and the new emphasis on childhood and the mother's role in nurturing children all served to enlarge middle-class women's responsibilities for reproduction at a time when technology had done little to reduce the sheer physical drudgery of housework.[8]

By all accounts middle-class women did not challenge the gender-based division of labor or the enlargement of their reproductive responsibilities. Indeed, middle-class women — as readers and writers of literature; as members and leaders of clubs, charitable organizations, associations, reform movements, and religious revivals; and as supporters of the cause of abolition — helped to elaborate the domestic code (Brenner and Laslett 1986).[9] Feminists seeking an expanded public role for women argued that the same nurturant and moral qualities that made women centers of the home should be brought to bear in public service. In the domestic sphere, instead of questioning the inequitable gender division of labor, they sought to slough off the more burdensome tasks onto more oppressed groups of women.[10]

Phyllis Palmer observes that at least through the first half of the twentieth century, "most white middle class women could hire another woman — a recent immigrant, a working class woman, a woman of color, or all three — to perform much of the hard labor of household tasks" (Palmer 1987, 182–83). Domestics were employed to clean house, launder and iron clothes, scrub floors, and care for infants and children. They relieved their mistresses of the heavier and dirtier domestic chores.[11] White middle-class women were thereby freed for supervisory tasks and for cultural, leisure, and volunteer activity or, more rarely during this period, for a career.[12]

Palmer suggests that the use of domestic servants also helped resolve certain contradictions created by the domestic code. She notes that the early twentieth-century housewife confronted inconsistent expectations of middle-class womanhood: domesticity and "feminine virtue." Domesticity—defined as creating a warm, clean, and attractive home for husband and children—required hard physical labor and meant contending with dirt. The virtuous woman, however, was defined in terms of spirituality, refinement, and the denial of the physical body. Additionally, in the 1920s and 1930s there emerged a new ideal of the modern wife as an intelligent and attractive companion. If the heavy parts of household work could be transferred to paid help, the middle-class housewife could fulfill her domestic duties, yet distance herself from the physical labor and dirt and also have time for personal development (Palmer 1990, 127–51).

Who was to perform the "dirty work" varied by region. In the Northeast, European immigrant women, particularly those who were Irish and German, constituted the majority of domestic servants from the mid-nineteenth century to World War I (Katzman 1978, 65–70). In regions where there was a large concentration of people of color, subordinate-race women formed a more or less permanent servant stratum. Despite differences in the composition of the populations and the mix of industries in the regions, there were important similarities in the situation of Mexicans in the Southwest, African Americans in the South, and Japanese people in northern California and Hawaii. Each of these groups was placed in a separate legal category from whites, excluded from rights and protections accorded full citizens. This severely limited their ability to organize, compete for jobs, and acquire capital (Glenn 1985). The racial division of private reproductive work mirrored this racial dualism in the legal, political, and economic systems.

In the South, African American women constituted the main and almost exclusive servant caste. Except in times of extreme economic crisis, whites and Blacks did not compete for domestic jobs. Until the First World War 90 percent of all nonagriculturally employed Black women in the South were employed as domestics. Even at the national level, servants and laundresses accounted for close to half (48.4 percent) of non-agriculturally employed Black women in 1930.[13]

In the Southwest, especially in the states with the highest proportions of

Mexicans in the population—Texas, Colorado, and New Mexico—Chicanas were disproportionately concentrated in domestic service.[14] In El Paso nearly half of all Chicanas in the labor market were employed as servants or laundresses in the early decades of the century (Garcia 1981, 76). In Denver, according to Sarah Deutsch, perhaps half of all households had at least one female member employed as a domestic at some time, and if a woman became a widow, she was almost certain to take in laundry (Deutsch 1987a, 147). Nationally, 39.1 percent of nonagriculturally employed Chicanas were servants or laundresses in 1930.[15]

In the Far West—especially in California and Hawaii, with their large populations of Asian immigrants—an unfavorable sex ratio made female labor scarce in the late nineteenth and early twentieth centuries. In contrast to the rest of the nation, the majority of domestic servants in California and Hawaii were men: in California until 1880 (Katzman 1978, 55) and in Hawaii as late as 1920 (Lind 1951, table 1). The men were Asian—Chinese and later Japanese. Chinese houseboys and cooks were familiar figures in late nineteenth-century San Francisco; so too were Japanese male retainers in early twentieth-century Honolulu. After 1907 Japanese women began to immigrate in substantial numbers, and they inherited the mantle of service in both California and Hawaii. In the pre–World War II years, close to half of all immigrant and native-born Japanese American women in the San Francisco Bay area and in Honolulu were employed as servants or laundresses (U.S. Bureau of the Census 1932, table 8; Glenn 1986, 76–79). Nationally, excluding Hawaii, 25.4 percent of nonagricultural Japanese American women workers were listed as servants in 1930.[16]

In areas where racial dualism prevailed, being served by members of the subordinate group was a perquisite of membership in the dominant group. According to Elizabeth Rae Tyson, an Anglo woman who grew up in El Paso in the early years of the century, "almost every Anglo-American family had at least one, sometimes two or three servants: a maid and laundress, and perhaps a nursemaid or yardman. The maid came in after breakfast and cleaned up the breakfast dishes, and very likely last night's supper dishes as well; did the routine cleaning, washing and ironing, and after the family dinner in the middle of the day, washed dishes again, and then went home to perform similar services in her own home" (Garcia 1980, 327). In southwest cities, Mexican American girls were trained at an early age to do domestic work and girls as young as nine or ten were hired to clean house.[17]

In Hawaii, where the major social division was between the haole (Caucasian) planter class and the largely Asian plantation worker class, haole residents were required to employ one or more Chinese or Japanese servants to demonstrate their status and their social distance from those less privileged.

Andrew Lind notes that "the literature on Hawaii, especially during the second half of the nineteenth century, is full of references to the open-handed hospitality of Island residents, dispensed by the ever-present maids and house-boys" (Lind 1951, 73). A public school teacher who arrived in Honolulu in 1925 was placed in a teacher's cottage with four other mainland teachers. She discovered a maid had already been hired by the principal: "A maid! None of us had ever had a maid. We were all used to doing our own work. Furthermore, we were all in debt and did not feel that we wanted to spend even four dollars a month on a maid. Our principal was quite insistent. Everyone on the plantation had a maid. It was, therefore, the thing to do" (Lind 1951, 76).

In the South, virtually every middle-class housewife employed at least one African American woman to do cleaning and child care in her home. Southern household workers told one writer that in the old days, "if you worked for a family, your daughter was expected to, too" (Tucker 1988, 98). Daughters of Black domestics were sometimes inducted as children into service to baby-sit, wash diapers, and help clean (Clark-Lewis 1987, 200–201).[18] White-skin privilege transcended class lines, and it was not uncommon for working-class whites to hire Black women for housework (Anderson and Bowman 1953). In the 1930s white women tobacco workers in Durham, Noth Carolina, could mitigate the effects of the "double day"—household labor on top of paid labor—by employing Black women to work in their homes for about one-third of their own wages (Janiewski 1983, 93). Black women tobacco workers were too poorly paid to have this option and had to rely on the help of overworked husbands, older children, Black women too old to be employed, neighbors, or kin.

Where more than one group was available for service, a differentiated hierarchy of race, color, and culture emerged. White and racial-ethnic domestics were hired for different tasks. In her study of women workers in Atlanta, New Orleans, and San Antonio during the 1920s and 1930s, Julia Kirk Black-welder reported that "anglo women in the employ of private households were nearly always reported as housekeepers, while Blacks and Chicanas were reported as laundresses, cooks or servants" (Blackwelder 1978, 349).[19]

In the Southwest, where Anglos considered Mexican or "Spanish" culture inferior, Anglos displayed considerable ambivalence about employing Mexicans for child care. Although a modern-day example, this statement by an El Paso businessman illustrates the contradictions in Anglo attitudes. The man told an interviewer that he and his wife were putting off parenthood because "the major dilemma would be what to do with the child. We don't really like the idea of leaving the baby at home with a maid . . . for the simple reason if the maid is Mexican, the child may assume that the other person is its mother. Nothing wrong with Mexicans, they'd just assume that this other person is its mother. There have been all sorts of cases where the infants learned Spanish before they learned English. There've been incidents of the Mexican maid stealing the child and taking it over to Mexico and selling it" (Ruíz 1987b, 71).

In border towns, the Mexican group was further stratified by English-speaking ability, place of nativity, and immigrant status, with non-English-speaking women residing south of the border occupying the lowest rung. In Laredo and El Paso, Mexican American factory operatives often employed Mexican women who crossed the border daily or weekly to do domestic work for a fraction of a U.S. operative's wages (Hield 1984, 95; Ruíz 1987a, 64).

## The Race and Gender Construction of Domestic Service

Despite their preference for European immigrant domestics, employers could not easily retain their services. Most European immigrant women left service upon marriage, and their daughters moved into the expanding manufacturing, clerical, and sales occupations during the 1910s and twenties.[20] With the flow of immigration slowed to a trickle during World War I, there were few new recruits from Europe. In the 1920s, domestic service became increasingly the specialty of minority-race women (Palmer 1990, 12). Women of color were advantageous employees in one respect: they could be compelled more easily to remain in service. There is considerable evidence that middle-class whites acted to ensure the domestic labor supply by tracking racial-ethnic women into domestic service and blocking their entry into other fields. Urban school systems in the Southwest tracked Chicana students into homemaking courses designed to prepare them for domestic service. The El Paso school board established a segregated school system in the 1880s that remained in place for the next thirty years; education for Mexican children emphasized manual and domestic skills that would prepare them to work at an early age. In 1909 the Women's Civic Improvement League, an Anglo organization, advocated domestic training for older Mexican girls. Their rationale is explained by Mario Garcia: "According to the league the housegirls for the entire city came from the Mexican settlement and if they could be taught housekeeping, cooking and sewing, every American family would benefit. The Mexican girls would likewise profit since their services would improve and hence be in greater demand" (Garcia 1981, 113).

The education of Chicanas in the Denver school system was similarly directed toward preparing students for domestic service and handicrafts. Sarah Deutsch found that Anglo women there persisted in viewing Chicanas and other "inferior-race" women as dependent, slovenly, and ignorant. Thus, they argued, training Mexican girls for domestic service not only would solve "one phase of women's work we seem to be incapable of handling" but it would simultaneously help raise the (Mexican) community by improving women's standard of living, elevating their morals, and facilitating Americanization (Deutsch 1987b, 736). One Anglo writer, in an article published in 1917 titled "Problems and Progress among Mexicans in Our Own Southwest," claimed, "When trained there is no better servant than the gentle, quiet Mexicana girl" (Romero 1988a, 16).

In Hawaii, with its plantation economy, Japanese and Chinese women were coerced into service for their husbands' or fathers' employers. According to Lind, prior to World War II:

> It has been a usual practice for a department head or a member of the managerial staff of the plantation to indicate to members of his work group that his household is in need of domestic help and to expect them to provide a wife or daughter to fill the need. Under the conditions which have prevailed in the past, the worker has felt obligated to make a member of his own family available for such service, if required, since his own position and advancement depend upon keeping the goodwill of his boss. Not infrequently, girls have been prevented from pursuing a high school or college education because someone on the supervisory staff has needed a servant and it has seemed inadvisable for the family to disregard the claim. [Lind 1951, 77]

Economic coercion also could take bureaucratic forms, especially for women in desperate straits. During the Depression, local officials of the federal Works Project Administration (WPA) and the National Youth Administration (NYA), programs set up by the Roosevelt administration to help the unemployed find work, tried to direct Chicanas and Blacks to domestic service jobs exclusively (Blackwelder 1984, 120–22; Deutsch 1987a, 182–83). In Colorado, local officials of the WPA and NYA advocated household training projects for Chicanas. George Bickel, assistant state director of the WPA for Colorado, wrote: "The average Spanish-American girl on the NYA program looks forward to little save a life devoted to motherhood often under the most miserable circumstances" (Deutsch 1987a, 183). Given such an outlook, it made sense to provide training in domestic skills.

Young Chicanas disliked domestic service so much that slots in the programs went begging. Older women, especially single mothers struggling to support their families, could not afford to refuse what was offered. The cruel dilemma that such women faced was poignantly expressed in one woman's letter to President Roosevelt:

My name is Lula Gordon. I am a Negro woman. I am on the relief. I have three children. I have no husband and no job. I have worked hard ever since I was old enough. I am willing to do any kind of work because I have to support myself and my children. I was under the impression that the government or the W.P.A. would give the Physical [*sic*] fit relief clients work. I have been praying for that time to come. A lady, Elizabeth Ramsie, almost in my condition, told me she was going to try to get some work. I went with her. We went to the Court House here in San Antonio, we talked to a Mrs. Beckmon. Mrs. Beckmon told me to phone a Mrs. Coyle because she wanted some one to clean house and cook for ($5) five dollars a week. Mrs. Beckmon said if I did not take the job in the Private home I would be cut off from everything all together. I told her I was afraid to accept the job in the private home because I have registered for a government job and when it opens up I want to take it. She said that she was taking people off of the relief and I have to take the job in the private home or none. . . . I need work and I will do anything the government gives me to do. . . . Will you please give me some work. [Blackwelder 1984, 68–69]

Japanese American women were similarly compelled to accept domestic service jobs when they left the internment camps in which they were imprisoned during World War II. To leave the camps they had to have a job and a residence, and many women were forced to take positions as live-in servants in various parts of the country. When women from the San Francisco Bay area returned there after the camps were closed, agencies set up to assist the returnees directed them to domestic service jobs. Because they had lost their homes and possessions and had no savings, returnees had to take whatever jobs were offered them. Some became live-in servants to secure housing, which was in short supply after the war. In many cases domestic employment became a lifelong career (Glenn 1986).

In Hawaii the Japanese were not interned, but there nonetheless developed a "maid shortage" as war-related employment expanded. Accustomed to cheap and abundant household help, haole employers became increasingly agitated about being deprived of the services of their "mamasans." The suspicion that many able-bodied former maids were staying at home idle because their husbands or fathers had lucrative defense jobs was taken seriously enough to prompt an investigation by a university researcher.[21]

Housewives told their nisei maids it was the maids' patriotic duty to remain on the job. A student working as a live-in domestic during the war was dumbfounded by her mistress's response when she notified her she was leaving to take a room in the dormitory at the university. Her cultured and educated mistress, whom the student had heretofore admired, exclaimed with annoyance: "'I think especially in war time, the University should close down the dormitory.' Although she didn't say it in words, I sensed the implication that she believed all the (Japanese) girls should be placed in different homes, making it easier for the haole woman."[22] The student noted with some bitterness that although her employer told her that working as a maid was the way for her to do "your bit for the war effort," she and other haole women did not, in turn, consider giving up the "conveniences and luxuries of pre-war Hawaii" as their bit for the war.[23]

The dominant group ideology in all these cases was that women of color — African American women, Chicanas, and Japanese American women — were particularly suited for service. These racial justifications ranged from the argument that Black and Mexican women were incapable of governing their own lives and thus were dependent on whites — making white employment of them an act of benevolence — to the argument that Asian servants were naturally quiet, subordinate, and accustomed to a lower standard of living. Whatever the specific content of the racial characterizations, it defined the proper place of these groups as in service: they belonged there, just as it was the dominant group's place to be served.

David Katzman notes that "ethnic stereotyping was the stock in trade of all employers of servants, and it is difficult at times to figure out whether blacks and immigrants were held in contempt because they were servants or whether urban servants were denigrated because most of the servants were blacks and immigrants" (Katzman 1978, 221). Even though racial stereotypes undoubtedly preceded their entry into domestic work, it is also the case that domestics were forced to enact the role of the inferior. Judith Rollins and Mary Romero describe a variety of rituals that affirmed the subordination and dependence of the domestic; for example, employers addressed household workers by their first names and required them to enter by the back door, eat in the kitchen, and wear uniforms. Domestics understood they were not to initiate conversation but were to remain standing or visibly engaged in work whenever the employer was in the room. They also had to accept with gratitude "gifts" of discarded clothing and leftover food (Rollins 1985, chap. 5; Romero 1987).

For their part, racial-ethnic women were acutely aware that they were trapped in domestic service by racism and not by lack of skills or intelligence. In their study of Black life in prewar Chicago, St. Clair Drake and Horace Cayton found that education did not provide African Americans with an entree into white collar work. They noted, "Colored girls are often bitter in their comments about a society which condemns them to the 'white folks' kitchen'" (Drake and Cayton 1962, 246). Thirty-five years later, Anna May Madison minced no words when she declared to anthropologist John Gwaltney: "Now, I don't do nothing for white women or men that they couldn't do for themselves. They don't do anything I couldn't learn to do every bit as well as they do it. But, you see, that goes right back to the life that you have to live. If that was the life I had been raised up in, I could be President or any other thing I got a chance to be" (Gwaltney 1980, 173).

Chicana domestics interviewed by Mary Romero in Colorado seemed at one level to accept the dominant culture's evaluation of their capabilities. Several said their options were limited by lack of education and training. However, they also realized they were restricted just because they were Mexican. Sixty-eight-year-old Mrs. Portillo told Romero: "There was a lot of discrimination, and Spanish people got just regular housework or laundry work. There was so much discrimination that Spanish people couldn't get jobs outside of washing dishes — things like that" (Romero 1988b, 86).

Similarly, many Japanese domestics reported that their choices were constrained because of language difficulties and lack of education, but they, too, recognized that color was decisive. Some nisei domestics had taken typing and business courses and some had college degrees, yet they had to settle for "school girl" jobs after completing their schooling. Mrs. Morita, who grew up in San Francisco and was graduated from high school in the 1930s, bluntly summarized her options: "In those days there was no two ways about it. If you were Japanese, you either worked in an art store ('oriental curios' shop) where they sell those little junks, or you worked as a domestic. . . . There was no Japanese girl working in an American firm" (Glenn 1986, 122).

Hanna Nelson, another of Gwaltney's informants, took the analysis one step further; she recognized the coercion that kept African American women in domestic service. She saw this arrangement as one that allowed white women to exploit Black women economically and emotionally and exposed Black women to sexual assaults by white men, often with white women's complicity. She says, "I am a woman sixty-one years old and I was born into this world with some talent. But I have done the work that my grandmother's mother did. It is not through any failing of mine that this is so. The whites took my mother's milk by force, and I have lived to hear a human creature of my sex try to force me by threat of hunger to give my milk to an able man. I have grown to womanhood in a world where the saner you are, the madder you are made to appear" (Gwaltney 1980, 7).

## Race and Gender Consciousness

Hanna Nelson displays a consciousness of the politics of race and gender not found among white employers. Employers' and employees' fundamentally different positions within the division of reproductive labor gave them different interests and perspectives. Phyllis Palmer describes the problems the YWCA and other reform groups encountered when they attempted to establish voluntary standards and working hours for live-in domestics in the 1930s. White housewives invariably argued against any "rigid" limitation of hours; they insisted on provisions for emergencies that would override any hour limits. Housewives saw their own responsibilities as limitless, and apparently felt there was no justification for boundaries on domestics' responsibilities. They did not acknowledge the fundamental difference in their positions: they themselves gained status and privileges from their relationships with their husbands — relationships that depended on the performance of wifely duties. They expected domestics to devote long hours and hard work to help them succeed as wives, without, however, commensurate privileges and status. To challenge the inequitable gender division of labor was too difficult and threatening, so white housewives pushed the dilemma onto other women, holding them to the same high standards by which they themselves were imprisoned (Kaplan 1987; Palmer 1990).

Some domestic workers were highly conscious of their mistresses' subordination to their husbands and condemned their unwillingness to challenge their husbands' authority. Mabel Johns, a sixty-four-year-old widow, told Gwaltney:

> I work for a woman who has a good husband; the devil is good to her, anyway. Now that woman could be a good person if she didn't think she could just do everything and have everything. In this world whatsoever you get you will pay for. Now she is a grown woman, but she won't know that simple thing. I don't think there's anything wrong with her mind, but she is greedy and she don't believe in admitting that she is greedy. Now you may say what you willormay [*sic*] about people being good to you, but there just ain' a living soul in this world that thinks more of you than you do of yourself. . . . She's a grown woman, but she have to keep accounts and her husband tells her whether or not he will let her do thus-and-so or buy this or that. [Gwaltney 1980, 167]

Black domestics are also conscious that a white woman's status comes from her relationship to a white man, that she gains privileges from the relationship that blinds her to her own oppression, and that she therefore willingly participates in and gains advantages from the oppression of racial-ethnic women. Nancy White puts the matter powerfully when she says,

My mother used to say that the black woman is the white man's mule and the white woman is his dog. Now, she said that to say this: we do the heavy work and get beat whether we do it well or not. But the white woman is closer to the master and he pats them on the head and lets them sleep in the house, but he ain' gon' treat neither one like he was dealing with a person. Now, if I was to tell a white woman that, the first thing she would do is to call you a nigger and then she'd be real nice to her husband so he would come out here and beat you for telling his wife the truth. [Gwaltney 1980, 148]

Rather than challenge the inequity in the relationship with their husbands, white women pushed the burden onto women with even less power. They could justify this only by denying the domestic worker's womanhood, by ignoring the employee's family ties and responsibilities. Susan Tucker found that southern white women talked about their servants with affection and expressed gratitude that they shared work with the servant that they would otherwise have to do alone. Yet the sense of commonality based on gender that the women expressed turned out to be one-way. Domestic workers knew that employers did not want to know much about their home situations (Kaplan 1987, 96; Tucker 1988). Mostly, the employers did not want domestics' personal needs to interfere with serving them. One domestic wrote that her employer berated her when she asked for a few hours off to pay her bills and take care of pressing business (Palmer 1990, 74). Of relations between white mistresses and Black domestics in the period from 1870 to 1920, Katzman says that in extreme cases "even the shared roles of motherhood could be denied." A Black child nurse reported in 1912 that she worked fourteen to sixteen hours a day caring for her mistress's four children. Describing her existence as a "treadmill life," she reported that she was allowed to go home "only once in every two weeks, every other Sunday afternoon — even then I'm not permitted to stay all night. I see my own children only when they happen to see me on the streets when I am out with the children [of her mistress], or when my children come to the yard to see me, which isn't often, because my white folks don't like to see their servants' children hanging around their premises."[24]

While this case may be extreme, Tucker reports, on the basis of extensive interviews with southern African American domestics, that even among live-out workers in the 1960s,

White women were also not noted for asking about childcare arrangements. All whites, said one black woman, "assume you have a mother, or an older daughter to keep your child, so it's all right to leave your kids." Stories of white employers not believing the children of domestics were sick, but hearing this as an excuse not to work, were also common. Stories, too, of white women who did not inquire of a domestic's family — even when that domestic went on extended trips with the family — were not uncommon. And work on Christmas morning and other holidays for black mothers was not considered by white employers as unfair. Indeed, work on these days was seen as particularly important to the job. [Tucker 1988, 99]

The irony is, of course, that domestics saw their responsibilities as mothers as the central core of their identity. The Japanese American women I interviewed, the Chicana day workers Romero interviewed, and the African American domestics Bonnie Thornton Dill interviewed all emphasized the primacy of their role as mothers (Dill 1980; Glenn 1986; Romero 1988b). As a Japanese immigrant single parent expressed it, "My children come first. I'm working to upgrade my children." Another domestic, Mrs. Hiraoka, confided she hated household work but would keep working until her daughter graduated from optometry school.[25] Romero's day workers arranged their work hours to fit around their children's school hours so that they could be there when needed. For domestics, then, working had meaning precisely because it enabled them to provide for their children.

Perhaps the most universal theme in domestic workers' statements is that they are working so their own daughters will not have to go into domestic service and confront the same dilemmas of leaving their babies to work. A Japanese American domestic noted, "I tell my daughters all the time, 'As long as you get a steady job, stay in school. I want you to get a good job, not like me.' That's what I always tell my daughters: make sure you're not stuck."[26]

In a similar vein, Pearl Runner told Dill, "My main goal was I didn't want them to follow in my footsteps as far as working" (Dill 1980, 109). Domestic workers wanted to protect their daughters from both the hardships and the dangers that working in white homes posed. A Black domestic told Drake and Cayton of her hopes for her daughters: "I hope they may be able to escape a life as a domestic worker, for I know too well the things that make a girl desperate on these jobs" (Drake and Cayton 1962, 246).

When they succeed in helping their children do better than they themselves did, domestics may consider that the hardships were worthwhile. Looking back, Mrs. Runner is able to say, "I really feel that with all the struggling that I went through, I feel happy and proud that I was able to keep helping my children, that they listened and that they all went to high school. So when I look back, I really feel proud, even though at times the work was very hard and I came home very tired. But now, I feel proud about it. They all got their education" (Dill 1980, 113). Domestics thus have to grapple with yet another contradiction. They must confront, acknowledge, and convey the undesirable nature of the work they do to their children, as an object lesson and an admonition, and at the same time maintain their children's respect and their own sense of personal worth and dignity (Dill 1980, 110). When they successfully manage that contradiction, they refute their white employers' belief that "you are your work" (Gwaltney 1980, 174).

## *The Racial Division of Public Reproductive Labor*

As noted earlier, the increasing commodification of social reproduction since World War II has led to a dramatic growth in employment by women in such areas as food preparation and service, health care services, child care, and recreational services. The division of labor in public settings mirrors the division of labor in the household. Racial-ethnic women are employed to do the heavy, dirty, "back-room" chores of cooking and serving food in restaurants and cafeterias, cleaning rooms in hotels and office buildings, and caring for the elderly and ill in hospitals and nursing homes, including cleaning rooms, making beds, changing bed pans, and preparing food. In these same settings white women are disproportionately employed as lower-level professionals (e.g., nurses and social workers), technicians, and administrative support workers to carry out the more skilled and supervisory tasks.

The U.S. Census category of "service occupations except private household and protective services" roughly approximates what I mean by "institutional service work." It includes food preparation and service, health care service, cleaning and building services, and personal services.[27] In the United States as a whole, Black and Spanish-origin women are overrepresented in this set of occupations; in 1980 they made up 13.7 percent of all workers in the field, nearly double their proportion (7.0 percent) in the work force. White women (some of whom were of Spanish origin) were also overrepresented, but not to the same extent, making up 50.1 percent of all "service" workers, compared with their 36 percent share in the overall work force. (Black and Spanish-origin men made up 9.6 percent, and white men, who were 50 percent of the work force, made up the remaining 27.5 percent.)[28]

Because white women constitute the majority, institutional service work may not at first glance appear to be racialized. However, if we look more closely at the composition of specific jobs within the larger category, we find clear patterns of racial specialization. White women are preferred in positions requiring physical and social contact with the public, that is, waiters/waitresses, transportation attendants, hairdressers/cosmetologists, and dental assistants, while racial-ethnic women are preferred in dirty back-room jobs as maids, janitors/cleaners, kitchen workers, and nurse's aides.[29]

As in the case of domestic service, who does what varies regionally, following racial-ethnic caste lines in local economies. Racialization is clearest in local economies where a subordinate race/ethnic group is sizable enough to fill a substantial portion of jobs. In southern cities, Black women are twice as likely to be employed in service occupations as white women. For example, in Atlanta in 1980, 20.8 percent of African American women were so employed, compared with 10.4 percent of white women. While they were less than one-quarter (23.9 percent) of all women workers, they were nearly two-fifths (38.3 percent) of women service workers. In Memphis, 25.9 percent of African American women compared with 10.2 percent of white women were in services; though they made up only a third (34.5 percent) of the female work force, African American women were nearly three-fifths (57.2 percent) of women employed in this field. In southwestern cities Spanish-origin women specialize in service work. In San Antonio, 21.9 percent of Spanish-origin women were so employed, compared with 11.6 percent of non-Spanish-origin white women; in that city half (49.8 percent) of all women service workers were Spanish-origin, while Anglos, who made up two-thirds (64.0 percent) of the female work force, were a little over a third (36.4 percent) of those in the service category. In El Paso, 16.9 percent of Spanish-origin women were service workers compared with 10.8 percent of Anglo women, and they made up two-thirds (66.1 percent) of those in service. Finally, in Honolulu, Asian and Pacific Islanders constituted 68.6 percent of the female work force, but 74.8 percent of those were in service jobs. Overall, these jobs employed 21.6 percent of all Asian and Pacific Islander women, compared with 13.7 percent of white non-Spanish-origin women.[30]

Particularly striking is the case of cleaning and building services. This category — which includes maids, housemen, janitors, and cleaners — is prototypically "dirty work." In Memphis, one out of every twelve Black women (8.2 percent) was in cleaning and building services, and Blacks were 88.1 percent of the women in this occupation. In contrast, only one out of every 200 white women (0.5 percent) was so employed. In Atlanta, 6.6 percent of Black women were in this field — constituting 74.6 percent of the women in these jobs — compared with only 0.7 percent of white women. Similarly, in El Paso, 4.2 percent of Spanish-origin women (versus 0.6 percent of Anglo women) were in cleaning and building services — making up 90.0 percent of the women in this field. And in San Antonio the Spanish and Anglo percentages were 5.3 percent versus 1.1 percent, respectively, with Spanish-origin women 73.5 percent of women in these occupations. Finally, in Honolulu, 4.7 percent of

Asian and Pacific Islander women were in these occupations, making up 86.6 percent of the total. Only 1.3 percent of white women were so employed.[31]

## From Personal to Structural Hierarchy

Does a shift from domestic service to low-level service occupations represent progress for racial-ethnic women? At first glance it appears not to bring much improvement. After domestic service, these are the lowest paid of all occupational groupings. In 1986 service workers were nearly two-thirds (62 percent) of workers in the United States earning at or below minimum wage.[32] As in domestic service, the jobs are often part-time and seasonal, offer few or no medical and other benefits, have low rates of unionization, and subject workers to arbitrary supervision. The service worker also often performs in a public setting the same sorts of tasks that servants did in a private setting. Furthermore, established patterns of race/gender domination-subordination are often incorporated into the authority structure of organizations. Traditional gender-race etiquette shapes face-to-face interaction in the workplace. Duke University Hospital in North Carolina from its founding in 1929 adopted paternalistic policies toward its Black employees. Black workers were highly conscious of this, as evidenced by their references to "the plantation system" at Duke (Sacks 1988, 46).[33]

Still, service workers, especially those who have worked as domestics, are convinced that "public jobs" are preferable to domestic service. They appreciate not being personally subordinate to an individual employer and not having to do "their" dirty work on "their" property. Relations with supervisors and clients are hierarchical, but they are embedded in an impersonal structure governed by more explicit contractual obligations and limits. Also important is the presence of a work group for sociability and support. Workplace culture offers an alternative system of values from that imposed by managers (Benson 1986).[34] Experienced workers socialize newcomers, teaching them how to respond to pressures to speed up work, to negotiate work loads, and to demand respect from superiors. While the isolated domestic finds it difficult to resist demeaning treatment, the peer group in public settings provides backing for individuals to stand up to the boss.

That subordination is usually not as direct and personal in public settings as in the private household does not mean, however, that race and gender hierarchy is diminished in importance. Rather, it changes form, becoming institutionalized within organizational structures. Hierarchy is elaborated through a detailed division of labor that separates conception from execution and allows those at the top to control the work process. Ranking is based ostensibly on expertise, education, and formal credentials.

The elaboration is especially marked in technologically oriented organizations that employ large numbers of professionals, as is the case with health care institutions. Visual observation of any hospital reveals the hierarchical race and gender division of labor: at the top are the physicians, setting policy and initiating work for others; they are disproportionately white and male. Directly below, performing medical tasks and patient care as delegated by physicians and enforcing hospital rules, are the registered nurses (RNs), who are overwhelmingly female and disproportionately white. Under the registered nurses and often supervised by them are the licensed practical nurses (LPNs), also female but disproportionately women of color. At about the same level are the technologists and technicians who carry out various tests and procedures and the "administrative service" staff in the offices; these categories tend to be female and white. Finally, at the bottom of the pyramid are the nurse's aides, predominantly women of color; housekeepers and kitchen workers, overwhelmingly women of color; and orderlies and cleaners, primarily men of color. They constitute the "hands" that perform routine work directed by others.

## The Racial Division of Labor in Nursing

A study of stratification in the nursing labor force illustrates the race and gender construction of public reproductive labor. At the top in terms of status, authority, and pay are the RNs, graduates of two-, three-, or four-year hospital or college-based programs. Unlike the lower ranks, registered nursing offers a career ladder. Starting as a staff nurse, a hospital RN can rise to head nurse, nursing supervisor, and finally, director of nursing. In 1980 whites were 86.7 percent of RNs even though they were only 76.7 percent of the population. The LPNs, who make up the second grade of nursing, generally have had twelve months' training in a technical institute or community college. The LPNs are supervised by RNs and may oversee the work of aides. Racial-ethnic workers constituted 23.4 percent of LPNs, with Blacks, who were 11.7 percent of the population, making up fully 17.9 percent. Below the LPNs in the hierarchy are the nurse's aides (NAs), who typically have on-the-job training of four to six weeks. Orderlies, attendants, home health aides, and patient care assistants also fall into this category. These workers perform housekeeping and routine caregiving tasks "delegated by an RN and performed under the direction of an RN or LPN." Among nurse's aides, 34.6 percent were minorities, with Blacks making up 27.0 percent of all aides.[35]

Nationally, Latinas were underrepresented in health care services but were found in nurse's aide positions in proportion to their numbers — making up 5.2 percent of the total. The lower two grades of nursing labor thus appear to be Black specialties. However, in some localities other women of color are concentrated in these jobs. In San Antonio, 48 percent of aides were Spanish-origin, while only 15.1 percent of the RNs were. Similarly, in El Paso, 61.5 percent of aides were Spanish-origin, compared with 22.8 percent of RNs. In Honolulu, Asian and Pacific Islanders who were 68.6 percent of the female labor force made up 72.3 percent of the NAs but only 45.7 percent of the RNs.[36]

**Familial Symbolism and the Race and Gender Construction of Nursing:** How did the present ranking system and sorting by race/ethnic category in nursing come about? How did the activities of white nurses contribute to the structuring? And how did racial-ethnic women respond to constraints?

The stratification of nursing labor can be traced to the beginnings of organized nursing in the 1870s. However, until the 1930s grading was loose. A broad distinction was made between so-called trained nurses, who were graduates of hospital schools or collegiate programs, and untrained nurses, referred to — often interchangeably — as "practical nurses," "hospital helpers," "nursing assistants," "nursing aides," or simply as "aides" (Cannings and Lazonik 1975; Reverby 1987).

During this period health work in hospitals was divided between male physicians (patient diagnosis and curing) and female nursing staff (patient care) in a fashion analogous to the separate spheres prescribed for middle-class households. Nurses and physicians each had primary responsibility for and authority within their own spheres, but nurses were subject to the ultimate authority of physicians. The separation gave women power in a way that did not challenge male domination. Eva Gamarinikow likens the position of the British nursing matron to that of an upper-class woman in a Victorian household who supervised a large household staff but was subordinate to her husband (Gamarinikow 1978). Taking the analogy a step further, Ann Game and Rosemary Pringle describe the pre–World War II hospital as operating under a system of controls based on familial symbolism. Physicians were the authoritative father figures, while trained nurses were the mothers overseeing the care of patients, who were viewed as dependent children. Student nurses and practical nurses were, in this scheme, in the position of servants, expected to follow orders and subject to strict discipline (Game and Pringle 1983, 99–100).

Like the middle-class white housewives who accepted the domestic ideology, white nursing leaders rarely challenged the familial symbolism supporting the gender division of labor in health care. The boldest advocated at most a dual-headed family (Reverby 1987, 71–75). They acceded to the racial implications of the family metaphor as well. If nurses were mothers in a family headed by white men, they had to be white. And, indeed, trained nursing was an almost exclusively white preserve. As Susan Reverby notes, "In 1910 and 1920, for example, less than 3% of the trained nurses in the United States were black, whereas black women made up 17.6% and 24.0% respectively of the female working population" (Reverby 1987, 71–75).

The scarcity of Black women is hardly surprising. Nursing schools in the South excluded Blacks altogether, while northern schools maintained strict quotas. Typical was the policy of the New England Hospital for Women and Children, which by charter could only admit "one Negro and one Jewish student" a year (Hine 1989, 6). Black women who managed to become trained nurses did so through separate Black training schools and were usually restricted to serving Black patients, whether in "integrated" hospitals in the North or segregated Black hospitals in the South.[37]

White nursing leaders and administrators justified exclusion by appeals to racist ideology. Anne Bess Feeback, the superintendent of nurses for Henry Grady Hospital in Atlanta, declared that Negro women under her supervision had no morals: "They are such liars. . . . They shift responsibility whenever they can. . . . They quarrel constantly among themselves and will cut up each other's clothes for spite. . . . Unless they are constantly watched, they will steal anything in sight" (Hine 1985, 101). Perhaps the most consistent refrain was that Black women were deficient in the qualities needed to be good nurses: they lacked executive skills, intelligence, strength of character, and the ability to withstand pressure. Thus Margaret Butler, chief nurse in the Chicago City Health Department, contended that Black nurses' techniques were "inferior to that of the white nurses, they are not punctual, and are incapable of analyzing a social situation." Apparently Black nurses did not accept white notions of racial inferiority, for Butler also complains about their tendency "to organize against authority" and "to engage in political intrigue" (Hine 1989, 99). Another white nursing educator, Margaret Bruesche, suggested that although Black women lacked the ability to become trained nurses, they "could fill a great need in the South as a trained attendant, who would work for a lower wage than a fully trained woman" (Hine 1989, 101). Even those white nursing leaders sympathetic to Black aspirations agreed that Black nurses should not be put in supervisory positions because white nurses would never submit to their authority.

Similar ideas about the proper place of "Orientals" in nursing were held by haole nursing leaders in pre–World War II Hawaii. White-run hospitals and clinics recruited haoles from the mainland, especially for senior nurse positions, rather than hiring or promoting locally trained Asian American nurses. This pattern was well known enough for a University of Hawaii researcher to ask a haole health administrator whether it was true that "oriental nurses do not reach the higher positions of the profession?" Mr. "C" confirmed this: "Well, there again it is a matter of qualification. There is a limit to the number of nurses we can produce here. For that reason we have to hire from the mainland. Local girls cannot compete with the experience of mainland haole girls. In order to induce haole nurses here we could not possibly put them under an oriental nurse because that would make them race conscious right at the start. And as I said before, Japanese don't make good executives."[38] Because of the racial caste system in Hawaii, Japanese American women who managed to get into nursing were not seen as qualified or competent to do professional work. The chairman of the Territorial Nurses Association noted that "before the war [started], our local nurses were looked down [upon] because they were mostly Japanese. . . . The Japanese nurses feel they can get along better with Mainland nurses than local haole nurses. That is true even outside of the profession. I remember hearing a Hawaiian born haole dentist say, 'I was never so shocked as when I saw a white man shine shoes when I first went to the Mainland.' Haoles here feel only orientals and other non-haoles should do menial work."[39]

The systematic grading of nursing labor into three ranks was accomplished in the 1930s and forties as physician-controlled hospital administrations moved to establish "sound business" practices to contain costs and consolidate physician control of health care.[40] High-tech medical and diagnostic procedures provided an impetus for ever-greater specialization. Hospitals adopted Taylorist principles of "scientific management," separating planning and technical tasks from execution and manual labor. They began to hire thousands of subsidiary workers and created the licensed practical nurse, a position for a graduate of a one-year technical program, to perform routine housekeeping and patient care. With fewer discriminatory barriers and shorter training requirements, LPN positions were accessible to women of color who wanted to become nurses.

The lowest level of nursing workers, nurse's aides, also was defined in the 1930s, when the American Red Cross started offering ten-week courses to train aides for hospitals. This category expanded rapidly in the 1940s, doubling from 102,000 workers in 1940 to 212,000 in 1950 (Cannings and Lazonik 1975, 200–201). This occupation seems to have been designed deliberately to make use of African American labor in the wake of labor shortages during and after World War II. A 1948 report on nursing told the story of how nurse's aides replaced the heretofore volunteer corps of ward attendants: "In response to this request for persons designated as nursing aides, the hospital discovered among the large Negro community a hitherto untapped reservoir of personnel, well above the ward attendant group in intelligence and personality" (Cannings and Lazonik 1975, 201).

One reason for their superiority can be deduced: they often were overqualified. Barred from entry into better occupations, capable, well-educated Black women turned to nurse's aide work as an alternative to domestic service.

In the meantime RNs continued their struggle to achieve professional status by claiming exclusive rights over "skilled" nursing work. Some nurses, especially rank-and-file general duty nurses, called for an outright ban on employing untrained nurses. Many leaders of nursing organizations, however, favored accepting subsidiary workers to perform housekeeping and other routine chores so that graduate nurses would be free for more professional work. Hospital administrators assured RNs that aides would be paid less and assigned non-nursing functions and that only trained nurses would be allowed supervisory roles. One administrator claimed that aide trainees were told repeatedly that "they are not and will not be nurses" (Reverby 1987, 194).

In the end, the leaders of organized nursing accepted the formal stratification of nursing and turned their attention to circumscribing the education and duties of the lower grades to ensure their differentiation from "professional" nurses. Indeed, an RN arguing for the need to train and license practical nurses and laying out a model curriculum for LPNs warned: "Overtraining can be a serious danger. The practical nurse who has a course of over fifteen months (theory and practice) gets a false impression of her abilities and builds up the unwarranted belief that she can practice as a professional nurse" (Deming 1947, 26). Hospital administrators took advantage of race and class divisions and RNs' anxieties about their status to further their own agenda. Their strategy of co-opting part of the work force (RNs) and restricting the mobility and wages of another part (LPNs and NAs) undermined solidarity among groups that might otherwise have united around common interests.

**Nursing Aides: Consciousness of Race and Gender:** The hierarchy in health care has come to be justified less in terms of family symbolism and more in terms of bureaucratic efficiency. Within the new bureaucratic structures, race and gender ordering is inherent in the job definitions. The nurse's aide job is defined as unskilled and menial; hence, the women who do it are, too. Nurse's aides frequently confront a discrepancy, however, between how their jobs are defined (unskilled and subordinate) and what they actually are allowed or expected to do (exercise skill and judgment). Lillian Roberts's experiences illustrate the disjunction. Assigned to the nursery, she was fortunate to work with a white southern RN who was willing to teach her. "I would ask her about all kinds of deformities that we would see in the nursery, the color of a baby, and why this was happening and why the other was happening. And then I explored with her using my own analysis of things. Sometimes I'd be right just in observing and putting some common sense into it. Before long, when the interns would come in to examine the babies, I could tell them what was wrong with every baby. I'd have them lined up for them" (Reverby 1979, 297–98).

The expertise Roberts developed through observation, questioning, and deduction was not recognized, however. Thirty years later Roberts still smarts from the injustice of not being allowed to sit in on the shift reports: "They never dignify you with that. Even though it would help you give better care. There were limitations on what I could do" (Reverby 1979, 298–99).

She had to assume a deferential manner when dealing with white medical students and personnel, even those who had much less experience than she had. Sometimes she would be left in charge of the nursery and "I'd get a whole mess of new students in there who didn't know what to do. I would very diplomatically have to direct them, although they resented to hell that I was both black and a nurse's aide. But I had to do it in such a way that they didn't feel I was claiming to know more than they did" (Reverby 1979, 298). One of her biggest frustrations was not being allowed to get on-the-job training to advance. Roberts describes the "box" she was in: "I couldn't have afforded to go to nursing school. I needed the income, and you can't just quit a job and go to school. I was caught in a box, and the salary wasn't big enough to save to go to school. And getting into the nursing schools was a real racist problem as well. So there was a combination of many things. And I used to say, 'Why does this country have to go elsewhere and get people when people like myself want to do something?'" (Reverby 1979, 299). When she became a union organizer, her proudest accomplishment was to set up a program in New York that allowed aides to be trained on the job to become LPNs.

While Roberts's experience working in a hospital was typical in the 1940s and 1950s, today the typical aide is employed in a nursing home, in a convalescent home, or in home health care. In these settings, aides are the primary caregivers.[41] The demand for their services continues to grow as treatment increasingly shifts out of hospitals and into such settings. Thus, even though aides have lost ground to RNs in hospitals, which have reorganized nursing services to recreate RNs as generalists, aides are expected to remain among the fastest-growing occupations through the end of the century (Sekcenski 1981, 10–16).[42]

Whatever the setting, aide work continues to be a specialty of racial-ethnic women. The work is seen as unskilled and subordinate and thus appropriate to their qualifications and status. This point was brought home to Timothy Diamond during the training course he attended as the sole white male in a mostly Black female group of trainees: "We learned elementary biology and how we were never to do health care without first consulting someone in authority; and we learned not to ask questions but to do as we were told. As one of the students, a black woman from Jamaica used to joke, 'I can't figure out whether they're trying to teach us to be nurses' aides or black women'" (Diamond 1988, 40).

What exactly is the nature of the reproductive labor that these largely minority and supposedly unskilled aides and assistants perform? They do most of the day-to-day, face-to-face work of caring for the ill and disabled: helping patients dress or change gowns, taking vital signs (temperature, blood pressure, pulse), assisting patients to shower or giving bed baths, emptying bedpans or assisting patients to [the] toilet, changing sheets and keeping the area tidy, and feeding patients who cannot feed themselves. There is much "dirty" work, such as cleaning up incontinent patients. Yet there is another, unacknowledged, mental and emotional dimension to the work: listening to the reminiscences of elderly patients to help them hold on to their memory, comforting frightened patients about to undergo surgery, and providing the only human contact some patients get. This caring work is largely invisible, and the skills required to do it are not recognized as real skills.[43]

That these nurse's aides are performing reproductive labor on behalf of other women (and ultimately for the benefit of households, industry, and the state) becomes clear when one considers who would do it if paid workers did not. Indeed, we confront that situation frequently today, as hospitals reduce the length of patient stays to cut costs. Patients are released "quicker and sicker" (Sacks 1988, 165). This policy makes sense only if it is assumed that patients have someone to provide interim care, administer medication, prepare meals, and clean for them until they can care for themselves. If such a person exists, most likely it is a woman—a daughter, wife, mother, or sister. She may have to take time off from her job or quit. Her unpaid labor takes the place of the paid work of a nurse's aide or assistant and saves the hospital labor costs. Her labor is thereby appropriated to ensure profit (Glazer 1988). Thus, the situation of women as unpaid reproductive workers at home is inextricably bound to that of women as paid reproductive workers.

## Conclusions and Implications

This article began with the observation that the racial division of reproductive labor has been overlooked in the separate literatures on race and gender. The distinct exploitation of women of color and an important source of difference among women have thereby been ignored. How, though, does a historical analysis of the racial division of reproductive labor illuminate the lives of women of color and white women? What are its implications for concerted political action? In order to tackle these questions, we need to address a broader question, namely, how does the analysis advance our understanding of race and gender? Does it take us beyond the additive models I have criticized?

## The Social Construction of Race and Gender

Tracing how race and gender have been fashioned in one area of women's work helps us understand them as socially constructed systems of relationships — including symbols, normative beliefs, and practices — organized around perceived differences. This understanding is an important counter to the universalizing tendencies in feminist thought. When feminists perceive reproductive labor only as gendered, they imply that domestic labor is identical for all women and that it therefore can be the basis of a common identity of womanhood. By not recognizing the different relationships women have had to such supposedly universal female experiences as motherhood and domesticity, they risk essentializing gender — treating it as static, fixed, eternal, and natural. They fail to take seriously a basic premise of feminist thought, that gender is a social construct.

If race and gender are socially constructed systems, then they must arise at specific moments in particular circumstances and change as these circumstances change. We can study their appearance, variation, and modification over time. I have suggested that one vantage point for looking at their development in the United States is in the changing division of labor in local economies. A key site for the emergence of concepts of gendered and racialized labor has been in regions characterized by dual labor systems.

As subordinate-race women within dual labor systems, African American, Mexican American, and Japanese American women were drawn into domestic service by a combination of economic need, restricted opportunities, and educational and employment tracking mechanisms. Once they were in service, their association with "degraded" labor affirmed their supposed natural inferiority. Although ideologies of "race" and "racial difference" justifying the dual labor system already were in place, specific ideas about racial-ethnic womanhood were invented and enacted in everyday interactions between mistresses and workers. Thus ideologies of race and gender were created and verified in daily life (Fields 1982).

Two fundamental elements in the construction of racial-ethnic womanhood were the notion of inherent traits that suited the women for service and the denial of the women's identities as wives and mothers in their own right. Employers accepted a cult of domesticity that purported to elevate the status of women as mothers and homemakers, yet they made demands on domestics that hampered them from carrying out these responsibilities in their own households. How could employers maintain such seemingly inconsistent orientations? Racial ideology was critical in resolving the contradiction: it explained why women of color were suited for degrading work. Racial characterizations effectively neutralized the racial-ethnic woman's womanhood, allowing the mistress to be "unaware" of the domestic's relationship to her own children and household. The exploitation of racial-ethnic women's physical, emotional, and mental work for the benefit of white households thus could be rendered invisible in consciousness if not in reality.

With the shift of reproductive labor from household to market, face-to-face hierarchy has been replaced by structural hierarchy. In institutional settings, stratification is built into organizational structures, including lines of authority, job descriptions, rules, and spatial and temporal segregation. Distance between higher and lower orders is ensured by structural segregation. Indeed, much routine service work is organized to be out of sight: it takes place behind institutional walls where outsiders rarely penetrate (e.g., nursing homes, chronic care facilities), in back rooms (e.g., restaurant kitchens), or at night or other times when occupants are gone (e.g., in office buildings and hotels). Workers may appreciate this time and space segregation because it allows them some autonomy and freedom from demeaning interactions. It also makes them and their work invisible, however. In this situation, more privileged women do not have to acknowledge the workers or to confront the contradiction between shared womanhood and inequality by race and class. Racial ideology is not necessary to explain or justify exploitation, not for lack of racism, but because the justification for inequality does not have to be elaborated in specifically racial terms: instead it can be cast in terms of differences in training, skill, or education.[44]

Because they are socially constructed, race and gender systems are subject to contestation and struggle. Racial-ethnic women continually have challenged the devaluation of their womanhood. Domestics often did so covertly. They learned to dissemble, consciously "putting on an act" while inwardly rejecting their employers' premises and maintaining a separate identity rooted in their families and communities. As noted earlier, institutional service workers can resist demeaning treatment more openly because they have the support of peers. Minority-race women hospital workers have been in the forefront of labor militancy, staging walkouts and strikes and organizing workplaces. In both domestic service and institutional service work, women have transcended the limitations of their work by focusing on longer-term goals, such as their children's future.

## Beyond Additive Models: Race and Gender as Interlocking Systems

As the foregoing examples show, race and gender constructs are inextricably intertwined. Each develops in the context of the other; they cannot be separated. This is important because when we see reproductive labor only as gendered, we extract gender from its context, which includes other interacting systems of power. If we begin with gender separated out, then we have to put race and class back in when we consider women of color and working-class women. We thus end up with an additive model in which white women have only gender and women of color have gender plus race.

The interlock is evident in the case studies of domestic workers and nurse's aides. In the traditional middle-class household, the availability of cheap female domestic labor buttressed white male privilege by perpetuating the concept of reproductive labor as women's work, sustaining the illusion of a protected private sphere for women and displacing conflict away from husband and wife to struggles between housewife and domestic.

The racial division of labor also bolstered the gender division of labor indirectly by offering white women a slightly more privileged position in exchange for accepting domesticity. Expanding on Judith Rollins's notion that white housewives gained an elevated self-identity by casting Black domestics as inferior contrast figures, Phyllis Palmer suggests the dependent position of the middle-class housewife made a contrasting figure necessary. A dualistic conception of women as "good" and "bad," long a part of western cultural tradition, provided ready-made categories for casting white and racial-ethnic women as oppositional figures (Davidoff 1979; Palmer 1990, 11, 137–39). The racial division of reproductive labor served to channel and recast these dualistic conceptions into racialized gender constructs. By providing them an acceptable self-image, racial constructs gave white housewives a stake in a system that ultimately oppressed them.

The racial division of labor similarly protects white male privilege in institutional settings. White men, after all, still dominate in professional and higher management positions where they benefit from the paid and unpaid services of women. And as in domestic service, conflict between men and women is redirected into clashes among women. This displacement is evident in health care organizations. Because physicians and administrators control the work of other health care workers, we would expect the main conflict to be between doctors and nurses over work load, allocation of tasks, wages, and working conditions. The racial division of nursing labor allows some of the tension to be redirected so that friction arises between registered nurses and aides over work assignments and supervision.

In both household and institutional settings, white professional and managerial men are the group most insulated from dirty work and contact with those who do it. White women are frequently the mediators who have to negotiate between white male superiors and racial-ethnic subordinates. Thus race and gender dynamics are played out in a three-way relationship involving white men, white women, and women of color.

## Beyond Difference: Race and Gender as Relational Constructs

Focusing on the racial division of reproductive labor also uncovers the relational nature of race and gender. By "relational" I mean that each is made up of categories (e.g., male/female, Anglo/Latino) that are positioned, and therefore gain meaning, in relation to each other (Barrett 1987). Power, status, and privilege are axes along which categories are positioned. Thus, to represent race and gender as relationally constructed is to assert that the experiences of white women and women of color are not just different but connected in systematic ways.

The interdependence is easier to see in the domestic work setting because the two groupings of women confront one another face-to-face. That the higher standard of living of one woman is made possible by, and also helps to perpetuate, the other's lower standard of living is clearly evident. In institutional service work the relationship between those who do the dirty work and those who benefit from it is mediated and buffered by institutional structures, so the dependence of one group on the other for its standard of living is not apparent. Nonetheless, interdependence exists, even if white women do not come into actual contact with women of color.[45]

The notion of relationality also recognizes that white and racial-ethnic women have different standpoints by virtue of their divergent positions. This is an important corrective to feminist theories of gendered thought that posit universal female modes of thinking growing out of common experiences such as domesticity and motherhood. When they portray reproductive labor only as gendered, they assume there is only one standpoint—that of white women. Hence, the activities and experiences of middle-class women become generic "female" experiences and activities, and those of other groups become variant, deviant, or specialized.

In line with recent works on African American, Asian American, and Latina feminist thought, we see that taking the standpoint of women of color gives us a different and more critical perspective on race and gender systems (Garcia 1989; Anzaldúa 1990; Collins 1990). Domestic workers in particular—because they directly confront the contradictions in their lives and those of their mistresses—develop an acute consciousness of the interlocking nature of race and gender oppression.

Perhaps a less obvious point is that understanding race and gender as relational systems also illuminates the lives of white American women. White womanhood has been constructed not in isolation but in relation to that of women of color. Therefore, race is integral to white women's gender identities. In addition, seeing variation in racial division of labor across time in different regions gives us a more variegated picture of white middle-class womanhood.

White women's lives have been lived in many circumstances; their "gender" has been constructed in relation to varying others, not just to Black women. Conceptualizing white womanhood as monolithically defined in opposition to men or to Black women ignores complexity and variation in the experiences of white women.

## Implications for Feminist Politics

Understanding race and gender as relational, interlocking, socially constructed systems affects how we strategize for change. If race and gender are socially constructed rather than being "real" referents in the material world, then they can be deconstructed and challenged. Feminists have made considerable strides in deconstructing gender; we now need to focus on deconstructing gender and race simultaneously. An initial step in this process is to expose the structures that support the present division of labor and the constructions of race and gender around it.

Seeing race and gender as interlocking systems, however, alerts us to sources of inertia and resistance to change. The discussion of how the racial division of labor reinforced the gender division of labor makes clear that tackling gender hierarchy requires simultaneously addressing race hierarchy. As long as the gender division of labor remains intact, it will be in the short-term interest of white women to support or at least overlook the racial division of labor because it ensures that the very worst labor is performed by someone else. Yet, as long as white women support the racial division of labor, they will have less impetus to struggle to change the gender division of labor. This quandary is apparent in cities such as Los Angeles, which have witnessed a large influx of immigrant women fleeing violence and poverty in Latin America, Southeast Asia, and the Caribbean. These women form a large reserve army of low-wage labor for both domestic service and institutional service work. Anglo women who ordinarily would not be able to afford servants are employing illegal immigrants as maids at below-minimum wages (McConoway 1987). Not only does this practice diffuse pressure for a more equitable sharing of household work but it also re-creates race and gender ideologies that justify the subordination of women of color. Having a Latino or Black maid picking up and cleaning after them teaches Anglo children that some people exist primarily to do work that Anglos do not want to do for themselves.

Acknowledging the relational nature of race and gender and therefore the interdependence between groups means that we recognize conflicting interests among women. Two examples illustrate the divergence. With the move into the labor force of all races and classes of women, it is tempting to think that we can find unity around the common problems of "working women."

With that in mind, feminist policymakers have called for expanding services to assist employed mothers in such areas as child care and elderly care. We need to ask, Who is going to do the work? Who will benefit from increased services? The historical record suggests that it will be women of color, many of them new immigrants, who will do the work and that it will be middle-class women who will receive the services. Not so coincidentally, public officials seeking to reduce welfare costs are promulgating regulations requiring women on public assistance to work. The needs of employed middle-class women and women on welfare might thus be thought to coincide: the needs of the former for services might be met by employing the latter to provide the services. The divergence in interest becomes apparent, however, when we consider that employment in service jobs at current wage levels guarantees that their occupants will remain poor. However, raising their wages so that they can actually support themselves and their children at a decent level would mean many middle-class women could not afford these services.

A second example of an issue that at first blush appears to bridge race and ethnic lines is the continuing earnings disparity between men and women. Because occupational segregation, the concentration of women in low-paying, female-dominated occupations, stands as the major obstacle to wage equity, some feminist policymakers have embraced the concept of comparable worth (Hartmann 1985; Acker 1989). This strategy calls for equalizing pay for "male" and "female" jobs requiring similar levels of skill and responsibility, even if differing in content. Comparable worth accepts the validity of a job hierarchy and differential pay based on "real" differences in skills and responsibility. Thus, for example, it attacks the differential between nurses and pharmacists but leaves intact the differential between nurses and nurse's aides. Yet the division between "skilled" and "unskilled" jobs is exactly where the racial division typically falls. To address the problems of women of color service workers would require a fundamental attack on the concept of a hierarchy of worth; it would call for flattening the wage differentials between highest- and lowest-paid ranks. A claim would have to be made for the right of all workers to a living wage, regardless of skill or responsibility.

These examples suggest that forging a political agenda that addresses the universal needs of women is highly problematic not just because women's priorities differ but because gains for some groups may require a corresponding loss of advantage and privilege for others. As the history of the racial division of reproductive labor reveals, conflict and contestation among women over definitions of womanhood, over work, and over the conditions of family life are part of our legacy as well as the current reality. This does not mean we give up the goal of concerted struggle. It means we give up trying falsely to harmonize women's interests. Appreciating the ways race and gender division of labor creates both hierarchy and interdependence may be a better way to reach an understanding of the interconnectedness of women's lives.

## NOTES

*Acknowledgments:* Work on this project was made possible by a Title F leave from the State University of New York at Binghamton and a visiting scholar appointment at the Murray Research Center at Radcliffe College. Discussions with Elsa Barkley Brown, Gary Glenn, Carole Turbin, and Barrie Thorne contributed immeasurably to the ideas developed here. My thanks to Joyce Chinen for directing me to archival materials in Hawaii. I am also grateful to members of the Women and Work Group and to Norma Alarcon, Gary Dymski, Antonia Glenn, Margaret Guilette, Terence Hopkins, Eileen McDonagh, JoAnne Preston, Mary Ryan, and four anonymous *Signs* reviewers for their suggestions.

1. For various formulations, see Benston (1969), Secombe (1974), Barrett (1980), Fox (1980), and Sokoloff (1980).

2. Recently, white feminists have begun to pay attention to scholarship by and about racial-ethnic women and to recognize racial stratification in the labor market and other public arenas. My point here is that they still assume that women's relationship to domestic labor is universal; thus they have not been concerned with explicating differences across race, ethnic, and class groups in women's relationship to that labor.

3. See, e.g., Reisler (1976), which, despite its title, is exclusively about male Mexican labor.

4. I use the term *racial-ethnic* to refer collectively to groups that have been socially constructed and constituted as racially as well as culturally distinct from European Americans and placed in separate legal statuses from "free whites" (c.f. Omi and Winant 1986). Historically, African Americans, Latinos, Asian Americans, and Native Americans were so constructed. Similarly, I have capitalized the word *Black* throughout this article to signify the racial-ethnic construction of that category.

5. Capitalism, however, changed the nature of reproductive labor, which became more and more devoted to consumption activities, i.e., using wages to acquire necessities in the market and then processing these commodities to make them usable (see Weinbaum and Bridges 1976; and Luxton 1980).

6. This is not to deny that family members, especially women, still provide the bulk of care of dependents, but to point out that there has been a marked increase in institutionalized care in the second half of the twentieth century.

7. For a discussion of varying views on the relative importance of control versus agency in shaping state welfare policy, see Gordon (1990). Piven and Cloward note that programs have been created only when poor people have mobilized and are intended to defuse pressure for more radical change (1971, 66). In their *Poor People's Movements* (Piven and Cloward 1979), they document the role of working-class struggles to win concessions from the state. For a feminist social control perspective, see Abramovitz (1988).

8. These developments are discussed in Degler (1980), Strasser (1982), Cowan (1983), and Dudden (1983, esp. 240–42).

9. See also Blair (1980); Epstein (1981); Ryan (1981); and Dudden (1983).

10. See, e.g., Kaplan (1987).

11. Phyllis Palmer, in her *Domesticity and Dirt*, found evidence that mistresses and servants agreed on what were the least desirable tasks — washing clothes, washing dishes, and

taking care of children on evenings and weekends — and that domestics were more likely to perform the least desirable tasks (1990, 70).

12. It may be worth mentioning the importance of unpaid cultural and charitable activities in perpetuating middle-class privilege and power. Middle-class reformers often aimed to mold the poor in ways that mirrored middle-class values but without actually altering their subordinate positions. See, e.g., Sanchez (1990) for discussion of efforts of Anglo reformers to train Chicanas in domestic skills.

13. U.S. Bureau of the Census 1933, chap. 3, "Color and Nativity of Gainful Workers," tables 2, 4, 6. For discussion of the concentration of African American women in domestic service, see Glenn (1985).

14. I use the terms *Chicano*, *Chicana*, and *Mexican American* to refer to both native-born and immigrant Mexican people/women in the United States.

15. U.S. Bureau of the Census 1933.

16. Ibid.

17. For personal accounts of Chicano children being inducted into domestic service, see Ruíz (1987a) and interview of Josephine Turietta in Elsasser, MacKenzie, and Tixier y Vigil (1980, 28–35).

18. See also life history accounts of Black domestics, such as that of Bolden (1976) and of Anna Mae Dickson by Wendy Watriss (Watriss 1984).

19. Blackwelder also found that domestics themselves were attuned to the racial-ethnic hierarchy among them. When advertising for jobs, women who did not identify themselves as Black overwhelmingly requested "housekeeping" or "governess" positions, whereas Blacks advertised for "cooking," "laundering," or just plain "domestic work."

20. This is not to say that daughters of European immigrants experienced great social mobility and soon attained affluence. The nondomestic jobs they took were usually low paying and the conditions of work often deplorable. Nonetheless, white native-born and immigrant women clearly preferred the relative freedom of industrial, office, or shop employment to the constraints of domestic service (see Katzman 1978, 71–72).

21. Document Ma 24, Romanzo Adams Social Research Laboratory papers. I used these records when they were lodged in the sociology department; they are currently being cataloged by the university archives and a finding aid is in process.

22. Ibid., document Ma 15, 5.

23. Ibid.

24. "More Slavery at the South: A Negro Nurse," from the *Independent* (1912), in Katzman and Tuttle (1982, 176–85, 179).

25. From an interview conducted by the author in the San Francisco Bay area in 1977.

26. Ibid.

27. The U.S. Labor Department and the U.S. Bureau of the Census divide service occupations into three major categories: "private household," "protective service," and "service occupations except private household and protective services." In this discussion, "service work" refers only to the latter. I omit private household workers, who have been discussed previously, and protective service workers, who include firefighters and police: these jobs, in addition to being male dominated and relatively well paid, carry some degree of authority, including the right to use force.

28. Computed from U.S. Bureau of the Census (1984), chap. D, "Detailed Population Characteristics," pt 1: "United States Summary," table 278: "Detailed Occupation of Employed Persons by Sex, Race and Spanish Origin, 1980.28."

29. Ibid.

30. Figures computed from table 279 in each of the state chapters of the following: U.S. Bureau of the Census (1984), chap. D, "Detailed Population Characteristics," pt. 6: "California"; pt. 12: "Georgia"; pt. 13: "Hawaii"; pt. 15: "Illinois"; pt. 44: "Tennessee"; and pt. 45: "Texas." The figures for Anglos in the Southwest are estimates, based on the assumption that most "Spanish-origin" people are Mexican, and that Mexicans, when given a racial designation, are counted as whites. Specifically, the excess left after the "total" is subtracted from the "sum" of white, Black, American Indian/Eskimo/ Aleut, Asian and Pacific Islander, and "Spanish-origin" is subtracted from the white figure. The remainder is counted as "Anglo." Because of the way "Spanish-origin" cross-cuts race (Spanish-origin individuals can be counted as white, Black, or any other race), I did not attempt to compute figures for Latinos or Anglos in cities where Spanish-origin individuals are likely to be more distributed in some unknown proportion between Black and white. This would be the case, e.g., with the large Puerto Rican population in New York City. Thus I have not attempted to compute Latino versus Anglo data for New York and Chicago. Note also that the meaning of *white* differs by locale and that the local terms *Anglo* and *haole* are not synonymous with *white*. The "white" category in Hawaii includes Portuguese, who, because of their history as plantation labor, are distinguished from haoles in the local ethnic ranking system. The U.S. Census category system does not capture the local structure of race/ethnicity.
31. Computed from tables specified in ibid.
32. The federal minimum wage was $3.35 in 1986. Over a quarter (26.0 percent) of all workers in these service occupations worked at or below this wage. See Mellor (1987, esp. 37).
33. Paternalism is not limited to southern hospitals; similar policies were in place at Montefiore Hospital in New York City. See Fink and Greenberg (1979).
34. See also many examples of workplace cultures supporting resistance in Sacks and Remy (1984) and Lamphere (1987).
35. American Nurses' Association 1965, 6. Reflecting differences in status and authority, RNs earn 20–40 percent more than LPNs and 60–150 percent more than NAs (U.S. Department of Labor 1987a, 1987b).
36. For the national level, see U.S. Bureau of the Census (1984), chap. D, "Detailed Population Characteristics," pt. 1: "United States Summary," table 278. For statistics on RNs and aides in San Antonio, El Paso, and Honolulu, see U.S. Bureau of the Census (1984), chap. D, "Detailed Population Characteristics," pt. 13: "Hawaii"; and pt. 45: "Texas," table 279.
37. For accounts of Black women in nursing, see also Hine (1985) and Carnegie (1986). Hine (1989, chap. 7) makes it clear that Black nurses served Black patients not just because they were restricted but because they wanted to meet Black health care needs. Blacks were excluded from membership in two of the main national organizations for nurses, the National League of Nursing Education and the American Nurses' Association. And although they formed their own organizations such as the National Association of Colored Graduate Nurses and enjoyed the respect of the Black community, Black nurses remained subordinated within the white-dominated nursing profession.
38. Document Nu21-1, p. 2, Romanzo Adams [Social] Research Laboratory papers, A1989-006, box 17, folder 1.
39. Document Nu10-1, p. 3, Romanzo Adams [Social] Research Laboratory papers, A1989-006, box 17, folder 4.
40. This was one outcome of the protracted and eventually successful struggle waged by

physicians to gain control over all health care. For an account of how physicians established hospitals as the main site for medical treatment and gained authority over "subsidiary" health occupations, see Starr (1982). For accounts of nurses' struggle for autonomy and their incorporation into hospitals, see Reverby (1987) and also Wagner (1980).

41. For example, it has been estimated that 80 percent of all patient care in nursing homes is provided by nurse's aides (see Coleman 1989, 5). In 1988, 1,559,000 persons were employed as RNs, 423,000 as LPNs, 1,404,000 as nurse's aides, orderlies, and attendants, and 407,000 as health aides (U.S. Department of Labor 1989, table 22). Nurse's aides and home health care aides are expected to be the fastest-growing occupations through the 1990s, according to Silvestri and Lukasiewicz (1987, 59).

42. For a description of trends and projections to the year 2000, see Silvestri and Lukasiewicz (1987).

43. Feminists have pointed to the undervaluing of female-typed skills, especially those involved in "caring" work (see Rose 1986).

44. That is, the concentration of minority workers in lower-level jobs can be attributed to their lack of "human capital" — qualifications — needed for certain jobs.

45. Elsa Barkley Brown pointed this out to me in a personal communication.

## REFERENCES

Abramovitz, Mimi. 1988. *Regulating the Lives of Women: Social Welfare Policy from Colonial Times to the Present*. Boston: South End Press.

Acker, Joan. 1989. *Doing Comparable Worth: Gender, Class, and Pay Equity*. Philadelphia: Temple University Press.

Adams, Romanzo. Social Research Laboratory papers. University of Hawaii Archives, Manoa.

American Nurses' Association. 1965. *Health Occupations Supportive to Nursing*. New York: American Nurses' Association.

Anderson, C. Arnold, and Mary Jean Bowman. 1953. "The Vanishing Servant and the Contemporary Status System of the American South." *American Journal of Sociology* 59: 215–30.

Anzaldúa, Gloria. 1990. *Making Face, Making Soul — Haciendo Caras: Creative Critical Perspectives by Women of Color*. San Francisco: Aunt Lute Foundation.

Barrera, Mario. 1979. *Race and Class in the Southwest: A Theory of Racial Inequality*. Notre Dame, Ind., and London: University of Notre Dame Press.

Barrett, Michèle. 1980. *Women's Oppression Today: Problems in Marxist Feminist Analysis*. London: Verso.

———. 1987. "The Concept of 'Difference.'" *Feminist Review* 26(July): 29–41.

Benson, Susan Porter. 1986. *Counter Cultures: Saleswomen, Customers, and Managers in American Department Stores, 1890–1940*. Urbana and Chicago: University of Illinois Press.

Benston, Margaret. 1969. "The Political Economy of Women's Liberation." *Monthly Review* 21(September): 13–27.

Blackwelder, Julia Kirk. 1978. "Women in the Work Force: Atlanta, New Orleans, and San Antonio, 1930 to 1940." *Journal of Urban History* 4(3): 331–58, 349.

———. 1984. *Women of the Depression: Caste and Culture in San Antonio, 1929–1939*. College Station: Texas A&M University Press.

Blair, Karen. 1980. *The Clubwoman as Feminist: True Womanhood Redefined, 1868–1914*. New York: Holmes & Meier.

Blauner, Robert. 1972. *Racial Oppression in America*. Berkeley: University of California Press.

Bolden, Dorothy. 1976. "Forty-Two Years a Maid: Starting at Nine in Atlanta." In *Nobody Speaks for Me! Self-Portraits of American Working Class Women*, ed. Nancy Seifer. New York: Simon & Schuster.

Boydston, Jeanne. 1990. *Home and Work: Housework, Wages, and the Ideology of Labor in the Early Republic*. New York: Oxford University Press.

Braverman, Harry. 1974. *Labor and Monopoly Capital: The Degradation of Labor in the Twentieth Century*. New York and London: Monthly Review Press.

Brenner, Johanna, and Barbara Laslett. 1986. "Social Reproduction and the Family." In *Sociology, from Crisis to Science?* Vol. 2, *The Social Reproduction of Organization and Culture*, ed. Ulf Himmelstrand, 116–31. London: Sage.

Brown, Elsa Barkley. 1989. "Womanist Consciousness: Maggie Lena Walker and the Independent Order of Saint Luke." *Signs: Journal of Women in Culture and Society* 14(3): 610–33.

Cannings, Kathleen, and William Lazonik. 1975. "The Development of the Nursing Labor Force in the United States: A Basic Analysis." *International Journal of Health Sciences* 5(2): 185–216.

Carnegie, Mary Elizabeth. 1986. *The Path We Tread: Blacks in Nursing, 1854–1954*. Philadelphia: Lippincott.

Chaplin, David. 1978. "Domestic Service and Industrialization." *Comparative Studies in Sociology* 1: 97–127.

Clark-Lewis, Elizabeth. 1987. "This Work Had an End: African American Domestic Workers in Washington, D.C., 1910–1940." In *"To Toil the Livelong Day": America's Women at Work, 1780–1980*, ed. Carole Groneman and Mary Beth Norton. Ithaca, N.Y.: Cornell University Press.

Coleman, Barbara. 1989. "States Grapple with New Law." *AARP News Bulletin*, 30(2): 4–5.

Collins, Patricia Hill. 1986. "Learning from the Outsider within: The Sociological Significance of Black Feminist Thought." *Social Problems* 33(6): 14–32.

———. 1990. *Black Feminist Thought: Knowledge, Consciousness, and the Politics of Empowerment*. New York: Allen & Unwin.

Cowan, Ruth Schwartz. 1983. *More Work for Mother: The Ironies of Household Technology from the Open Hearth to the Microwave*. New York: Basic.

Davidoff, Lenore. 1979. "Class and Gender in Victorian England: The Diaries of Arthur J. Munby and Hannah Cullwick." *Feminist Studies* 5(Spring): 86–114.

Degler, Carl N. 1980. *At Odds: Women and the Family in America from the Revolution to the Present*. New York: Oxford University Press.

Deming, Dorothy. 1947. *The Practical Nurse*. New York: Commonwealth Fund.

Deutsch, Sarah. 1987a. *No Separate Refuge: Culture, Class, and Gender on an Anglo-Hispanic Frontier in the American Southwest, 1880–1940*. New York: Oxford University Press.

———. 1987b. "Women and Intercultural Relations: The Case of Hispanic New Mexico and Colorado." *Signs* 12(4): 719–39.

Diamond, Timothy. 1988. "Social Policy and Everyday Life in Nursing Homes: A Critical Ethnography." In *The Worth of Women's Work: A Qualitative Synthesis*, ed. Anne Statham, Eleanor M. Miller, and Hans O. Mauksch. Albany, N.Y.: SUNY Press.

Dill, Bonnie Thornton. 1980. "The Means to Put My Children Through: Childrearing Goals and Strategies among Black Female Domestic Servants." In *The Black Woman*, ed. La Frances Rodgers-Rose. Beverly Hills and London: Sage.

———. 1988. "Our Mothers' Grief: Racial Ethnic Women and the Maintenance of Families." *Journal of Family History* 12(4): 415–31.

Drake, St. Clair, and Horace Cayton. (1945) 1962. *Black Metropolis: A Study of Negro Life in a Northern City*, vol. 1. New York: Harper Torchbook.

Dudden, Faye E. 1983. *Serving Women: Household Service in Nineteenth Century America*. Middletown, Conn.: Wesleyan University Press.

Elsasser, Nan, Kyle MacKenzie, and Yvonne Tixier y Vigil. 1980. *Las Mujeres: Conversations from a Hispanic Community*. Old Westbury, N.Y.: Feminist Press.

Engels, Friedrich. 1972. *The Origins of the Family, Private Property, and the State*. New York: International Publishers.

Epstein, Barbara. 1981. *The Politics of Domesticity: Women, Evangelism, and Temperance in Nineteenth-Century America*. Middletown, Conn.: Wesleyan University Press.

Fields, Barbara. 1982. "Ideology and Race in American History." In *Region, Race, and Reconstruction: Essays in Honor of C. Vann Woodward*, ed. J. Morgan Kousser and James M. McPherson. New York: Oxford University Press.

Fink, Leon, and Brian Greenberg. 1979. "Organizing Montefiore: Labor Militancy Meets a Progressive Health Care Empire." In *Health Care in America: Essays in Social History*, ed. Susan Reverby and David Rosner. Philadelphia: Temple University Press.

Fox, Bonnie, ed. 1980. *Hidden in the Household: Women's Domestic Labour under Capitalism*. Toronto: Women's Press.

Gamarinikow, Eva. 1978. "Sexual Division of Labour: The Case of Nursing." In *Feminism and Materialism: Women and Modes of Production*, ed. Annette Kuhn and Ann-Marie Wolpe, 96–123. London: Routledge & Kegan Paul.

Game, Ann, and Rosemary Pringle. 1983. *Gender at Work*. Sydney: Allen & Unwin.

Garcia, Alma. 1989. "The Development of Chicana Feminist Discourse, 1970–1980." *Gender and Society* 3(2): 217–38.

Garcia, Mario T. 1980. "The Chicana in American History: The Mexican Women of El Paso, 1880–1920: A Case Study." *Pacific Historical Review* 49(2): 315–39.

———. 1981. *Desert Immigrants: The Mexicans of El Paso, 1880–1920*. New Haven, Conn.: Yale University Press.

Glazer, Nona. 1988. "Overlooked, Overworked: Women's Unpaid and Paid Work in the Health Care Services' 'Cost Crisis.'" *International Journal of Health Services* 18(2): 119–37.

Glenn, Evelyn Nakano. 1985. "Racial Ethnic Women's Labor: The Intersection of Race, Gender and Class Oppression." *Review of Radical Political Economy* 17(3): 86–108.

———. 1986. *Issei, Nisei, Warbride: Three Generations of Japanese American Women in Domestic Service*. Philadelphia: Temple University Press.

Gordon, Linda. 1990. "The New Feminist Scholarship on the Welfare State." In *Women, the State, and Welfare*, ed. Linda Gordon, 9–35. Madison: University of Wisconsin Press.

Gwaltney, John, ed. 1980. *Drylongso: A Self-Portrait of Black America*. New York: Random House.

Hartmann, Heidi I., ed. 1985. *Comparable Worth: New Directions for Research*. Washington, D.C.: National Academy Press.

Hield, Melissa. 1984. "Women in the Texas ILGWU, 1933–50." In *Speaking for Ourselves: Women of the South*, ed. Maxine Alexander, 87–97. New York: Pantheon.

Hine, Darlene Clark, ed. 1985. *Black Women in the Nursing Profession: A Documentary History*. New York: Pathfinder.

———. 1989. *Black Women in White: Racial Conflict and Cooperation in the Nursing Profession, 1890–1950*. Bloomington: Indiana University Press.

Janiewski, Delores. 1983. "Flawed Victories: The Experiences of Black and White Women Workers in Durham during the 1930s." In *Decades of Discontent: The Women's Movement, 1920–1940*, ed. Lois Scharf and Joan M. Jensen, 85–112. Westport, Conn., and London: Greenwood.

Kaplan, Elaine Bell. 1987. " 'I Don't Do No Windows': Competition between the Domestic Worker and the Housewife." In *Competition: A Feminist Taboo?*" ed. Valerie Miner and Helen E. Longino. New York: Feminist Press at CUNY.

Katzman, David M. 1978. *Seven Days a Week: Women and Domestic Service in Industrializing America*. New York: Oxford University Press.

Katzman, David M., and William M. Tuttle, Jr., eds. 1982. *Plain Folk: The Life Stories of Undistinguished Americans*. Urbana and Chicago: University of Illinois Press.

Kessler-Harris, Alice. 1981. *Women Have Always Worked: A Historical Overview*. Old Westbury, N.Y.: Feminist Press.

———. 1982. *Out to Work: A History of Wage-earning Women in the United States*. New York: Oxford University Press.

King, Deborah K. 1988. "Multiple Jeopardy, Multiple Consciousness: The Context of a Black Feminist Ideology." *Signs* 14(1): 42–72.

Lamphere, Louise. 1987. *From Working Daughters to Working Mothers: Immigrant Women in a New England Industrial Community*. Ithaca, N.Y.: Cornell University Press.

Lasch, Christopher. 1977. *Haven in a Heartless World: The Family Besieged*. New York: Basic.

Laslett, Barbara, and Johanna Brenner. 1989. "Gender and Social Reproduction: Historical Perspectives." *Annual Review of Sociology* 15: 381–404.

Lind, Andrew. 1951. "The Changing Position of Domestic Service in Hawaii." *Social Process in Hawaii* 15: 71–87.

Luxton, Meg. 1980. *More than a Labour of Love: Three Generations of Women's Work in the Home*. Toronto: Women's Press.

McConoway, Mary Jo. 1987. "The Intimate Experiment." *Los Angeles Times Magazine*, February 19, 18–23, 37–38.

Marx, Karl, and Friedrich Engels. 1969. *Selected Works*, vol. 1. Moscow: Progress.

Mellor, Earl F. 1987. "Workers at the Minimum Wage or Less: Who They Are and the Jobs They Hold." *Monthly Labor Review*, July, 34–38.

Omi, Michael, and Howard Winant. 1986. *Racial Formation in the United States*. New York: Routledge.

Palmer, Phyllis. 1987. "Housewife and Household Worker: Employer-Employee Relations in the Home, 1928–1941." In *"To Toil the Livelong Day": America's Women at Work, 1780–1980*, ed. Carole Groneman and Mary Beth Norton, 179–95. Ithaca, N.Y.: Cornell University Press.

———. 1990. *Domesticity and Dirt: Housewives and Domestic Servants in the United States, 1920–1945*. Philadelphia: Temple University Press.

Piven, Frances Fox, and Richard A. Cloward. 1971. *Regulating the Poor: The Functions of Public Welfare*. New York: Pantheon.

———. 1979. *Poor People's Movements: Why They Succeed, How They Fail*. New York: Pantheon.

Reisler, Mark. 1976. *By the Sweat of Their Brow: Mexican Immigrant Labor in the United States, 1900–1940*. Westport, Conn.: Greenwood.

Reverby, Susan M. 1979. "From Aide to Organizer: The Oral History of Lillian Roberts." In

*Women of America: A History*, ed. Carol Ruth Berkin and Mary Beth Norton. Boston: Houghton Mifflin.

——. 1987. *Ordered to Care: The Dilemma of American Nursing, 1850–1945*. Cambridge: Cambridge University Press.

Rollins, Judith. 1985. *Between Women: Domestics and Their Employers*. Philadelphia: Temple University Press.

Romero, Mary. 1987. "Chicanas Modernize Domestic Service." Unpublished manuscript.

——. 1988a. "Day Work in the Suburbs: The Work Experience of Chicana Private House-keepers." In *The Worth of Women's Work: A Qualitative Synthesis*, ed. Anne Statham, Eleanor M. Miller, and Hans O. Mauksch, 77–92. Albany: SUNY Press.

——. 1988b. "Renegotiating Race, Class and Gender Hierarchies in the Everyday Inter-actions between Chicana Private Household Workers and Employers." Paper presented at the 1988 meetings of the Society for the Study of Social Problems, Atlanta.

Rose, Hilary. 1986. "Women's Work: Women's Knowledge." In *What Is Feminism?* ed. Juliet Mitchell and Ann Oakley, 161–83. Oxford: Basil Blackwell.

Ruíz, Vicki L. 1987a. "By the Day or the Week: Mexicana Domestic Workers in El Paso." In *Women on the U.S.–Mexico Border: Responses to Change*, ed. Vicki L. Ruíz and Susan Tiano, 61–76. Boston: Allen & Unwin.

——. 1987b. "Oral History and La Mujer: The Rosa Guerrero Story." In *Women on the U.S.–Mexico Border: Responses to Change*, ed. Vicki L. Ruíz and Susan Tiano, 219–32. Boston: Allen & Unwin.

Ryan, Mary P. 1981. *Cradle of the Middle Class: The Family in Oneida County, New York, 1790–1865*. Cambridge: Cambridge University Press.

Sacks, Karen Brodkin. 1988. *Caring by the Hour: Women, Work, and Organizing at Duke Medical Center.* Urbana and Chicago: University of Illinois Press.

Sacks, Karen Brodkin, and Dorothy Remy, eds. 1984. *My Troubles Are Going to Have Trouble with Me: Everyday Trials and Triumphs of Women Workers.* New Brunswick, N.J.: Rutgers University Press.

Sanchez, George J. 1990. " 'Go after the Women': Americanization and the Mexican Immi-grant Woman, 1915–1929." In *Unequal Sisters: A Multicultural Reader in Women's History*, ed. Ellen Carol DuBois and Vicki L. Ruíz, 250–63. New York: Routledge.

Secombe, Wally. 1974. "The Housewife and Her Labour under Capitalism." *New Left Review* 83 (January–February): 3–24.

Sekcenski, Edward S. 1981. "The Health Services Industry: A Decade of Expansion." *Monthly Labor Review* (May): 10–16.

Silvestri, George T., and John M. Lukasiewicz. 1987. "A Look at Occupational Employment Trends to the Year 2000." *Monthly Labor Review* (September): 46–63.

Smuts, Robert W. 1959. *Women and Work in America*. New York: Schocken.

Sokoloff, Natalie J. 1980. *Between Money and Love: The Dialectics of Women's Home and Market Work*. New York: Praeger.

Starr, Paul. 1982. *The Social Transformation of American Medicine*. New York: Basic.

Strasser, Susan. 1982. *Never Done: A History of American Housework*. New York: Pantheon.

Tucker, Susan. 1988. "The Black Domestic in the South: Her Legacy as Mother and Mother Surrogate." In *Southern Women*, ed. Carolyn Matheny Dillman, 93–102. New York: Hemisphere.

U.S. Bureau of the Census. 1932. *Fifteenth Census of the United States: 1930, Outlying Territo-ries and Possessions*. Washington, D.C.: Government Printing Office.

———. 1933. *Fifteenth Census of the United States: 1930, Population*. Vol. 5, *General Report on Occupations*. Washington, D.C.: Government Printing Office.

———. 1984. *Census of the Population, 1980*. Vol. 1, *Characteristics of the Population*. Washington, D.C.: Government Printing Office.

U.S. Department of Labor. 1987a. *Industry Wage Survey: Hospitals, August 1985*. Bureau of Labor Statistics Bulletin 2273. Washington, D.C.: Government Printing Office.

———. 1987b. *Industry Wage Survey: Nursing and Personal Care Facilities, September 1985*. Bureau of Labor Statistics Bulletin 2275. Washington, D.C.: Government Printing Office.

———. 1989. *Employment and Earnings, January 1989*. Bureau of Labor Statistics Bulletin. Washington, D.C.: Government Printing Office.

Wagner, David. 1980. "The Proletarianization of Nursing in the United States, 1932–1945." *International Journal of Health Services* 10(2): 271–89.

Watriss, Wendy. 1984. "It's Something Inside You." In *Speaking for Ourselves: Women of the South*, ed. Maxine Alexander. New York: Pantheon.

Weinbaum, Batya, and Amy Bridges. 1976. "The Other Side of the Paycheck." *Monthly Review* 28: 88–103.

## Chapter 7

# Family, Gender, and Business in Direct Selling Organizations

- Nicole Woolsey Biggart

An Amway distributor described the usual separation between people's work lives and their family lives and the problem he saw with that arrangement:

> In today's structure, the man goes to work here, and the woman goes to work there, and they come home at night and they're tired. It's been a long day, and a lot of the time they can't even share what's going on in each other's day because it's so different. There comes to be a separation between the husband and wife.

His network DSO [Direct Selling Organization], on the other hand, promises an alternative relationship between work and family.

> With the Amway business you have continuity, and both people can work together to achieve a goal that's going to benefit them and their family. And the kids too. They like to come around and serve cookies at the meetings, or clean the products on the shelf. So there's a real strong moral attitude in this business that everyone [in the family] should become involved.

Most businesses today, as this distributor described, exclude workers' families from the place and process of work. People in the United States now

Excerpted from *Charismatic Capitalism: Direct Selling Organizations in America* by Nicole Woolsey Biggart (Chicago: University of Chicago Press, 1989), chap. 4, pp. 70–97. © 1989 by The University of Chicago. Reprinted by permission.

generally accept that bringing one's personal life into the office is improper and disrupts the efficient conduct of business.[1] Moreover, firms often have nepotism rules about employing members of the same family. Corporations fear that selection and promotion on merit might be compromised if employees are related to each other. Businesses can also lose control of important processes: members of a family can favor each other or band together in decision making. The impersonal, economically efficient running of firms is predicated on the separation of work from family — if not absolutely, then as an ideal.[2]

This separation of the public sphere of work from the private sphere of domestic life is a strategy for managing the tension between two powerful, commitment-seeking units. Although work organizations cannot make employees give up all outside commitments (as a convent or military organization can), they can require that employees leave their families behind when they walk through the door at work. Rosabeth Kanter describes the compromise that modern business organizations exact from workers: "While you are here, you will *act as though* you have no other loyalties, no other life."[3]

Network DSOs, however, though they have no less need for members' loyalty than firms do, employ a radically different strategy for controlling the tension between work and family: *they manage the family*, making its powerful emotions and social unity serve organizational ends or actively manipulating the pull of family ties. The affective bonds and authority relations of the family are directed toward profit-making ends.

I discuss two overlapping topics in this chapter. First, I analyze the means by which network DSOs manage the family, either through its integration into business practice or by directly overcoming it as an obstacle. I suggest how the strategy represents a break from the recent past of family/work relations. Second, I examine the relation between gender and organization in direct selling. I argue that the integration of family, both in reality and as metaphor, creates a "feminine" form of organization qualitatively distinct from "masculine" firms. Finally, I consider how women's interests are, and are not, served by organizing in a feminine manner.

## Historical Background

Although the separation between one's private life and one's life as a worker is commonplace in this country today, this was not always so. In fact there have been several different work/family arrangements and a number of different forms of the "typical" family. Many scholars, though, recognize three relationships between the economic and domestic spheres that were important in the push toward modernity: a unified family economy centered in the home; a transitional period where family members worked together both inside and outside the home; and a separation between economic life and family life.[4] Direct selling organizations claim to offer an alternative to the model of separate spheres.

In this country's preindustrial economy of largely agrarian and craft workers, the family represented an economic unit. In this first arrangement, parents worked closely together and children were important contributors to families' livelihoods, for example, as farmhands and apprentices. As Ann Oakley writes, "The [preindustrial] unit of production is the unit of kin relationships, and life is not divided into what one does to earn a living — called work — and what one does the rest of the time."[5] Modern distinctions between work and play, adulthood and childhood, were very much blurred.

Seventeenth-century American families, typical of preindustrial economies, often had a sexual division of labor: men and women typically performed different household and money-raising tasks. This division was very flexible, though, as pointed out by Rosalyn Baxandall and her colleagues:

> In the Colonial Period the husbands of poor or middling women were usually farmers, artisans or small shopkeepers, and in these cases the men did their work at or near home also. Craft or retail shops were usually part of the home, and women often assisted in their husbands' work. Furthermore, the closeness of communities and absence of mechanical devices made sharing and cooperation, even in housework tasks, necessary.[6]

Even where work was divided by sex, the contributions of both men and women were understood to be critical to their mutual livelihood. Men's labor produced income while women's work conserved money that otherwise would be spent in the marketplace on goods and services.

A second work/family relationship came about with the rise of early industrial capitalism from about 1770 to 1830. In this period a few early factories were established in urban areas. More frequently, women took in piecework manufacturing in their homes. Organized production, both in the first American factories and by home-workers, began to produce for the marketplace goods that previously had been made only for personal consumption. According to Alice Kessler-Harris, "By 1800 [the family] had begun to turn to manufactories for some of its essentials. In an uneven pattern, beginning in the settled northeastern areas about 1790 and extending west and south over the next fifty years, manufactured products — yard goods, candles, brooms — began to replace those formerly made in the household."[7]

The transition from an agrarian economy to an industrial one was spurred in part by the demand for goods produced only laboriously at home, such as textiles, and for laborsaving farm machinery. These purchases required money — scarce in a barter economy.

Families, taking advantage of the new implements and manufactures, no longer needed the labor of all their members all the time. Moreover, they needed the cash that wage labor would bring to service new debts. During this transition from a preindustrial to a fully industrial economy, women and children were especially important sources of wage labor, both in factories and as pieceworkers at home. They worked for cash while some men worked at their traditional occupations. Over these decades more men entered the factories as full-time workers.

In this early industrial era the family was still the important economic unit, even as members moved outside the home to work. Rosabeth Kanter describes the system in which "spinners in textile mills chose their wives, children, and near relatives as assistants, generally paying them from their own wages. Children entering the factory at eight or nine worked for their fathers, perpetuating the old system of authority and the traditional values of parents training children for occupations."[8] Families performed many of the tasks we associate with management today: recruiting, supervision, and discipline.[9]

By the 1890s the spilling over of the family onto the factory floor was becoming less common, and a third work/family relationship developed. The rapidly growing industrial economy created more opportunities for men to earn income off the farm, and capitalist ideology urged the movement of young men into the wage-labor force. In this period approaching the turn of the century, Janet Clark says, men's "success or failure was identified with their skillful ability to support their own nuclear family."[10] Men were expected to be "good providers" to their wives and children.

Professional management increasingly replaced kinship as an important means of labor discipline. Unmarried and widowed women continued to work in the factories, but the new norm for middle-class families became the wage-earning husband and the wife at home.

It was the blossoming of industrial capitalism that produced the separation of spheres we associate with the modern family. Men went "out into the world" to earn a wage, and middle-class women were pressured to stay at home, largely isolated from the public world of politics and the economy. Just as an important ideology sustained men in the "good provider" role, new ideas developed in the Victorian era to justify women's new place. The "cult of true womanhood" supported the notion that women were a critical counterbalance to the harsh public life of industrial capitalism. Women were seen as uniquely able to provide nurturing and respite for men, and they were expected to cultivate the moral and spiritual realms for their families. Though women were understood to be men's moral superiors, they became legal and economic inferiors. Although less affluent women continued to perform wage labor, a new social ideal denigrated their work outside the home.

The domestic labor of married middle-class women, now frequently aided by employed domestic workers, made it possible for men to enter the paid work force. Middle-class women's privatized and unpaid labor, however, lost status in a now moneyed economy. Women became dependent on men's wages, while their own labor became economically invisible.[11]

Although this arrangement served industrial capitalism well for decades, it had substantial drawbacks for both men and women, at least viewed retrospectively. Women lost marketable skills and the psychological benefits that accrue from publicly recognized work. They lost economic and social independence; the course of their lives was determined by making a "good" marriage. Men now had the entire economic burden of the family on their shoulders. More than that, a man's entire selfhood was dependent on his success as a breadwinner. "Success in the good-provider role came in time to define masculinity itself," says Jessie Bernard, and men were less valued for their performance as fathers and mates.[12] Men, as economic heads of households, encroached on women's decision making in the domestic sphere, often conserving the right to control the purse and to make other significant household decisions.[13] Sociologists have debated whether, on balance, this role served men's interests, but it certainly further undermined the unity of the family.[14] Moreover, the entire family lost the subtle benefits of closeness, of joint effort in securing their livelihood.

This separation of spheres characteristic of industrial capitalism began to break down in the 1940s and 1950s when increasing numbers of women entered the "men's world" of the labor force. By the 1970s more than 40% of American women were in the public sphere of work. The transition since then to a new, more egalitarian model for work and family may be emerging to accommodate this economic shift, but if so, it is only in fits and starts. As women enter the public sphere they expect their husbands to assume domestic chores and to perform some of the emotional labor in the family. Numerous studies show, though, that even as women enter the work force they continue to do most of the housework.[15] While a more caring role model for men may be developing, it is at best half-formed. For many men, giving up the good provider role means giving up self-control and control of the family.

Network DSOs grew at precisely the moment when a family/work relationship predicated on a separation of spheres was under tension. Direct selling organizations offered an alternative vision of work and family to a population seeking new solutions: an *integration* of the domestic and economic spheres reminiscent of preindustrial America. Direct selling offers flexible work arrangements to women and sometimes allows them to work and care for children at the same time; it lets women "have it all." In network DSOs that attract both men and women, direct selling promises a shared work life and the emotional benefits to marriage that ensue from economic partnership. For women whose entry into a firm-dominated labor force has been less than happy, DSOs promise working conditions that emulate the nurturing character of the domestic sphere they are familiar with. The promise and the reality, however, are not always the same.

## A Family Business

The preoccupation with "family" among network DSOs is nothing less than extraordinary when compared with the whole of American business. All the DSOs I studied expressed concern with the effect of work on family. Many of them have an ideology of family participation that permeates their literature and public meetings. An A. L. Williams distributor told me that "as a company, there's no question that A. L. Williams is absolutely committed to producing more successful families than any other company in the history of the world," not only through product sales, but through organization.

Many network DSOs integrate the family into the business of selling, using its powerful emotions and authority structure to serve economic ends, not unlike the factories of the 1800s. In some instances DSOs manage the obstacle that competing family ties present. Unlike most firms, network DSOs recognize the power of the family and attempt to harness or actively divert it. Not all DSOs stress the work/family linkage to the same extent, and they vary in how they solicit family participation or acceptance, but four family-management strategies are common in the industry.

*1. Network DSOs encourage the recruitment of family members.* The "family tree" of a DSO line is often filled with actual relatives who have sponsored each other into the business. Nephews, sisters, brothers, and cousins are prime targets for sponsorship. There are many mother and daughter units in Mary Kay Cosmetics. In DSOs where both men and women sell, such as Amway and Shaklee, there is very strong pressure for spouses to build an organization together. Recognition awards and promotion through status levels are often given to couples, not individuals. Attendance at meetings by only one spouse raises eyebrows in some lines. The Amway and Shaklee house organs are filled with pictures of couples who have achieved success together. An A. L. Williams distributor described his preferred recruits:

Although we have some very successful single people, we try to stay away from single people. A lot of times, if they want to become involved, they do so. If we're going to pick and choose, we will pick people who are married and have similar lives, families.

A Shaklee distributor, a divorcee, described her status in that organization:

[As a single person] I'm looked at as kind of rare. In fact, the home office has called me and had me talk to a group about what it is like to build a Shaklee business as a single person.

Recruiting people with whom there is an existing social bond, such as relatives, creates a good basis for business relations in direct selling. When mothers encourage daughters and cousins support each other in their selling, the act reproduces their nonbusiness relations. Support in selling appears to spring from a long-term foundation of caring, and the financial self-interest of sponsors is obscured. In fact, for distributors who are committed to the ideology of direct selling, there is no separation between the interest of the loved one and self-interest: they truly want to share their commitment with those they love.

Recruiting spouses utilizes the emotions and authority relations of marriage for business purposes, as I discuss further below. However, even in DSOs where only women sell, husbands are sometimes a co-optive target of the organization. In Mary Kay Cosmetics, for example, gaining husbands' support is an explicit corporate goal. Husbands are invited to attend Seminar, the annual meeting for beauty consultants, and are given a parallel three-day schedule of activities. They are briefed by the company's executives, paid a visit by Mary Kay Ash, and treated to a recreation program that may include a top sports figure such as Arnold Palmer. Winners of the sports competitions, including a bowling tournament with pink bowling pins, are given recognition at a ceremony not unlike those for beauty consultants. One distributor described the purpose of including husbands in Seminar:

They are treated so royally and so wonderfully that they want their wives to belong to this organization. So that is kind of a psychology on Mary Kay's part. These men are really treated with kid gloves. I mean, you couldn't imagine how it must make them feel for Mary Kay to say how wonderful they are.

Husbands who do not attend Seminar are not neglected. Mary Kay Ash sends a telegram to the husband of each participating woman thanking him for, as one beauty consultant put it, "eating scrambled eggs and frozen dinners" and taking care of the children.

The president of another DSO said it is crucial to gain the husband's acceptance of his wife's work and is an important management strategy in direct selling.

> A lot of [our talk to husbands] is very casual, but it's very direct. It starts with top management, and [then] our regional managers see how we handle the husbands. So when they start recruiting people, one of the first things they do is bring the husbands in. They take them to dinner. They bring them to sales meetings and make them a part of it. At a high-level convention or meeting with top-level awards, we call both husband and wife up, and we let [the audience] know that this woman could not be successful without his support and backing.

This same company uses the husbands of successful distributors to explain to the husbands of new recruits how they can assist their wives. The subliminal message is that other "real men" accept their wives' selling. "And so they begin to realize, 'Well, gosh, that's no big deal if I baby-sit and fix dinner. Sure, I can do it.'"

Husbands' approval is critical in companies such as Mary Kay and Tupperware. Much selling takes place at night, and husbands must handle child care alone and accept the absence of their wives.

*2. Network DSOs espouse an ideology that claims family is more important than work.* For many people who feel guilty because their work leads them to neglect spouses and children, an industry that encourages the subordination of work to family seems worthy of commitment. Mary Kay Cosmetics, Home Interiors and Gifts, A. L. Williams, and a number of other DSOs support the aphorism "God first, family second, career third." This phrase was recited frequently in interviews. For example:

> I want to succeed financially. That's not the most important thing in my life. My God's first, and my family is second. My wife knows that I could quit A. L. Williams in a minute if it meant losing her and my family.

DSOs' professed support of this formula for organizing one's life is comforting to people who believe its tenets. The reality does not always match the formula, however.

> There was a time there when I was going crazy with Mary Kay. That's all I thought about. I ate it, I drank it, I slept it. Everything, OK? And

things were getting just crazy for me. I was feeling guilty. I was feeling like I was taking time away from my family.

Sometimes it is hard to put Mary Kay third, sometimes the others get shoved down the line a bit. . . . It is just a continuing effort remembering to put it third instead of first.

It is not clear that distributors, especially committed ones, organize their lives differently than they would if they had other attractive occupations.[16] Direct selling is seductive, and for some distributors it becomes the center of their lives. That revered founders such as Mary Kay Ash and Art Williams profess commitment to families, however, is comforting to distributors struggling to reconcile work and home.

3. *Network DSOs argue that a commitment to direct selling can strengthen marriages.* The promise of a closer marital bond is an important recruiting point in some DSOs, including Amway. What direct selling can do for a marriage is "a big carrot," as one distributor put it. "The greatest marriages, the most absolutely blissful relationships I have ever witnessed, have been in this business." DSOs hold out the possibility of a shared enterprise that will bring not only riches, but emotional closeness.

Even DSOs where only women sell promote direct selling as healthful for marriages. Women who become entrepreneurs are described as more interesting to their husbands. These wives have another way to strengthen the marriage bond. A number of women, in fact, said their husbands took an interest in their businesses. One woman described how her Mary Kay business gave her some influence with her husband:

We have a new line of communication. We got to talking the other night about customer service and were just sitting there really going at it. I have a little more clout. If I had talked to him about customer service five years ago, I didn't have a lot of clout because where was I coming from? You know, I might have been on the tennis court all day long.

The breakdown of the good provider role has left many families struggling both with the problem of generating new income and with maintaining the "face" of husbands whose paychecks are insufficient for family needs. This problem is widespread, but most corporations treat it as a private concern. A number of DSOs, however, deal with this emotional issue quite openly, although they vary in how they manage it. Some urge recognition of pressure on husbands to recruit wives into selling. Direct selling becomes a way of expressing wifely love.

Mary Kay says there's a lot of men out there who are going to go to their graves earlier because they have to work so hard. What's wrong with helping your husband out and sharing? In this day and age most women work, so why not work and get the most out of it, plus have time for your family?

Some companies, particularly those that recruit women largely from blue-collar families, such as Tupperware, downplay the "career" character of direct selling. Selling is presented as a way to make money that does not threaten the essential position of the husband as head of household.

Yet others actively attempt to preserve the good provider role for families that fear its loss. These companies, including to varying degrees Amway, A. L. Williams, and Shaklee, maintain an image of the family as one with the husband in control and the wife as a submissive helper. A sexual division of labor is encouraged within the couple's direct selling business: men go out to demonstrate the business opportunity to prospects, while women do the inside work of managing product sales and demonstrations. Women are supposed to encourage their husbands to greater efforts, to help them be "winners." Stephen Butterfield, a former distributor, described an Amway leadership seminar that included separate lectures for husbands and wives trying to build successful businesses:

The male leader told the husbands to be gentle and considerate in their sexual approaches to their wives; the lady should be wooed with furs, jewelry and candlelight dinners in expensive restaurants. The female leader told the wives to submit to their husbands cheerfully, even if they thought it was unpleasant sometimes, because a man needed to feel like a winner in the bedroom as well as out in that livingroom showing the Plan. The year was 1980. I wondered if I had been caught in some time-[warp].[17]

As Butterfield describes it, some DSOs attempt to stop the clock of social change at a familiar, reassuring time while maintaining the modern rhetoric of economic partnership.

Direct selling organizations are aggressive in attempting to manage families, but they are not always successful. Those with women distributors routinely fail at co-opting husbands, according to my interviews. A Tupperware distributor, a Mary Kay sponsor, and an industry executive spoke of how husbands posed significant hurdles to achieving business goals:

My husband, the only way he supports me is baby-sitting and helping me spend the money. Otherwise I get no support from him at all.

That's a real drain. I'm always just running, trying to get everything done so he doesn't have anything to complain about when I leave. I don't know if I'm going to get to go to Jubilee [Tupperware's annual meeting], because if he throws too big a stink about it, it's just not worth the fight.

The consultants who are doing well, they're either single and don't have a husband, or if you're married, you've got to hope that your husband is supportive. It's that middle husband, the one who is insecure himself, the one who has to have dinner on the table at five and never wants to baby-sit [who is a problem]. There are a lot of men who are like that, and there are women who cater to that.

If a husband is the type where his ego needs the glory, the applause, and he has to be center stage with the spotlight on him, it won't work. Because all those [downline recruits] are there because of her, not him. What will work is if the guy is smart enough to realize that he has to keep her in the spotlight. She's the number one, and he sits back and gives her tips.

A wife's absences from home and her business success are sometimes tolerated by otherwise recalcitrant husbands because of the income she earns. Mary Kay Ash has a much-repeated saying for beauty consultants: "If you want to keep your husband excited, stay thin and make bank deposits."

4. *Children are a fourth way DSOs solicit distributors' commitment.* All stress that flexible work arrangements allow parents to put their children's schedules before work. Some distributors like being able to work with their children present — for example, when they deliver products, or solicit business. One Mary Kay beauty consultant approaches women with her young son:

My little boy, he got so used to me approaching women at the shopping mall that he would ask the ladies first, "Do you use Mary Kay cosmetics?" He was only four years old at the time. Of course I would bring my card out and I would say, "Could I have your name and number?" And he would say, "Address, too." I had to calm him down a bit.

Women, especially, cite the ease of integrating their roles as mother and worker as a reason for doing direct sales. For some, particularly blue-collar women who treat direct selling as a sideline and not a "real job," they can have the happy combination of making money and being an "at home" mother. One Tupperware dealer put it this way:

I was driving my son and four friends to a birthday party, and I heard them talking in the back about their moms working. And one of the kids says, "Say, does your mommy work?" And he goes, "No." That's what I want. I don't want them to think I work. They don't even think that I have a job because I'm not gone from eight to five.

Network DSOs that recruit husband-and-wife teams usually try to integrate the children into the business in some way. Children sometimes attend meetings held in parents' homes and are occasionally included at conventions and other events.[18] Many children of Amway and Shaklee distributors are paid to deliver products, take telephone orders, and otherwise participate in their parents' business. The ideology of a family business is realized in some homes, with all members participating in some fashion.

In DSOs with strong entrepreneurial ideologies, the parents' continuing commitment is often sustained because of their belief in the importance of teaching their children the moral principles of capitalist enterprise. This is not unlike parents' going to church because it sets a good example for their children. A father and a mother spoke about the influence of direct selling on their children's development:

I have a ten-year-old son. He's my partner. Most of our social life revolves around either his school or A. L. Williams. He's very, very supportive. As a matter of fact, for a ten-year-old, he's one of my best recruiters. He'll talk to his friends about asking if their parents could use extra money. . . . It's teaching him how to set his goals and what he wants out of life.

I have bought a division under Avacare for my daughter and have it on ice because she's only twenty. But I figured when she gets older she will have that division. I have sponsored my son into another multilevel marketing company, and I'm helping him develop that business. . . . What I'm doing with my children is much more than earning money [for them]. It's teaching them. They will be totally self-sufficient by the time they get married. They will never go on welfare. That would just break my heart.

Some DSOs actively encourage parents to see their selling as a critical part of their children's moral education. One Amway tape, for example, encourages children to be their parents' paid helpers and to view unearned allowances as "welfare for children."

The inclusion of children in the business is sometimes more illusory than real, however. Although children may perform some business-related work at home, by its very nature direct selling requires parents to be away from home a lot. Direct selling is also hard work, and active distributors find it demanding. Some parents spoke of this problem:

> I'm not there all the time—I can't be. I've got to work harder now than I've ever worked in my life. But when I do take off I spend quality time. I don't go home and watch television like I used to do five years ago. I can afford to do some things and spend time that the kids are going to remember.

> A lot of beauty consultants have kids. . . . I sort of have this uncomfortable feeling. . . . I don't know. There is sort of that superwoman consciousness about it all. You can do it. You can look beautiful and sell products and work full time and get home on time.

Children are actively co-opted by some DSOs. Amway, for instance, encourages parents to let children choose an item from their product catalog as a "goal." The picture of the item is taped to the refrigerator, along with a calendar. Each night that their father goes out to show the business plan to a prospective recruit, the children check off a space. When enough spaces are checked, they receive the item. The parent's absence is made to serve children's material interests. As an Amway distributor put it, eventually "there will be freedom for us from jobs, and we'll be able to be together as a family," but in the meantime "there are rewards for them."[19]

Direct selling's flexible schedule does make it possible for family needs to be accommodated. As more wives and mothers enter the labor force, part-time jobs, flex-time, temporary work, and other new work arrangements are appearing. Corporate America is beginning to recognize and make some adjustment to the nonwork lives of its employees. Most firms, though, offer these new arrangements not so that the barrier between family and work can be lowered, but so that it can remain high.[20]

Direct selling uses a very different strategy. It begins by recognizing the pull of family obligations and certifying them as real and important. In some instances it uses those ties to serve business purposes, for example, by encouraging the recruitment of relatives and sustaining commitment for the children's sake. The industry even uses the desire to be with loved ones to urge work outside the home. The contradiction inherent in this ploy may be blatant, but the appeal is effective precisely because of the strong commitment people feel to their families. In an industry that cannot rely on bureaucratic controls, harnessing the emotions, aspirations, and fears of families is an important business strategy.

## The Metaphorical Family

By integrating the family into business activity, direct selling organizations use existing social ties for economic purposes. The industry also does the reverse, making the economic ties of sponsorship the basis for familylike social relations. DSOs are "metaphorical families." The result of both strategies is to create a double-stranded bond far stronger than either one alone. Moreover, pecuniary self-interest and affective interest in the other are indistinguishable.

Metaphorical expressions of kinship, what anthropologists call "fictive relations," are widely employed in network DSOs. The expressions vary by individual and by organization, but distributors commonly understand themselves as "family" or, in Tupperware, as "close friends." For example, Mary Kay Cosmetics is a "sisterhood."

Whereas individuals employed by firms tend to describe their positions in the organization by function or level, such as "accountant" or "supervisor," in DSOs people use kinship terms to describe their place. Lines in companies such as Amway and Shaklee are often spoken of as branches on a "family tree." People trace their "genealogies" by identifying their upline sponsors. Amway lines have "family reunions." Women in Mary Kay are "sisters," but Tupperware distributors are "daughter dealers" to their "mother managers." In Cameo Coutures, a recruit's sponsor is likewise her "mother," and the mother's sponsor is the recruit's "grandmother." When a Mary Kay distributor has enough recruits to form her own unit, she becomes the "offspring" of her director. Movement up the director ranks is measured in part by the number of offspring a woman gives birth to.

The overlay of a metaphorical family on top of blood ties and marital bonds creates some interesting organizational relations. For example, one Mary Kay beauty consultant's real sister is her "offspring." Her mother remains in her unit as a consultant. Thus all three are "sisters" in the larger enterprise.

Family metaphors also describe organizational activities. In Amway and a number of other DSOs, recruiting people to set up their own business is called "duplication." Duplication means doing exactly as the upline does, but it also refers to an organizational growth strategy reminiscent of biological asexual reproduction. Tupperware uses the terminology of courtship to describe securing appointments for home parties: these are "dates." "Dating" future hostesses is understood to be a crucial job at a party. In Shaklee and some other DSOs, a distributor whose line becomes inactive is known as an "orphan." There are "adoption" rules that regulate the incorporation of orphans into active lines.

Family metaphors refer not only to positional relations and activities, but also to the *content* of ties between distributors. "Family" establishes an ideal of loving, nurturing relations between distributors; the metaphor establishes normative expectations. For example, distributors assume familylike obligations toward each other in their conduct of business. The obligations typically extend beyond the economic sphere, too. Amway and Mary Kay distributors described this situation:

> I found a family I had never had. There was a tremendous amount of support to achieve. I went through a divorce about five years after I got into the business, and I took five years off from actively building my organization. In that time period I was never forgotten. I would get postcards once in a while, and it made me feel like I was still part of something. There was a tremendous amount of love and acceptance, support in growing.

> There is a sisterhood charisma between all the consultants. I have been stranded at airports and know for a fact [it's true]. One time I was stranded two days in Denver because of a storm. All I did was look in the phone book under "Mary Kay Cosmetics," and the [local] director came over to have lunch with me. I know that anywhere I go I can call up a sister consultant and I'll be taken to her home.

"Family" provides a powerful model for intraorganizational relations. It is a satisfying conceptualization for distributors who are welcomed into a network of emotional ties and not seen merely as "workers" or financially significant "recruits." There is a preservation of personhood in some DSOs that is conspicuously absent in many corporations. "Family" also provides a well-understood model for interpersonal relations, especially useful to people without significant paid work experience. Direct selling puts them in familiar interactional territory by importing the logic of one institution — the family — for use in another — business.

"Family" has distinctive management advantages.[21] In an industry that cannot oversee intraorganizational relations very effectively, the metaphor provides a flexible guide to relations for distributors. For example, while all distributors are formally competitors for sales to consumers and all believe in free enterprise and competition, the notion of "family" mutes destructive competitive practices. "Mothers" do not compete with "daughters." Internecine warfare is thwarted by distributors' embracing family norms. Caring relations are typically interpreted to mean helping each other to be successful — that is, generating profit for the individual and the company.

The management of Mary Kay Cosmetics discovered the force with which the family metaphor is held when it completed a leveraged buy-out. Mary Kay

Ash and her son Richard Rogers, cofounders of the company, bought back all publicly owned stock in 1985, returning the company to family ownership. The company had faced a decline in the period just before the buy-out, and management was concerned with the beauty consultants' interpretation of the financial transaction, hoping they would not understand it as an act of weakness. One executive described how the family metaphor provided a useful interpretive vehicle for the sales force:

> The word "family" in Mary Kay means something. People consider themselves part of the family. All of a sudden they're asking, "What does this buy-out mean?" [They've come up with the answer]: "Everything's back and owned by the family." All of a sudden they feel like — I don't know what's going through their minds — "We weren't family before, but now we're back?" "All of those outsiders had stock, we got rid of them?" If I've heard it once, I've heard it a thousand times, "It's great to be family again."

A family strategy, in both its "real" and its metaphorical forms, utilizes strong emotional bonds and social patterns to inspire and channel economic activity. It also sustains an interactional character within the industry that is wholly distinctive.

## A "Feminine" Organization

The organization men described by C. Wright Mills and William F. Whyte in the 1950s were rational beings, outwardly calm if inwardly anxious. While the prototypical white collar worker of the 1980s may inhabit a looser corporate culture and exhibit a friendlier mien, today's corporate worker is clearly a descendant of the forebears Mills and Whyte described.

The character of corporate workers, then and now, is shaped in important part by the world of work they inhabit. Bureaucratically organized corporations establish norms for interaction that flow from their roots in economic rationality. Workers are urged to be analytic and results oriented. Interpersonal relations are typically impersonal and segmental; people relate to each other primarily in terms of the positions they occupy. The hierarchical ranking of positions makes everyone aware of even subtle power differences, discouraging collegiality. Promotion on the basis of merit pits employees against one other and supports an atmosphere of aggressive individualism. Individual success in firms is a zero-sum proposition: if I win the promotion to manager, everyone else loses. These conditions combine to create a work environment distinctive to firms. Not surprisingly, as Mills put it, workers' "very self-images, what they do and what they are, are derived from the enterprise."[22]

This corporate world is a man's world in more than one sense. The valued pattern of relations is "masculine," as we understand that concept in this society. Social action among bureaucratic officials is characterized by aggressive individualism and instrumentalism; the structure of the firm rewards independence and competition. These are social traits that we associate with men. Paul Hirsch's fascinating study of the history of takeovers and mergers in the United States shows how the standards of business activity have changed in the past twenty-five years "from the world of a gentleman's club toward that of a street-fighter's brawl."[23] Though changed, it remains a man's world.

The character of relations mirrors and supports the structure of power. If possessing "masculine" interactional skills is critical to making it up the ladder of success, then women are clearly disadvantaged. If men control the top positions in corporate America — and they do — they can maintain the conditions that sustain their dominance. Feminist scholars have argued, in fact, that bureaucracy is inherently patriarchal, not a neutral tool for getting work done. They argue that the structure of firm organization, including its patterns of control and its reproduction of men's culture, excludes women as a class. Numerous studies show that women workers tend to inhabit occupational categories that do not lead to important decision making positions. They have "women's jobs," less-valued positions that utilize stereotypical female traits of support and nurturing.

Even if the evidence shows that women as a group disproportionately occupy lower-level, less well-paid positions, individual women have made it to top jobs. The number of highly educated young women with M.B.A. degrees has increased women's presence in managerial circles. Even such privileged women, however, face the choice of conforming to the machismo model of management or being branded as "soft," a corporate synonym for "inept."[24] Marilyn Loden, a consultant who has studied women executives, finds that some are resisting the pressure to remake themselves to fit male models of competence. "Many talented women find that the sacrifices required of them so outweigh the potential rewards that they decide to leave corporate life altogether."[25] The corporate world gives women a tough choice: use their womanly skills in the less-valued, subordinate "women's jobs," or act like men.

Some feminists have argued that if women are to achieve power in the economy it is critical to pursue a third strategy: create organizations that utilize and value women's cultural preferences and competencies.[26] Such organizations would have minimal hierarchies, encourage participative decision making, and value intuitive as well as analytic approaches to work. Relations would be characterized as nurturing and cooperative rather than instrumental and individualistic. Indeed, some women's organizations, including *Ms.* magazine, have consciously adopted such organizational forms in an effort to empower women on their own terms.[27]

This feminist agenda for organizations parallels in important ways the reality of network DSOs. DSOs have a status hierarchy but no hierarchy of authority. While there is ideological support for the idea of the "independent entrepreneur," distributors in fact see themselves as connected in a network of social relations. There are strong norms in DSOs for encouraging others in both practical and emotional ways. A Tupperware distributor and an Amway distributor described this ethic:

> Everybody wants everybody else to succeed. It's not like competition that you get in some jobs where I don't want you to know what I know because if you do, then you can take my job. I want to share with you what made me successful, so you can be successful too.

> You don't find some one-star general encouraging some colonel to go ahead [of him] and say, "Hey, I'll help you and you can become a four-star general over me." No, you don't find that. But in this business we encourage people to go ahead of us. We don't care where they go. If they want to make eight times more money than I made, that's great.

The financial structure of direct selling does not result in zero-sum relations: one distributor's success may directly contribute to the earnings of upline sponsors. That distributors' mutual encouragement may be self-interested in no way negates the "feminine" character of relations that result, however. People applaud and are genuinely happy when others do well. There are hugs and kisses for even small successes. In DSOs tears accompany disappointment and pleasure without people's feeling shame or appearing weak. Cooperation is far more efficacious than competition as a form of economic action in DSOs. As a Tupperware dealer put it, "In this business you don't get to the top unless you take a lot of people with you."

Feminists, in urging the formation of organizations that celebrate and utilize women's skills, see this as a strategy of empowering women. Feminine organizations create a world of work where women are able to pursue success as themselves, not by adopting an alien masculine orientation. This strategy is an attempt to take the pattern of social relations that characterizes the domestic sphere, in which women are skilled, and use it to women's advantage in the public sphere of the economy and the polity.

Direct selling, with its stress on nurturing and cooperation, its absence of authority differences, is clearly feminine when compared with the bureaucratic firm. Indeed, it is in part the character of its interpersonal relations that attracts so many women: DSOs feel familiar, feel "right," to women distributors. Network DSOs' co-opting of the family and their creation of a metaphorical family reproduce to an extraordinary extent the social structure of the private sphere within an economic organization.

## Does Direct Selling Empower Women?

Is an organization that accords so well with women's experiences and abilities feminist? Does it lead to more power for women as individuals and as a class? The answer that comes from this study of the direct selling industry is clearly mixed. My interviews suggest that network DSOs empower women as individuals in significant ways. They also suggest that the industry does not challenge, and sometimes reinforces, the patriarchal structure of society.

Women distributors spoke of at least three ways direct selling gives them influence. First, they describe the power that an independent income gives them in marriage. This sort of power is not granted exclusively by direct selling, of course, but women who would not or could not do other types of work find DSOs a possible route to economic strength. As a Tupperware dealer put it, "My husband has this claw on the checkbook, and he doesn't like to share it. So having my own income gives me a little bit more freedom." She established her own checking account, an act of independence, at the encouragement of her "mother manager."

Although most women do direct selling part time and earn very modest amounts, it does provide a route to a good, even substantial income for very hardworking women with a talent for this form of business. The fifty-nine national sales directors in Mary Kay Cosmetics earn over $100,000 each—some two or three times that figure—and there are women in other established DSOs who have large incomes. The nurturing skills these women used to achieve success in direct selling would not have been valued in corporate settings.

Distributors spoke, second, of how their work in direct selling is a source of influence with their children. Many believe that direct selling allows them to be more than "just a mom" in a society that values economic achievement and allows them to be role models to their daughters. As one woman said, "[my daughter] sees me in a very independent role, yet whenever she needs me I'm always there."

Third, and perhaps most important, direct selling gives women the *experience* of being powerful. Women who have been in subordinate positions all their lives and, further, had seen other women only as dependents, spoke of the pleasure of being thought of as skilled and able. For many, direct selling gave them their first glimpse of their own sex in the role of competent adult. A Mary Kay beauty consultant described her first direct selling function:

> I couldn't believe it. [These women] were just bubbling. I had never been around a bunch of women who were not talking about their kids, not talking about so-and-so running around with so-and-so, you know, all the negative things and about household chores. You see, that's what I had been around because I had been home for a while. Housewifey things. These women were talking about *business*.

The entrance to the Mary Kay Cosmetics headquarters in Dallas, Texas, is an impressive sight for the thousands of women who visit each year. The vestibule has the requisite oil painting of the founders, Mary Kay Ash and Richard Rogers, in a prominent place. Where one would expect to find pictures of pinstriped male executives or corporate directors, there are large paintings of the national sales directors, the industrious women who sustain the sales force. The display of fifty-nine images of hugely successful women is jarring because it so thoroughly violates expectations. Women who see other women succeed begin to imagine the possibility for themselves.

Women's DSOs, such as Mary Kay Cosmetics, Home Interiors and Gifts, and Tupperware, celebrate women's abilities in business. They are unabashedly women's worlds where pink Cadillacs, fur coats, and warm hugs are as much a part of the organizational culture as aggressive individualism is part of a firm's. While they differ from one other, they all have the character of sororities: women's spheres where women enjoy each other and act "naturally." In DSOs where men also sell, the atmosphere is different but still familylike and expressive.

Although women distributors have been empowered personally and economically by direct selling, and though women's DSOs celebrate women's abilities as a whole, direct selling does not challenge existing social arrangements in which women are subordinate.[28] In particular, the model of the family that DSOs embrace includes a submissive wife.

The submissive wife role is expressed most overtly in DSOs that recruit husband-and-wife teams. For example, A. L. Williams recruits the whole family, but the expectation is that only the husband will sell insurance. The wife will do her part by giving her husband moral support and encouragement and by not complaining when he is out at night trying to bolster their income.

A. L. Williams has a Partners' Organization run by Williams's wife Angela. Angela Williams is, like her husband, a gifted orator and tells a very moving story about how her support of Art's business was critical to his success against great odds. She urges the "partners" in rally audiences to do the same and, further, to participate in her auxiliary organization.

There are women A. L. Williams agents, but the model the organization supports is clearly that of the traditional family.

> [Angela Williams] runs a great Partners' Organization, which is the wives' side of things. And we have some male partners, too. They get together for monthly meetings on how to support us. Next week they're doing a pep rally. They're going all out — they make costumes, pom-poms. So my wife is just loving the business too.

> [My wife doesn't sell insurance], definitely not. She's not licensed. Some wives get licensed, just so they can talk about it a little more, but they don't have to be licensed. That doesn't mean they can't go out and actively crusade our concepts. They can recruit people. They can talk about what we do a little bit, and then refer them to us. But my wife's taking an active role in building up the Partners' Organization.

Amway, Shaklee, and United Science of America distributors similarly follow a sexual division of labor. The husband shows the business plan while women sell vitamins or cosmetics to their friends and keep the books.[29]

More than one woman said her husband paid no attention to her business at first, but after she began to make a good income he became involved. A Shaklee wife said it was not uncommon for retired husbands to take over the businesses their wives had built.

In fact, Tupperware has institutionalized this practice. Only women are dealers, the beginning level of distributor. Managers, the next level, may be single women or husband-and-wife teams. Such teams, in which a husband quits any other job, are called Total Tupper families and are regarded favorably by the company. The next level, a distributorship, for a long time could be assigned *only* to a husband-and-wife team. A woman's mobility was thus constrained by her husband's career choice. Although there have been exceptions to this practice in recent years, according to informants it remains the rule.

Occasionally, too, the Tupperware headquarters fills executive positions by recruiting from among the distributors. The husband always becomes the employee, although the wife may consider herself part of the team and travel with him at company expense. The paycheck, though, has only the husband's name on it. According to former Tupperware president Joe Hara, "We have to pay it to somebody. What we are trying to do is decide what is in the interest of good marital relations. . . . I know of no situations that involve a gal who doesn't want more free time."[30]

Even women's DSOs assume that a wife's duty is first to support her husband's needs and only then to care for her business. For example, Mary Crowley's book of aphorisms includes, "Don't marry a man you aren't willing to adjust to" and "Let the husband be the HEAD of the household and the wife be the neck. You never saw a head turn without the neck."[31] Mary Kay Ash's advice to beauty consultants is less religious and more witty. She is a sort of Erma Bombeck to working women, convinced of women's extraordinary abilities but urging women to coddle their way to autonomy. Her autobiography is filled with tidbits on how to gain a husband's support and manage a direct selling business so as to interfere as little as possible with a man's life at home. For example, she says she sometimes fooled her husband by putting a frozen dinner on a plate and heating it in the microwave oven: "Mel used to brag that I never served him a TV dinner, but I did sometimes — on a plate!"[32]

Mary Kay beauty consultants are urged to gain a husband's permission for a new recruit to begin work. A beauty consultant described how she did this:

> Because it's a family business, there is no way I want to recruit a lady without talking to her husband. Because eventually she is going to have to go to him for money or guidance and there'll be customers calling and coming, so he's going to have to get involved. I ask her, "Do you feel I need to sit down and talk with your husband?" If so, we will stop the interview right there and set another time so I can go and talk with them.

In truth, Mary Kay urges women to recognize that social realities such as divorce and the husbands' early death can leave women financially and socially on their own. She prompts women to learn to take care of themselves, but first to secure their husbands' support for such an undertaking. As one former beauty consultant put it, "Everything [Mary Kay] says, even listening to her inspirational tapes, is all directed to women. It has an undertone of 'we are capable, but we still have our place.' "

Traditional marital ties are also used to support profits in DSOs. Romantic love as the ideal bond between spouses emerged with the rise of industrial capitalism and the separation of spheres.[33] No longer tied by shared activities, husbands and wives were cemented by a new romantic model of mutual affection. Love is the critical social glue that holds the family together under the conditions of modern capitalism. There is an implicit exchange model in romantic love: women provide affection and sex, and men give their wives money and status.[34] Butterfield argues that the Amway line he belonged to exploited this exchange relationship and that sexual impulses, alternately suppressed and titillated, fueled economic activity:

> Despite their unintentional parody of Bible school sexual ethics, a great deal of subliminal — and perverted — sexuality goes on at Amway functions. Audiences are led in mass denunciations of soap operas dealing with the theme of adultery, husbands and wives are instructed from the stage to kiss and hold hands. Dexter Yager jokingly refers to the "other woman" in his life, who turns out to be his daughter; the wife of a prominent Diamond[-level distributor] calls the ladies to Christ by describing Jesus as a wonderful "hunk" of a man. But just beneath these comfortably square plugs for the monogamous "Christian" nuclear family lurks the tail of the serpent: the men strutting in their suits, leaving business cards on the chairs like dogs peeing on fire hydrants to mark their territories; the women arrayed in alluring and expensive costumes, turning heads as they pass; the equation of attractiveness with pin level ("I'm so glad my man is a *Winner*"); [and] the salacious play on the word "excited" (Are you *excited?* Show me how *excited* you are!).[35]

According to Butterfield, Amway distributors are encouraged to read books about preserving love in marriage.

Historians and sociologists who study the development of the family over time have debated whether the separation of spheres served women's interests.[36] Many agree that, at the least, the domestic sphere did create a world in which women could develop expertise and exercise a degree of independence and authority. It was a world in which women's values and culture were preserved. This arrangement, while to an extent liberating, did not threaten the essentially patriarchal character of the economy or the husband as head of the family.

I think this judgment fits the direct selling industry too. Network DSOs give women a sphere in which they can develop competence, a degree of economic independence, and the opportunity to interact in ways that do not do violence to their sense of themselves as women. But DSOs, even one led by such an obvious booster of women as Mary Kay Ash, do not challenge the prevailing sociopolitical arrangements of society. In fact, it is probably the compromise direct selling represents that has made it attractive to so many women. They can be personally empowered — *feel* liberated and modern — without upsetting the traditional premises of their lives.

Whether a women's organization is feminist depends not only on its grounding in women's culture, but on its political and ideological bases. Women's DSOs might be characterized as *prefeminist*, celebrating womanly abilities and values but not challenging dominant social structures.[37] It is also clear that creating economic organizations that emulate the domestic sphere can be used not only to empower women, as women's organizers hope, but to maintain their submission.

A quick look at network DSOs might lead an observer to conclude that they are an anachronism, a throwback to a preindustrial model of social organization where husbands, wives, and children worked and played together. In fact, direct selling organizations are a product of today. They are a response to families' desire to be together in an economy that keeps them apart and to a world of work that disadvantages women in several ways. Network direct selling organizations are one industry's opportunistic response to the segmented and gender-divided arrangements of postindustrial society.

## NOTES

1. The rhetoric and the reality are not always the same. For example, bureaucratic workers may be expected to bring work home at night and on weekends. The Lynds called this "the long arm of the job" (Lynd and Lynd 1959: chap. 7).
2. Weber saw patrimonialism as a direct inhibitor of the instrumentalism critical to development of rational administration and a capitalist economy (Roth and Wittich 1978: 237–41). Although impersonality is a professed ideal in firms, it does not always exist in practice precisely because families are such useful political resources. For example, as Charles Perrow (1986) describes it, "Relatives who work for you can be expected to hide your mistakes and incompetence, warn you about threats to your position, and support you in conflicts with others" (p. 7). Moreover, even where work and family are kept formally separate they influence each other indirectly. For example, work usually determines a family's economic and social status, the amount of scheduling of their time together, and the presence or absence of stress in the household. See Mortimer and London (1984: 20–42).
3. Kanter (1977: 15).
4. An important history of the family is Degler (1980). Although based on the European experience, Louise A. Tilly and Joan W. Scott's (1978) work clearly shows the relationship between the shape of the family and the shape of the economy under capitalist development.
5. Oakley (1976: 10).
6. Baxandall, Gordon, and Reverby (1976: 15).
7. Kessler-Harris (1982: 24–27).
8. Kanter (1977: 10).
9. See also Nelson (1975: chap. 5). Nelson argues that factories relied on families and ethnic communities as a recruiting source for unskilled labor into the early twentieth century, until the rise of scientific management.
10. Clark (1984).
11. The isolation of women as homemakers in the late nineteenth century and early twentieth century was not uniform. In general it occurred among middle-class women. Im-

migrant women, black women, and working-class women often continued to work outside the home. See Kessler-Harris (1982: chaps. 3–5).

12. Bernard (1984: 48).

13. The United States census assumed that the man was the head of household until the 1980 census.

14. Bernard (1984: 54–57).

15. Maret and Finley (1984) and Weiss (1985).

16. Other types of work outside the home might be said to make women more interesting to men. What is important, though, is that direct selling makes this argument and most other businesses do not.

17. Butterfield (1985: 116).

18. Children are welcome at some A. L. Williams rallies but typically not at Amway functions. Nor does Amway provide day care at events. Butterfield (1985) claims that day care is viewed as "creeping socialism," and "hiring babysitters is more consistent with the ideal of the nuclear family motivated by the pursuit of wealth: couples provide for their own, the lines are kept apart, and the distributor must strive harder to boost his [sales] in order to meet the cost" (p. 123).

19. This is an instance of what Bennett Berger (1981) calls "ideological work," that is, reconciling beliefs with the exigencies of living.

20. The family ideology of DSOs and other organizations that promote home work has a material basis too. These businesses profit by imposing on family members who answer phones, pack orders, baby sit, and otherwise sustain home workers. DSOs try to make a virtue of what is in their economic interests.

21. Direct selling is not the only form of enterprise to use the family metaphor. Large Japanese firms are also metaphorical families. Not coincidentally, Japanese business practice, like DSOs, stresses cooperation and mutes individualism.

22. Mills (1953: 109).

23. Hirsch (1986: 815).

24. Graduate business programs give middle-class women a chance to learn the instrumental-rational skills valued in corporations. Most women I interviewed did not have even this chance, of course.

25. Loden (1986: sec. 3, p. 2).

26. This separatist strategy was pursued with vigor by American women from 1870 to 1930. They developed an extensive institutional network known as the "women's club movement" that was both a response to rejection by men's public-sphere organizations and a desire for more feminine forms of organizing. See Freedman (1979) and Robinson (1985).

27. The studies of sociologist Nancy Chodorow (1978) and psychologist Carol Gilligan (1982) suggest reasons for some women's rejection of bureaucracy: girls' developmental experiences lead them to nurturing interpersonal orientations, in contrast to boys' being directed toward concern with individual rights and abstract responsibilities. The organizational implications of these developmental outcomes are profoundly different. For a review of extant literature on gender and organization see Hearn and Parkin (1983). Kathy E. Ferguson (1984) has written an analysis of bureaucracy as a patriarchal system.

28. Of course, network DSOs are capitalist enterprises, not social movement organizations dedicated to the emancipation of women. In fact, I argue below that their success stems in part from their not challenging prevailing arrangements in a substantial way.

29. The sexual division of labor is the reverse in women's DSOs. When men become involved they do the "inside" tasks of bookkeeping while women do the sales management.

30. Quoted by Wedemeyer (1975). This interesting article explores the congruence of
women's gender and working-class culture in Tupperware.

31. Crowley (1974: 46–47).

32. Ash (1981: 75).

33. See Degler (1980: 14–19).

34. This exchange is not an equal one. According to Francesca M. Cancian (1985), defining
love only as romantic and expressive "exaggerates women's dependence on men," who
are assumed to need romantic love less (men depend on women for sex, practical help,
and other loving activities that are not generally labeled as love in our society). Defining
love only in romantic terms further devalues women's domestic sphere by associating
love with sentimentalism, unappreciated in a society that prizes instrumental activity.

35. Butterfield (1985: 117).

36. Cf. Lantz, Keyes, and Schultz (1975) and Degler (1980: chap. 7).

37. This is a term suggested by Estelle Freedman (1979: 527). A prefeminist organization
may become feminist if "the group experience leads to insights about male domination"
and if the group is relatively autonomous from control by men. My study suggests that
the former condition holds in some women's DSOs but the latter does not.

## REFERENCES

Ash, Mary Kay. 1981. *Mary Kay.* New York: Harper and Row.

Baxandall, Rosalyn, Linda Gordon, and Susan Reverby. 1976. *America's Working Women: A
Documentary History 1600 to the Present.* New York: Random House Vintage Books.

Berger, Bennett. 1981. *The Survival of the Counter Culture: Ideological Work and Everyday Life
among Rural Communards.* Berkeley: University of California Press.

Bernard, Jessie. 1984. "The Good-Provider Role: Its Rise and Fall." In Patricia Voyandoff,
ed., *Work and Family: Changing Roles of Men and Women.* Palo Alto: Mayfield.

Butterfield, Stephen. 1985. *Amway: The Cult of Free Enterprise.* Boston: South End Press.

Cancian, Francesca M. 1985. "Gender Politics: Love and Power in the Private and Public
Spheres." In Alice Rossi, ed., *Gender and the Life Course* (pp. 253–64). New York:
Aldine.

Chodorow, Nancy. 1978. *The Reproduction of Mothering: Psychoanalysis and the Sociology of
Gender.* Berkeley: University of California Press.

Clark, Janet. 1984. "Women and Their Work: A Theory of Sexual Division of Labor and
Growth of Women in the Labor Force." *Social Science Journal* 21(4).

Crowley, Mary C. 1974. *Be Somebody . . . God Doesn't Take Time to Make a Nobody.* Dallas:
Crescendo.

Degler, Carl N. 1980. *At Odds: Women and the Family in America from the Revolution to the
Present.* Oxford: Oxford University Press.

Ferguson, Kathy E. 1984. *The Feminist Case against Bureaucracy.* Philadelphia: Temple University Press.

Freedman, Estelle. 1979. "Separatism as Strategy: Female Institution Building and American Feminism, 1870–1930." *Feminist Studies* 5(3): 512–29.

Gilligan, Carol. 1982. *In a Different Voice.* Cambridge, MA: Harvard University Press.

Hearn, Jeff, and P. Wendy Parkin. 1983. "Gender and Organizations: A Selective Review and a Critique of a Neglected Area." *Organization Studies* 4(3): 219–42.

Hirsch, Paul M. 1986. "From Ambushes to Golden Parachutes." *American Journal of Sociology* 91(4).

Kanter, Rosabeth Moss. 1977. *Work and Family in the United States: A Critical Review and Agenda for Research and Policy.* New York: Russell Sage Foundation.

Kessler-Harris, Alice. 1982. *Out to Work: A History of Wage-Earning Women in the United States.* Oxford: Oxford University Press.

Lantz, Herman R., Jane Keyes, and Martin Schultz. 1975. "The American Family in the Preindustrial Period: From Base Lines in History to Change." *American Sociological Review* 40(1): 21–36.

Loden, Marilyn. 1986. "A Machismo That Drives Women Out." *New York Times*, February 9, sec. 3.

Lynd, Robert S., and Helen Merrell Lynd. 1959. *Middletown: A Study in Contemporary American Culture.* New York: Harcourt, Brace.

Maret, Elizabeth and Barbara Finley. 1984. "The Distribution of Household Labor among Women in Dual-Earner Families." *Journal of Marriage and the Family* 46(2): 357–64.

Mills, C. Wright. 1953. *White Collar.* New York: Oxford University Press.

Mortimer, Jeylan T., and Jayne London. 1984. "The Varying Linkages of Work and Family." In Patricia Voyandoff, ed., *Work and Family: Changing Roles of Men and Women.* Palo Alto: Mayfield.

Nelson, Daniel. 1975. *Managers and Workers: Origins of the New Factory System in the United States, 1880–1920.* Madison: University of Wisconsin Press.

Oakley, Ann. 1976. *Woman's Work.* New York: Random House Vintage Books.

Perrow, Charles. 1986. *Complex Organizations: A Critical Essay.* New York: Random House.

Robinson, Patricia. 1985. "The Organizational Contrast of Past and Present Women's Groups: A Comparison of the Women's Committee of the Council of National Defense and the National Organization of Women." Paper presented at the meetings of the Pacific Sociological Association, Albuquerque, April.

Roth, Gunter, and Claus Wittich, eds. 1978. *Economy and Society.* Berkeley: University of California Press.

Tilly, Louise A., and Joan W. Scott. 1978. *Women, Work, and the Family.* New York: Holt, Rinehart and Winston.

Wedemeyer, Dee. 1975. "There's a Tupperware Party Starting Every Ten Seconds." *Ms.* 4(2).

Weiss, Robert. 1985. "Men and the Family." *Family Processes* 24: 49–58.

*Chapter 8*

# Reproducing Gender Relations in Large Law Firms: The Role of Emotional Labor in Paralegal Work

- Jennifer L. Pierce

## *Introduction*

S arah's boss, Richard, considers her to be an excellent paralegal. Richard, who is a highly successful partner in the legal department at Bonhomie Corporation, describes her as "highly organized, efficient, hard working, and possessing a terrific mind for details." But more importantly, he thinks she's one of the most intuitive people he's ever known: "She anticipates my every move. It's almost as though she reads my mind." Sarah does not share the glowing evaluation of herself: "I always feel like I'm in over my head, constantly playing catch-up, putting out one fire after another." Part of what makes her job so difficult is that in addition to mental tasks such as summarizing depositions or analyzing documents, she must also expend energy taking care of people at the office. This becomes evident in her description of a typical day at work:

> I got back to my office just in time to pick up my ringing phone. It turned out to be two of the witnesses I had been trying to contact — they conference-called me. Neither had any idea why I had been trying to contact them. They had received the notification letter I'd sent, but neither knew anything about the case of the plaintiff. So, I had to explain who the plaintiff was, why he initiated the lawsuit, the nature of the lawsuit, and why we wanted them to be witnesses. . . .

Anyway, I bet I was on the phone for half an hour or so just *reassuring* these clowns about what was going on. Oy!

[Later] I sailed into Richard's office and said, "I just wanted to drop off your weekend reading material." When he looked up at the accordion file, he groaned and said, "What's this — more weekend reading material? I just got a repeat request on another case, and I have all this other stuff to read. . . ." So, I went into my *reassuring routine*: "It's really not as bad as it looks — most of the materials are charts, graphs, and tables. There's very little actual text." I flipped through the charts for emphasis. He said with ironic emphasis, "Thanks for the *reassurance!*"

I spent the rest of the morning working on a document production [this involves going through boxes and boxes of written material to locate those responsive to the plaintiff's legal request for the production of documents relevant to the case]. . . . It's the most boring and exhausting kind of work legal assistants do. And predictably, twenty minutes before her court appearance, Diane [an attorney] called me asking for a copy of a report from the documents to support a legal argument she wanted to make. . . . I hate these last-minute rushes — it always makes me nervous. I found a report and ran upstairs, but it turned out to be the wrong one. Diane was *furious* with me. She started *grilling me*: "What kind of reports do we have? What's in the correspondence? Was there anything damaging?" I started panicking about whether I'd ever find the right report, but said *I'd take care of it* and ran back downstairs to continue my search.

The minute I hit the document room, the phone rang. It was Diane telling me to drop the search and call Greg [the client] and ask him what he knew about the report. I sighed inwardly — Greg had been less than cooperative in previous attempts to gather information. . . . [So, I called him and] I told him it was an emergency request for Diane and *convinced him* that we were desperate. He responded immediately to the request.

Then I ran back upstairs to tell Diane. As I explained the contents of the report to her, she filled her briefcase and shut it. She *barraged me* with questions as we walked down the hall to the bathroom. Inside, she stood looking in the mirror, making last-minute adjustments to her hair and suit, and mumbling about how her suit looked, while I carefully tried to answer all her questions, told her she looked fine, and reminded her that it was time to go. She walked out the door, and I went back downstairs to try and finish reviewing the documents.

The phone rang again. This time it was Richard, who wanted another report from the documents that I hadn't placed in the accordion file. He was completely vague about what was in the report, when it had been written, but he knew that I would find it as soon as possible. I started looking again with that sinking feeling. Suddenly, I felt completely exhausted. (Emphasis added.)

These excerpts highlight not only the frenetic pace and variety of tasks found in paralegal work, but its socioemotional dimension as well. Sarah reassures witnesses for the upcoming trial and attorneys about their work—"reassuring these clowns" and "I went into my reassuring routine." While she is working on the document production, she allays the panic of the attorney, convinces the client of their desperate need for information, relays information between client and attorney, and props up the attorney's sense of self, all the while quelling her own panic beneath a cheerful exterior. At the same time, she must contend with being barraged with questions and constantly interrupted.

Sarah's emotional role is not unique. My fifteen months of field work from 1988 to 1989 at two large law firms in San Francisco—six months at a private firm (Lyman, Lyman, and Portia) and nine months in the legal department of a large corporation (Bonhomie Corporation)—provide a daily record of the variety of socioemotional tasks found in paralegal work.[1] The interviews I conducted with twenty legal assistants further corroborate these findings. Surprisingly, the one major study done on paralegals, by Quintin Johnstone and Martin Wenglinsky (1985), overlooks the emotional requirements of the job. Their survey of paralegals in various law practice settings in New York City describes where paralegals work, what they do, who they are, and where they come from, but does not address this emotional dimension of labor. Despite the invisibility of "emotional labor" (Hochschild 1983),[2] this aspect of paralegal work has significant consequences for the reproduction of the labor process in the large bureaucratic firm and for the psychological well-being of paralegals. These legal workers function to support and maintain the emotional stability of lawyers they work for through deferential treatment and caretaking. By affirming the status of lawyers, paralegals also reproduce gender relations in the law firm. Most attorneys who receive caretaking and support are men, and the majority of legal assistants who provide these emotional services are women. In this way, the emotional labor required of paralegals serves to reproduce the gendered structure of the law firm.

Theoretically, this research builds upon Michael Burawoy's (1979) argument that the organization of work relations can "manufacture consent" at the site of production. In his view, the limited autonomy workers have to make decisions on the shop floor serves to reproduce the labor process because their power to control minor matters engages their interests at the same time that it mitigates their discontent with hierarchical structures. Burawoy's argument is important because it provides an account of social reproduction where structure is both the medium and outcome of social practice. In his view, the labor process places constraints on workers' choices at the same time that workers actively participate in maintaining and reproducing the labor process.

My theoretical account reconceptualizes Burawoy's argument in two ways. First, unlike Burawoy, I argue that the workplace is a site for the reproduction of gender relations. The fact that male and female paralegals work in a female-dominated occupation that serves predominantly male attorneys poses divergent consequences for the ways women and men are treated by their employers and for their consent or resistance to organizational practices. Here, I draw from feminist theories of organizations (Acker 1990), symbolic interactionism (West and Zimmerman 1987), and feminist theories of gender identity (Chodorow 1978) to argue that the gendered structure of law firms shapes paralegals' practices at the same time that legal workers participate— wittingly or not—in the reproduction of gender relations.[3] Second, unlike Burawoy, my focus is on emotional labor. In my view, the labor process in law firms is reproduced not only through mental and physical labor but through emotional labor as well. Thus, emotional labor is the lens through which I explore the complex patterns of work relations that give rise to gendered forms of consent and resistance among women and men paralegals.

The remainder of this chapter consists of four sections. First, I compare the demographic background of the paralegal work force in this study to national statistics and discuss the reasons for the emergence of this new occupational category. Second, I outline two main components of emotional labor performed by paralegals—deference and caretaking behavior—and provide examples from my field work and interviews. Next, I consider how the experiences of male and female paralegals differ at the level of both the organizational structure and individual behavior and identity. Being a paralegal is not the same job for women and for men. Male and female paralegals are treated differently by attorneys, face divergent expectations, and do different kinds of emotional labor. Finally, I consider the strategies paralegals utilize to resist emotional degradation on the job and argue that women confront a double bind that men do not.

## The Paralegal Work Force

In the late sixties, paralegals or legal assistants emerged as a new occupational category in the legal profession. These semiprofessional workers[4] played and continue to play an intermediate role between secretaries and attorneys in the law firm hierarchy, performing such tasks as conducting legal research; summarizing court transcripts, depositions, and other detailed material; and reviewing and analyzing the thousands of documents produced in large litigation cases. Before 1968 this position did not exist as a formal job category in law firms (Shirp 1989). Today over one hundred thousand people are employed as legal assistants (U.S. Department of Labor 1989). What kind of people become paralegals? How did this occupation emerge? This section outlines the demographic background of paralegals in this study, comparing it to national statistics, and briefly discusses the reasons for the emergence of this occupation.

During the peak of the paralegal professionalization movement—from about 1968 to 1975—a legal assistant was typically a legal secretary turned paralegal after years of experience in a law firm or other law-related job (Larbalestrier 1986). Additionally, paralegals were housewives and mothers reentering the labor force who were trained in-house at large firms. By contrast, in the eighties and nineties legal assistants come directly from college and are trained on the job or from a paralegal certificate program. They are predominantly white, middle-class, college-educated women, somewhere between the ages of 22 and 35 (Johnstone and Wenglinsky 1985: 67–72).

The paralegal work force from the two field sites in this study approximates this pattern.[5] At Lyman, Lyman and Portia, 87 percent of the legal assistants were women, and in the legal department at Bonhomie Corporation, 83 percent. However, in terms of class background, paralegals from the private firm were more likely to come from middle- to upper-middle-class backgrounds (84 percent), whereas at Bonhomie Corporation a larger percentage came from working-class backgrounds (37 percent). Quintin Johnstone and Martin Wenglinsky (1985: 67) found that different types of law offices employ different types of paralegals. Private firms, for example, are more likely to employ legal assistants from backgrounds with college degrees similar to those of the attorneys for whom they work, that is, from the upper middle class with degrees from elite colleges and universities. This difference in educational background also held in my study. Although 93 percent of the paralegals overall had college degrees and several had graduate degrees, the types of institutions they had attended varied greatly. At the private firm, they were more likely to come from elite schools (54 percent) such as Stanford, whereas at Bonhomie Corporation they came from four-year state colleges (64 percent).

Paralegals were also slightly younger at the private firm, where most were concentrated in the twenty-two to twenty-eight age bracket; in the legal department, the majority were between twenty-six and thirty-five years of age. The relatively youthful overall age is attributed in part to the newness of the occupation and to its high dropout rate. The difference between sites can be accounted for by hiring practices. Bonhomie Corporation tended to hire people with previous experience, whereas Lyman, Lyman and Portia often hired people without experience and trained them in-house. Finally, the paralegal work force at both sites was predominantly white.[6]

What kind of work do paralegals perform? Although legal assistants have not been admitted to the practice of law, they execute many of the same tasks done by lawyers, such as performing legal and factual research, drafting discovery motions and other pleadings, summarizing depositions, reviewing and organizing documents from large document productions, and locating and preparing witnesses for trial and deposition. However, as members of a "satellite occupation," they must work under the supervision and control of lawyers (Johnstone and Wenglinsky 1985: 2). Like other semiprofessional workers, such as nurses, paralegals lack exclusive control and autonomy over their own work (Etzioni 1969). In fact, the tasks performed by paralegals and other semiprofessionals have a direct and independent relationship on a profession. Semiprofessionals often act in the service of a profession. As Natalie Sokoloff (1980) observes, "The fact that it is women serving men is of crucial importance to understanding why women work in these areas and why male professionals have accepted large-scale female employment in these areas" (p. 57). As I will argue in the following section, the emotional labor that paralegals perform provides an emotional service for a predominantly male profession — trial lawyers.

Because they do not possess law degrees, paralegals are invariably paid less than attorneys with comparable years of experience. According to the *1989 Survey* of the San Francisco Association for Legal Assistants (1989), the average salary for beginning paralegals was $22,000 a year. First-year associates at the private firm averaged $58,500. Thus, beginning lawyers at the private firm were paid between two and three times as much as the beginning paralegals in the same office. These disparities in income widen as the two groups become more experienced. At both firms paralegals with seven-plus years experience averaged $35,000 a year. Partners in the legal department at Bonhomie Corporation made $100,000 to $150,000, and at the private firm, partners could earn up to $250,000, plus earnings from profit sharing.

In addition to being members of a new occupation, paralegals belong to one of the fastest-growing occupations in the country (Shapiro and Walsch 1987; Uchitelle 1988). The percentage growth in paralegal employment anticipated by the U.S. Department of Labor (1989) between 1986 and 2000 is

104 percent. This ranks legal assistants first among growth areas of employment, followed by medical assistants (90%) and physical therapists (86 percent). This exponential growth is related to the growth of large bureaucratic law firms (Johnstone and Wenglinsky 1985). Law, like many other professions, has become increasingly bureaucratized to serve larger and more complex case loads more efficiently (Larson 1977; Nelson 1988; Smigel 1969). As a result, paralegals have become highly desirable as "lawyer adjuncts." A recent article in the *National Law Journal* reported that "competitive pressures" on law firms are forcing them to manage their "partner time" more strategically; "a law firm maximizes its financial performance by allocating a partner's legal skills to legal matters that can be priced at premium rates, and by delegating routine legal matters . . . to other law firm personnel such as paralegals" (Granat and Saewitz 1989: 19). Thus, legal assistants can perform many of the tasks that lawyers do, but their services cost clients less money, making them more cost effective for many projects.

The expanded reliance on paraprofessionals is not unique to law. Such workers have become increasingly important in medicine as physician's assistants, x-ray and lab technicians, and nurse practitioners. Together they have changed medicine from an individual-based practice to a largely hospital-based one in which technology and extensive support staff make a bureaucratic division of labor possible (Appel and Lowin 1975; Schneller 1976). Similarly, work in the legal profession is no longer based on the solo practitioner; it takes place in the large law firm with an extensive computer-assisted library and research facilities as well as word-processing capabilities, electronic mail and fax machines, and an extensive support staff consisting of secretaries, paralegals, case clerks, library assistants, photocopier operators, and junior associates.

At the two field sites where I worked, labor is divided according to the "team concept."[7] Several attorneys, paralegals, secretaries, and filing clerks are assigned to a given team to work on a specific case. The size of the team and the type of technology needed depend on the size of the case. Large civil litigation cases, for example, with thousands upon thousands of documents, require extensive review and analysis as well as computerized retrieval and indexing facilities. Typically, in a given team tasks are assigned by occupational category. Secretaries are primarily responsible for typing, copying, and filing legal documents and correspondence. Some paralegals review and analyze documents for the case. Others locate and interview witnesses. Still others summarize lengthy transcripts. Young junior associates are each assigned to research different areas of law as they relate to the case. Supervision of the team lies within the responsibility of the senior partner.[8]

## Paralegals and Emotional Labor

In contrast to Max Weber's (1946) classic conception of a rationalized, deper-sonalized bureaucracy, the relationship between paralegal and attorney in the large law firm is a highly personal one.[9] This fact is supported by the numerous statements lawyers made to me emphasizing the importance of personality traits over work skills in hiring decisions. Richard, for example, highlights Sarah's "intuitive qualities" as being most important to him. Personnel direc-tors discussed the importance of being "pleasant" and being able to work with "difficult" attorneys. Similarly, when I asked attorneys what qualities they considered important for a good legal assistant, they invariably listed personal characteristics such as "pleasant" or "unflappable" before they mentioned task-related skills such as "good organizer" or "detail oriented."

Another source that suggests that paralegal work involves emotional labor comes from the evaluation forms used by law firms to assess a given legal assistant's job performance for annual salary reviews. In the legal department at Bonhomie Corporation, the standardized form had the following nine parts: (1) writing; (2) oral presentations; (3) legal research; (4) legal knowledge; (5) technical and operational knowledge; (6) judgment and problem-solving; (7) relationship to clients or professionalism; (8) work habits and relation-ships to others; and (9) managerial ability. In my view, the last three often include substantial amounts of emotional labor.

These forms were taken quite seriously by management in determining "salary treatment." One of the paralegals I worked with, Diana, was unhappy with her evaluation. Whereas she had received a 5 on a scale of 1 to 5 for her technical expertise in the first six categories, she received 3s for her ability to get along with other people. She was told that she did not work well with at-torneys, caused friction with the client, and needled secretaries and support staff unnecessarily. Although her boss agreed with her assessment of the situa-tion—that she had criticized attorneys, secretaries, and clients when such comments were, in fact, warranted—he told her that she had to learn how to give criticism in a positive manner that would not offend other people, and added that she needed to "work on her interpersonal skills." As a result, the overall performance evaluation was pulled down to a 4, and she did not receive the raise she would have gotten had she scored more highly on her "people skills."

The occupation itself appears to recognize the emotional dimension of the job. Conferences for legal assistants often hold special sections on "Stress and the Paralegal" that underscore the emotional demands of the job and provide lessons on individualized coping strategies for dealing with stress, such as deep breathing exercises, visualization techniques, and physical exercise. For example, at one conference I attended in San Francisco, the psychologist lecturing on stress suggested that when an attorney screams at a paralegal, the legal assistant could alleviate stress by jumping rope for ten minutes.[10]

From my field work and interviews, I identified two specific components of emotional labor — deference and caretaking behavior. The first component reflects the structure of the relationship between the attorney and the paralegal — the attorney is the authority and the paralegal, the subordinate. As such, legal assistants are expected to be deferential.[11] Erving Goffman (1956) defines "deference" as a type of ceremonial activity that "functions as symbolic means by which appreciation is regularly conveyed to the recipient" (p. 477). For Goffman, the distinctive element of deferential behavior between subordinate and superordinate is that it reproduces the hierarchical nature of the relationship by confirming each person's position within it. This is also true of legal assistants and attorneys; however, for paralegals, deference involves not only a facial display of subservience but an emotional one as well. A paralegal may show deference by averting the eyes, but must also suppress feelings such as anger or irritation to make the attorney feel competent, knowledgeable, and powerful.

Although deferential behavior is required of workers in other service occupations (e.g., Leidner 1993; Rollins 1985), in paralegal work it reflects the adversarial nature of the legal profession itself, which requires that paralegals be treated by attorneys as if they were adversaries.[12] Just as opposing counsel, clients, and witnesses are interrogated, intimidated, grilled, and regarded with great suspicion and distrust, so too are legal assistants. Marguerite, a twenty-six-year-old paralegal, describes her discussions with Eric, a partner, in this way:

> I feel like I am on the witness stand when I am talking to him about the trial. After I give him detail after detail to his questions, he says, "Anything else? Anything else?" in this aggressive way. . . . I think what's weird about Eric is how he can't turn off this adversarial style. . . . He just persists in cross-examining me.

A male paralegal characterized the pretrial behavior of Mark, an attorney: "Mark asks question after question like a rapid-fire machine gun . . . and he stares intently at you while he's asking the questions. I think it's one of those strategies they teach lawyers to intimidate witnesses . . . and [I feel like] he's practicing on me." Janice, another legal assistant, commented bitterly: "I hate the adversarial relationship. You can never have a normal discussion about a case. It's always an argument, and I just get pushed to the other side. Sometimes I want to say, 'Hey, I'm on our side, remember?'"

Although paralegals are subjected to adversarial practices, they are not allowed to respond in a like manner. As subordinates, they are not true adversaries. They must recognize the attorney as the authority, not challenge him or her as an equal. Thus, they affirm the attorney's status by enduring the degradation of being treated as, one legal assistant told me, "the lawyer's emotional punching bag."

To do so, paralegals must manage anger — their own and that of the attorney. Whenever a lawyer is angry about something, the paralegal is liable to be the recipient of that anger — even when it was not his or her fault. For example, Greg, a paralegal, had brought a client into his office to wait until Chris, the attorney, got off the phone. Greg had been specifically instructed to sit with the client rather than leaving him to wait in the reception area. While they were waiting, Greg received an important and long-awaited call for business on another case. Rather than discuss the business in front of the client, he forwarded the call to a more private line and retreated to a nearby empty conference room. In his absence, the impatient client began to wander the halls and happened into the lawyer's office. The attorney immediately got off the phone, welcomed the client, and commenced their business. After the client left, Chris yelled at the paralegal for leaving the client alone. Greg explained what had happened. Rather than apologizing for her outburst, the attorney angrily replied: "Well, I just had to yell at someone, and you were there." The implication is that the lawyer has the right to yell at Greg and that Greg's job is to submit to the outburst.

Greg's story was not unusual, for the majority of legal assistants I interviewed reported similar incidents of managing anger. Law firms recognize this aspect of the job, since they specifically seek to hire legal assistants who can deal gracefully with irate attorneys. When I was interviewing for paralegal positions, the question that came up in each of the five interviews was: "How do you feel about working with a difficult attorney?" In fact, in one office, I was asked this question by the personnel director, her administrative assistant, and one of the interviewing attorneys. An experienced paralegal told me the question implied the attorney I was to work with "must be a jerk." Employers, on the other hand, were trying to discern how a prospective employee would handle such a personality: "We like to hire people who know how to get along with the lawyers. The litigation department is a pressure cooker; we don't have time for girls who take everything personally" (personnel director, Bonhomie Corporation).

Whereas deference is the first major component of emotional labor, playing a caretaking role vis-à-vis the attorneys and, to a certain extent, witnesses and clients, is the second. This form of emotional labor also reflects the asymmetry of the attorney/paralegal relationship: the attorney is the recipient of care, the paralegal is the caregiver. It also reflects a particular cultural construction of motherhood—what Nancy Chodorow and Susan Contratto (1982) as well as Jessica Benjamin (1989) refer to as the "mother as object." This cultural representation is the "fantasy of the perfect mother," who meets all her children's needs and wishes while suppressing her own. She is the ultimate caregiver, but no one takes care of her. Thus, caretaking, like deference, serves to reproduce the hierarchical nature of the relationship between attorneys and paralegals.

One element of the caretaking dimension of emotional labor is being pleasant. As one paralegal described her job: "I was trying to be pleasant, pay attention, and take notes [while the witness was talking]. Not an easy feat, [because] I felt like I was next to a human time bomb [the attorney]." Being pleasant or cheerful is an attitude paralegals are expected to convey while trying to accomplish other aspects of their jobs. As the personnel director for the private firm told me in a job interview, "It's important to maintain a pleasant manner while attending to the not-so-pleasant side of the job, don't you think?" Being pleasant not only involves inducing a feeling—being cheerful—but it also calls for a specific facial display—a smile. Many women paralegals (but not men) grimly reported the consequences of not smiling: "Why aren't you smiling today?" "What's the matter with you—give me a smile!" "You look like someone just died." Such remarks were typically made by male attorneys, clients, and witnesses to female legal assistants. However, the personnel director for the private firm, who was a woman, could also be counted on for making comments about one's demeanor. A female paralegal wryly observed, "Sometimes I think she thinks smiling is supposed to be part of my job."

Another element of caretaking is providing reassurance by alleviating the anxiety of the attorneys for whom one works. For example, Jenna spent most of an afternoon doing what she called "hand holding." By this she meant repeatedly reassuring John, the attorney, that he would make his 5:00 P.M. filing deadline. Similarly, Debbie spent a lot of her time acting as Michael's "therapist." She listened patiently to all his work-related anxieties and concerns, gently asked questions, and offered reassurance. Of course, this form of emotional labor went only one way. Lawyers rarely, if ever, reassured paralegals about work-related matters.

These findings suggest not only that there is a strong socioemotional dimension to paralegal work but that deference and caretaking serve to reproduce the gendered, hierarchical structure of the law firm. In the next section, I demonstrate how the experiences of male and female paralegals differ both at the macro level of occupational structure and at the micro level of interactions and identity.

## Gendering Constraint and Consent

According to Rosabeth Kanter (1977), tokenism emerges in groups that are highly skewed, with a preponderance of one group of workers, the dominants, over another, the tokens.[13] Male paralegals, like women lawyers, are tokens — they represent the numerical minority in this feminized occupation. Kanter's thesis suggests that tokens face greater performance pressures in jobs because they encounter more scrutiny than their counterparts in the numerical majority. For example, in response to their greater conspicuousness, women managers in her study attempted to limit their visibility by being more secretive, less independent, and less oppositional. In both the private firm and in the legal department at Bonhomie Corporation, male legal assistants as token members of the occupation are treated in dissimilar ways from women, face divergent expectations, and do different kinds of emotional labor. However, upon closer examination these differences do not concur with Kanter's explanations about organizational behavior. Unlike the female managers in Kanter's study, male paralegals do *not* attempt to limit their visibility or conform to the behavior of the numerically dominant group. Nor do they encounter the exclusionary practices Kanter's women executives faced.

These findings corroborate recent feminist scholarship that suggests that the experiences of male and female tokens are not equivalent (Williams 1989, 1993; Zimmer 1988). Chris Williams (1989), for example, finds that male nurses, unlike female marines, strive to be visible in their field by emphasizing their masculinity and by occupying the few high-status positions within the occupation. Like Williams's study, my research also considers how male tokens reproduce gender in a feminized occupation. Further, it shares her psychoanalytic interpretation of gender identity. However, my argument departs from hers in theorizing a dynamic relationship between occupational structure, behavior, and gender identity. I argue that gender shapes the experiences of paralegals in law firms at the same time that paralegals reproduce gender through their interactions with lawyers and other legal workers. Such a theoretical account improves upon structural explanations such as Kanter's, which deny agency to social actors, as well as social-psychological explanations such as Williams's, which neglect the way individual behavior is related to larger institutions.

The first gender difference among paralegals' work is reflected in the stratification of the occupation: male paralegals were more likely to be found in positions of authority or influence than female paralegals. This suggests that among paralegals, much like other occupations and professions, an "internal stratification" exists wherein men occupy the "good" jobs and women occupy the "bad" ones (Bielby and Baron 1986; Reskin and Roos 1987). Among paralegals this finding is especially striking given that this occupation is female dominated and that only a few of the more important paralegal positions exist in any one firm. For example, at both the private firm and in the legal department at Bonhomie Corporation, male paralegals held the most influential, highly valued, and highly paid positions.

Men not only found themselves in different positions within the occupational hierarchy, but they were also treated differently by virtue of their status as males. Male paralegals were often mistaken for attorneys because they were men. Because most secretaries were women, female paralegals were often mistaken for secretaries. Many female paralegals reported that they were asked to type for attorneys. Not surprisingly, women resented this assumption. The male legal assistants frequently viewed this behavior as humorous. These examples illustrate how the gender of a paralegal affected the perception of their occupational roles. Being male inflated the perception of one's occupational status, whereas being female deflated it.

These status differences were also played out on a more informal level. Male attorneys often invited male legal assistants to join them after work to go out for drinks, to play on the firm softball team, or to go to sporting events. These informal "get-togethers" served an important function. They became a means of getting to know the attorney who might write a letter of recommendation for professional school or provide more interesting work assignments. One male paralegal, for example, managed to finagle his way out of a boring case into a more interesting assignment. Women were rarely included in these social events. These differences in informal patterns of socializing also contradict Kanter's analysis. In her account, secretaries and other workers in positions of blocked mobility tended to socialize among themselves, whereas managers moving up the corporate ladder tended to socialize upward in an effort to advance their careers. Female paralegals socialized together and sometimes with secretaries; however, male legal assistants often chose not to do so.

The males' choice not to socialize within their own occupational group challenges Kanter on a related point. She describes how members of a dominant group heighten boundaries between themselves and the tokens to exaggerate differences. This is not the case, however, with both female and male paralegals. Women actively sought to include the men in lunches, breaks, and other social activities. Although there was some socializing, men often opted out because they were bored with women's discussions. Others said they preferred to see friends outside the office. Thus although male paralegals were included, they chose to emphasize their difference as men and downplay any presumption of similarity.

These differences in status also resulted in a gendered division of labor. Women were expected to be more nurturing than men. Attorneys were more likely to confide their personal problems in women paralegals. Several women, in fact, were referred to as this or that attorney's "therapist." Men were not relied upon as therapists but as political advisers and "yes men." They were expected to provide political information and gossip to protect their boss' interests. Theirs was a less personal, more rational mode of conduct. This does not mean emotional labor was not required of them, however. As Peter Lyman (1982) reminds us, "Rationality is not a dispassionate emotional state, but takes its latent structure in the repression of anger" (p. 1). Thus, men and women were expected to do different kinds of emotional labor.

The basis for gender-appropriate emotional labor among legal assistants lies in the degree of affective engagement. Being affectively neutral or polite is acceptable for men but not for women. As a consequence, men must put a lid on expressing deep emotion. For example, attorneys repeatedly criticized one male paralegal for his "giddy" and "flamboyant" behavior. While other paralegals and secretaries found his imitations of the "Church Lady" from the television show "Saturday Night Live" amusing, the attorneys did not. As he said to me in his interview, "They're always telling me to tone it down. Attorneys are so serious. . . . You'd think this place was a funeral parlor or something." This "feeling rule" for male inexpressivity reflects larger cultural conceptions of masculinity (Connell 1987; Pleck 1981; Sattel 1982).

By contrast, women are expected to be affectively engaged. This can be demonstrated through behavior such as "being nice" or facial displays such as smiling. As I mentioned in the previous section, women were repeatedly admonished to express their engagement by smiling. Similarly, women were also prodded to humor attorneys, flirt with them, or pay "special" attention to them. One twenty-seven-year-old woman said, "David [the attorney] always says things like, 'Did you notice my new tie or my new office furniture or my new car. . . ?' He's always trying to get me to pay attention to him!" Another woman commented, "After Mark [a twenty-six-year-old associate] gives me an assignment, he just stands around in my office like this little boy waiting for something. . . . When I ask, 'What's up?' he'll say, 'Oh, nothing.' But he keeps standing there looking hopeful." Yet another woman complained about the partner she works for: "Jerry drives me absolutely crazy — he's such a blabbermouth, he never shuts up. He hates it when I ignore him and try and do my own work; he just can't stand not to be noticed."

These descriptions are reminiscent of the early mother-child relationship. Mothers coo and smile at their babies, and babies coo and smile back. As the infant gets older and begins to take its first steps away from mother, she or he continues looking back to the mother for recognition and support (Mahler, Pine, and Bergman 1975). Similarly, male attorneys look to female paralegals for recognition—"Notice me, smile at me"—as if they were actually their mothers. As Arlie Hochschild (1983) writes, "The world turns to women for mothering, and this fact silently attaches itself to many a job description" (p. 170).

While smiling and being nice are required of women, anger is prohibited. The job requires that paralegals manage anger—their own and that of attorneys. For example, when attorneys yell at paralegals, legal assistants are not expected to respond in the same way but to suppress their own anger. However, as Hochschild (1983) observes, there is a double standard in the perception of anger: "When a man expresses anger, it is deemed rational. . . . When women express an equivalent degree of anger, it is more likely to be interpreted as a sign of emotional instability" (p. 173). In my findings, this double standard appeared in the form of an invisible threshold. Both men and women paralegals were expected to manage their anger. However, men were given more leeway than women to express anger. For male paralegals, it was not until they blew up in response to an attorney's needling that they were sanctioned for their behavior. For women, this threshold was reached sooner. Women were much more likely than men to be sanctioned simply for responding coolly to an attorney's unreasonable request.

Status differences also translated into differential expectations about intellectual ability. Men were taken more seriously than women were. Although both women and men had to contend with being treated as if they could not understand the finer points of the law, women tended to be denigrated more frequently than men. Male attorneys referred to various women paralegals as "bimbos," "ditzy," and "Barbie dolls," implying that they were sexually attractive but dumb. Male paralegals were sometimes criticized for being "weird" or lacking social skills, but no one called them names that implied they lacked intelligence. This corroborates Muriel Schultz (1975) and Robin Lakoff (1975), who found that terms applied to women contain sexual connotations. Schultz argues that this process of "derogation," like racial and ethnic slurs, suggests that women are viewed as the proper subjects for ridicule.

Some men felt embarrassed or defensive about being a legal assistant. For them, being a member of a female-dominated profession did not approximate the masculine ideal of success. When I asked a twenty-six-year-old what he told people he did for a living, he laughed nervously and said, "I just tell them I work for Lyman, Lyman and Portia, and they're impressed. You know it's a big

San Francisco financial district law firm. If I told them I was just a paralegal, they wouldn't be." Another male legal assistant told me that he believed male paralegals were treated quite favorably compared to women. "The attorneys always asked me *when* I planned to go to law school," he said, which he interpreted as a sign of their confidence in his abilities. On the other hand, a thirty-year-old who described himself as an artist and *not* as a paralegal said, "Lawyers always think you should be a lawyer. I used to be offended. Now, I think they lack imagination—they can't imagine anybody would want to be anything else!" Thus, lawyers made assumptions about the career goals of male paralegals that were not made about female paralegals.

The differences paralegals faced in expectations correspond roughly to actual gender differences in emotional labor. Women performed what I term a more relational or feminine style of emotional labor that emphasized their concern for others. Men, on the other hand, had a masculine style of emotional labor that underscored their difference from others as well as their own achievements.

One of the main features of deference for paralegals involves holding a noncritical stance vis-à-vis attorneys. In fact, one of the emotional requirements of being is paralegal is to support the attorney, but women and men do this in different ways. Women do what Pamela Fishman (1978) calls "interaction work." For example, during team meetings, women paralegals listened attentively by nodding their heads and saying, "Uh huh," and "Um hmm," a lot. Men listened but not as actively. They did not offer as much verbal assurance, but were more likely to be silent and occasionally ask questions about the case in a polite, reserved manner. Women were also more likely to support the attorneys they worked for by saying enthusiastically, "You're doing great," or "You're doing fine." Men said authoritatively, "I think you're doing great." This subtle difference has important implications. To say, "I think you're doing great," is an egocentric form of support. It underscores what *I think* about your behavior. On the other hand, the phrase, "You're doing great," reflects a concern with the other person. Although both men and women show their support, they do so in different ways.

Paralegals are also expected to take care of their bosses, but men and women do this differently as well. Women were more likely to be what I call "nice" or affectively engaged, whereas men were more likely to be polite or affectively neutral. Lisa, for example, was the prototypically "nice" female paralegal. She was warm, friendly, and outgoing. Whenever I saw her in the office hallways, she was always cheerful. She tried to please people by remembering their birthdays and cheering them up when they were down. After our interview, she came back several times the following day to tell me more personal stories that she thought might be "helpful." Bill, on the other hand, was the ideal of the polite male paralegal. He was always tactful, courteous, and considerate of other people's feelings but never overly solicitous. Although he didn't smile much, he gave the appearance of being interested and concerned. However, I never saw him standing in the hallways to socialize with co-workers.

Being polite is more aloof than being nice. The male paralegal is pleasant but distant. He does what Hochschild (1983) calls "surface acting" (p. 37), which involves acting as if one has a certain feeling by using facial display, body movement, or tone of voice. Daniel, a paralegal, described his behavior toward Mark, an attorney, in this way:

> I was waiting outside his door to talk to him while he was on the phone. As he talked, I began to imagine the face I wanted to present—calm, serious, competent. I watched my reflection in the plate-glass window and tried out various looks. As Mark said good-bye and hung up the telephone, I entered with what I imagined to be the proper politesse: "Can I have a word with you, Mark? It's about the American Bank case."

Greg, another male legal assistant, who was far more outgoing than either Bill or Daniel, greeted paralegals and secretaries with a booming "Hello!" Whereas he was openly flirtatious with women paralegals and secretaries, with attorneys he was subdued: "I turn down the volume with them and put on my serious face."

Whereas men do "surface acting" by presenting a particular face or turning down the volume, women do what Hochschild (1983) calls "deep acting" (p. 38), that is, actually evoking the feeling itself. Lisa does not just smile but "psyches" herself up to be cheerful and friendly to those around her. In describing herself, she says, "Everyone thinks I'm nice and cheerful all the time, but I'm not. On my bad days I try and think about how they're feeling and what I can do to make them feel better." When I asked Marsha, a twenty-eight-year-old single mother, how she coped with her boss's temper, she said, "I try and remember that he's stressed out about the trial. It's not me he's mad at—it's the craziness of the pretrial schedule. So when he starts sniping at me, I don't let myself get upset. I try to be nice and considerate."

In addition to surface acting, male paralegals also distance themselves from the niceness required of paralegals through criticism and contempt. Most men regarding "being nice" as "taking shit." For example, Tony, a paralegal, was openly contemptuous of Jane's behavior. He denigrated her for being "sugar sweet" and for refusing to stand up for herself when the attorneys treated her badly. When Jane received a higher raise than Tony did, he was furious: "She doesn't even deserve the raise. She just pretends to be nicey-nice and sweet." He then went to the managing partner and complained politely about his raise, arguing that he was as qualified, if not more so, than Jane. He also threatened to quit if he didn't get the raise. He received the raise.

Men could get away with being polite instead of nice and with bowing out of some of the caretaking, but women could not. Karen was a bright, competent paralegal whose behavior in many ways more closely resembled that of the men. She was somewhat aloof and businesslike in her presentation of herself. She did not smile much and expressed no interest in the personal problems of the attorneys she worked for. Nor did she do "interaction work" in meetings. She was regarded by the partner for whom she worked as "uncooperative" and was given a raise that reflected as much. When she inquired about what had happened, she was told that she had an "attitude problem." Concerned that she might have severed working relations, Karen pressed to find out precisely what this meant: "If they think I'm not doing my job, I'd like to know about it, and if I've hurt someone's feelings, I'd like to know about that too." However, neither her boss nor anyone else would tell her anything more specific. She eventually left the firm.

Women were well aware of this gendered division of labor and how it affected them psychologically. Many women complained about the implicit expectation that they would "mother" attorneys. A thirty-four-year-old woman who had worked at the private firm said: "It's a lot of stress trying to figure these people out all the time. Their personalities are like that of small children, and we're like their mothers or their servants. 'Get me this, Get me that. . . .' It's disgusting." A thirty-two-year-old woman from the legal department at Bonhomie Corporation grumbled: "I hate that ["mothering" expectation]. But with some attorneys, it's very significant that you be that way." Some women, like Karen, did not even attempt to make the effort. Mary Ann, for example, said: "To him [the attorney], a paralegal is a mother. He could never understand why I didn't want to play 'mom.' He didn't like that about me. A lot of attorneys are like that." Despite their complaints, most women found themselves engaged *to some degree* in this type of emotional labor. At one end of the continuum were women like Karen or Mary Ann, who refused to have any part in it. (Ten percent of the women fall into this category.) Next were the women who grudgingly went through the motions but complained. (They represented over half of the women.) And finally, at the other end of the continuum, there were the women like Lisa, who were the prototypes of "niceness."

Why do some women feel compelled to perform this aspect of emotional labor and others do not? To answer this question, the experiences of women paralegals must be theorized as a dynamic relationship between the macro level of occupational structure and micro level of behavior and identity. Structurally, a female-dominated job such as paralegal work demands specific types of emotional labor from women. Not only are women expected to be deferential and caretaking, but they are further expected to be cheerful, reassuring, and attentive to the moods and feelings of others. On the most basic level, women must perform such emotional labor if they intend to keep their jobs. A woman who is not friendly, pleasant, and nurturing develops bad working relations with attorneys, is regarded as uncooperative, may not receive raises, or may be forced out of the law firm altogether. Thus, women comply with "feeling rules" because they cannot afford to do otherwise.

The structural part of my argument outlines the gendered constraints women paralegals encounter in the occupation. Further, it suggests powerful economic incentives for women to comply with "feeling rules." However, reliance on structural explanations alone denies agency to social actors. It assumes that legal assistants are in some sense forced to perform emotional labor. As Burawoy (1979) reminds us, under monopoly capitalism workers are not forced but rather consent to the labor process. To improve upon this theoretical weakness, I introduce a behavioral component to my structural explanation: women perform different kinds of emotional labor as a way of "doing gender," that is, as Candace West and Don Zimmerman (1987) suggest, as a way of interacting that is consistent with their notions of gender-appropriate behavior. In this explanation, the feminized structure of paralegal work sets gendered limits on women's behavior. Unlike male legal workers, they are expected to be affectively engaged. Women like Lisa remain safely and unambivalently within these boundaries by doing gender in accordance with the traditional female caregiving role. Others do gender by adopting a more distanced relation to these limits, performing the requisite feminized labor nonetheless. And finally, a small group of women, like Karen, cross over these boundaries, refusing to heed the limits. These women do gender by being professional — in other words, by acting more like their male counterparts — and by downplaying any association with the traditional female role.

Despite this variation in behavior, these women share a common concern with relationships. For those who conform to the feminized socioemotional requirements, ambivalently or not, a relational or feminine style of emotional labor serves to emphasize connection with others through language, reassurance, attentiveness to the moods and feelings of others, and "niceness." On the other hand, women like Karen who do not behave relationally remain psychologically preoccupied with these issues. Although her behavior approximates that of male paralegals, when relationships break down she still expresses concern. Nancy Chodorow's (1978) theory of gender identity helps us to understand this common concern. In her psychoanalytic understanding, women develop a sense of self as empathic and nurturant through the early mother-daughter relationship. As a consequence, feminine identity comes to be defined through attachment and relation to others. For some women paralegals, this sense of self is expressed through the performance of emotional labor and for others, in their continuing preoccupation with relational issues.

Chodorow's theory alone cannot explain why women are relational in some contexts and not in others. Her theory cannot address such behavior because it does not theorize the relationship between occupational structure and personality. However, by integrating her concept of gender identity within this specific occupational context, the continuity and variation in women's behavior can be explained by theorizing a dynamic relationship between occupational structure, behavior, and gender identity. In a dynamic understanding, the paralegal occupation places gendered limits on behavior. Women respond actively and creatively to these limits to construct an emotional style that is congruent with their notion of gender-appropriate behavior. Furthermore, their choice of doing gender is in some way informed by their sense of self as relational or feminine. In this dynamic account, gender shapes the structure of the occupation by setting limits on women's behavior. At the same time, women negotiate within and around these limits, reproducing gender in their interactions with others by being nice, reassuring, and attentive to the feelings of others or simply by being preoccupied with relational issues.

This argument also applies to the behavior of male paralegals. In structural terms, men must also comply with emotional norms. However, as male workers in this female-dominated occupation, men have different experiences compared to those of women. As I have shown, there is a double standard in terms of how women and men are treated by lawyers. Male paralegals, for example, are assumed to be more qualified for positions of authority within the occupation, more career oriented, and more intelligent. Consequently, men are often able to get away with doing different kinds of emotional labor than women do (e.g., being polite rather than nice and playing the role of political adviser rather than nurturing therapist). Furthermore, they also accrue a number of advantages simply by virtue of being male. Informal socializing with male attorneys sometimes leads to more interesting work assignments, letters of recommendation for professional school, and personal recognition and affirmation for their work.

Doing gender in a female-dominated job means that male paralegals, unlike women, must contend with the contradictions of being a man in a woman's job. Their contradictory location explains, in part, why they choose to exclude themselves from women's social activities as well as why they express contempt for their "nicey-nice" female counterparts. They do gender in these ways to emphasize their differences as men and to downplay any similarity to their women co-workers.

The men's concept of doing gender is further informed by the assumption that they have a gender-specific identity. In other words, men do gender because they have a sense of self as masculine. Chodorow's (1978) theory of gender identity suggests that masculine gender identity emerges through a definition of self as separate from the mother—as "not female." A masculine style of emotional labor emphasizes difference and self-assertion through emphatic language such as, "I think," and through mechanisms such as contempt, politeness, and surface acting, which distance men from the feminine aspects of the job. Moreover, men further emphasize their difference by choosing to exclude themselves from informal all-female social activities. While men accrue benefits structurally by engaging in such exclusionary practices, at the same time doing gender in this way also serves to affirm and enhance their gender identity as masculine.

Such an explanation analyzes the experiences of paralegals at the level of occupational structure, behavior, and identity. Gender is an integral part of this analysis. The occupational structure itself is gendered, which poses divergent experiences for women and men. Being a paralegal is not the same job for women and men. Men are the minority in this female-dominated occupation. Despite this fact, men are located within the few visible positions of authority within the workplace. By virtue of their status as male, they are often mistaken for attorneys, taken more seriously than women, and assumed to be career oriented. They are also included in both male and female social activities, but choose to exclude themselves from women's groups. In addition, men and women confront divergent expectations about gender-appropriate emotional labor. Women are expected to be affectively engaged, whereas men are expected to be affectively neutral.

Consent to this organizational process is also gendered. Women and men perform different kinds of emotional labor. Women perform a relational or feminine style of emotional labor. They do gender by performing "interaction work" in meetings, emphasizing their concern for others through language, "being nice," being attentive to the moods of others, and offering reassurance. By contrast men perform a masculine version of emotional labor. They do gender by emphasizing difference through language and through distancing mechanisms such as surface acting, politeness, and contempt. While female and male paralegals encounter gender-specific occupational norms for engaging in such behavior, at the same time the gendered forms of emotional labor they perform also serve to affirm their identities as women and as men. In this way, gender shapes the experiences of legal workers at the same time as paralegals themselves reproduce gender.

## Gendered Strategies of Resistance

> In the Legal Department, there are two kinds of employees: the attorneys and nonattorneys. When you fill out all forms, vouchers, overtime slips, and work requests, designate your status. *Status determines priority.*
> — Personnel director, Bonhomie Corporation (emphasis added)

> When I first started working at the private firm, I overheard one attorney ask another who I was. "Oh, her," he said, "she's *just* a paralegal."
> — A female paralegal (emphasis in original)

> Kill the lawyers.                                          — Plaque on paralegal's desk

The reproduction of gender in corporate law firms and legal departments is not a smooth or uncontested process. Because the designation "nonattorney" connotes subordinate status, paralegals, like other support staff such as secretaries, library assistants, case clerks, and photocopier operators, have fewer rights to entitlement and respect on the job than attorneys do, and many express dissatisfaction about this inequity. Female legal assistants, in particular, resent the gendered division of emotional labor. As a result, paralegals do not comply to feeling rules without some ambivalence, conflict, or resistance.

The majority of paralegals in this study reported feelings of strain, anger, ambivalence, and alienation about their jobs. Surveys done by regional paralegal organizations across the country[14] as well as Johnstone and Wenglinsky's (1985) sociological study also find that members of this occupation experience a high rate of dissatisfaction. Johnstone and Wenglinsky (1985: 84) found, for example, that 47 percent disliked their current position because it was a boring or dead-end job. In this study, legal assistants' dissatisfaction with the dead-end nature of the job was colored heavily by the demeaning character of their working relations with attorneys. A thirty-one-year-old woman who had previously been a primary school teacher said: "Lots of jobs are dead-end, that's not what makes them so difficult. It's the people you work with who make the difference." Another woman in her late twenties told me what she disliked most about her job: "It's a dead-end job. I mean, where do I go from here? Of course, that wouldn't be an issue if lawyers weren't such a pain to work with." And another woman described what she liked least about her job: "The work is boring, but the attitude of lawyers is the hardest thing you have to put up with in the law biz." In their view, it is not only the structure of the job that they dislike but the nature of working relations in law firms.

Over three-quarters of the paralegals interviewed described burnout as the major occupational hazard for the litigation legal assistant. To deal with this problem, many invoked what was called the "two-year rule." Joe described it in this way: "After two years, you make a decision. Either you move out of litigation into probate [this specialty was considered less stressful], you take a job at another firm, or you check in at Napa [the state mental hospital]." In actuality, paralegals not only move with frequency *between* and *within* firms, but many eventually move out of the occupation altogether. The average job tenure for both field sites approximates the average for the occupation as a whole — five years (Johnstone and Wenglinsky 1985).[15] Those who left became licensed as private investigators, opened their own businesses, or hired themselves out to lawyers on a contract-by-contract basis. Despite the commonly held assumption that the job is a stepping stone to law school, only 7 percent actually went on to professional school.[16]

Given that the levels of job dissatisfaction and turnover are so high, how do legal assistants maintain their sense of self-worth? Hochschild (1983) argues that workers in jobs that require emotional labor constantly renegotiate the boundaries between self and work role to maintain their self-respect. In both the private firm and in the legal department at Bonhomie Corporation, paralegals constructed a variety of strategies (Bourdieu 1979)[17] to resist the "feeling rules" implicit in their occupational roles and, at the same time, resolve dilemmas about self-respect on the job. The underlying purpose of resistance strategies lies in answering two questions: How can I make myself feel important in a job where I am required to be deferential and do caretaking at the same time that I am denigrated for doing so? And, how can I maintain my core sense of gendered self under these conditions?

The remainder of this section describes the five coping and resistance strategies that paralegals employ to deal with these questions about emotional degradation on the job: (1) infantilizing the attorneys; (2) personalizing the relationship; (3) being "nice"; (4) defining oneself as an occupational transient; and (5) rationalizing one's career goals and life-style choices. These strategies are not always mutually exclusive, and legal assistants sometimes utilize a combination of them; however, women tend to rely on the first three strategies, whereas men more frequently manifest the latter two. Finally, I explain why women and men paralegals adopt divergent strategies and argue that women confront a double bind in the performance of emotional labor that men do not.

The first strategy — employed primarily by women workers — is infantilizing the attorney. This social-psychological strategy became evident when I sat in on "gripe" sessions that paralegals held when lawyers were not around. In these sessions, attorneys were frequently denigrated as egotistical jerks, petty tyrants, drones, dweebs, workaholics with no social skills, and so forth. But what came up with equal frequency was the tendency to describe an attorney as a baby or a child, and to describe one's job as a paralegal as "babysitting." Debbie, a paralegal, was even referred to as Michael's (an attorney) "security blanket." Michael's secretary said about Debbie and Michael's working relationship: "Michael is like Linus. He needs her to go everywhere [court, settlement conferences, depositions, etc.] with him — it makes him feel more secure." Young associates fresh out of law school were most frequently called "baby attorneys." In fact, they were considered the "biggest babies of all" because they often had to be trained not only in the basics of brief writing, local court rules, and firm politics but in social etiquette, since many of them had never before held full-time jobs.

This strategy serves an interesting psychological function by reversing the asymmetrical relationship between the attorney and the paralegal. The powerful attorney becomes the powerless, helpless, ineffectual, demanding baby, whereas the paralegal becomes the all-powerful, all-knowing, competent mother. In the short run, such a characterization makes legal assistants feel better about themselves and their work. By making fun of their bosses, they can feel superior, knowledgeable, and competent — feelings their work rarely gives them. It also serves as an ironic twist on the attorneys' implicit assumption about "mothering." Rather than refusing to take care of them altogether, Marilyn, a thirty-four-year-old paralegal, said: "So they want me to be their mother? Fine! Then I'll treat them just like they are little kids."

The first move in this strategy is both cognitive and emotional. It involves a redefinition of the attorney/paralegal relationship and an emotional tone — contempt. These women do not like or respect the people they work for. The second move, which is behavioral, entailed actually treating the lawyers as if they were children. Paralegals accomplished this in a number of ways. Some talked to attorneys like they were two-year-olds: "Did Jimmy forget his briefcase today?" "Did Stevie remember to wear matching socks to court today?" Others pinned or taped reminder notes on attorneys' overcoats, suit jackets, or books, or inside their brief bags: "Don't forget your meeting with Smith tomorrow." "Sign this voucher for your lunch money." "Read this case for the meeting tomorrow." One paralegal told me she had gotten on the elevator one evening and seen the attorney she was working for wearing a note pinned to his coat that read, "Sign my overtime slip!" She stood behind him, stifling a giggle, because she had put the note on his coat herself, and he, in his absentminded way, had not noticed it. Others nagged their bosses for being messy. One left a cartoon on the attorney's desk that depicted a man sitting at his desk in an office inundated with papers, books, and office supplies. The caption read, "Life is rough for the organizationally impaired."

These moves involve a careful balancing act on the part of paralegals. As long as the attorneys thought their comments or actions humorous or even useful, they were successful. Paralegals continued to feel superior and contemptuous, and attorneys received the assistance and support they needed. However, paralegals could not push the strategy too far. Those who did were quickly reminded of their appropriate place in the law firm hierarchy. One attorney yelled at a legal assistant who had previously worked as a first-grade teacher, "Stop talking to me like I'm a five-year-old." She immediately backed down, saying: "Sorry, I used to be a schoolteacher. It's hard to lose that tone of voice." Nevertheless, she managed to retain her sense of dignity. As she said to me later, "What he doesn't know is that I didn't even talk to my first-graders that way."

Another strategy utilized by female paralegals was to personalize their professional relationships with attorneys by redefining them as personal friendships. In contrast to the women who adopted the babysitting strategy, these women often said they liked the attorneys for whom they worked. Although they recognized that many attorneys were difficult, they thought the lawyers they worked for were "different." In recasting their working relations as personal ones, these women sought to make themselves feel "indispensable," "important," or "special." The actual extent of the personal relationship and the degree of emotion work done to accept its terms varied from relationship to relationship.

One example is Debbie, a twenty-nine-year-old paralegal who works for John, a senior partner in the legal department of Bonhomie Corporation. At 5:00 one winter evening, John told Debbie to do an urgent project for him as he was leaving the office. Debbie did not realize how time-consuming the project was until she started working on it and ended up staying at the office all night to finish it. The next day, she bragged to many of her paralegal and secretary friends that she had stayed up all night to complete the work, sleeping for only a few hours on a couch in the attorney's office. Her continual bragging served to advertise the importance of her work to others in the office. It also hinted at the closeness of her relationship with John. After all, she had spent the night on the couch in his office. The significance of this last detail was not lost on her audience. Some immediately responded, "You slept on his couch!" Debbie invariably giggled and said, "Yes, yes, I slept all night on the couch." Despite the obvious sexual overtones, John had not even been in his office that night. Nor did he and Debbie have any romantic involvement. In fact, he and Debbie did not even socialize together. Nevertheless, Debbie delighted in telling and retelling the story. And, when anyone commented that it was a lot to expect on such short notice, she proudly exclaimed, "But I did it because I really like John." No one made her do it; she did it because she chose to do something nice for John, whom she liked. Thus, she characterized her fondness for her work in terms of interpersonal relationships with others.

The following day John graciously thanked Debbie for finishing the project on time. However, he never apologized for asking her to drop everything at the last minute. Nor did he inquire whether it had been an inconvenience. When she told him that she had stayed up all night in the office to complete the work, he did not express any concern about her spending the night alone in a dark, deserted office building, but said, "What would I do without you!" In acknowledging his dependence upon her, John's comment satisfied Debbie's need to be recognized as indispensable and important. She repeated it over and over to others in the office throughout the day. He and Debbie seemed to have reached a tacit agreement. She was willing to tolerate John's interruptions and his inconsiderate requests as long as the relationship was a "personal" one. On the other hand, John was willing to tolerate her personal innuendos — he considered them "innocuous, but childish" — as long "as the work gets done."

Debbie as well as many other female paralegals personalized work relationships to cope with emotional degradation on the job. The first move in this strategy is both cognitive and emotional. It entails redefining the relationship as friendship rather than work and its emotional tone as personal rather than impersonal. The strategy seemed to work when attorneys also participated in this process. It made paralegals feel important and special. However, attorneys had different interests in pursuing this strategy than paralegals did. In his interview, John explicitly stated that he "put up with it" to get work done. And another described encouraging such relationships as a means to "lubricate the squeak in the wheel." As Judith Rollins (1985) has observed, personalizing relationships between employer and employee is a subtle form of psychological exploitation. Treating workers as if they are friends when in fact they are not obscures the asymmetrical nature of the relationship. Further, it becomes difficult for the paralegal to complain about mistreatment when the attorney encourages a personal relationship.

The third and final gender strategy often adopted by women is simply "being nice." This is similar to the personalizing strategy in that it involves creating personal relationships, but it operates on a more general level. These women are not simply interested in creating exclusive friendships with their bosses, but in creating a pleasant and humane working environment. This strategy implicitly challenges the main assumptions underlying the adversarial relationship. Rather than regarding other workers as the "enemy or opposing counsel," they insist on being pleasant, kind, and thoughtful. In this light, the insistence on being nice can be seen as a protest or a refusal to accept the terms and conditions of adversarial practice. It can also be viewed as a means for making women feel important: by taking an active role in making the office a nice place, they are organizing the workplace in ways that feel comfortable to them. The first move in this strategy is both cognitive and emotional: it involves a redefinition of the working relationship and a particular emotional stance.

The second move in the strategy entails a behavioral component. These women attempted to please attorneys and other office workers by doing "nice" things such as remembering birthdays with cards or flowers, throwing anniversary luncheons for various employees, and having baby showers. Others did excessive amounts of overtime and ran personal errands for attorneys. For example, during the holiday season Anna did enormous amounts of overtime, spent her lunch hours helping an associate with his Christmas shopping, and baked cookies for everyone in her team (five attorneys, three secretaries, and two paralegals). Only one of the attorneys reciprocated by giving her a Christmas present, and she was devastated: "I tried so hard to please everyone and they didn't seem to care." Cindy, another legal assistant, expressed a similar dissatisfaction:

> No matter what I do, it's never enough. It's always, "Cindy do this," and "Cindy do that." No one ever expresses any thanks for all the weekends I've spent at the office. They [attorneys] seem to think that since they spend so much time at the office, I should too. They seem to forget that they get paid about ten times what I do.

These women workers seemed to think that if they were nice, the attorneys would eventually be nice back. This was especially true for younger women who hadn't been paralegals for very long. However, as these examples illustrate, their relational style was often used against them. This is what I call the "tyranny of niceness" — the nicer and more uncomplaining paralegals are, the more work gets dumped on them. And if paralegals are not nice, they are quickly typed by attorneys as being troublemakers and uncooperative. This is the double bind emotional labor presents for women paralegals, because if they are nice, they are exploited, and if they aren't, they are considered problematic.

Male paralegals adopted a different style of resisting than did women. One tactic was to define oneself as an occupational transient: "I'm planning to go to law school [or business school or graduate school] after working as a legal assistant for a few years. This is a good way to get experience." For men, being a paralegal was a means to an end — money, experience, and a letter of recommendation to graduate or professional school. They were willing to tolerate the job because it was temporary. Although almost half of the men I interviewed said they planned to go to professional school, only two actually did.[18] This suggests that even if they did not go to law school, it was important to define themselves in this way.[19]

Some of the men, however, had no interest in going to professional school. They, rather than defining themselves as occupational transients, described themselves in terms of their "real" interests and accomplishments. Over half told me that they were artists, writers, actors, or photographers, and that they took the job just for money. In fact, during my interviews, several men insisted upon showing me their art, which was prominently displayed on the walls of their offices or apartments. For them, being a paralegal was not part of their occupational identity: they were *artists* — not paralegals. As a consequence, they did not take the job very seriously. Jonathan, a twenty-five-year-old paralegal said: "I don't let all the firm politics get to me — I don't care about those people [the attorneys]. It's not my life!" Another said, "I have seen the gamesmanship and I do feel manipulated at times, but I don't take it that seriously." Like Goffman's (1959) strategic actors in *The Presentation of Self in Everyday Life*, these men viewed social interaction with attorneys as a carefully stage-managed affair. The performance was conveyed through the proper dramatic props — a Brooks Brothers look-alike suit, purchased at a thrift shop, the proper demeanor, and the proper tone of voice. Such an instrumental, pragmatic approach made life at the law firm bearable — "I'm just waiting 'til 5:00 so that I can go home and do my 'real' work" — and their real interests and accomplishments that lay outside the office made them feel important.

Another strategy utilized by male paralegals is the rationalization of one's career and life-style choices. As one male paralegal said: "Most attorneys [here] hate their jobs. They work long hours, do boring work, make a lot of money, and have absolutely no social life — that's not for me. I may not have a lot of money — but at least I have fun!" When I asked another male paralegal why he had decided not to go to law school, he said:

> I'm just not interested in that kind of life style . . . [with] the workaholic attitude — plus I'm very skeptical about law at this point in my life. It really comes down to whoever has the most money wins. Life style is important to me, so is my job, but I'm not willing to work sixty hours a week for the rest of my life. I have other interests besides my job.

And another reported on a more somber note: "I saw an attorney I worked for have a heart attack once. They don't pay me enough to get that stressed out. I just know how to set limits."

Such rationalizations served to legitimate the choices legal assistants make about choice of career and life style: they preferred meaningful work and an active social life even if it meant less money. Of course, these choices meant a *lot* less money. The attorneys in this study earned two, three, sometimes even ten times what the average paralegal made. Some legal assistants admitted to feeling envious about this income differential. Tony said, "I'd like to have a lot of money, a car that doesn't break down all the time, no end of the month scramble." However, he was quick to add, "But I'd hate the kind of work attorneys do."

Attorneys seemed to sense the potential for envy and reacted with a defensive maneuver. John, a young associate recently out of law school, said to me: "It must be nice to have weekends off. Not only do you have weekends off, but you probably even make more money than I do on an hourly basis, because I work so many more hours than you do." And another male lawyer said to the paralegal who worked for him: "I resent the fact that you do the same kind of work I do without going to law school. You don't have to put in long hours or pay your dues like I do." In expressing their own envy or even hostility for the advantages of the paralegal's leisure time, they effectively denied that legal assistants had any reason to envy attorneys. They seemed to be saying, "I made the trade-off and I am not so happy about it," yet implicit in this was the message, "You made your choices, so why envy me?"

Why did men and women adopt different resistance strategies? For men, the answer lies in understanding the dilemma posed by being male in a female-dominated occupation. In American society, men are expected to be career- and goal-oriented, hardworking, and financially successful (Kimmel 1987; Pleck 1981). As Williams (1989) found in her study on male nurses, men in nontraditional occupations are often under pressure to explain why they work in this field and not another one. The male paralegals I interviewed faced similar pressures from lawyers, colleagues, and peers. In response to this assault on their masculinity, they struggled to maintain their self-esteem.

Other studies provide insight into the ways in which men may build up their self-esteem. Elliot Liebow (1967) described how black streetcorner men sheltered their self-esteem behind a set of "shadow values" in his classic *Tally's Corner*. For example, streetcorner men who had moved from one failed marriage to another described themselves as oversexed, incapable of limiting their sexual desires to one woman. Failure in marriage thus became a virtue, the result of the manly "flaw" of being too virile to be satisfied with just one woman. In her study on downward mobility, Katherine Newman (1989) described how downwardly mobile executives also developed a "theory of manly flaws" (p. 72). These men thought they had been laid off or dismissed because they were too smart, too aggressive, or too principled. These qualities were simply too threatening to their superiors. In this way, former managers transformed their failure into a virtue.

Male paralegals are not unemployed, but they are, in a sense, *unusually* employed because they work in a female-dominated occupation. And like the men in Newman's and Liebow's studies, they attempt to transform this "failure" into a "manly flaw." Some assert that they are preparing for a career and that the job is only temporary. Others keep the job to make money to enable them to pursue other, more appropriate, male-occupational identities, such as that of the "virtuous artist." Still others transform their "failure" into a virtue through excessive rationalization: "I'm sacrificing financial well-being because I'd rather have a social life." For men, these strategies entail locating the sources of one's identity and self-esteem somewhere outside this strongly feminized occupation. At the same time, these strategies serve as ways of doing gender. By defining themselves as occupationally transient in a female-dominated occupation, emphasizing other, more appropriate, male occupational identities, or downplaying their loyalty to the firm, male paralegals emphasize their differences as men. In Chodorow's (1978) psychoanalytic understanding, such behavior serves to maintain their core sense of self as "not female." In this way, they make their work tolerable by defining what they do outside the office as important to themselves and others.[20] For these reasons, strategies that women utilized, such as personalizing professional relationships, cannot work for men precisely because they entail locating one's identity in relationships at work within a feminized occupation.

Women confronted a different dilemma in this occupation. Because it was a female-dominated field, there was no pressure to explain why they held these positions. It was presumed that women would hold them. For them, the problem lay in defining themselves through these work relationships. On the one hand, attorneys expected women to be personally engaged and to play "mother." Women, on the other, attempted to maintain their self-esteem by personalizing work relationships, by being nice, or by "babysitting." These strategies all involve doing gender as traditional female caregivers. When these strategies worked, they also served to maintain what Chodorow (1978) terms women's core sense of self as relational.[21] By locating their identity within relationships at work, women such as Debbie, Jenna, and Cindy defined themselves through their concern for and their attachments to others. However, these strategies were not always successful. Babysitting involved a careful balancing act. If pushed too far, attorneys became critical of the women. Personalizing work relationships was successful when women received some recognition for their efforts, but quickly broke down when they could no longer deny that attorneys regarded them as subordinates. And finally, as a strategy, being nice fell through when women realized these relationships were not reciprocal.

When female paralegals gave up on defining themselves through relationships or chose not to become affectively engaged, they encountered the "tyranny of niceness." In other words, they were sanctioned in some way whether they were nice or not. Similarly, women who attempted to adopt male strategies such as being the occupational transient or defining one's self through their "real interests" found that they were not taken seriously. For example, Diana, who was an artist, was teased about her "dilettante interest in finger painting." And, although many attorneys knew that I was in graduate school, they could never remember what field I was in: "Social work, isn't it?" Nor could they ever recall that I was getting a Ph.D.: "What are you getting your master's in again?"[22] Herein lies the double bind that emotional labor poses for women paralegals. If they define themselves through relationships, they are exploited as nurturing women; if they do not, they are considered problematic or uncooperative, or alternately are viewed as "dilettantes."

## Conclusion

Paralegals play a crucial socioeconomic role in the reproduction of the labor process in the large, bureaucratic law firm. These legal workers simultaneously function to support and maintain the emotional stability of the lawyers through deferential treatment and caretaking. By affirming the lawyers' status, paralegals also reproduce gender relations in the law firm. Most attorneys who receive these emotional services are men, and the majority of legal assistants who provide them are women. At the same time, even when paralegals resist the "feeling rules" implicit in their occupational life, they reproduce their own emotional labor through gendered strategies such as being nice (for the women) and defining oneself as an occupational transient (for the men). Just as Burawoy's (1979) factory workers unwittingly reproduce the labor process by defying the factory time clock and working at their own pace, women reproduce the feminized socioemotional requirements of paralegal work by being nice, personalizing relationships with attorneys, and "babysitting." On the other hand, by defining their identities somewhere outside the feminized occupation, men reinforce the notion that they are men and hence unsuited for this job. My account departs from Burawoy's, however, in elaborating how the labor process in law firms as well as the resistance strategies paralegals employ are gendered. Such an account increases our understanding of the different experiences women and men have *even* when they work in the same job.

My theoretical framework also departs from Burawoy's in its focus on emotional labor. As Hochschild (1983) observes, service work has created a new site for the exploitation of workers — their emotions. Paralegals' gendered strategies for resistance underscore the qualitative difference in the emotional exploitation of women and men. Women, and not men, face a double bind in selecting coping and/or resistance mechanisms. If they are nice, they are overworked and unappreciated, but if they fail to be nice, they are viewed as uncooperative. Men, on the other hand, can get away with failing to be nice and can pass themselves off as attorneys, thus utilizing the informal "old boys" network to their advantage. They can luxuriate as well in the privilege of defining themselves as occupationally transient and free from familial obligations. And finally, by virtue of being male they can and must distance themselves from the paralegal role. Male paralegals are doing a female-typed job, which requires certain stereotypical feminine elements, such as caretaking and deference behaviors. Because they are not female, they can distance themselves from the role. This is expressed through their contempt, their excessive rationalizations, or their repeated assertions of other, more appropriate, male occupational identities. Women find it more difficult to distance themselves from being a paralegal; it is not a role they can pick up and drop at will. As Chodorow (1978) argues, gender identity provides a fundamentally deep-rooted sense of who we are. For the women in this study, this identity is often tied to relations with others, and being a paralegal exploits precisely this capacity. As a consequence, on a very fundamental psychological level, emotional labor poses a double bind for women paralegals. As a woman, to distance oneself from the role of legal assistant means in some sense distancing oneself from one's feminine identity. On the other hand, to embrace the role means emotional exploitation of relational skills. Their ultimate form of resistance to this double bind is to leave the job, as many paralegals frequently do.

## NOTES

1. This chapter is excerpted from two chapters in my book *Gender Trials: Emotional Lives in Contemporary Law Firms* (1995), which compares the experiences of both trial lawyers and paralegals in large firms. Names or organizations and individuals have been changed throughout to protect confidentiality.
2. I am relying on Hochschild's (1983) definition of emotional labor as paid labor that "requires one to induce or suppress feelings in order to sustain an outward countenance that produces the proper state of mind in others" (p. 7).
3. This theoretical account is more fully developed in "Gendering Occupations and Emotions in Law Firms" in Pierce (1995: 4–14).
4. Sociologists distinguish professionals from other types of workers on the basis of their acquisition and creation of specialized knowledge and their relative autonomy vis-à-vis other occupations (Friedson 1970). By contrast, semiprofessionals apply knowledge derived from the profession rather than creating it, and have less status and little control or autonomy over their own work (Etzioni 1969; Simpson and Simpson 1969).
5. There were 37 paralegals at the private firm and 34 in the legal department at Bonhomie Corporation.
6. One African American man and one Japanese American woman worked as paralegals in

the private firm. In the legal department at Bonhomie Corporation, there were two Asian American women, one Chicana, and an African American woman.

7. The designation "team" or "team effort" connotes an equitable division of responsibility. However, in this context, the word is a misnomer, because, as I will demonstrate in the following sections, the emotional division of labor is far from democratic.

8. This division of labor is rarely as neat as I have described it. Just as a good paralegal must know something about the law in order to analyze the documents she or he reviews, a good lawyer must know what is in the documents before burying his or her head in case law. Ideally, the team facilitates this overlap in responsibilities by sharing information. However, overlap sometimes leads to difficulties. Legal assistants often resent doing work that associates pass off as their own. Thus, these boundaries are constantly being renegotiated in the workplace and within the profession itself. The controversy in California over whether "legal technicians" should be licensed — the paralegal position — or regulated by the state bar — the attorney position — exemplifies this conflict (*Alameda County Bar Association Bulletin* 1990; Hall 1988; Meyberg 1989).

9. Rollins (1985) also discusses the centrality of a "personal relationship" in the domestic worker's relationship to her boss. Similarly, Kanter (1977) describes the secretary's relationship to the boss as "patrimonial."

10. One female legal assistant told me that she could "think of better things to do with a rope," which she demonstrated by holding an imaginary noose around a lawyer's neck and tightening it.

11. Rollins (1985; see also Chapter 9) makes a similar argument about the deference required in domestic work. However, she does not use the concept "emotional labor."

12. Under the American adversarial model, the main objective of the lawyer or the "zealous advocate" is to persuade an impartial third party (the judge) that the client's interests should prevail (Luban 1988; Menkel-Meadow 1989). The adversarial model contrasts sharply with the inquisitorial model in Germany, which is a judge-driven system. The German system is considered to be less adversarial and less controlled by combative attorneys (Schwartz 1979).

13. For Kanter (1977: 209), tokenism occurs in situations where dominants outnumber tokens in a ratio of up to 85 : 15.

14. See Larson and Templeton (1980; 1981); San Francisco Association for Legal Assistants (1989); and Stibelman (1988).

15. According to the U.S. Department of Labor, the average tenure for *all careers* was 6.6 years as of August 1989. Barbers had the highest tenure — 24.8 years; fast-food workers, the lowest — 1 year. Lawyers averaged 10.1 years, and secretaries, 7.5 years. Paralegals rank higher than fast-food workers, but still fall below the average listed for all careers.

16. One male paralegal went to an M.B.A. program, and another went to night law school but later dropped out. One woman paralegal went to law school and recently completed her degree.

17. I use "strategy" in Bourdieu's (1979) sense of the term to emphasize that a strategy is not simply a purposive pursuit of goals, but rather the active deployment of an object-oriented "line of action" that obeys regularities and forms systematic patterns even though it does not necessarily flow from preplanned objectives.

18. One left to get an M.B.A., and another went to night school to get his law degree.

19. The fact that these men defined themselves as occupational transients to other people in the law firm as well as to me further underscores this point.

20. This sentence paraphrases sociologist Everett Hughes's (1951) argument about how

men make "their work glorious, and hence, tolerable to themselves and others" (p. 342).
Although I find Hughes's insight useful, our theoretical perspectives diverge. His work
falls squarely within the symbolic interactionist tradition, whereas mine is more eclectic,
drawing from feminist psychoanalytic theory, symbolic interaction, and theories of the
labor process.

21. In her study on service workers, Leidner (1993: 210) argues that women are unlikely to
affirm their identity through their work for two reasons. First, femininity, unlike masculinity, is not typically seen as something that can be achieved through paid work.
Second, because most female-typed jobs involve servility and deference, they are not
likely to provide women with personal satisfaction. By contrast, my research suggests
that women legal workers do try to define themselves through their work, but are often
frustrated because they encounter a double bind.

22. This seemed to be a rather effective denial, since most attorneys knew that I was interviewing people to complete my dissertation.

## REFERENCES

Acker, Joan. 1990. "Hierarchies, Jobs, Bodies: A Theory of Gendered Organizations." *Gender and Society* 4(2): 139–58.

*Alameda County Bar Association Bulletin.* 1990. (February).

Appel, Gary, and Aaron Lowin. 1975. *Physician's Extenders: An Evaluation of Policy-Related
Research.* Minneapolis: Interstudy.

Benjamin, Jessica. 1989. *The Bonds of Love: Psychoanalysis, Feminism, and the Problem of Domination.* New York: Basic Books.

Bielby, William, and James Baron. 1986. "A Woman's Place Is with Other Women: Sex
Segregation within Organizations." In Barbara Reskin and Heidi Hartmann, eds.,
*Women's Work, Men's Work: Sex Segregation on the Job* (pp. 67–80). Washington, DC:
National Academy Press.

Bourdieu, Pierre. 1979. "The Sense of Honor." In Pierre Bourdieu, *Algeria 1960* (pp. 123–
49). Cambridge: Cambridge University Press.

Burawoy, Michael. 1979. *Manufacturing Consent: Changes in the Labor Process under Monopoly Capitalism.* Chicago: University of Chicago Press.

Chodorow, Nancy. 1978. *The Reproduction of Mothering: Psychoanalysis and the Sociology of
Gender.* Berkeley and Los Angeles: University of California Press.

Chodorow, Nancy, and Susan Contratto. 1982. "The Fantasy of the Perfect Mother." In
Barrie Thorne with Marilyn Yalom, eds., *Rethinking the Family: Some Feminist Questions*
(pp. 54–75). New York: Longman Press.

Connell, Robert. 1987. *Gender and Power: Society, the Person, and Sexual Politics.* Stanford:
Stanford University Press.

Etzioni, Amitai. 1969. *The Semiprofessions and Their Organization.* New York: Free Press.

Fishman, Pamela. 1978. "Interaction: The Work Women Do." *Social Problems* 25(4): 397–
406.

Friedson, Eliot. 1970. *Profession of Medicine: A Study of Sociology of Applied Knowledge.* New
York: Dodd, Mead.

Goffman, Erving. 1959. *The Presentation of Self in Everyday Life.* New York: Anchor Books.

———. 1956. "The Nature of Deference and Demeanor." *American Anthropologist* 58: 473–
502.

Granat, Richard, and Dana Saewitz. 1989. "Paralegals Move up to Management." *National Law Journal*, January 30, p. 19.

Hall, Michael. 1988. "Paralegal Advocates See Firms in Future." *San Francisco Banner*, September 12, p. 5.

Hochschild, Arlie Russell. 1983. *The Managed Heart: Commercialization of Human Feeling.* Berkeley and Los Angeles: University of California Press.

Hughes, Everett. 1951. "Work and Self." In Everett C. Hughes, ed., *The Sociological Eye: Selected Papers of Everett C. Hughes* (pp. 173–193). New Brunswick, NJ: Transaction.

Johnstone, Quintin, and Martin Wenglinsky. 1985. *Paralegals: Progress and Prospects of a Satellite Occupation.* Westport, CT: Greenwood Press.

Kanter, Rosabeth Moss. 1977. *Men and Women of the Corporation.* New York: Basic Books.

Kimmel, Michael. 1987. *Changing Men: New Directions in Research on Men and Masculinity.* Newbury Park, CA: Sage Publications.

Lakoff, Robin. 1975. *Language and Woman's Place.* New York: Harper & Row.

Larbalestrier, Deborah. 1986. *Paralegal Practice and Procedure.* 2nd ed. Englewood Cliffs, NJ: Prentice Hall.

Larson, J., and D. Templeton. 1980. "Job Satisfaction of Legal Assistants." *Legal Assistant Update '80* 4(2): 1.

——. 1981. "Legal Assistants and Job Satisfaction: A Further Analysis." *Legal Assistant Update '81* 5(2): 1.

Larson, Magali Sarfatti. 1977. *The Rise of Professionalism: A Sociological Analysis.* Berkeley and Los Angeles: University of California Press.

Leidner, Robin. 1993. *Fast Food, Fast Talk: Service Work and the Routinization of Everyday Life.* Berkeley and Los Angeles: University of California Press.

Liebow, Elliot. 1967. *Tally's Corner: A Study of Negro Streetcorner Men.* Boston: Little Brown.

Luban, David. 1988. *Lawyers and Justice: An Ethical Study.* Princeton: Princeton University Press.

Lyman, Peter. 1982. "Be Reasonable: Anger and Technical Reason in Middle-Class Culture." Paper presented at the meeting of the Society for Social Problems, San Francisco.

Mahler, Margaret, Fred Pine, and Anni Bergman. 1975. *The Psychological Birth of the Human Infant.* New York: Basic Books.

Menkel-Meadow, Carrie. 1989. "The Feminization of the Legal Profession: The Comparative Sociology of Women Lawyers." In Richard Abel and Philip Lewis, eds., *Lawyers and Society.* Vol. 3, *Comparative Theories* (pp. 196–238). Berkeley and Los Angeles: University of California Press.

Meyberg, A. 1989. "Not a Pocketbook Issue: Unregulated Legal Technicians Put Indigent Clients at Risk." *The Recorder*, August 30, p. 6.

Nelson, Robert. 1988. *Partners with Power: The Social Transformation of the Large Law Firm.* Berkeley and Los Angeles: University of California Press.

Newman, Katherine. 1989. *Falling from Grace: The Experiences of Downward Mobility in the American Middle-Class.* New York: Vintage Books.

Pierce, Jennifer L. 1995. *Gender Trials: Emotional Lives in Contemporary Law Firms.* Berkeley and Los Angeles: University of California Press.

Pleck, Joseph. 1981. *The Myth of Masculinity.* Cambridge, MA: MIT Press.

Reskin, Barbara, and Patricia Roos. 1987. "Status Hierarchies and Sex Segregation." In Christine Bose and Glenna Spitze, eds., *Ingredients for Women's Employment Policy* (pp. 55–76). Albany: State University of New York Press.

Rollins, Judith. 1985. *Between Women: Domestics and Their Employers*. Philadelphia: Temple University Press.

San Francisco Association for Legal Assistants. 1989. *1989 Survey*. San Francisco: San Francisco Association for Legal Assistants.

Sattel, Jack. 1982. "The Inexpressive Male: Tragedy or Sexual Politics?" In Rachel Kahn-Hut, ed., *Women and Work* (pp. 79–93). New York: Oxford University Press.

Schneller, Eugene. 1976. "The Design and Evolution of the Physician's Assistant." *Sociology of Work and Occupations* 3: 455–71.

Schultz, Muriel. 1975. "The Semantic Derogation of Women." In Barrie Thorne and Nancy Henley, eds., *Language and Sex: Difference and Domination* (pp. 151–174). Towely, MA: Newbury House.

Schwartz, Murray. 1979. *Lawyers and the Legal Profession: Cases and Materials*. Indianapolis: Bobbs-Merrill.

Shapiro, Robert, and Maureen Walsch. 1987. "The Great Job Mismatch." *U.S. World and News Report*, September 7, p. 24.

Shirp, A. R. 1989. "Paralegals Show Strength in Numbers." *San Francisco Banner*, August 30, p. 2.

Simpson, Richard, and Ida Harper Simpson. 1969. "Women and Bureaucracy in the Semi-professions." In Amitai Etzioni, *The Semiprofessions and Their Organization* (pp. 25–43). New York: Free Press.

Smigel, Erwin. 1969. *The Wall Street Lawyer: Professional or Organizational Man?* 2nd ed. New York: Free Press.

Sokoloff, Natalie. 1980. *Between Money and Love: The Dialectics of Women's Home and Market Work*. New York: Praeger.

Stibelman, Arleen. 1988. "Paralegal Group Releases Survey." *San Francisco Banner*, October 5, p. 5.

Uchitelle, Louis. 1988. "As Jobs Increase, So Does Insecurity." *New York Times*, May 1, p. 25.

U.S. Department of Labor, Bureau of Statistics. 1989. *Bulletin 70*. Washington, DC: Government Printing Office.

Weber, Max. 1946. "Bureaucracy." In H. H. Gerth and C. Wright Mills, eds., *From Max Weber: Essays in Sociology*, trans. H. H. Gerth and C. Wright Mills (pp. 196–266). New York: Oxford University Press.

West, Candace, and Don Zimmerman. 1987. "Doing Gender." *Gender & Society* 1(2): 125–51.

Williams, Chris. 1989. *Gender Differences at Work: Men and Women in Nontraditional Occupations*. Berkeley and Los Angeles: University of California Press.

——, ed. 1993. *Doing "Women's Work": Men in Nontraditional Occupations*. Newbury Park, CA: Sage Publications.

Zimmer, Lyn. 1988. "Tokenism and Women in the Workplace: The Limits of a Gender-Neutral Theory." *Social Problems* 35(1): 64–77.

# Part III

## Worker Resistance, Organizing, and Participation

## Chapter 9

# Invisibility, Consciousness of the Other, and *Ressentiment* among Black Domestic Workers

• Judith Rollins

### *Being a Domestic*

D omestic work is obviously a form of physical labor. The work yields some of the same satisfactions (for example, a sense of accomplishment) as well as many of the same problems (for example, exhaustion and physical disabilities). But domestic work is far more: . . . to maneuver oneself into a satisfactory position — one not overly physically demanding, with more than minimal material benefits and with job security — one must have a pleasing personality as well as, if not more than, good housework skills.

Being a domestic means knowing the work and knowing the employers. It was not surprising that domestics had much more to say about housework, their employers, and the nuances of their relationships with them than employers did about housework and their relationships with domestics — so much of domestics' lives was spent intensely involved in these activities and relationships. Nor was it surprising that domestics considered the treatment they received from employers the most important aspect of the work. Research on women's values and morality indicates that women place more emphasis on the quality of their interpersonal relationships than on achievement. From the people in this historically degraded occupation, one which is further degraded when women or despised ethnic groups do it, it is not unexpected that we hear cries for dignity and humane treatment. Listen, for example, to Esther Jones . . .

She didn't think I was human, the way she worked me.

Reprinted from Judith Rollins, *Between Women: Domestics and Their Employers* (Philadelphia: Temple University Press, 1985), pp. 131–32, 207–32.

. . . and to Edith Lincoln . . .

> How you get along with your employer is everything. If she treats
> you bad, your job's impossible.

. . . and to Nancy Clay:

> I just wanted them to treat me like a human being. That's all I asked.

Clearly, for most domestics, as for most employers, the relationship established with the other played a critical role in their satisfaction with the work
situation. (The few exceptions were women — both domestics and employers — who seemed to prefer and create more distant, businesslike relationships,
not usually possible or desired in a live-in, childcare, or full-time situation, rare
even in part-time "day work.") How do domestics see their employers? What
kind of relationship do they desire? What are their lives as domestics like? . . .

## Invisibility

My field notes from my first day cleaning a large house in West Newton
describe this scene:

> Mrs. Thomas and I were both cleaning in her large kitchen when her
> sixteen-year-old came in to make a sandwich for lunch. They talked
> openly as if I weren't there — about where he had gone the night be-
> fore, who he had seen and how angry his father was about his staying
> out too late. I was surprised at how much rather personal information
> they exposed. During their conversation, he asked her if cats took
> vitamins. (The family recently got a kitten.) She answered she didn't
> know but she didn't think so. Despite the fact that I knew there were
> vitamins for cats, I said nothing because I felt that that was what was
> expected of me. This situation was the most peculiar feeling of the
> day: being there and not being there. Unlike a third person who chose
> not to take part in a conversation, I knew I was not expected to take
> part. I wouldn't speak and was related to as if I wouldn't hear. Very
> peculiar.

At a spacious house in Belmont where I worked a full eight-hour day during
December and January (when the temperature was regularly below freezing),
the psychiatrist husband and his non-working wife usually left the house in

mid-morning and returned in the late afternoon. My notes from the first day describe a pattern that would be repeated every time they left the house:

> About a half an hour after they left, I noticed the house getting cooler. The temperature continued to drop to, I would guess, 50°–55° — not comfortable even with my activity. I realized that they had turned the heat down as if there were no one there! I looked for a thermostat but couldn't find it. Worked in that temperature until 5:00 when I left.

And at a more humble ranch home in Needham, where I cleaned half a day each week for a retired accountant and his wife, this event took place:

> They left around 9:30 to make a doctor's appointment for her at 10:00. About forty-five minutes after they had left, the doorbell rang. When I went to open it, I was unable to. I could see through a small circular window in the middle of the door that it was a man delivering a plant. I gestured for him to leave it outside. I remembered that Mrs. Brown had always unlocked the door from the inside when I arrived, so I started a futile search for the key. I realized that when leaving the house, they must have locked it as they would when leaving it empty and that the only way I could get out would be to climb through a window. When they returned, I explained why the plant was sitting outside. He laughed and said, "Oh, I hadn't thought about that. You couldn't get out, could you?"

Similar kinds of incidents in which I felt I was treated as though I were not really there happened repeatedly during my seven months of domestic work. On one occasion, while sitting in a kitchen having my lunch while a couple walked and talked around me, my sense of being invisible was so great that I took out paper and started writing field notes. I wrote for about ten minutes, finished my lunch, and went back to work. They showed no evidence of having seen their domestic doing anything unusual; actually, they showed no evidence of having seen their domestic at all. (As Ralph Ellison has observed, "it is sometimes advantageous to be unseen."[1])

But such incidents were always disconcerting. It was this aspect of servitude I found to be one of the strongest affronts to my dignity as a human being. To Mrs. Thomas and her son, I became invisible; their conversation was as private with me, the black servant, in the room as it would have been with no one in the room. For the couples in Belmont and Needham, leaving me in the house was exactly the same as leaving the house empty. These gestures of ignoring my presence were not, I think, intended as insults; they were expressions of the employers' ability to annihilate the humanness and even, at times, the very existence of me, a servant and a black woman. Fanon articulates my reaction concisely: "A feeling of inferiority? No, a feeling of nonexistence."[2]

The servant position is not the only "non-person" role, but, as Erving Goffman has suggested, it may well be "the classic type of non-person in our society. . . . In certain ways [s]he is defined by both performers and audience as someone who isn't there."[3] Other categories of people sometimes treated as though they were not present include the very young, the very old and the sick. What is important about all of these groups of people is that their non-person role relates to their subordination and carries with it some disrespect. Thus the servant as non-person is a perfect fit: the position is subordinate by definition, the person in it disrespected by centuries of tradition.

It has been suggested that it was during the nineteenth century that Europeans began to consider their servants as non-persons.[4] Clearly invisibility was a desirable quality in an American domestic by the late nineteenth century. Writing about this period, David Katzman states:

> One peculiar and most degrading aspect of domestic service was the requisite of invisibility. The ideal servant as servant (as opposed to servant as a status symbol for the employer) would be invisible and silent, responsive to demands but deaf to gossip, household chatter, and conflicts, attentive to the needs of mistress and master but blind to their faults, sensitive to the moods and whims of those around them but undemanding of family warmth, love, and security. Only blacks could be invisible people in white homes.[5]

Thus Katzman leads us to the other, race-related, dimension of invisibility: blacks (and, I would submit, all people of color) are more easily perceived by whites as invisible or non-human than are other whites. This is an aspect of racism that has been discussed by many writers. Ralph Ellison wrote of white America's inability to see blacks because of "a matter of the construction of the inner eye, those eyes with which they look through their physical eyes upon reality." For James Baldwin, the "inner eye" of white America is constructed in such a way that despite an Afro-American presence of over four hundred years, the nation "is still unable to recognize [the black person] as a human being." From his examination of the treatment of Third World people in films, Asian scholar Tom Englehardt concluded that such films promote "the overwhelmingly present theme of the nonhumanness of the nonwhite," thus perpetuating that idea in the minds of the viewing audience.[6]

Even observers of interracial relations in the overseas colonies have pointed to dehumanization as fundamental to such relations. Albert Memmi explained how this mechanism facilitated the control of the colonized Arabs by the French: "What is left of the colonized at the end of this stubborn effort to dehumanize him? . . . He is hardly a human being . . . [and] one does not have a serious obligation toward an animal or an object."[7] But Frantz Fanon, writing of the same colonial dynamic, added the important point that the conceptualizations of those of the more powerful group create reality only for themselves and not for the people they choose to define as other than human.

> At times this Manicheism goes to its logical conclusion and dehumanizes the native, or to speak plainly, it turns him into an animal. . . . The native knows all this, and laughs to himself every time he spots an allusion to the animal world in the other's words. For he knows that he is not an animal. . . . [During decolonization] the "thing" which has been colonized becomes man during the same process by which it frees itself.[8]

Have I gone too far? Are the conceptual leaps from the mistress ignoring the presence of her servant to Asians being portrayed as non-humans in films to the colonizer treating the colonized as an animal or an object too great? I think not. I submit that all of these behaviors are manifestations of similar mental processes. What all of these writers are describing is the reality that, having been socialized into cultures that define people of color as worth less than whites and having observed material evidence that seems to corroborate this view of them as inferior, whites (particularly those in societies with large Third World populations) do, to varying degrees, devalue the personhood of such people. This devaluation can range from the perception of the persons as fully human but inferior to conceptualizing of them as subhuman (Fanon's colonized "animal") to the extreme of not seeing a being at all. And though this mechanism is functioning at all times when whites and people of color interact in this society, it takes on an exaggerated form when the person of color also holds a low-status occupational and gender position — an unfortunate convergence of statuses for the black female domestic servant.

## Consciousness of the Other

Yet the domestics I interviewed appeared to have retained a remarkable sense of self-worth. Like the colonized described by Fanon, domestics skillfully deflect these psychological attacks on their personhood, their adulthood, their dignity, these attempts to lure them into accepting employers' definitions of them as inferior. How do they do it? How do they cope with demands for deference, with maternalism, with being treated like non-persons? It seemed to me that their most powerful protections against such treatment were their intimate knowledge of the realities of employers' lives, their understanding of the meaning of class and race in this country, and their value system, which measures an individual's worth less by material success than by "the kind of person you are," by the quality of one's interpersonal relationships and by one's standing in the community.

Domestics were able to describe in precise detail the personalities, habits, moods, and tastes of the women they had worked for. (The descriptions employers gave were, by comparison, less complex and insightful — not, it seemed to me, because employers were any less capable of analyzing person-alities but rather because they had less need to study the nuances of their domestics.) Domestics' highly developed observational skills may grow out of the need for maneuvering and for indirect manipulation in this occupation, but the resulting knowledge and understanding [are] critically beneficial to their maintenance of their sense of self worth vis à vis their employers. Domes-tics' answers to my questions about their feeling jealousy about their em-ployers' better material conditions gave insight into not only their assessments of their employers but also their value system. Elizabeth Roy's, Ellen Samuel's, and Joan Fox's answers were particularly revealing:

> I used to feel envy of all the things they have. When I was younger, I did have a little envy. I wondered why they could have it all and we didn't have any. But I don't anymore because as I got older and took a good look at them, I realize material gains don't necessarily mean you're happy. And most of those women aren't happy, you know. I feel like I've done a good job. All three of my children came here to me to Boston. They're doing well. I'm proud of what I've done. I don't have any regrets. (Ms. Roy)

> Even today — and he's [her employer's son] a big doctor now — you know, when she wants to tell him something important, she calls me and asks me to call him. 'Cause he'll hang up on her! He hates her! When I was there [when the son was a teenager] he used to yell at her. He never yelled at me. Said then and he says now that I'm more of a mother to him than she is. I still get a birthday card and a Mother's Day card from him every year. Never sends her one. Now isn't that an awful way to live? (Ms. Samuel)

> I wouldn't want to be in her place. She's got nothing to do with herself. The older ones are the worst off. Just go to the hairdresser, go

to this meeting, sit around. If you look close, you see they're very lonely. I would never want to stop working, for one thing, even if I could. I would never want to live like that, sitting around, talking foolishness, and doing nothing. (Ms. Fox)

Working in the most private sphere of their employers' lives, domestics see their human frailties and problems. Sometimes employers volunteer the information. I was surprised by the revealing frankness of one of my employers (a Wellesley mother of two small children) the first day I worked for her. My field notes read:

> While I had my tea and she puttered in the dining area, she talked about her switch to health foods and her husband's still eating junk food. For example his breakfast, she said, is usually a Coke and a Baby Ruth bar. I commented lightly that that must be hard for a person into health foods to live with and she said, quietly and seriously, "You learn to live with it. If you want your children to have a father, you have to." She looked blankly at the wall as she spoke and when she realized that I was looking at her (with my surprise at her frankness probably showing), she nervously and quickly moved out of the room. I think she had revealed more about marital discontent to the stranger who'd come in to clean than she'd intended to.

And sometimes domestics just observe the contradiction between what employers want to present to the public and what the reality is. . . .

Thus, domestics' stronger consciousness of the Other functions not only to help them survive in the occupation but also to maintain their self-respect. The worker in the home has a level of knowledge about familial and personal problems that few outsiders do. It is not surprising that domestic workers do not take the insulting attitudes and judgments of employers seriously; they are in a position to make scathing judgments of their own. Regrettably, some of the best evidence of their evaluation of their employers cannot be captured in print: it was the cynicism and humor displayed in their derisive imitations of their employers. Raising their voices to little girl pitch, adding hand and facial gestures suggesting confusion and immaturity, my interviewees would act out scenes from their past experiences—typically scenes in which the employer was unable to cope with some problem and had to rely on the guidance and pragmatic efficiency of the domestic. It was interesting that these domestics, described historically and by some of the employers interviewed as childlike, perceived their employers as "flighty" and childlike. How *could* they buy into the evaluations of women they so perceived? When I asked a group of six domestics if they felt like "one of the family" when they heard themselves referred to as such, they laughed in agreement with Elizabeth Roy's cynical answer: "No! Of course not! [Employers] just say that in order to get more work out of you. It's just like that old Southern terminology: 'She's a good old nigger. That's my nigger. I just don't know what I'm going to do without that nigger.'"

The domestics I interviewed knew the importance of knowledge of the powerful to those without power. This significant element in relationships of domination has been discussed by writers as diverse as Nietzsche, Hegel, and Fanon.[9] Nietzsche was extreme in his view that the "slave" is a dependent lacking originality and genuine creativity.

> Slave ethics . . . begins by saying *no* to an "outside," an "other," a non-self, and that *no* is its creative act. This reversal of direction of the evaluating look, this invariable looking outward instead of inward, is a fundamental feature of rancor. Slave ethics requires for its inception a sphere different from and hostile to its own. Physiologically speaking, it requires an outside stimulus in order to act at all; all its action is reaction.[10]

Likewise Fanon, in his early writings, considered the consciousness of the colonized to be totally dependent. Colonized people, he said, "have no inherent values of their own, they are always contingent on the presence of the Other. . . . Everything that [he] does is done for the Other because it is the Other who corroborates him in his search for self-validation."[11] And at the beginning of his famous discussion of "Lordship and Bondage," Hegel appears to agree: "The one is independent, and its essential nature is to be for itself; the other is dependent, and its essence is life or existence for another. The former is the Master, or Lord, the latter the Bondsman."[12]

Domestics have been perceived as a dependent labor group in the past and, in some parts of the world, even today. (In fact, Memmi states that this is the reason servants are the only poor who have always been despised by other poor.[13]) Unquestionably, material dependence has characterized this occupation throughout time; in only a few parts of the world have the labor options of low-income women weakened this material dependence. But I suspect that the psychological independence displayed by the women I interviewed has also existed, to varying degrees, throughout time. Hegel and Fanon both recognized this as a countervailing energy within the apparent dependence — an energy, for Hegel, that developed out of the slave's labor and its effects on his or her consciousness:

> Through work and labour, however, this consciousness of the bonds-
> man comes to itself. . . . Labour is desire restrained and checked,
> evanescence delayed and postponed. . . . The consciousness that toils
> and serves accordingly attains by this means the direct apprehension
> of that independent being as itself. . . . Thus precisely in labour where
> there seems to be merely some outsider's mind and ideas involved, the
> bondsman becomes aware, through this re-discovery of himself by
> himself, or having and being a "mind of his own."[14]

The master, on the other hand, because of his desire-and-consumption
pattern of activity, becomes weaker in skills, self-discipline, and overall human
development. "It is not an independent, but rather a dependent consciousness that he has achieved."[15] Fanon, too, later recognized the existence of
inner-directedness and the importance of tradition in shaping the colonized's
thoughts and behaviors. However, Fanon maintained his view that the extensive control exercised by the European colonizer forced the colonized to be in
a state of constant awareness when among the colonizers: "The native is always on the alert. . . . The native and the underdeveloped man are today
political animals in the most universal sense of the word. . . . The emotional
sensitivity of the native is kept on the surface of his skin like an open sore."[16]
This view of the powerless as exhibiting the elements of dependence and
independence and always acutely aware of the powerful is consistent with the
information my interviews yielded. While domestics were indeed "invariably
looking outward," carefully scrutinizing the personality, habits, and moods of
their employers, they were also inner-directed, creative, and, like Hegel's slave,
"having and being a 'mind of [their] own.'"

Domestics, indeed, know the Other. And domestics know the meaning of
their own lives. They know they have held down jobs typically since they were
teenagers; they know they had the strength to move *alone* from the country or
the South or the Islands in order to better themselves; they know they can
successfully maneuver in black and white, working and middle-class worlds;
they know they are respected by their neighbors for being able to maintain a
regular job in a community plagued by unemployment, for their position in the
church or the Eastern Star or the Elks, and, most important, for raising good
children. Domestics also know the limitations placed on them in this country
because of their class and race in a way employers do not, because they need
not, know. And they know they have survived and transcended obstacles their
employers could not imagine. Free of illusions about equal social opportunity,
domestics neither blame themselves for their subordinate economic position
nor credit their female employers' superordinate position to any innate superi-

ority of theirs. This ability to assess their employers' and their own lives based on an understanding of social realities and on a distinct moral system is what gives domestics the strength to be able to accept what is beneficial to them in their employers' treatment while not being profoundly damaged by the negative conceptualizations on which such treatment is based. (Odette Harris, who put herself through high school and two years of college while taking from her exceptionally low-paid domestic job what she needed: "I was getting a little bit of love there. . . . And I needed that.") And the fact that all the domestics I interviewed who had worked in both the North and the South said they preferred Southern white women as employers further attests to this extraordinary "filtering" ability.

It may be assumed that most Southern white women are more conservative politically than most Northern white women. Certainly, on the group level, the Northerner's "aversive" racism would be less obviously oppressive than the Southerner's "dominant" style.[17] Yet, the Southern white woman's style of relating to the domestic worker was preferred.

Eleanor Preston-Whyte encountered a similar phenomenon in two sections of Durban, South Africa.[18] Relationships between servants and their employers were far more intimate, familiar, and maternalistic in the lower-income, more politically conservative area than in the higher-income, politically liberal neighborhood. Preston-Whyte attributed the familiarity in the low-income homes to the physical closeness of the women (because of small houses), the more informal family interaction style, which carried over into relationships with servants, and more cultural and experiential similarities between the low-income employers (frequently of rural backgrounds) and their servants. In the higher income areas

> it was not only culture which divided them but social class, experience and ambition. In the lower-income area, on the other hand, the white and African women may be said to have shared something of common social environment. They could appreciate the other's problems and offered each other genuine sympathy in times of crisis and insecurity.[19]

The apparent paradox of the conservative, apartheid-favoring white who permits intimacy in her home with her servant is explained by

> the very clear acceptance of both parties of the inferior position of the employee. . . . If the groups to which individuals belong are clearly differentiated and unequal to each other, the closest contact may not only be allowed, but it may even be thought fitting. . . . In South Africa . . . close contact between employer and servant may occur at

certain levels since it is thought impossible for a relationship of equality to exist between Black and white. There is thus no need for the employer "to keep his or her distance."[20]

Similarly in the American South where, until recently, racial segregation and domination were firmly embedded, the social distance between mistresses and servants, between blacks and whites, was unquestioned. Katzman states that, "since individual white action could not affect the subordinate role of blacks — Southern racial etiquette ensured this — whites could develop a far greater intimacy with their black servants than could mistresses in the North with their servants."[21] Additionally, as in Preston-Whyte's low-income area, Southern white and black women share a great deal in common culturally, certainly more than do Northern white employers and Southern black domestics. Katzman considered this to be one of the differences between the North and the South around the turn of the century:

> For all the differences between black and white in the South, they had in common Southern cultural traditions. The cultural differences between whites and blacks in the South were far fewer than the dissimilarities between native-born white mistresses in the North and their immigrant or black servants.[22]

And recall that many of my interviewees had worked in the South for blue-collar families (factory workers, small farmers). Because of the availability of a large cheap servant pool, Southerners of fairly low incomes — that is, with incomes close to that of their servants — can afford household help. One Southern-born domestic referred to the two groups as "co-related":

> There's quite a difference [between Northern and Southern white women employers]. From the Southern point of view, we're kind of co-related, you know. I say "co-related" meaning the Southern black and the Southern white understand each other — whether they like one another or not. You understand their goings and comings. And you feel a little easier with them. And they understand us more than Northern whites do. And treat us better.

Closer in class and culture, operating within a clearly defined system of social and racial inequality, sharing an acceptance of maternalistic behaviors as a necessary and appropriate element of domestic service, Southern black and white women developed a kind of mistress-servant relationship that was psychologically satisfying, to some degree, to both groups of women. Northern employers, on the other hand, operating in communities with unclear rules of race relations, typically having had less experience with blacks than their Southern counterparts, administering to an employee different not only in color but in culture and class, had to struggle to create rules to define domestics' proper place in their homes and psyches. If the Northern employer was also new to the role, the struggle was one of creating both class and racial distance. In any case, this need to create the behavioral norms of racism, since they were not given to Northern employers ready-made as in the South, is part of the explanation for Northerners' treating domestics more coldly. I interpret my interviewees' preference for Southern employers as an expression of both their comfort with the familiar and their desire for a more personal kind of relationship in their work situation — typically a high value, as stated, for all women. Like Odette Harris in her situation in Boston, these women were able to accept and benefit from the supportive elements in Southern maternalism while at the same time rejecting the destructive belief system on which such behavior was based.

## Lack of Identification

One might expect domestics' keen consciousness of employers to lead to their identifying with them. Certainly, the characterization of domestics as inevitably identifying with their mistresses is a prevalent theme in the literature on servitude throughout the world. From the upper-level servants of eighteenth-century England to the house slaves of the American South, identification has been seen as a characteristic of this occupation which brings the worker into such constant and intimate contact with the employer.

But identification is, of course, not unique to servitude. The phenomenon is a mode of coping with a situation of powerlessness that precludes overt attack against those with power. By identifying with the persons in power, one is permitted "a vicarious sharing of some of his or her strength."[23] However, this coping mechanism has the unhealthy elements of self-delusion and an admiration for one's oppressor. Bruno Bettelheim discerned it among some Nazi concentration camp prisoners:

> When a prisoner had reached the final stage of adjustment to the camp situation, he had changed his personality so as to accept various values of the SS as his own . . . from copying the verbal aggressions of the SS to copying its form of bodily aggressions. . . . They would try to acquire old pieces of SS uniforms . . . [because] . . . the old prisoners admitted that they loved to look like the guards. . . . [They] accepted

Nazi goals and values, too, even when these seemed opposed to their own interests.[24]

But Bettelheim added this significant observation: "These same old prisoners who identified with the SS defied it at other moments, demonstrating extraordinary courage in doing so."[25]

Likewise, writers have discussed such identification on the part of the colonized toward the colonizer. Unlike in the concentration camp, the identification in this situation is a result of direct efforts on the part of the dominant group: the culture of the colonizer is forced upon the colonized through institutions such as the educational and religious. Fanon observed:

> There is always identification with the victor. . . . The black schoolboy in the Antilles, who in his lessons is forever talking about "our ancestors, the Gauls," identifies himself with the explorer, the bringer of civilization, the white man who carries truth to savages — an all-white truth. There is identification — that is, the young Negro subjectively adopts a white man's attitude.[26]

And writers on the antebellum South, like Jessie Parkhurst and Eugene Genovese, have also commented on the identification of house slaves with their owners. But, like Bettelheim, Genovese sees that this identification had its limits: "On occasion . . . a servant decided he or she had had enough and murdered the white family."[27] What the concentration camp, the colonial situation, and house slavery have in common is the extreme dominance of one group over another and sufficient contact between members of the two groups for those in the less powerful position to have enough knowledge of the ideas and behaviors of the powerful to be able to adopt them to some degree. The existence of contact is critical; it explains why field slaves or the less assimilated colonized are less likely to identify. And it suggests why domestic servants, more than other blue-collar workers, might identify with their employers.

Undoubtedly, servants' identifying with their employers has existed in recent history. Identification may still exist to some degree in the American South and Far West, where servants are less sophisticated and dependency more encouraged. It may even exist in the Northeast among some live-in workers. But the women I interviewed expressed no hint of it. A discussion of the phenomenon was considered appropriate because so many writers have associated it with domestic service and because, frankly, I expected to encounter it. Rather, the domestics I interviewed see themselves, their lifestyles, their values, as distinct from and, in some ways, superior to that of their employers.[28] The closest phenomenon to identification I could discern, and it is quite distinct to be sure, was the extreme consciousness of the Other. As stated, domestics as a group were far more aware of and concerned with the subtleties of personality and habits of their employers than vice versa. But this awareness was that of a distant and somewhat judgmental observer, fully cognizant of her disadvantaged position in the relationship and the society, and conscious that the greater her understanding of those wielding power over her life the greater her potential for maneuvering skillfully and profitably within the employer's world. It was the keen awareness of one who knows that knowledge is power, not the envious and hungry stare of the sycophant. Powerlessness necessitates a state of acute awareness and a stance ready to react; these qualities are not, however, synonymous with identification.

Today's domestic (or at least, the American-born woman in the Northeast), fully aware of an egalitarian philosophy of human worth and opportunity, more psychologically and materially independent than her predecessors (and less fortunate segments of the contemporary pool), defines herself by her family, her church, her organizations, her place in her community. She neither buys into the employer's definition of her nor does she base her own definition of herself on her work situation. Like other blue-collar workers who consider their "real" lives that part that is away from their jobs, domestics' "real" identities come from other than work-related activities. But while the domestics of today are, in fact, more psychologically and materially independent than domestics of the past, they are nevertheless still asked for some semblance of the traditional subservient performance, a performance, it is clear, far removed from their view of their real selves. It is this contradiction of contemporary American servitude that explains why the women I interviewed exhibited such a high degree of *ressentiment*.


## Ressentiment

*Ressentiment*, a French term adopted by Nietzsche into the German language and later thoroughly explored by Max Scheler, denotes

> an attitude which arises from a cumulative repression of feelings of hatred, revenge, envy and the like. . . . When a person is unable to release these feelings against the persons or group evoking them, thus developing a sense of impotence, and when these feelings are continuously re-experienced over time, then *ressentiment* arises.[29]

> *Ressentiment* can only arise if these emotions are particularly powerful and yet must be suppressed because they are coupled with the feeling

that one is unable to act them out — either because of weakness, physical or mental, or fear. Through its very origin, *ressentiment* is therefore chiefly confined to those who serve and are dominated at the moment.[30]

A critical element of *ressentiment* is the sense of injustice based on the belief that one does not deserve to be in the subordinate position. It is not surprising, then, that *ressentiment* would be "strongest in a society like ours, where approximately equal rights (political and otherwise) or formal social equality, publicly recognized, go hand in hand with wide factual differences in power, property, and education."[31]

Scheler felt that certain positions within a social structure were especially prone to produce *ressentiment*-filled people: the feminine role (especially the spinster), the mother-in-law, and the priest, for example. Individuals in these positions have a sense of deprivation relative to others' power or benefits, with no opportunity to express the anger and envy caused by the deprivation. Clearly, domestic servants are in a similar type of position; they may be, in fact, the epitome of "those who serve and are dominated." And to the degree that they do not believe in their inferiority and therefore see their situation as unjust, they too should feel *ressentiment*. And, indeed, they do.

Despite domestics' knowledge that material comforts do not bring happiness and their assessments of themselves by other than job-related criteria, their awareness of employers' unearned privileges in the society (because of their class and race) and their having to endure employers' demeaning treatment cause feelings of *ressentiment* in even the most positive domestics. Many writers on servitude, from Lewis Coser to Jean Genet, have commented on the hostility that must exist in those who serve.[32] But *ressentiment* is more than hostility; it is a long-term, seething, deep-rooted negative feeling toward those whom one feels unjustly have power or an advantage over one's life. A domestic illustrates her *ressentiment* while describing her "kind" employer:

> She was the kind of person who made up for their dullness by a great show of pride, and she got every bit of her "Yes, Ma'am, Miss Annes" from each and everybody. Since she was that kind of person, I used to see if I could feed her enough of that to choke her. . . . She was, by white standards, a kind person, but by our standards she was not a person at all.[33]

Domestics know that employers have had the power to make the relationship mainly what they want it to be. Domestics may reject the degrading ideas behind the demanded "games," but, like Elizabeth Roy, they also know they have little choice but to play: "Domination. That's the name of the game. The more you know, the more you make the employer uneasy. . . . They want to dominate, exploit." If domestics do not pretend to be unintelligent, subservient, and content with their positions, they know the position could be lost. Esther Jones expresses an understanding all domestics share: "She always said I was one of the family, but I knew better. I knew just what was going on and how they could change. If you don't do the way they want, they'll change overnight!"

Thus, part of their *ressentiment* is caused by the psychological exploitation that my research indicates is intrinsic to this work relationship and part of it is caused by domestics' knowledge of how employers have used their power to also exploit them materially. For domestics are aware of this simple fact: if employers paid better, the quality of their (domestics') lives would be better. Even egalitarian interpersonal relationships (which are non-existent, in any case) could not fully compensate for the hardships caused by not making enough money to provide adequately for oneself and one's family. I heard a Newton employer speak warmly about Mary Dixon, her domestic of fifteen years, who was "one of the family now," who worries about her employer's husband dressing warmly enough, and whom "we love and trust." I later visited Ms. Dixon's clean but rundown apartment near Franklin Park in Roxbury and heard her talk about her minister's unsuccessful efforts to get her Medicaid coverage (she was fifty-two at the time), about having to make partial payments on her bills again in order to make a vacation trip home to South Carolina, about not declaring two of her six employers in order to be eligible for food stamps, which never seem to get her through to the end of the month. And I realized what this "caring" employer's wages of $3.50 an hour meant to the quality of the domestic's life. Ms. Dixon knew, of course, far better than I:

> Ya, they're all right [her six employers]. As long as I do what I'm supposed to, they're fine. And even then, they don't always do right. Like they go on vacation for two weeks without telling me ahead of time. Or they go for two months in the summer and not even try to help me find some other work. They're not people I consider friends. They're takers. Take as much as you let them. And then grab a little more.

I visited a sixty-four-year-old domestic's apartment heated only by a kitchen stove, and a sick domestic's efficiency heated by only a small space heater. I saw thirty-seven-year-old Edith Lincoln's face when she told me how she'd like to put her daughter in pre-school but because of her financial situation had to leave her with relatives. And I heard domestics' dreams, like Nell Kane's . . .

> I would have liked to get training for better jobs than just domestic work, maybe secretarial work or bookkeeper or something that would be upgrading.

. . . Dorothy Aron's . . .

> If I'd been able to get the education, I would have preferred to teach. I always thought I would be good at that. And I love children. But I just didn't have that opportunity.

. . . and Elizabeth Roy's:

> I always wanted a brick home. I always wanted my family together. But didn't any of that materialize.

In addition to having to cope with low pay, most domestics have experienced or heard about outright cheating by employers. Mary Dixon was one of the domestics who told me about a new practice in the Boston area:

> What's happening now, you have to be careful about checks. I won't take a check on the first day any more. This woman in West Newton was very nice but she gave me a check for thirty-five dollars and it bounced. So I called her and she said I should redeposit the check, she just forgot to put money into her account. So I redeposited it and it bounced again. That's what they're doing today. It's happened to a lot of the girls.

*Did you go to her house to get your money?*

> No, I didn't have the time for that. They know you're not going all the way back out there. That's why they know they can get away with it. They found a new way to get a free day's work for nothing.

Stories of such trickery are part of the ugly folklore of domestic service. The worst and most pervasive of such practices were apparently during the Depression in the notorious "Bronx slave markets," but stories of cheating by employers persist and are passed around in this labor group, feeding the anger shared among workers toward "these white people." Domestics do not forget

employers' abuse of their power even when it is, from the employer's point of
view, a minor infraction. Sixty-five-year-old Nell Kane vividly remembered an
experience she had in the 1940's:

> She was a wealthy lady. They owned a gladiola farm. I had already
> learned to cook and serve when I went to work for her. My regular
> people were away so I went to work for her for the holidays.
>
> From my working in different wealthy homes, I used to write up
> my own recipes. If I got an idea of something nice to serve, I would
> build a recipe up and try it. And if it was a success, I'd put it in this
> little book. I had created a lot of little decorations for their teas and
> dinners that I had written in there too. Whenever the ideas came, I'd
> write them down. And whenever you do, it's like a precious little
> thing that you do because you want to show your work.
>
> And I worked for her and she took my book. I remember her
> asking the evening I was packing to leave if she could borrow the
> book and copy some of the recipes. I said, "Well, these are the recipes
> I built from the time I began working and it's kind of precious to me,"
> I said, "but you can take a look at it." My brother drove me out there a
> few days later to pick it up and she says, "Nell, I've looked everywhere
> for that book and can't find it." So I looked around but I didn't see it.
> Do you know, they moved away and I never got that book back. That
> was one of the most upsetting experiences I've had. That book was so
> valuable to me. I wanted my children to read it.
>
> I think she took it deliberately. It hurt me. I cried. At that age, I
> didn't think anyone would do that to you. But some of these women!
> She had so much more than I did and that little book was my joy. It
> was a history I would like to have kept.

Telling me this story almost forty years after it happened, Nell Kane once again
cried. As Nietzsche said, the *ressentiment*-filled person inevitably becomes "expert in silence, in long memory, in waiting."

Employers' exploiting their advantaged position has been both institutionalized (as in the pay system) and underhanded, both material and psychological. But domestics recognize the exploitation for what it is and know their
comparative powerlessness to change it. This knowledge of their powerlessness as a group combines with their inability to express their outrage to those
who have caused it to form the basis of the deep and pervasive *ressentiment* in
the women I interviewed. The presence of such *ressentiment* attests to domestics' lack of belief in their own inferiority, their sense of injustice about their

treatment and position, and their rejection of the legitimacy of their subordination.

Domestics' ways of coping with employers' degrading treatment have been effective, then, in protecting them from the psychological damage risked by accepting employers' belief system but have not been effective in changing the behaviors themselves. All of the behaviors that are generated from the mistress — the demands for various forms of deference, treating domestics as nonpersons or children, the encouragement of unattractiveness and of performances of low intelligence and general incompetence (except for physical labor) — all of these conventions of the mistress-servant relationship have in common the quality of affirming the employer's belief in or of her asking for evidence of the domestic's inferiority. The behaviors and feelings that emanate genuinely from domestics (those not demanded by the mistress) indicate their rejection of the ideas of their own inferiority, of the greater worth of the mistresses, and of the legitimacy of the hierarchical social system.

Domestics do not identify with their employers; they evaluate themselves by criteria other than the society's and their employers' views of those who do domestic work; they show no evidence of considering themselves inferior because of the work they do. But domestics do exhibit the extreme consciousness of the Other that is characteristic of those in a subordinate position; and they do express the *ressentiment* of oppressed who do not accept the justness of their oppression. The elements in the relationship generated by domestics, however, form a weak counterpoint to the deference rituals and maternalism that are the essence of the dynamic between employers and domestics. The employer, in her more powerful position, sets the essential tone of the relationship; and that tone, as we have seen in this . . . chapter, is one that functions to reinforce the inequality of the relationship, to strengthen the employer's belief in the rightness of her advantaged class and racial position, and to provide her with justification for the inegalitarian social system.

## NOTES

1. Ellison (1972: 3).
2. Fanon (1967: 139).
3. Goffman (1959: 151). Although the terms "invisible," "non-person," or "object" to describe servants are not synonymous, I will discuss them without distinguishing between the subtle differences in their meaning. This is because writers use the terms differently but are, in my opinion, referring to closely related mental and social processes (for example, Goffman's use of "non-person" is quite similar to Ellison's use of "invisible person").
4. McBride (1976: 29).
5. Katzman (1978: 114).

6. Ellison (1972: 3); Baldwin (1963: 114); Englehardt (1975: 522–31).
7. Memmi (1965: 86).
8. Fanon (1963: 43 and 37).
9. Elsewhere, I have discussed in greater detail the ideas of these three writers on the consciousness of the Other and *ressentiment* of those in a subordinate position. See Rollins (n.d.).
10. Nietzsche (1956: 171).
11. Fanon (1967: 212–13).
12. Hegel (1967: 234).
13. Memmi (1968: 178–79).
14. Hegel (1967: 238–39).
15. Hegel (1967: 237). I did not, however, detect dependence in most of the employers I interviewed. This may have been because most had held jobs outside their homes and none currently had full-time domestic help. The few whose personalities suggested dependence were older women of less than good health (including two widows). Their dependency seemed to stem from these factors rather than overreliance on their domestics.
16. Fanon (1963: 45).
17. For a full discussion of aversive and dominant racism, see Kovel (1972: esp. chap. 2).
18. Preston-Whyte (1976: 71–89).
19. Preston-Whyte (1976: 82).
20. Preston-Whyte (1976: 86–87).
21. Katzman (1978: 200).
22. Katzman (1978: 200).
23. Lindesmith, Strauss, and Denzin (1977: 420).
24. Bettelheim (1979: 77–79).
25. Bettelheim (1979: 82).
26. Fanon (1967: 146–47).
27. Genovese (1976: 337).
28. The area of employers' lives most frequently criticized by domestics was their childrearing practices. Domestics described seeing children grow up who no longer speak to their parents; a number said their female employers had expressed envy of the respect and caring the domestic's children demonstrated. For a fuller discussion on comparative childrearing practices and the women's views on it, see Dill (1979).
29. Coser (1961: 23–24).
30. Scheler (1961: 48).
31. Scheler (1961: 50).
32. See Coser (1973) and Genet (1954).
33. Gwaltney (1981: 6).

## REFERENCES

Baldwin, James. 1963. *The Fire Next Time*. New York: Dial.
Bettelheim, Bruno. 1979. *Surviving and Other Essays*. New York: Alfred A. Knopf.
Coser, Lewis. 1973. "Servants: The Obsolescence of an Occupational Role." *Social Forces* 52(1): 31–40.
———. 1961. "Introduction." In Max Scheler, *Ressentiment*, trans. William Holdheim. Glencoe, IL: Free Press.

Dill, Bonnie Thornton. 1979. "Across the Boundaries of Race and Class: An Exploration of the Relationship Between Work and Family Among Black Female Domestic Servants." Ph.D. dissertation. New York University.

Ellison, Ralph. 1972. *Invisible Man*. New York: Vintage.

Englehardt, Tom. 1975. "Ambush at Kamikazee Pass." In Norman R. Yetman and C. Hoy Steele, eds., *Majority and Minority*, 2nd ed. Boston: Allyn & Bacon.

Fanon, Frantz. 1967. *Black Skin, White Masks*. New York: Grove.

———. 1963. *Wretched of the Earth*. New York: Grove.

Genet, Jean. 1954. *The Maids*, trans. Bernard Frechtman. New York: Grove.

Genovese, Eugene. 1976. *Roll, Jordan, Roll: The World the Slaves Made*. New York: Vintage.

Goffman, Erving. 1959. *The Presentation of Self in Everyday Life*. Garden City, NY: Doubleday Anchor.

Gwaltney, John L. 1981. *Drylongso*. New York: Vintage.

Hegel, G.W.F. 1967. *The Phenomenology of Mind*, trans. J. B. Baillie. New York: Harper Colophon.

Katzman, David. 1978. *Seven Days a Week: Women and Domestic Service in Industrializing America*. New York: Oxford University Press.

Kovel, Joel. 1971. *White Racism: A Psychohistory*. New York: Vintage.

Lindesmith, Alfred, Anselm Strauss, and Norman Denzin. 1977. *Social Psychology*. 5th ed. New York: Holt, Rinehart & Winston.

McBride, Theresa. 1976. *The Domestic Revolution*. New York: Holmes & Meier.

Memmi, Albert. 1968. *Dominated Man*. New York: Orion Press.

———. 1965. *The Colonizer and the Colonized*. Boston: Beacon.

Nietzsche, Friedrich. 1956. *The Birth of Tragedy and the Genealogy of Morals*, trans. Francis Golffing. New York: Doubleday Anchor.

Preston-Whyte, Eleanor. 1976. "Race Attitudes and Behaviour: The Case of Domestic Employment in White South African Homes," *African Studies* 35(2).

Rollins, Judith. n.d. "And the Last Shall Be First: The Master-Slave Dialectic in Hegel, Nietzsche, and Fanon." In Hussein A. Bulhan, ed., "The Legacy of Frantz Fanon," unpublished manuscript.

Scheler, Max. 1961. *Ressentiment*, trans. William Holdheim. Glencoe, IL: Free Press.

*Chapter 10*

# Shadow Mothers: Nannies, *Au Pairs*, and Invisible Work

• Cameron Lynne Macdonald

*A*lthough scholars have long studied relations between domestic work-ers and their employers in the United States,[1] they have focused their attention on defining domestic work as housework and as service to the master and mistress; only recently have they begun to look upon domestic work as labor that includes child care and service to the children. Lynet Uttal (1993) addresses this discrepancy, stating that "significant differences be-tween commodified housework and commodified child rearing have not been previously recognized" (p. 222). This essay begins to bridge this gap by examining the working conditions and resistance strategies of live-in child care providers, and by comparing their experiences with those documented in other studies of domestic workers.

The critical question for this essay is if and how domestic work changes when it is defined primarily as child care rather than as housework. Because children are considered more socially valuable than clean houses, is child care then considered more skilled and more essential? Do in-home child-care work-ers have more or less autonomy than other domestic workers? To explore these questions, this paper will examine the work lives of nannies and *au pairs*,[2] their struggles with their employers for dignity and autonomy in their work, and how these differ from strategies employed by other domestics. Some domestic workers are responsible for all tasks related to the family and household. Others are more specialized: they may be responsible for cleaning only, some-times working in teams and performing specific tasks for a variety of em-ployers. Others, such as the nannies and *au pairs* discussed in this study, are primarily responsible for their employers' children; although they may also cook, clean, and do laundry, their primary duty is child care. For the purposes of this essay, workers whose primary occupation is cleaning and care of the home will be referred to as maids,[3] and workers whose primary occupation is child care will be termed nannies, or if they are European, *au pairs*.

The nannies and *au pairs* in this study are all white women, as are their employers. Maids in comparable studies are all women of color. Therefore this paper compares white child-care workers with women of color who perform other domestic work, and does not systematically address how the race or legal status of the job holder shapes the job. Judith Rollins (1985) and others have found that domestic work tends to be defined as "child care" when it is performed by white women and as "housework" when it performed by women of color, regardless of the actual tasks involved. Likewise Shellee Colen (1989) found that legal immigrant workers were more likely to hold child-care jobs, and that illegal immigrants were more likely to be cleaners. And although others (Uttal 1993; Wrigley 1995) have investigated the effects of race on perceptions of child care, no studies have systematically compared how race and ethnicity affect the working conditions of in-home child-care providers.[4] The larger study of which this is a part will make this comparison.

*Au pairs* work an average of 45 hours per week and earn $100–$115 per week in addition to room and board, a plane ticket, and basic health coverage.[5] The nannies I interviewed earn $150–$400 per week in addition to room and board, but generally without insurance or other benefits, for a 45–70-hour work week. Both nannies and *au pairs* sometimes also receive the use of a car.[6] By comparison, the median weekly earnings in 1993 for all domestic workers was $183, exclusive of room and board (U.S. Bureau of the Census 1994: 429, Table 665).

Given the addition of room and board, it seems evident that nannies and *au pairs* are somewhat better paid than other domestic workers, and given their specialized job descriptions, they are likely to perform a narrower range of the "dirty work" of housekeeping. These considerations, however, are not the only useful criteria for understanding the meaning and worth of domestic work. It is important to note that while nannies and *au pairs* may perform the same tasks as other domestic workers, how the job is *defined*—by both the employer and the employee—is crucial in determining demands associated with it and how workers respond to them.

## Child-Care Workers and the Ideology of Intensive Mothering

Although we tend to view the large-scale use of paid child-care providers as a relatively recent phenomenon, it is not. Working-class and poor women have always engaged in wage labor, often working as domestics for other women, and in order to do so, have had to leave their own children in the care of kin or other child-care providers. Additionally, in earlier eras, middle- and upper-class mothers did not hesitate to leave their children in the care of servants or other care givers. For centuries, European nobility and landed gentry left their children in the care of peasant wet nurses and lower-class serving women. In the United States, Southern slave women and children reared their future masters. In the North, mothers of all classes who were busy running the household economy brought "hired girls," domestic servants, and boarders into their homes to look after their children (Dudden 1983; Katzman 1978; Macdonald 1992; Palmer 1989; Sutherland 1981).

Since the turn of the century, however, middle-class mothers have increasingly heeded the advice of child-rearing experts who admonished them to supervise their own children, and, if they must hire domestic help, to delegate them the less crucial tasks of cooking and cleaning. This shift is partly a function of industrialization: as women's "productive" household labor (e.g., growing and preserving food, producing essential goods such as fabric, clothing, and candles) was appropriated by market enterprises, they had less cause to delegate child care to helpers (Cowan 1983; Ehrenreich and English 1978; Strasser 1982). In addition, the rise of psychological child-rearing ideologies in the late nineteenth and early twentieth centuries increased the perceived value of children's emotional well-being as well as the socialization and "bonding" that could only be successfully accomplished by the mother (Eyer 1992; Margolis 1984; Thurer 1994). Thus, the rise of "mother-intensive" child-rearing ideologies gradually eroded mothers' reliance on the assistance of others in caring for their children, especially during the first five years of life.

In the latter half of the twentieth century, the view that child rearing should ideally be "child centered, expert guided, emotionally absorbing, labor intensive, and financially expensive" (Hays 1993: 15) and performed by the mother herself became widely accepted. As a result, the child-rearing ideology of white middle-class America has room for only one primary care giver — the mother, with perhaps the addition of an enlightened participatory father or partner, but not a household employee. Influenced by this ideology, many working mothers do not know where to place paid care givers in the context of their families: whether to think of them as a younger sister, an elder daughter, or a wage worker. They are also confused about how to define the relationships between providers and children, relationships based on the cash nexus, not on blood ties, not on "real" family.[7]

Despite the predominance of mother-intensive child rearing as a cultural value, the practice of motherhood in the 1990s for most women includes the use of paid care givers, given that 60 percent of married mothers with young children work outside the home (U.S. Bureau of the Census: 402). The working mothers in this study, who hire in-home child-care workers, are generally professional or managerial workers who are single parents or whose partners have equally demanding careers. Thus, they cite as key benefits of this form of child care the flexibility of having a nanny "on call" who can adapt her work schedule to the exigencies of their careers, and the sense of control over their children's care that comes from bringing a provider to live and work under their supervision.[8]

These working mothers negotiate a compromise between demanding careers and their desire to provide the best possible care for their children by hiring a mother-surrogate to take their place during the working day. They seek to *hire* an individual who will provide a nurturing environment for their children rather than to *be* that nurturing individual. In so doing, they shift their focus from the mother-intensive child-rearing ideology to a belief in the importance of a child-centered home. As one mother pointed out:

> It's my observation that she [her four-year-old] was much happier to be at home. But I don't know if that's my projection. You know to have the whole family leave in the morning and come home at night, the house doesn't get lived in and I think that makes a difference. I mean she runs around her own house all day and no matter what she feels about the baby-sitter at least she's around her bedroom and her toys.

The mothers in this study combine providing a child-centered home and hiring the best available mother-substitute to approximate the care of a stay-at-home mother. The nannies and *au pairs* in this study work to create and sustain a child-centered home for their employers, while at the same time carefully refraining from supplanting them as the primary parents.

### Domestic Work as Invisible Labor

Ivan Illich (1981) coined the term "shadow work" to refer to "that entirely different form of unpaid work which an industrial society demands as a necessary complement to the production of goods and services" (pp. 99–100). Often referred to as reproductive labor, or "women's work," shadow work is devalued, frequently invisible, and unpaid. Arlene Kaplan Daniels (1987) elaborates this distinction by pointing out that our common-sense understanding of what "counts" as work obscures work that is unpaid, work that takes place in the private sphere, and interactive work that is traditionally performed by women. Many of the tasks understood as shadow work, far from being inconsequential, are in fact essential to the maintenance of family life.

Our failure to recognize certain tasks as work deprives those who undertake them of validation. Daniels (1987) notes that "any recognition of an activity as work gives it a moral force and dignity — something of importance in a society" (p. 408). Thus conceptual distinctions between productive and reproductive labor, labor for money and labor for love, market work and shadow work, devalue tasks not easily commodified or understood as part of an economy based on market exchange. Daniels argues that one reason that reproductive labor is "invisible work" is because much of it is difficult to conceptualize in market exchange terms. For example, specific tasks such as preparing food, cleaning a room, or doing the laundry can be understood as labor having exchange value and thus a market price. Planning these tasks and tailoring them to the needs of particular individuals, however, cannot.

Because many activities included in reproductive labor are also viewed as "naturally" feminine and therefore not skilled labor but the simple enactment of innate propensities, we tend not to view many of women's skills as valuable or requiring effort (Daniels 1987: 408). Thus we expect women to be "naturally" good listeners; maids' employers often expect them to be "naturally" deferent; nannies' employers expect them to "naturally" love the children in their care. As Daniels (1987: 410) argues, relegating these qualities to the realm of private exchange and natural human behavior obscures the effort entailed in producing them.

Domestic work is quintessential shadow work. Not coincidentally, 95 percent of the 900,000 private household workers documented in 1993 U.S. labor statistics are women, and the majority of these are minority women (U.S. Bureau of the Census 1994: 409). Aside from gender, these workers have three things in common: they work inside their employers' homes, they perform a range of tasks that are typically understood as women's responsibilities, and they generally work under the supervision of the woman who employs them. The fact that they work in the informal economy also distinguishes domestic workers from other service-sector workers. Working in employers' homes, hidden from the purview of normal workplace customs and regulations, domestic workers find their job descriptions subject to employers' whims and much of their labor designated as invisible, or shadow, work.

Research on maids and their resistance strategies (Colen 1989; Dill 1988; Glenn 1986; Rollins 1985; Romero 1993; Salzinger 1991) indicates that maids and housekeepers face two primary sets of demands for invisible labor: to tailor their work to meet flexible "family norms" and to display a perpetually deferential demeanor. For example, in the case of family norms, Bonnie Thornton Dill (1988) notes that because domestic work centers around the performance of personal services, it becomes difficult to distinguish "between work-related duties and those necessitated by the eccentricities of certain employers" (p. 35). The tasks included in a maid's day can range from doing light housekeeping to scrubbing floors on hands and knees, from baby-sitting to cooking and running household errands, depending on employer demands. Thus, a maid's working day includes the paid labor of cooking, cleaning, and laundry, and also the unpaid, and invisible, labor of anticipating and meeting employers' individualized needs.

Even more frustrating for maids is the expectation that they perform deferential "emotional labor" to enhance their employer's sense of status and innate superiority. The term "emotional labor," coined by Arlie Hochschild (1983), describes a process in which "rules about how to feel and how to express feelings are set by management, when workers have weaker rights to courtesy than customers do, when deep and surface acting are commodities to be sold" (p. 89). Researchers on domestic labor have found that employers routinely expect maids to perform symbolic acts of deference such as wearing uniforms, accepting unwanted gifts in lieu of fair pay, and engaging in what Colen (1989) describes as "asymmetrical first naming" (pp. 181–82). For example, a domestic may be referred to as "Leona," but her employer is always "Mrs. Helmsley." Regarding demands for deference, Rollins (1985) states:

> The presence of the "inferior" domestic, an inferiority evidenced by
> the performance she is encouraged to execute and her acceptance of
> demeaning treatment, offers the employer justification for materially
> exploiting the domestic, ego enhancement as an individual, and a
> strengthening of the employer's class and racial identities. (p. 203)

The deference expected of maids reinforces the hierarchical nature of the domestic-employer relationship and is also typical of invisible work in that it is assumed by the employer to emerge "naturally" from the domestic's racial or class status.

These characteristics combine to create an employer-employee relationship that is symbolically structured around the subordination and objectification of the worker. As Colen (1989) points out, "having involved the worker in intimate aspects of their lives, employers rarely acknowledge either the degree to which this is the case or their dependence on the worker" (p. 180). At the same time that the domestic is expected to provide ego gratification for her employer through displays of deference, she must also shore up her employer's sense of superiority by not reminding her of her reliance upon the worker. As a result, her emotional labor is both demeaning work and work that is unrecognized and unpaid; in short, it is shadow work.

Shadow work also exists in the occupational lives of nannies and *au pairs*, although it takes a different form from that of maids. Their shadow work is generated by several contradictions implicit in commodified child care. For example, the mother's desire to control her children's care can conflict with the nanny's need for autonomy and with her wish that her employer appreciate her expertise. In addition, the mother's expectation that her nanny care for and love her children as she would herself frequently collides with her *own* desire to be the primary care giver and with her belief in the ideology of mother-intensive child rearing; it also conflicts with the assumption that the quality of the mother-child relationship should be the same as if she were at home full-time and someone else were not doing the bulk of the actual care.

As a result of these contradictory impulses, the mothers I studied frequently wanted a "shadow mother," an extension of herself who would stay home as if she were the mother and then vanish upon the real mother's return, leaving no trace of her presence in the psychic lives of the children they shared. One mother described this expectation concerning her relationship with her one-year-old son's *au pair*:

> I wanted her to love him and adore him during the day when she was with him, and at night or any time that I was home, I wanted her to *not* be loving and adoring towards him. I wanted her to just take a step back and be very "hands off." Which is sort of impossible to ask a person to shut off all the time, but I think she was very understanding and really tried to help me with that.

The "shadow motherhood" of nannies and *au pairs*, therefore, is not so much their recognized, paid labor of physical care for children, but the emotional labor of simultaneously building and concealing affective ties, of creating and maintaining the family while at the same time shoring up the myth of nuclear family self-sufficiency.

In contrast to the employers, who wanted a "shadow mother," the nannies and *au pairs* I interviewed wanted recognition for precisely those elements of their work that employers chose not to recognize: their strong attachment to and responsibility for the children in their care. This aspect of their work is what they find the most rewarding, and they look for recognition of their importance in children's lives from their employers. They frequently want "third-parent"[9] status in the families of their employers: they seek the autonomy and authority they feel are commensurate with their daily responsibilities.

As a result, nannies and *au pairs* are caught between conflicting impulses: to do their work well yet to avoid threatening their employer's sense of supremacy as the primary care giver.

## *Resistance: Restructuring and Reinterpreting*

Both maids and live-in child-care providers resist demands for shadow labor by using two sets of strategies: restructuring their work and redefining the meanings associated with it.[10] Maids resist employers' demands for flexibility and personalized service by restructuring the work relationship and imposing their own, professionalized definition of the work. They create a businesslike relationship with employers by minimizing personal contact and moving from live-in to day work. In addition, they frequently refuse to work for employers who are at home during the day. They also work in teams and work for multiple employers. In short, they attempt to change the terms of the work from an "exchange of labor power to [an exchange of] labor services" (Romero 1992: 147). Through redefining the work as labor by "task rather than time," maids can then exert control and authority in the decision-making process and as a result, can increase their wages and reduce their working hours (Romero 1992: 31).

Some, such as the Chicana maids in Mary Romero's (1993) study, choose to become housecleaning experts, and refuse to perform personal tasks such as cooking, mending, and child care. Others, such as the West Indian women studied by Colen (1989), refuse to do heavy housework and define themselves primarily as child-care providers. How they renegotiate this definition depends on their perceptions of their value to their employer, their own sense of other options (e.g., whether they are legal aliens and can find other work), and their view of what aspects of the work are more or less demeaning (Colen 1989: 191; Romero 1992: 155).

In addition, maids redefine the meaning associated with the work and its place in their lives. Rather than accepting their employers' definitions of themselves as subordinate family members, maids find other sources of identification, primarily through active involvement in ethnic communities and with their own families, and by valuing aspects of their lives other than their work (Colen 1989: 188; Dill 1988: 48). African-American domestic workers began this process in the early twentieth century by making the transition from live-in to live-out work; by the end of World War I, day work was the most prevalent form of domestic service. The benefits to workers of this shift were many:

Day workers are able to retain family and social life outside of the work site, so they are less vulnerable to being manipulated by employer's personalistic appeals to family ideology — to see themselves "like one of the family." (Hondagneu-Sotelo 1994: 52)

Even maids who live in frequently find a way to live out on their days off. For example, the immigrant domestics Rina Cohen (1991) studied in Canada typically live in during the week but spend weekends with their family, or if they have no local relatives, in a rented apartment shared by five to ten workers.

Drawing sustenance from nonwork identity requires maintaining strict boundaries between work and nonwork selves. This division can take the shape of constructing a nonwork social support network, as in the cases above, or of refusing to perform certain tasks that are charged with emotional meaning — that is, tasks that they might perform for family but not for outsiders. For example, Romero (1992: 158) cites Chicana maids who cooked for their employers but refused to prepare Mexican food, reserving their native cuisine for family and friends.

Maids also reinterpret their unequal status vis-à-vis their employers through denigration and ridicule. As Rollins (see Chapter 9) points out, they use their intimate status within employers' homes to gain a superior "consciousness of the other" that enables them to resist subordination both internally and interactively. Derogatory comments, mockery, gossip, and caricature are common resistance strategies used behind the scenes to enable workers to maintain a sense of self-respect. As Cohen (1991) remarks, "One way to assert humanity and dignity is to perform little tricks, privately or with other maids, and celebrate small triumphs while still retaining the employer's favor" (p. 211). Thus, maids use both negotiation and re-interpretation as forms of resistance. They negotiate to restructure the work to make it more profitable, more flexible, and less personal. They use internal strategies such as "consciousness of the other" to reinterpret the work and to resist its intrusions into their lives and their definitions of self.

Because of the intimate nature of their work, nannies and *au pairs* cannot implement many of the resistance strategies developed by other domestic workers. Whenever possible, however, they do attempt to restructure their work: they prefer to work for mothers who work full-time outside of the home, they attempt to negotiate live-out situations, and they try to delimit their assigned duties to tasks associated with child care. But many of these conditions are not open to negotiation. Their work is, by definition, to live and work exclusively for one family in one household. In addition, their wages are frequently predetermined by agency contracts, their hours are subject to the exigencies of their employers' work schedules, and their tasks, although generally designated as child care, can include a variety of other housekeeping chores.

The nannies and *au pairs* I studied also found their ability to renegotiate the terms of their work hampered by a relative dearth of alternatives. *Au pairs* come to the United States through agencies that closely monitor their hours and working conditions. If an *au pair* is exploited by her host family (for example, if she is forced to work too many hours or to perform housework that is not in her contract), the agency will intervene and attempt to mediate. If mediation is unsuccessful and an *au pair* chooses to leave a family, she can only work for another family from the same agency, and if one is not available, she is sent home. She also forfeits the $500 deposit she gave the agency to guarantee her one-year contract.

U.S. nannies also find employers through agencies, but in these cases, the agency has no responsibility to monitor the terms of the contract or to see that they are followed. Further, the agency's fee is contingent on the nanny's completion of the one-year contract, so the agency has an economic interest in ensuring that she remains. However, American nannies forfeit nothing if they leave an employer and generally have very little difficulty finding another. So while *au pairs* are more protected from potential exploitation, they have fewer options should they choose to leave; nannies have virtually no protections, but if they quit and test the market, they often find they have many options.

Nonetheless, most nannies and *au pairs* find that loyalty, either to the children or to the family in general, prevents them from testing their worth on the child-care market. One nanny told of staying an extra year in a job she detested because of loyalty to the children:

> I was there for two years only because she got pregnant with Jason and I didn't see the point in [leaving] the three [other children] — they were all really insecure and I didn't want to see them have to get used to a new nanny and then get used to a new baby brother. So it was just easier to stay and let them get used to Jason before I left.

Nannies and *au pairs* also find that their sense of obligation to the children prevents them from confronting employers about unfair labor practices. As one remarked:

> They ask you to do a few extra things now and then, and they're always slipping in extra stuff that's not really in your contract — and how far do you go? There's the situation where they have to work late

and you have to cancel important plans — if they can't get home, you're it — you have to stay unless they have a different baby-sitter, but most families don't have a back-up.

Therefore, they find that many of the restructuring tactics used by other domestic workers are not easily enacted within the context of their work lives.

Nannies and *au pairs* most resemble the maids discussed above in their use of denigration as an internal strategy of resistance. They value and dignify their work by comparing themselves with their employers, generally finding their employers' mothering skills wanting. One nanny told me:

> [The baby] would cry when his mom would walk in the door, and when I would go in and pick him up he would stop crying, just because he was so used to me and not used to her. And it would make her angry and she would stomp off. . . . He was so used to me that he didn't know his mom. She should have spent more time around him and have him get used to her. . . . It was sad, really sad.

Another referred to her employer as a contaminating influence on the children: "It seems like there's only so much you can do. . . . I spend so much time with them, but no matter how much time I spend with them, it's corrupted every night, you know, it just goes backwards." By comparing themselves with their employers, they give themselves the recognition their employers deny them. In addition, these comparisons enable nannies and *au pairs* to define their work as skilled, and to view themselves, in opposition to their employers, as child-care experts, and in fact, as *the* experts concerning their employers' children.

In sum, maids' resistance strategies aim to modernize their work and structure it to resemble work in the formal service sector. They seek to remove the pseudofamilial bond with their employers and establish the work agreement on a fee-for-service rather than a servant-mistress basis. This strategy enables maids to remove invisible labor from their work: no longer does their work include the creation and maintenance of a semi-intimate relationship, the need to adjust to employers' idiosyncratic demands, or the performance of rituals of deference. By modernizing and formalizing their work, they eliminate the employer's ability to demand and expect invisible work.

When domestic work is child care, however, employees approach employer demands, and specifically demands for invisible labor, quite differently. As mentioned, a sense of loyalty to the children often prevents nannies and *au pairs* from negotiating for better wages or working conditions, and can prevent them from leaving employers they would otherwise abandon. In addition, nannies and *au pairs* use very different strategies regarding invisible labor from those used by maids. The invisible work demanded of them is not so much the performance of deference or the deciphering of individual employer's quirks, although these may play a role; instead, nannies and *au pairs* are asked to perform the invisible work of masking the effects of their care on the children, of simultaneously forging and concealing affective ties. Since these affective ties are, for many nannies and *au pairs*, one of the most rewarding aspects of their work, they seek not to remove invisible labor from their jobs but to render their invisible work visible.

### Shadow Mothers and the Third-Parent Ideal

Because of the intimate nature of their work and because the essence of this work is to love and bond with the children in their care, the distancing strategies used by other domestics seem not only unavailable to the care givers I interviewed but generally unnecessary. For the most part, nannies and *au pairs* do not view child care as essentially demeaning work. They value the emotional labor required of them — to love the children — and they relish the attachments they develop. One nanny told me, "Some nannies consider the kids theirs, and I felt the same way; I felt those kids were mine." She also referred to herself as the "third parent" in her employer's household, as did several others.

The third-parent ideal meant being recognized as important adults in the children's lives, being consulted about questions of discipline and care, being invited to parent-teacher conferences or visits to the pediatrician, and being trusted to care for the children in their own way when they were on duty. One nanny described the autonomy and freedom she experienced on her job this way:

> At Dan and Karen's, when I got there, they set up a house account in my name and they just put money in it and any time we needed anything, if the baby went to a new size of clothes and needed new undershirts, I would go out and buy them for him. . . . I mean I did everything, and I liked it . . . and having the freedom to do what you want when you wanted made it better.

She also worked 60 to 70 hours per week and did all the housework, errands, cooking, and a host of other "motherly" duties. In her mind, the loss of delineated on-duty and off-duty time and the extra work she did were fair exchange for the autonomy and recognition she received as the "third parent" in the family.

Achieving third-parent status was the ideal for most of the nannies and *au pairs* I interviewed. However, the primary rule of emotional labor in child-care work often prevented them from attaining this recognition. In her study of family day-care providers, Margaret Nelson (1990) termed this the "detached attachment" rule (p. 76). Detached attachment is really three rules in one: the first and most obvious component is a mandate to love the children in one's care and to form a stable bond with them that resembles mother care. Second, the care giver must maintain some emotional distance while loving the child so that she can prepare herself and the child for the day when they will eventually say good-bye. Finally, providers need to be careful not to usurp the mother's position as primary care giver, regardless of the amount of time they might spend with the children or the strength of the bond between them.

This rule, while rarely explicitly stated, has several sources. First, it is prompted by the provider's need to preserve herself from the pain of eventual separation. This was more of a concern for the *au pairs* I interviewed, who faced a predetermined end to their relationship with the children, than it was for the nannies, who did not. Second, and more importantly, it was subtly imposed by parents, especially mothers, who viewed nannies' involvement with their children as a threat. As one nanny remarked:

> When I was off duty I was off duty, and Elaine thought it was strange that I would want to spend time with the baby on weekends — she would say, "Well, I'm sure you have more important things you could be doing." But I wanted to be with him. It was kind of like she was pushing me away.

Parents also viewed their employees as a threat to their privacy and to their sense of themselves as a self-sufficient, nuclear family unit. Often they seemed to view the child's attachment as a zero-sum game — love for the nanny being automatically subtracted from the mother's side of the ledger.

As a result of anxieties over closeness between care giver and child, nannies and *au pairs* find themselves in the awkward position of wanting to do their jobs well but unobtrusively. For the most part, the nannies and *au pairs* I interviewed did not strive for emotional detachment; on the contrary, they wanted recognition for the degree and efficacy of their emotional attachment and its importance in children's lives. In most cases, however, they were careful not to make waves. One nanny explained:

> When [the baby] does things, I don't tell her [the mother] . . . — you know, "I noticed his tooth and I got him to stand up by himself," but I

don't tell her that because . . . I wouldn't want somebody to tell me my child did this, I'd like to see it myself first — so I let her see the things before — . . . I could see if I were telling her every day, "Well, he did this today, and he did that," it would be like I'm the one who's learning all these things about her child before she is, but it's not like that because I don't tell her anything [laughs], I just let her find out for herself so that she can be happy.

Given the constraints of the "detached attachment" rule, they often found that not only was their importance in the children's lives unrecognized, they had to take pains to render their efforts invisible.

Care givers cope with the tensions caused by having to render invisible the most rewarding and important aspects of their work by trying to make a lasting emotional mark on the children in their care, even if the positive effects of their care are unrecognized or denied by their employers. Their efforts to make a mark in their children's lives are often doomed, however, especially if the children are very young, which care givers sadly recognize:

When he [the seven-month-old] got a new nanny — all he did for the first week was cry. . . . But I mean, he'll never even remember it. I was gone a month, I came back, and he had no idea who I was. It kind of hurt at first, but then I understood — he didn't recognize me at all. But [the other nanny] is good with him, and I trusted her [pause] to take care of my baby.

Some nannies, primarily those who stay with their employers for longer than the initial one-year contract, do make a mark: "It's just cool to know that no matter what happens, you know, whoever comes in and out of their house and who comes in and out of their lives, I'm always going to be there." However, most do not have the satisfaction of a long-term bond. Despite the fact that they know they will not be remembered by their youngest charges, most of the nannies and *au pairs* I interviewed keep up correspondence with former employers in the hope that they will not be completely forgotten and their work erased.

In some cases, the attachment between care giver and child is recognized and valued by her employer. Even though the mothers in this study feel strongly about viewing themselves as the primary parent in their families, they depend on their care givers for stability and consistency in their children's lives, and, if the children love the care provider, no matter how uncomfortable that might be to the mother, that love is the ultimate currency in the family's child-care economy. One mother explained to me why she had been willing to make changes in her work schedule to enable her nanny to attend college, and to make other personal and financial concessions in order to keep the same nanny for five years:

> The fact that [the children] grow to love someone and that person leaves and they never see them again, it can make them not trust the next relationship or not be so open on the next relationship. . . . You know you get jealous a little bit, but, you know I just say hey, you're gonna work, you want someone they're gonna love, and whose gonna love them, you know. Because if you're not there, you want someone who really cares about them and you're going to be their mother for the rest of their lives [laughs]. . . . You know I mean, they love them and they love you, it's nice that they have another person who cares about them. . . . They are getting sort of an extra dose.

A nanny described a similar negotiation based on a child's reaction to her impending departure:

> This summer I was going to leave. And I actually had a job and everything. . . . I was going to go work in a day-care center . . . and it was all set, but [the six-year-old] was just not handling it well. He was like turning into, I don't know, somebody else. . . . All of a sudden he was a baby again and he needed me to do everything that I hadn't been doing for him. And the only thing that we could figure out was that he just really didn't want me to leave and . . . they decided that if I wanted to stay, they'd still pay me as though I was full-time and even though I was only working part-time, so I decided, hey, I can't beat that!

When the value of her attachment is openly recognized by her employer, a nanny can find she is in a position to bargain to restructure the job, using the child's attachment to her as leverage.

However, it is frequently not the economic or work-reduction aspects of this bargain that are the most meaningful to the care giver. In fact, the nanny quoted above moved from a live-in situation in which she was paid $300 per week plus room and board for a sixty-hour work week, to a live-out situation in which she was paid the same amount for a forty-five-hour week, minus the room and board. Although this hardly represents a raise in pay or reduction in work for her, she counted it as a victory because her importance to the family was openly recognized: "[The mother] actually said, 'We'll do what it takes to keep you here because we really want you here,' and she was very nice about it, and she really made it seem like she wanted me here. Not anybody specifically, but me." Another nanny described her decision to stay a second year in a situation in which she had felt overworked, underpaid, and unrecognized:

> [The money] wasn't it, though. I mean I could have gone elsewhere and gotten that amount of money — I think it was more that they gave me what I wanted emotionally. Like, they praised me — constantly . . . and they were amazed at all the things I could do, like getting the kids to do stuff they didn't want to do and, well . . . I was very attached to the kids.

As she points out, she stayed not because her employers offered her improved working conditions, but because they recognized and made visible her shadow labor.

Ironically, the same attachment that can lead employers to offer incentives to stay on for a period of years can also lead nannies and *au pairs* to stay longer than they want in unsatisfactory working conditions. Ultimately, nannies and *au pairs* seek to change not the material but the emotional conditions of their work lives. They feel satisfied when their shadow labor is acknowledged, and although they sometimes use this acknowledgment to renegotiate some of their working conditions, their emphasis on the emotional conditions of their work can just as easily lead them to sacrifice fair wages and decent hours for loyalty and attachment.

## Conclusion

How can we account for the differences between the strategies used by maids and those used by nannies and *au pairs*? Three factors seem salient: the workers, the work, and the meanings associated with the work. The nannies and *au pairs* studied here are white women who see themselves as temporary domestic workers. Whether realistic or not, they view domestic work as a transition phase on the way to greater social and career mobility, regardless of how many years it may consume. Therefore, they tend not to view their wages, hours, and benefits as reflective of their ultimate worth on the labor market. Since they have little or no other work experience, they compare their salary and working conditions to those of other nannies and *au pairs*, not to other workers of similar skill levels. And, because they are white women, they are not expected to reproduce racial hierarchies within the homes of their employers. Nor do they feel that they are relegated to child care or domestic labor as "caste" work.

Further research is needed to determine if this difference is a function of race, of the job description, or of a combination of both.[11]

Second, the highly emotional nature of the work itself prevents nannies and *au pairs* from using the kinds of distancing techniques used by other domestic workers. Instead, they distinguish between the work they consider rewarding (work for the children) and the work they consider degrading (work for the parents and the house). To the extent that they attempt to restructure the work at all, they try to delimit and reduce the latter forms of work while increasing the former.

Third, child care, although poorly paid, carries a high moral and social value. Therefore, nannies and *au pairs* do not perceive the work itself as inherently degrading. They generally enjoy the children in their care and the work of raising them. More importantly, they have an allegiance, not to their employers, but to the children and to the third-parent ideal. As the third parent, they take pride in creating a child-centered home and in putting the children's needs before their own.

Nannies and *au pairs* seek not to reduce their child-care responsibilities but to increase them, and more importantly, to gain recognition for them. Unlike other domestic workers, they try to gain recognition for their invisible labor rather than to do away with it. Their "professionalization project" entails reframing their work as skilled labor and redefining themselves as third parents rather than as mother's helpers. Ironically, allegiance to the third-parent ideal can lead them to forgo viewing their work as an exchange for services, and instead to view it in terms of love and self-sacrifice. As a result, they often neglect their own interests as workers in negotiations with employers.

Their "professionalization project" involves them intimately in renegotiating the division of mothering labor and the meanings associated with it. Working in concert with and in opposition to their employers, nannies and *au pairs* forge a particular type of shared mothering. This shared mothering is created, however, within the context of a dominant cultural ideology that values only mother-intensive child rearing performed by the biological or adoptive mother, and not by a hired provider. Struggles over domination and resistance, over fair wages for fair work, and over market versus family norms, are anathema to this ideology of good motherhood. Therefore, in attempting to redefine the meanings that frame their work and their negotiations with their employers, nannies and *au pairs* use this cultural ideal as a bargaining tool, as a form of resistance, and as a "higher authority" to which they can appeal in negotiations with employers. Ultimately, however, they too capitulate to this ideal, which both shapes the contours of their work and constrains their attempts to change it.

## NOTES

*Acknowledgments:* An earlier version of this chapter was presented at the 1995 annual meeting of the Eastern Sociological Society in Philadelphia. The author would like to thank the following individuals for their valuable comments on earlier drafts: Karen V. Hansen, Betsy Hayes, Henry Rubin, Carmen Sirianni, and Gregory Williams.

1. For example, historians have investigated the transformation of domestic labor during industrialization. See Dudden (1983); Katzman (1978); Palmer (1989); and Sutherland (1981). In addition, sociologists and historians have studied how domestic service continues to re-create class and race oppression within households, and how domestic workers have developed resistance strategies against the indignities of personal service. See Colen (1989); Dill (1988); Glenn (1986) and Chapter 6 in this volume; Rollins (1985) and Chapter 9 in this volume; Romero (1992); and Salzinger (1991).

2. This study is a part of a larger research project, based on interviews with nannies, *au pairs*, and mothers who employ them, that examines the nature of shared mothering within the home, how mothers and providers divide mothering work within this context, and the implications of this division for personal and cultural meanings associated with motherhood.

   This paper draws specifically on the pilot study for this project, which consists of in-depth interviews with 5 *au pairs*, 5 nannies, and 5 mothers, as well as interviews with the owner of a nanny placement agency, the local coordinator for an *au pair* placement program, and the president of the International Nanny Association. To be included in this pilot study, a family situation had to include at least 1 child under age 5 and a mother who worked at least 35 hours per week outside of the home as well as a live-in care giver. Some nannies and *au pairs* were interviewed more than once over the course of their work lives. The study also draws on my own experiences as a former live-in child-care provider. And, although this pilot study is based on interviews with 15 *au pairs*, nannies, and mothers, most had experienced more than one care giver–employee relationship, so the data include stories from 28 family situations.

   Thus far, I have interviewed only European *au pairs* and Caucasian American nannies. Therefore, this chapter does not reflect the full range of live-in child-care providers, since no women of color are included in this study at this stage. Although the term "maid" may be considered somewhat demeaning, I chose to use it rather than the broader term "domestic" because of the need to refine further the categories of domestic service. Within household service, there are various types of workers with different responsibilities, previously understood under the catchall category of "domestic worker," which is too broad to be of analytic use in this essay. At the same time, other terms, like "house cleaner," seem too narrow. Therefore, to designate those workers whose responsibilities are primarily cleaning, I chose, like Romero (1992), to use the designation "maid."

4. Uttal's (1993) study includes child-care arrangements of all types, including care by family members and friends. Wrigley's (1995) study attempts to analyze how race shapes relationships between in-home care givers and their employers, yet it includes both housekeepers and nannies, and thus fails to distinguish how job description and title are affected by race.

5. On new legislation regulating *au pair* earnings and training, see Greenhouse (1995).

6. There are no current systematic data on the wages of immigrant care givers. Wrigley (1995: 6) found wages of $150–$200 per week among immigrant care givers who

worked for middle-class families. It is not clear, however, whether they also received full-time room and board, or whether their jobs were defined primarily as child care or as housekeeping.

7. For more on this dilemma, see, for example, Macdonald (1993); Nelson (1990); Wrigley (1995).

8. Hertz (1986: esp. 156, 174) notes the same preferences among the two-income couples she studied.

9. Or second-parent status, in the case of a single-parent family.

10. Romero (1992: 136–43) makes this useful distinction between the types of resistance strategies used by domestics.

11. As mentioned, since the nannies and *au pairs* in this study are white women, and the maids in other studies are all women of color, these groups are mutually exclusive and cannot be compared along ethnic lines.

## REFERENCES

Cohen, Rina. 1991. "Women of Color in White Households: Coping Strategies of Live-in Domestic Workers." *Qualitative Sociology* 14(2): 197–215.

Colen, Shellee. 1989. "'Just a Little Respect': West Indian Domestic Workers in New York City." In Elsa M. Chaney and Maria Garcia Castro, eds., *Muchachas No More: Household Workers in Latin America and the Caribbean* (pp. 171–197). Philadelphia: Temple University Press.

Cowan, Ruth Schwartz. 1983. *More Work for Mother: The Ironies of Household Technology from the Open Hearth to the Microwave.* New York: Basic Books.

Daniels, Arlene Kaplan. 1987. "Invisible Work." *Social Problems* 34(5): 403–26.

Dill, Bonnie Thornton. 1988. "Making Your Job Good Yourself." In Ann Bookman and Sandra Morgen, eds., *Women and the Politics of Empowerment* (pp. 33–52). Philadelphia: Temple University Press.

Dudden, Faye. 1983. *Serving Women: Household Service in Nineteenth-Century America.* Middletown, CT: Wesleyan University Press.

Ehrenreich, Barbara, and Deirdre English. 1978. *For Her Own Good: 150 Years of the Experts' Advice to Women.* Garden City, NY: Doubleday.

Eyer, Diane. 1992. *Mother-Infant Bonding: A Scientific Fiction.* New Haven: Yale University Press.

Glenn, Evelyn Nakano. 1986. *Issei, Nissei, War Bride: Three Generations of Japanese American Women in Domestic Service.* Philadelphia: Temple University Press.

Greenhouse, Stephen. 1995. "U.S. Sets Rules on *Au Pairs.*" *The New York Times,* February 16, sec. D, p. 21.

Hays, Sharon. 1993. "The Cultural Contradictions of Intensive Motherhood." Ph.D. dissertation, University of California, San Diego.

Hertz, Rosanna. 1986. *More Equal Than Others: Women and Men in Dual-Career Marriages.* Berkeley: University of California Press.

Hochschild, Arlie. 1983. *The Managed Heart: Commercialization of Human Feeling.* Berkeley: University of California Press.

Hofferth, Sandra, April Brayfield, Sharon Deich, and Pamela Holcomb. 1991. *National Child Care Survey, 1990.* Washington, DC: Urban Institute Press.

Hondagneu-Sotelo, Pierrette. 1994. "Regulating the Unregulated? Domestic Workers' Social Networks." *Social Problems* 41(1): 50–64.

Illich, Ivan. 1981. *Shadow Work*. Boston, MA: M. Boyars.

Katzman, David. 1978. *Seven Days a Week: Women and Domestic Work in Industrializing America*. New York: Oxford University Press.

Kenny, Charles. 1993. "More Illegal Aliens Find Work in Area as Nannies." *Boston Globe*, January 17, p. 28.

Macdonald, Cameron Lynne. 1993. "'Three Parents Instead of Only Two': Nannies, *Au Pairs*, and the Social Construction of Mothering." Brandeis University Women's Studies Program Working Papers Series, No. 7.

———. 1992. "'One to Hold Me, the Other to Look At': Mothers, Servants, and Others Performing Child Care in Nineteenth-Century New England." Unpublished paper.

Maitland, Leslie. 1990. "A Tribute to Nannies by One of Their Own." *The New York Times*, July 5.

Margolis, Maxine. 1984. *Mothers and Such: Views of American Women and Why They Changed*. Berkeley: University of California Press.

Nelson, Margaret K. 1990. *Negotiated Care: The Experiences of Family Day Care Providers*. Philadelphia: Temple University Press.

Palmer, Phyllis. 1989. *Domesticity and Dirt: Housewives and Servants in the United States, 1920–1989*. Philadelphia: Temple University Press.

Rollins, Judith. 1985. *Between Women: Domestics and Their Employers*. Philadelphia: Temple University Press.

Romero, Mary. 1992. *Maid in the U.S.A.* New York: Routledge.

Salzinger, Leslie. 1991. "A Maid by Any Other Name: The Transformation of 'Dirty Work' by Central American Immigrants." In Michael Burawoy et al., eds., *Ethnography Unbound: Power and Resistance in the Modern Metropolis* (pp. 139–60). Berkeley: University of California Press.

Sontag, Deborah. 1993. "Increasingly, Two-Career Family Means Illegal Immigrant Help." *The New York Times*, January 24.

Strasser, Susan. 1982. *Never Done: A History of American Housework*. New York: Pantheon Books.

Sutherland, Daniel. 1981. *Americans and Their Servants: Domestic Service in the United States from 1800 to 1920*. Baton Rouge: Louisiana State University Press.

Thurer, Shari L. 1994. *The Myths of Motherhood: How Culture Reinvents the Good Mother*. Boston: Houghton Mifflin.

U.S. Bureau of Labor Statistics. 1993. "Civilian Employment in Fastest Growing and Fastest Declining Occupations: 1992 to 2005." *Monthly Labor Review* (November).

U.S. Bureau of the Census. 1994. *Statistical Abstract of the United States*. Washington, DC: U.S. Government Printing Office.

Uttal, Lynet. 1993. "Shared Mothering: Reproductive Labor, Child Care, and the Meanings of Motherhood." Ph.D. dissertation. University of California at Santa Cruz.

Wrigley, Julia. 1995. *Other People's Children*. New York: Basic Books.

## Chapter 11

# Resisting the Symbolism
# of Service among Waitresses

## • Greta Foff Paules

> In the public world of work, it is often part of an individual's job to accept uneven exchanges, to be treated with disrespect or anger by a client, all the while closeting into fantasy the anger one would like to respond with. Where the customer is king, unequal exchanges are normal, and from the beginning customer and client assume different rights to feeling and display.
> — Arlie Hochschild, *The Managed Heart* [1983]

> [The customer] jumps up, he pushes me out of the way, and he goes, "You just blew your tip! I'm going to have your *job*! That's what I'm going to have." . . . I don't take that. . . . I have to tell people off. When they're degrading me personally, then I will tell them, "I don't have to put up with your shit. I don't have to wait on you. I don't have to. You can leave."
> — Route waitress

Studies of women in low-level jobs typically focus on the constraints and hardships of the work, on what is denied and demanded of the women, and on how the work disempowers the workers.

When I began an eighteen-month participant-observation study of waitresses at Route, a small family-style restaurant in New Jersey, I expected to follow this well-trod path of inquiry. What clearer symbol of exploited woman could there be than the harried waitress racing among tables of cranky cus-

Reprinted from Greta Foff Paules, *Dishing It Out* (Philadelphia: Temple University Press, 1991), pp. 131–66, with revisions.

tomers with crying babies, her arms stacked with plates of dripping pancakes and cold eggs, her polyester apron smeared with yesterday's mashed potatoes and clinking with the nickels and dimes she receives as pay?

Besides, before waitressing, observing, and doing interviews at Route, I had waitressed on and off for five years, working full- and part-time, on the west and east coasts. I knew these ropes, and they were rough.

But what I found, once I learned to tune out my own griping and really listen to the women I worked with in the course of the study, was that, for all the grit and grind of their work, these waitresses were not passive victims of exploitive processes. (Without formally challenging the conditions of their work, and without unionizing, they nonetheless succeeded in improving the quality of their work lives in very real ways.)

Nowhere, perhaps, was this more apparent than in their rejection of the complex symbolism of servitude that pervades the work of waitresses and of many service employees. Employees of service industries are encouraged to treat customers with unflinching reverence and solicitude; to regard their concerns and needs as paramount; to look upon them as masters and kings. But to accept this image of the other requires that one adopt a particular image of self. If the customer is king (or queen), the employee by extension is subject, or servant. In the restaurant, a complex system of symbolism encourages customer and worker alike to approach service as an encounter between beings of vastly different social standing, with unequal claims to courtesy, consideration, and respect. (Though the customer accepts the imagery of servitude and adopts an interactive posture appropriate to the role of master, the waitress rejects the role of servant in favor of images of self in which she is an active and controlling force in the service encounter. Perhaps because of this, she is able to control the feelings she experiences and expresses toward her customers, and she is neither disoriented nor self-alienated by the emotional demands of her work.)

## *Waitress as Servant:*
## *Company- and Customer-Backed Metaphors*

### Conventions of Interaction

The image of waitress as servant is fostered above all by the conventions that govern interaction between server and served. Much as domestic servants in the nineteenth century did not dine with or in the presence of masters, so today waitresses are forbidden to take breaks, sit, smoke, eat, or drink in the presence of customers.[1] At Route, employees are not allowed to consume so much as a glass of water on the floor, though they are welcome to imbibe unlimited quantities of soda and coffee out of sight of customers. The prohibition against engaging in such physically necessary acts as eating, drinking, and resting in the customer's presence functions to limit contact between server and served and fortify status lines. It is, in addition, a means of concealing the humanness of those whom one would like to deny the courtesies of personhood. When indications of the server's personhood inadvertently obtrude into the service encounter, customers may be forced to modify their interactive stance. One Route waitress commented that when her parents ate at the restaurant her customers treated her with greater respect.

> They look at me like, "Oh my God. They have *parents?*" It's sometimes like we're not human. It's like they become more friendly when my parents are there and I get better tips off them. And I've never gotten stiffed when my parents have been sitting there. . . . They see that outside of this place I am a person and I have relationships with other people.

## Physical Setting and Costumes of Waitress Work

The architecture of nineteenth-century houses reinforced class distinctions by ensuring physical segregation of master and servant (Sutherland 1981: 30). Servants were charged to enter and exit through back doors and were exiled to live and work in isolated and barren quarters.[2] Special care was taken to conceal or separate the kitchen from family living areas. Similarly, in restaurants, employees may be required to enter through back doors or don street clothes, and so assume the status of customer, if entering through the front door. They are assigned separate bathrooms and separate rooms to eat and rest in, and the kitchen is carefully camouflaged behind swinging doors or staggered partitions. Even then, proximity to the kitchen diminishes the desirability of a table, indicating that the polluting force of servants cannot be contained by physical barriers.

The demarcation between the quarters of server and served is marked in the restaurant, as in a house, by a change in decor: (the carpet stops abruptly at the boundary between front and back house; the soft lighting of the dining room is replaced by a fluorescent glare; and no music is piped into the employees' working areas, break room, or bathrooms.) As one moves into the work areas of lower-ranking employees the decor becomes increasingly barren. Like scullery maids who "never entered family quarters, . . . and ate and slept in nooks and crannies" (Sutherland 1981: 30), dishwashers and other back-house employees rarely appear on the floor but are kept out of sight in rooms with no windows, no air conditioning, and drains in the floor. It may be symbolically significant that at Route, as in many restaurants, the managers' office is located in the bowels of the back house, squeezed between the employee bathroom, the dish room, and the cooks' line.

Dress is another symbolically rich realm. Restaurants often discourage waitresses from adorning themselves in ways that might appear cheap — from wearing heavy make-up, for instance, or wearing their skirts too short. Waitresses, and other service workers, are also discouraged from dressing above their stations. The common interdiction in service dress codes against conspicuous jewelry may serve the same purpose as medieval decrees forbidding low-ranking persons to wear gold (Simmel 1950: 343). In each case those of subordinate status are prohibited from assuming symbols of wealth or status that might obscure their position and blur class lines. The aggressively plain uniform of the waitress underscores status distinctions between those who render and those who receive service in the same way that the black dress and white cap of the nineteenth-century domestic acted as a "public announcement of subservience" (Rothman 1987: 169; Sutherland 1981: 29–30). Today the standard uniform of the waitress (plain dress and apron or pinafore) and that of a maid are similar enough that it is difficult to determine whether certain drawings in school textbooks represent waitresses or maids (Federbush 1974: 181). In the modern service encounter, the need to underscore the server's inferiority may be especially strong as the status differential between server and served is intrinsically tenuous. The superiority of customer to waitress is limited temporally to the duration of the encounter and spatially to the boundaries of the restaurant. Rigidly defined dress codes, which eliminate all clues of the server's nonwork status, may serve to put the customer at ease in issuing orders to one whose subordination is so narrowly defined.

It is in their implications for the worker's status that the dress codes of direct services differ from those of other categories of work. As the titles suggest, blue- and white-collar workers are also subject to dress codes, but the primary function of these codes is not to proclaim the worker's low social standing or control her projected personality. The appearance regulations of factory workers are designed at least partly with the security of the company and the safety of the worker in mind.[3] The appearance codes of service workers are concerned primarily with image and status delineation and may actually interfere with the worker's ability to perform her job safely or effectively. Some flight attendants are required to wear heels, which decrease their stability and increase their fatigue (Hochschild 1983). And in some restaurants, waitresses who carry plates on their arms rather than on trays are required to wear short-sleeved, and hence less authoritative uniforms.[4] Because plates are heated (by heat lamps or in the oven) to keep the food warm, waitresses must allow the plates (and the food) to cool, or pad their arms with napkins before delivering orders. Both strategies waste time and produce lukewarm food, and the latter can lead to burned arms, as napkins tend to absorb heat or fly away en route to the table.

The businesswoman who would "dress for success" is, like the waitress, subject to dress regulations of remarkable specificity. She is advised by a best-selling dress manual to wear a wool skirt with ample hem, reinforced waist, and zipper the same color as the fabric. She is counseled to wear dark pumps, closed at the heel and toe, with one-and-a-half-inch heels, and she is urged to carry an umbrella with at least ten spokes, preferably solid (Molloy 1977). While the waitress's maidlike uniform functions to diminish her status, however, the executive's "uniform" is designed for status enhancement. A basic dress-for-success guideline is "always wear upper-middle-class clothing" (Molloy 1977: 186).[5] The uniform of the executive also differs from that of the service worker in that it is at least ostensibly voluntary, indicating that however strictly the businessperson's appearance is controlled by her work, this control is not recognized as a right.

## Linguistic Conventions of Service

The linguistic conventions of the restaurant and, in particular, the unilateral use of first names, further emphasize status differences between customer and waitress. Like the nonreciprocal use of terms of endearment (Wolfson and Manes 1980), the unilateral use of first names signals the subordinate status of the addressee; thus, African Americans, children, and household domestics have traditionally been addressed by first names by those whom they in turn address as *sir*, *ma'am*, *Mr.*, or *Mrs.* Restaurants perpetuate this practice by requiring servers to wear name tags which, regardless of the worker's age, bear only her first name, and by requiring servers to introduce themselves by first name to each party they wait on. Waitresses generally have no access to the customer's first or last name (the customer's larger "information preserve" prohibits inquiry) and are constrained to resort to the polite address forms *sir* and *ma'am* when addressing their parties.[6]

The etymological nearness of the terms *service worker* and *server/servant* to *servile* (Hollander 1985: 56) contributes to the imagery of servitude by providing linguistic continuity between historically stigmatized and modern forms of service. Throughout the nineteenth century domestic workers rebelled against the label *servant*, which carried connotations of serfdom, indentured servitude, and slavery. As a result of this rebellion, euphemisms such as *help* were gradually substituted for the implicitly demeaning *servant* (Sutherland 1981: 125). The term *server*, a relatively new innovation in the restaurant industry (Jerome n.d.), is thus anachronistic rather than conservative and suggests a desire to resurrect more traditional forms of service.

The symbolism of service is not a creation of Route, or of other service industries in which it is found. The symbolic similarities between direct-service work and domestic servitude are the product of actual historical connections between past and present forms of service. The proliferation of restaurants in the early twentieth century coincided with the appearance of smaller, mechanized houses and the corresponding disappearance of the domestic servant as an essential fixture in middle- and upper-middle-class homes (Sutherland 1981: 182–99). (It seems likely that the symbolism of service was simply transported along with the physical and social functions of the domestic from private home to private enterprise.)

Even so, modern service organizations must be charged with actively perpetuating the conventions of servitude and, in some cases, inventing new conventions that restate ties with the past. The restaurant requires the waitress to dress as a maid and introduce herself by first name; the restaurant commissions the building of separate bathrooms for employee and customer; and the restaurant promotes the degrading term *server.* In preserving the conventions of servitude the company encourages the waitress to internalize an image of self as servant and to adopt an interactive stance consistent with this image. In promoting an image of server as servant to the public, the restaurant encourages customers to treat, or mistreat, the waitress as they would a member of a historically degraded class.

## Public Perceptions of Service as Servitude

That customers embrace the service-as-servitude metaphor is evidenced by the way they speak to and about service workers. Virtually every rule of etiquette is violated by customers in their interaction with the waitress: the waitress can be interrupted; she can be addressed with the mouth full; she can be ignored and stared at; and she can be subjected to unrestrained anger. Lacking the status of a person she, like the servant, is refused the most basic considerations of polite interaction. She is, in addition, the subject of chronic criticism. Just as in the nineteenth century servants were perceived as ignorant, slow, lazy, indifferent, and immoral (Sutherland 1981), so in the twentieth century service workers are condemned for their stupidity, apathy, slowness, incompetence, and questionable moral character. The full range of criticism commonly directed toward service workers is captured in a 1987 *Time* cover story entitled "Pul-eeze!

Will Somebody Help Me?" (Koepp 1987). The article and its accompanying cartoons portray service workers as ignorant: cabdrivers do not know where Main Street is, and bookstore cashiers have never heard of Dickens; incompetent: a clerk in an appliance store "does not know how to turn on the tape recorder he is trying to sell"; lazy: men at work play cards and smoke, while painters snooze; and immoral: cabin attendants "stand by unconcerned, aloof and bored, while old folks and children struggle with their bags." The *Time* story is not unique. Television commercials regularly caricature the ineptitude of service workers, and newspapers and magazines are inundated with articles bemoaning the service problem, as newspapers and magazines in the last decades of the last century were flooded with articles on the "servant problem" (Sutherland 1981: 169–71).[7]

Criticism of service is not confined to television or to the pages of popular journalism. One of the most impassioned denunciations of service workers is found in Marvin Harris's anthropological text, *America Now*. Harris (1981: 39–59) describes service workers as hostile, physically and vocally abusive, disinterested, incompetent, arrogant, snarling, evasive, unreliable, unrepentant, bored, apathetic, rude, and threatening. He accuses service workers of crimes commensurate with their moral and mental deficiencies: bus drivers drive recklessly, caterers poison food, filling station attendants assault customers, doctors and nurses send families home with the wrong babies and let patients bleed to death.[8] Harris's commentary confirms that service workers have inherited the negative stereotypes as well as the physical and social functions of their nineteenth-century predecessors, and demonstrates that anthropologists are as much imprisoned by the values and beliefs of their culture as are those they study.

As service workers have inherited the negative stereotypes of servants, so modern customers have inherited a belief in a "golden age" of service. In the past the date of this golden age was not fixed, but according to Daniel Sutherland (1981: 6), seemed to advance with the passing of generations: "By the mid-1870s, the golden age was estimated to be around 1850. . . . In the twentieth century, those halcyon days were remembered as being in the decade after the Civil War, and by 1920, they had progressed as far as 1900." Stephen Koepp (1987) identifies the early post–World War II era as the "heyday of personal service," indicating that the golden age of service continues to advance — or retreat. Still more recently, the ideal of personal service has come to be located, not in the past, but in other countries, most notably Japan (Barron 1989).

The imagery of servitude is the most insidious and perhaps, therefore, the most dangerous of hazards the waitress encounters. It pervades every aspect of her work, pressuring her to internalize a negative perception of self and assume a corresponding posture of submission; yet, because it is symbolically conveyed and not, for the most part, explicitly advocated, it cannot be directly confronted and may not even be consciously recognized. Nevertheless, the Route waitress successfully resists the symbolism of service, counterpoising company-supported understandings of her role as servant with her own images of self as a soldier confronting enemy forces, or alternatively, as an independent businessperson, working in her own interests, on her own territory. )

## *Waitress as Soldier*

If asked, a waitress would certainly agree that waiting tables is much like doing battle, but waitresses do not voluntarily make the comparison explicit. Rather, the perception of waiting tables as waging war and accordingly, the self-perception of waitress as soldier, is expressed implicitly in the waitress's war-oriented terminology: groups of tables under the control of individual waitresses are referred to as *stations*; the cooks' work area is referred to as the *line*; simultaneously adding several checks to the cooks' wheel is *sandbagging*; to receive many customers at once is to *get hit*; a full station or busy line is *bombed out*; old food and empty restaurants are *dead*; customers who leave no tips, *stiff*; abbreviations used by the waitress to communicate orders to the cook are *codes*; to get angry at someone is to *go off on* or *blow up at* her; to be short an item of food on an order is to *drag* the item; the number of customers served is a *customer count*; the late shift is *graveyard* or *grave*; to provide assistance to a co-worker (especially a cook) is to *bail him out*. Waitresses occasionally devise new uses of the war idiom. One waitress commented that when she was pregnant she had her friend *run* the eggs while she went to throw up. Later, when her manager refused to let her go home, the waitress responded by handing him her book and walking out: "I walked off my — I abandoned ship," she recalled. Explaining why she objected to a manager having an affair with a waitress, another waitress commented that managers "don't supposed to infiltrate the treaty."

Though much of this is official company terminology, it assumes the connotations of battle only in connection with the waitress's informal, and more blatantly war-oriented language. To refer to the nucleus of the kitchen as the *line* does not in itself convey a sense of combat; there are assembly lines and bus lines as well as lines of fire and battle. Only when the cooks' line is regularly said to be *bombed out*, or when stations are repeatedly referred to as *getting hit*, does the battle-oriented meaning of these terms become apparent.

Several of the war idioms used by waitresses are not specific to restaurant work but are used in other occupations, or are common slang. The point here is not that the waitress's view of her work is unique, but that it is a view very different from that promoted by the physical props and interactive conventions of the restaurant. Like many people, and seemingly to a greater degree, the waitress views her work as something of a battle and those with whom her work brings her into contact as the enemy. More important, (she views herself, not as a servant who peacefully surrenders to the commands of her master, but as a soldier actively returning fire on hostile forces.) The waitress's capacity to sustain this self-image while donning the costume of a maid and complying with the interpersonal conventions of servitude, attests to her strength of will and power of resistance. The same may be said of all subordinate persons who are forced to resist without openly violating the symbolic order (Scott 1985: 33).

## Waitress as Private Entrepreneur

During a rush, when the restaurant looks and sounds like a battle zone, the metaphor of service as war and waitress as soldier is most salient. During more peaceful periods, a different image of self assumes prominence: that of waitress as private entrepreneur. While these perceptions of self can be viewed as divergent and even opposed, both convey a sense of power and action.[9]

(Evidence that the waitress perceives herself as a private entrepreneur is found in her conceptual isolation of herself from the company and in her possessiveness toward people and things under her jurisdiction.) The waitress's self-isolation may be expressed relatively directly, as in the following comments of a Route waitress:

> When she [a dissatisfied customer] was getting ready to pay her check, I was ringing it up and she was asking me my name, she was asking my manager's name, she was writing down the regional office's number. So I said, "Look. Do you have a problem? I'm a grown woman. If you have a problem with me, talk to me. If you have a problem with Route, call the region. Fine. If you have a problem with me, talk to me."

(It is also expressed in the waitress's ambivalence toward performing tasks not directly related to the business of making tips.) As an independent businessperson, the waitress views her responsibilities to the company as extremely limited. The company pays her a minor retainer, but it is felt to cover few duties beyond those immediately related to waiting tables. Accordingly, *side-work* (stocking supplies and cleaning other than that involved in bussing tables) is performed by the waitress with an air of forbearance as though it were understood that such work was above the call of duty.

The term *sidework* fosters the view that these tasks are peripheral to the waitress's work, but in fact, the thorough completion of sidework duties is critical to the smooth functioning of each shift—and to peaceful relations between shifts. The failure of swing waitresses to stock chocolate fudge spells disaster for grave waitresses faced with twenty orders for sundaes and no supplies. Likewise, the neglect of grave waitresses to fill the syrup dispensers and stock butter creates chaos for the day shift. There is rarely time to stock the necessary items while waiting tables: supplies are often packed in boxes under other boxes on shelves in locked rooms or freezers; they are packaged in jumbo cans and jars, which are heavy and difficult to open; and they sometimes require heating or defrosting before they can be used. Still, stocking and cleaning for the next shift are peripheral to the waitress's work in the sense that they do not directly enhance her tip earnings, and this is the sense that is most significant for the waitress as entrepreneur.

The waitress may, in addition, consider it beyond the call of duty to intervene on the company's behalf to prevent theft of restaurant property.

> I constantly tell Hollinger [a manager] he's a jerk. Constantly. 'Cause he's an ass. Because, people came in and ripped off place mats on graveyard, and he came in giving me heck. . . . And I said, "Let me tell you something, Hollinger. I don't *care* if they rip off the place mats. If you want somebody to stand by that door, and by that register, then you'd better hire somebody just to do that. 'Cause that's not my job. I'm here to wait on the people. I take the cash.[10] I can't be baby-sitting grown adults."

The place mats referred to here were being sold by Route as part of a promotional campaign; waitresses do not use place mats to set tables. The point is significant because, as will be seen, waitresses are extremely possessive of, and so likely to protect, restaurant property that they use in their work.

The waitress's tendency to isolate herself from the company, which she perceives as neither liable for her faults nor warranted in requiring her to do more than wait tables, indicates that she does not see herself as an employee in the conventional sense. Her sense of independence is fostered by the tipping system, which releases her from financial dependence on the company, and by the circumscription of managerial authority, which indirectly augments the scope of her autonomy. At the same time, the waitress's perception that she is in business for herself may prompt her to assert her independence more strongly.)

In keeping with her self-image as entrepreneur, the waitress refers to restaurant property as though it belonged to her. She speaks of *my* salt and peppers, my coffee, my napkins, my silverware, my booths, my catsups, my sugars. Linguistically, people too belong to the waitress who talks of *my* customers, my district manager, and my manager. The inclusion of managers among the waitress's possessions reflects(her view of managers as individuals hired by the company to maintain satisfactory working conditions so she can conduct her business efficiently. Cooks, dishwashers, and hostesses, on the other hand, tend to be viewed as employees hired by and accountable to managers and are referred to more inclusively as *our* or *their*)(the managers').

The waitress also exhibits possessiveness in the way she treats her belongings and the belongings of others. Though she is unwilling to discourage customers from stealing company place mats, she may protect items she uses, and so regards as her own, literally to the knife:

> [A customer] comes in, and he wanted a to-go order of a steak and so forth and he had a steak knife, and silverware. . . . I watched him take it [the silverware]. And I told him . . . "I won't give you your food until you give me back *my* silverware." I was determined not to give his to-go order until he gave me back my silverware, and he was determined he was taking it with the silverware. So he pulled a knife [his own] on me and told me, how would I like my pretty little face all cut up? And not to get smart with him and so forth. So I just yelled for Calvin [a cook] and said, "I'm not getting smart with you. You give me back my silverware, you'll get your food." (emphasis added)

If waitresses are adamantly protective of their own property, they are equally respectful of the property of others. In the restaurant, ownership is determined by location: supplies located in a waitress's station belong to her for the duration of the shift. (Customers who pilfer napkins, silverware, and salt and pepper shakers from nearby tables are often inadvertently stealing from another waitress's station.) A waitress who wishes to borrow a co-waitress's catsups, silverware, napkins, or coffee must ask to do so. If she cannot locate the owner and is in desperate and immediate need of the item, she may take it but will apologetically inform the owner as soon as possible that she "stole" the needed article. Borrowing or stealing customers is never acceptable. Apart from those rare occasions when she has obtained her co-worker's consent beforehand, a waitress will not take the order of a party seated in a co-worker's station no matter how frantically the customers wave menus, or how impatiently they glare at passing employees. (If, as frequently happens, the "owner" of the party has disappeared, or if there is some confusion concerning the party's ownership, a waitress will search the corners of the restaurant and question other employees in an effort to locate or identify the rightful owner, rather than take the order herself and risk being accused of theft.[11] Indeed, waitresses avoid becoming involved with their co-workers' customers, even in the interests of lending assistance.) One waitress recalled that a co-waitress and friend had been caught in the cross fire of a customer food fight and had been doused with orange soda. Asked if she had intervened on behalf of her friend and reprimanded the customers, the waitress responded, "No. I didn't say nothing. 'Cause that's Mary's people."

If a waitress does lend assistance to a co-worker's party, she is likely to approach the party's owner immediately afterward and explain what she has done and why (for example, "I gave table six some napkins, 'cause the kid spilled his water"). This allows the party's owner to keep track of what her customers have and still need and ensures that chargeable items will be added to the check. Equally important, by explaining her presence in a co-worker's domain, the waitress concedes that she has trespassed and acknowledges her co-worker's right to sovereignty on her own territory.

A waitress who is flagged down by a particularly aggressive party in a co-worker's station is liable to lose substantial time from her own parties listening to the customers' questions or complaints, tracking down their rightful waitress, or fulfilling their requests personally. In these instances, the waitress may inform the party's owner of her assistance as a means of pointing out that, by virtue of her negligence, the owner has trespassed on the assisting waitress's time. The negligent waitress typically apologizes (sincerely) and then goes on to criticize the party for its relentless requests or complaints. The assisting waitress agrees that the customers appeared rude or picky, or simply expresses sympathy with her co-worker and so demonstrates that the waitress's negligence is forgiven. These interchanges do not function to establish a balance of debt between servers. A waitress who lends assistance in such cases does not expect and will not ask for a return favor at a later date. These relatively formalized interactions serve only to reaffirm the sanctity of each waitress's time and territory by acknowledging that a violation of the possessive order has taken place.

The emphasis waitresses place on respecting one another's property and territorial boundaries is part of a broader code of noninterference. (As entrepreneurs operating on their own and in their own interests, waitresses do not expect to be interfered with by others.) The anger that the waitress experiences in response to managerial intervention in her work may arise, in part, because such intervention is at variance with her understanding of her status in the restaurant as an independent businessperson. Waitresses also expect each other to respect their autonomy and rarely meddle with the work habits of co-workers. Some waitresses apparently define good relations with co-workers and management as those involving minimum contact. One former Route waitress commented:

> I got along with all the managers [at Route]. Nobody bothered me.

Another waitress remarked:

> Route right now, it's fun. I don't get any abuse, I don't get any hassles. It's just fun. And I don't really pay attention to anybody.

And another said:

> Graveyard staff, they're the easiest to get along with. They mind their own business, and they're not as petty as any of the other staffs.

One of the clearest manifestations of the waitresses' code of noninterference is the diversity of methods they employ to carry food. Some Route waitresses can stack ten or more plates on one arm and carry two in their spare hand; others can barely manage three plates at a time, and still others resort to carrying plates on beverage trays. Some waitresses can hold five full water glasses in one palm or carry two brimming coffee cups on saucers in one hand without spilling a drop; others can manage only three glasses or two cups with both hands and are still prone to slosh and spill their beverages en route to the table. There is a proper, or optimally efficient, method of carrying plates and glasses, and it is fairly easy to learn; yet those who are familiar with the technique do not attempt to teach it to less-skilled workers, and these in turn do not solicit instruction from their more efficient co-waitresses. This is not a case of seasoned workers guarding trade secrets, for some experienced, high-ranking waitresses carry plates relatively inefficiently, and there is no attitude of condescension or mystery among those who possess the skill. It would simply be inconsistent with the waitress's emphasis on protecting her autonomy, and respecting that of others, to correct or even comment on the carrying practices or other work habits of her co-workers.

One of the few instances in which a waitress directly interfered with the work of a co-waitress ended in a physical confrontation. In this incident a longtime Route waitress advised a relative newcomer not to scoop ice from the ice bin with a glass, since the glass might break, and the bin would then have to be emptied and flushed. The newcomer advised the waitress to mind her own business and continued to use the glass to scoop ice, dragging it along the metal bottom of the bin in the process. The first waitress then called in a manager to back her up, and the two waitresses continued to exchange sharp words while he stood between them. Finally, tempers peaked and the newcomer reached around the manager and slapped her co-worker in the face. There were other issues underlying this conflict, including quite possibly racial tensions, but it is significant that the final confrontation took the form of a dispute over the right of one waitress to intervene in the work of another. In discussing the incident with her co-workers afterward, the senior-ranking waitress took great care to justify her initial interference, pointing out that not only were customers likely to get glass slivers in their soda, but she herself was in danger of suffering injuries since she used ice from that bin for her own drinks.

## *Freedom of Emotion*

(As she resists company efforts to influence her perception of self, so the waitress maintains control over the emotions she experiences and, to some degree, expresses in the service encounter.)The waitress may adopt a submissive or energetically friendly manner toward those she serves, but she recognizes this manipulation of self as a means of manipulating the other. The boundary between front and backstage, between manufactured and spontaneous emotion, remains distinct; even in the midst of a performance, the waitress does not lose herself in her role or lose sight of her objective.

> This is my motto: "You sit in my station at Route, I'll sell you the world. I'll tell you anything you want to hear." Last night I had this guy, wanted my phone number. He was driving me nuts. And I wasn't interested. . . . He goes, "Well, how come you and your husband broke up?" I said, "Well, he found out about my boyfriend and got mad. I don't know. I don't understand it myself." And he started laughing. And I'm thinking, *"This is my money.* I'll tell you anything." . . . I got five bucks out of him. He didn't get my phone number, but *I got my five-dollar tip.* I'll sell you the world if you're in my station. (emphasis added)

The waitress does not sell her customer the world, only a moment of cheerful banter and an illusion of friendship. For this sale she is adequately compensated: "I got my five-dollar tip" — as though she had settled beforehand on a fair price for her illusion.

The success of such an encounter is not measured by monetary rewards alone, however. For the waitress as for all social actors, skillful dissimulation may be an exercise in autonomy, an expression of control.

> By easily showing a regard that he does not have, the actor can feel that he is preserving a kind of inner autonomy, holding off the ceremonial order by the very act of upholding it. And of course in scrupulously observing the proper forms he may find that he is free to insinuate all kinds of disregard by carefully modifying intonation, pronunciation, pacing, and so forth. (Goffman 1967: 58)

The degree of control the waitress maintains over her inner state is suggested by the ease with which she turns on and off the facade of subservience or conviviality: a smile becomes a sneer even as she turns away from the table; "yes, ma'am, yes, sir" become vehement expletives as soon as she disappears behind the lines.

> I can cuss like a wizard now. Because when they get on your nerves you go in the back and before you know it you saying, "You mother-fucker, you God damn bastard, you blue-eyed faggot." . . . I came out with some names I ain't never thought I knew.

Many servers commented that waitressing had made them tougher and had, in addition, altered their perception of the public.

> It's changed me a lot. I have less patience with the public. I found out how rude and cruel people today are. . . . I seen two faces of the public, and I don't like it. I don't like their evil side. . . . After you been working with the public for X amount of years, you start seeing the good and the bad in people, and the bad outweighs the good.

> My thoughts on people went downhill after being on graveyard for a while. . . . I was never hit with ignorance or someone speaking to me gruffly or roughly and ordering around, and snapping their fingers. . . . People basically are not nice people.

> I never knew that people were so low-down, rotten, and whatever that goes along with it until you start waitressing. . . . I never knew in my life how rude and nasty and obnoxious people can be. Until you start waitressing and you have to wait on these people. . . . [later] They act like animals! Like, like they starving. Like they ain't never had a piece of gristle or toast in their mouth!

(As the waitress comes to see the public in an increasingly negative light, she comes to interpret her customers' rudeness and impatience, like their low tips, as evidence of their "evil side," and not a reflection on her waitressing or social skills. In turn, she becomes less willing to tolerate impatience and irritation which she no longer accepts responsibility for provoking. In the terms of her own idiom of war, the waitress claims the right to return fire on what she has come to regard as inherently aggressive, hostile forces.)

The worst experience I had as far as a customer was when I worked graveyard and a family came in . . . two girls and a man and a woman. She obviously was a foreigner, cause she spoke broken English. . . . And she was very rude, very nasty to me. . . . First thing that she did when she sat down was complain. From the time she sat down to the time they ended up walking out, she complained left and right. And she embarrassed me. She tried to embarrass me. She tried everything in the book. She degraded me. But I stood up to her, and I wouldn't let that happen. I stood up to her regardless of whether they were customers, regardless of whether I lost my job.[12] Nobody's going to degrade me like that because I'm a waitress. . . . And then she started getting loud. And boisterous. . . . I said, "Look." And then I put my book down. I slammed my book down. I put my pen on the table. . . . I said, "Look. If you can do a better job than me, then you write your damn order down yourself and I'll bring it back to the kitchen. When it's ready I'll let you know, and you go back there and pick it up." *Then* she called me a foreigner. And that's when the shit hit the fan. I said, "How dare you have the gall to call me a foreigner? *You're* the one that's in America. *You're* the foreigner. The problem with you for-eigners, is *you* come in this country and *you* try and boot Americans out of their *own* jobs, their *own* homes, and you try and take over this country." I said, "Don't you *ever* call me a foreigner, lady. Because I'll take you right by your collar now. I don't care whether I lose my job or not." *Then* she started cursing at me, and then I cursed right back at her. . . . Then she started arguing with her husband. . . . Called him a MF, bad, bad, vulgar language, right? . . . And he said, "If you call me that one more time . . . I'm going to knock you right in your MFing mouth. And I'll put you on the ground in front of everybody." And she deserved it, and when he said it, I applauded him. I said, "Boy, I'll tell you. If I was married to a bitch like her, I would have knocked her out a long time ago." And he just smiled at me and turned around and walked out. (emphasis added)

(The waitress slams down her book immediately before releasing her anger on the woman, thereby signaling that she is no longer willing to play the role of compliant servant: she is going to take a stand as a person.)In breaking character and expressing her anger she defies company- and customer-supported conceptions of the waitress as one obligated to endure mistreatment at the hands of her supposed social betters. Occasionally the waitress will make this challenge explicit, by proclaiming emphatically that the customer cannot or should not speak to her abusively.

> There was a white male. He was white. I shouldn't use the word "white," but it was a white male. . . . He came in and he was a very type hyper person looking [hyper-looking type person] to me. And he wanted a cup of coffee to go. . . . And he asked me if the manager was in . . . because he wanted to fill out an application to get hired. I replied to this man, I said, "Are you kidding? Six o'clock in the morning?" . . . He wanted to fill out an application to get a *job* at six o'clock in the morning, Greta. After he left, I'm assuming this guy felt very bad the way I approached him about the job, so he came *back*, and he said to me, "What's the matter with you? Are you stupid or something? I asked you for regular coffee," and he used the palm of his hand as the color the coffee should be. "*White*. Can't you tell *white*? . . . Don't you know, this is white, this is white? Can't you understand? Are you stupid?" And from that type of remark that he made to me, I went off. . . . With the way I am now, okay, I don't take any nonsense from no one. . . . Customers included, waitress, waiters, dishwashers, management, you name the team of Route, I don't take no junk from them, because I demand to make sure that I treat you fair, you treat me fair. . . . Had he been an intelligent person, he would not even applied himself in *person*. Let more [let alone] ask a waitress for an application at six o'clock in the morning. What a idiot. So anyway, what I did was, I said to this guy, I said, "Who in the Hell do you think you are?" . . . I told him, I said, "Don't you dare talk to me this way, cause I take this pot of water and I throw it right into your damn face." And I was serious, because at that moment, I felt that I don't need this guy in here bugging me early in the morning for a job. (emphasis added)

Another waitress recounted the following episode that occurred after she had accidentally spilled water into the lap of a customer:

> He jumps up, he pushes me out of the way, and he goes, "You just blew your tip! . . . I'm going to have your *job*! That's what I'm going

to have." And I turned around and looked at him. I said, "*Excuse me?* . . . *You're* going to have *my* job? *You* don't even have a job, and you're going to have *my* job? No. You're not going to have *my* job." . . . Because I don't take that. I told him, I said, "If you think I'm some stupid bimbo, don't know how to do nothing but wait tables, you're a *fool*. So don't even talk to me like that." . . . I have to tell people off . . . if they got a problem. When they're degrading me personally, then I will tell them, "I don't have to put up with your shit. I don't have to wait on you. I don't have to. You can leave." (emphasis added)

Another waitress recalled:

I had brought out this lady's chicken fried steak and the middle of it wasn't cooked enough for her. . . . Instead of her saying, "Ma'am, would you please take this back to the kitchen and have it cooked a little bit more?" she slide that shit over to me and said, "You take this shit back in the kitchen 'cause it ain't cooked." I turn around to her, I said, "Who the Hell you think you're talking to?" I said, "Do you know who you're talking to?" I said, "Do I look like one of your children? 'Cause if I do, you better take another look. Now I can understand that you upset 'cause the middle of your chicken ain't done. . . . But. In the same token, I think you better learn to tone that voice of yours down. 'Cause you don't talk to me or nobody else like that." "Well" [the woman said], "I don't have to take this. I talk to the mana" — I said, "Damn you, lady, you talk to any damn person you want to talk to." 'Cause I by that time I'd about had it. She [could] kiss my ass far as I was concerned.

These comments illustrate the waitress's concern with contesting the belief that a server who is rude to a customer will lose her job. The waitress who related the incident above described the customer's view as follows:

They figure they say what they want and do what they want; figure that you might be afraid to say anything. . . . You know, "She ain't going to say nothing because . . . I go to the boss and tell her boss and she'll lose her job, so she ain't going to say nothing to me."

When assumptions like these surface, in the form of reckless rudeness or threats to contact supervisors, the waitress responds by informing the customer or demonstrating by her actions that she is confident no action will be taken against her.

The following exchange concluded a heated interchange between a waitress and customer regarding the waitress's failure to remember that the customer's boyfriend had not ordered sausage with his breakfast. Note that the waitress volunteers her name to the customer, underscoring her lack of concern with being reported.

> She [the customer] said, "Well, I would like to call in the morning and talk to your manager." I said, "Fine. My name is Mae Merrin. You can call him. I been here seven years. I ain't going nowhere. Especially over a couple pieces of meat."

Regardless of whether the waitress directly confronts the issue of her own expendability, her decision to retaliate against an offensive customer challenges the view that she, like a servant, is constrained to submit to abuse as part of her job. The promptness and intensity of her reaction indicate the degree to which this conception diverges from her own perception of self as an independent, but to the company indispensable, businessperson.

## *Hazards of Personality Control*

Within the service sector, the process of rationalization has not been confined to the physical tasks of work. Attempts have also been made to control the personality the employee projects and the emotions she expresses. As with the physical tasks of service (making change, pouring drinks), rationalization of the worker's interactive stance is achieved by transferring control over the decisions of work from employee to service "expert." C. Wright Mills (1956: 180) describes the process as it has affected salesmanship:

> What he [the salesperson] says and what he can't say is put down for him in his sales manual. . . . His very presentation of proposition, product, and self is increasingly given to him, increasingly standardized and tested. Sales executives, representing the force that is centralizing and rationalizing salesmanship, have moved to the top levels of the big companies. The brains in salesmanship, the personal flair, have been centralized from scattered individuals and are now managed by those who standardize and test the presentation which the salesmen memorize and adapt.

In the airline industry, efforts to shape the worker's projected personality begin before an individual has been hired. A career guide for flight attendants

includes a section on mannerisms in which prospective attendants are instructed on how long to maintain eye contact and how much enthusiasm to display during the interview (Hochschild 1983: 96). Like appearance codes, regulation of workers' mannerisms, facial expressions, tone of voice, and choice of words requires them to subordinate part of themselves to company control.    W-M
(The intention in both cases is to ensure that workers will convey the desired image of the company to the public, and that this image will elicit the desired response — satisfaction and continued patronage — from consumers. )

The demand that those who serve assume a personality prescribed by their employer is not an innovation of modern service industries. In the past, a domestic's ability to present a submissive persona was considered a more decisive determinant of his worth than his ability to cook or serve (Sutherland 1981: 37). Nor is the need to project a false self limited to interaction strictly defined as service. James Scott (1985: 284) suggests that dissimulation, and in particular the expression of false deference to those in power, is the requisite pose of all subordinate classes. Erving Goffman (1967: 10) goes further, arguing that the need to maintain an expressive order consistent with one's assumed self-image or face "make[s] of every man his own jailer."

While interpersonal activity may always and everywhere have demanded maintenance of a facade, individuals are increasingly pressured to experience, rather than merely express appropriate emotions. In *The Managed Heart*, Hochschild (1983) proposes that(organizations are no longer content that their workers engage in surface acting, which relies on technical maneuvers to portray feelings, and in which "the body, not the soul, is the main tool of the trade" (1983: 37). Today, workers are encouraged to engage in deep or method acting, in which the worker draws on a reservoir of "emotion memories" to produce an appropriate response (empathy, cheerfulness) for a given role and scene. Toward this end, workers are urged to adopt a view of the service encounter and of the consumer that will evoke a suitable interactive stance.)Flight attendants are counseled to look upon the cabin as a living room and passengers as guests, and to regard difficult passengers as children who need attention. The assumption is that flight attendants will feel sincerely sympathetic with passengers they perceive as guests or children and will not be inclined to reciprocate their anger or impatience (Hochschild 1983).

By furnishing the waitress with the script, costume, and backdrop of a servant, the restaurant encourages her to become absorbed in her role or, in Hochschild's terms, to engage in deep acting. In so doing, the company may hope to enhance the authenticity of the performance and reduce the possibility that the server will break character and express emotions incongruous with the role she is expected to play. As one who perceives herself as a servant, the waitress should willingly abdicate her claim to the courtesies of interaction between equals; she should absorb abuse with no thought of retaliation; she should fulfill requests however trivial and unreasonable, and accept blame however misdirected, because as a servant it is her job to do so.

Several researchers have commented on the potential for an individual who is subject to personality or emotion control to become estranged from her feelings, and ultimately from herself. Mills (1956: 184) argues that the salesperson whose personality is transformed into an "instrument of an alien purpose" will become "self-alienated." Hochschild (1983) warns that workers whose emotions are consistently managed for commercial purposes may become estranged from their feelings, much as factory workers become estranged from their bodies. Even when emotional estrangement or detachment serves defensive functions, it is injurious, "for in dividing up our sense of self, in order to save the 'real' self from unwelcome intrusions, we necessarily relinquish a healthy sense of wholeness. We come to accept as normal the tension we feel between our 'real' and our 'on-stage' selves" (Hochschild 1983: 183–84). David Riesman (1953) argues in *The Lonely Crowd* that workers who are constrained to engage in false personalization (roughly equivalent to Hochschild's "emotional labor") may lose the capacity to distinguish between coerced and genuine friendliness (1953: 305).[13] Riesman identifies the demand for false personalization, with co-workers as well as consumers, as "a principal barrier to autonomy in the sphere of work" and advocates increased automatization as a means of alleviating the emotionally coercive element from the workplace (1953: 302). Presumably being replaced by a machine is preferable to making an instrument of one's self.

More than anything else, the waitress's ability to withstand the symbolic machinery of her work without suffering emotional estrangement testifies to her power of resistance. Though constrained to comply with the interactive conventions of master and servant, while clad in a domestic's uniform, the waitress does not internalize an image of service as servitude and self as servant. In times of stress she sees her work as war and herself as soldier. In times of peace she sees her work as a private enterprise and herself as entrepreneur. Like all social actors, the waitress monitors her projected personality and manipulates her feelings in the course of social interaction, but she does so knowingly and in her own interests. This manipulation of self does not induce self-alienation or emotional disorientation. The waitress distinguishes clearly between emotions expressed in order to please or appease a potential tipper, and emotions that arise spontaneously and are genuine. With experience her ability to separate front and backstage expressions of subservience and conviviality increases and she may silently applaud her powers of deception even as she stands before her audience of customers. To some extent, too, the waitress determines the degree to which she is willing to put up with rudeness in the interests of protecting a potential tip. In the terms of Hochschild's dramaturgical metaphor, she reserves the right to break character; (in terms of her own idioms of war and private enterprise, she retains the right to reciprocate the aggressions of her opponents in battle and business.)

All this is not to deny that waitressing and other direct-service jobs are emotionally taxing and exploitive. Work that regularly provokes outbursts of anger and engenders an embittered view of those with whom one must daily interact, off and on the job, is both injurious and in the strictest sense, coercive. It is not my intention to exonerate organizations that perpetuate rituals of deference that threaten the dignity and deny the personhood of those who serve. Though the waitress rejects the symbolic implications of these rituals, her customers do not. The symbolism of service encourages the customer to assume the posture of master to servant, with all accompanying rights of irrationality, condescension, and unrestrained anger. The resulting conflict of perspectives is a constant source of friction between server and served, friction that diminishes the quality of the waitress's work environment and periodically erupts into open fire.

Nonetheless, it is important to acknowledge and explore the ways in which the waitress confronts the emotionally coercive demands of her work. (Researchers of emotion-controlling labor, like many observers of women, have tended to focus on the exploitive policies of the workplace, while de-emphasizing the ways in which workers respond to or protect themselves against exploitation.) When the responses of women are considered at all, it is the injuries suffered that receive attention. Hochschild, for example, argues that

> the more often "tips" about how to see, feel, and seem are issued from above and the more effectively the conditions of the "stage" are kept out of the hands of the actor, the less she can influence her entrances and exits and the nature of her acting in between. The less influence she has, the more likely it is that one of two things will occur. Either she will overextend herself into the job and burn out, or she will remove herself from the job and feel bad about it. (1983: 189)

Route waitresses demonstrate that women may respond to the adverse conditions of their work not merely in the passive sense of suffering injuries, but by actively resisting, reformulating, or rejecting the coercive forces they encounter. Like the flight attendant, the waitress is pressured to see and feel about her work in company-endorsed ways; and like the flight attendant, she has little influence over the setting of the stage on which she must act out her work role. And yet the waitress does not overextend herself into her work, and when she distances herself from her job she does not "feel bad about it."

Analysts of emotion labor may have been led to deemphasize the ways in which women respond to the hazards of their work by the often silent or hidden nature of women's resistance. The waitress sometimes breaks character and rejects the role of servant, but for the most part her resistance is unseen, taking place behind a facade of subservience or behind the lines, out of sight of customers. What remains to be determined is why those who serve do not more often openly reject the degrading symbolism of servitude. Scott provides a possible answer.

> Open insubordination in almost any context will provoke a more rapid and ferocious response than an insubordination that may be as pervasive but never ventures to contest the formal definitions of hierarchy and power. For most subordinate classes, which, as a matter of sheer history, have had little prospect of improving their status, this form of resistance has been the only option. What may be accomplished *within* this symbolic strait-jacket is nonetheless something of a testament to human persistence and inventiveness. (1985: 33)

The truth of this statement is demonstrated in those instances in which waitresses do contest the formal definition of hierarchy and power and engage in open insubordination. Customers who find their anger reciprocated by a waitress typically respond with intensified displays of anger or ominous demands to see the manager. Contrary to customer belief, the waitress is not liable to lose her job or be censured as a result of her defiance. In truth, the manager is likely to express sympathy with the waitress, to apologize to her for the customers' misconduct, and to join with her in verbally disparaging the departed party. Still, the waitress's defiance is damaging to her. In withdrawing from the role of servant by retaliating against abusive customers or informing them that they cannot "degrade" her, the waitress releases them from their obligation to fulfill the requirements of their role as customers. In short, she provides them with a license to stiff. For this reason, and not for fear she will lose her job, the waitress strives to suppress her anger and her negative views of the public behind a mask of subservience. Silent resistance may not be the only option open to her, but it is the most profitable.

An alternative explanation for the apparent compliance of women with exploitive or demeaning conditions is provided by Shirley Ardener.

> While professing to support the values and codes of behaviour embodied in the dominant system, perhaps their own sense of value derives from a muted counterpart system, of which they may not themselves even be completely aware. For instance, the principal measure for social success or for other satisfactions in the counterpart model may differ from that of the model of the dominant group, and therefore their acquiescence at being placed low down on the latter's scale for success may occur because the placing seems unimportant or irrelevant to them, since they may not necessarily be "unsuccessful" or "unsatisfied" according to the logic of their own muted model. (1975: xvii)

In the waitress's counterpart model she is not a servant, but an independent businessperson or a soldier. Success and satisfaction in these occupations are predicated on the individual's ability to control the behavior of those with whom she enters into business transactions or does battle. By upholding the symbolic order and complying with the rituals of servitude, the waitress, as businessperson, achieves success in the form of greater tip income. As soldier, the waitress achieves success by refusing to let enemy fire penetrate her facade; by deflecting the aggressions of her opponents with a shield of stoicism.

## NOTES

1. Though servants are still employed in some households, domestic service is referred to here in the past tense because it is no longer a commonplace of middle- and upper-middle-class life, as it was in the last century.
2. Hortense Powdermaker (1939: 48) notes that in the deep South, whites lock the back door against thieves when they leave the house, but leave the front door open on the assumption that "no colored person would go in the front way and, apparently, that no white person would steal." This gives some indication of how seriously conventions of interaction may be taken by the superordinate class or caste.
3. Factory dress codes may also serve to diminish the employee's status, but hard hats and protective goggles are more easily justified on practical grounds than chef's hats or blue eye shadow for female flight attendants.
4. Hochschild (1983: 178) reports that the management of one airline "objected to a union request that men be allowed to wear short-sleeved shifts on warm days, arguing that such shirts 'lacked authority.'" John Molloy (1977: 50) contends that long sleeves are essential to the standard "success suit."
5. The uniform of the female executive serves additionally to conceal her femininity. Molloy (1977: 50) recommends that women wear "man-tailored" jackets, cut to "cover the contours of the bust," and man-tailored shirts as well as carry attaché cases. A full-blown "imitation man look" (complete with pinstriped suit and tie) is discouraged on the grounds that "when a woman wears certain clothes with male colors or patterns, her femaleness is accentuated" (1977: 28).

6. Goffman's (1971: 38–40) "information preserve" roughly corresponds to Georg Simmel's (1950: 322–24) notion of "intellectual private-property." Both encompass biographical facts about the individual, in which category first names may be included. As in the case of dress codes, the server's formal lack of control over the borders of this territory of self reflects her low status.

7. For current examples see "Service with a Sneer" (Lanpher 1988), "Getting Serious about Service" (Barron 1989), "Sure Ways to Annoy Customers" (Wessel 1989), "Guerrilla Tactics for Shoppers" (Franzmeier 1987), and "Friendly Waiters and Other Annoyances" (Burros 1989). A common motif in service articles, and one which is commonly portrayed in the accompanying illustrations, is the service worker who eats, reads, or watches television while a long line of customers gathers cobwebs, grows old, or undergoes bodily decay while waiting to be served. In his examination of factors that contribute to the anxiety of waiting, David Maister (1985) suggests that the sight of service workers not serving while customers wait in line is irritating, because to the customer, the wait is "unexplained." He remarks that "the explanation that the 'idle' personnel are taking a break or performing other tasks is frequently less than acceptable," but does not indicate why this should be the case. In light of the argument presented here, it might be hypothesized that customers become anxious or angry at least partly because the server's behavior challenges their perception of service as an encounter between master and servant. By subordinating the customer's needs to her own need or right (if on break) to drink, eat, or rest, the server violates the customer's self-image as master whose needs are by definition paramount. Further, by openly engaging in such blatantly human acts as eating, the worker flaunts her personhood and her equality to those accustomed to looking upon those who serve as nonpersons or as beings of a lower order.

8. Harris's failure to distinguish direct service from other forms of service work leads him to confuse emotions springing from opposite sources. The anger felt toward waitresses and bus drivers is akin to the sentiments of master toward servant; the anger and distrust felt toward doctors and government officials more closely resemble the feelings of servant toward master. While the former reflects impatience with the supposed mental and moral deficiencies of the powerless, the latter stems from the belief that money, knowledge, and authority are being misused by those in power. One is the anxiety of the oppressor, the other of the oppressed.

9. It could be argued that the soldier is no more than a pawn of high-order military strategists. Still, soldiers are armed and commissioned to fight, rather than passively absorb the aggressions of enemy forces. Though they may be formally powerless, they wield power; though their actions are dictated from above, they are active.

10. *Take the cash* (usually *take cash*): ring up a check, take the customer's payment, and return the appropriate change. Many waitresses do not see this as part of their job, in part because there is a separate job code for hostessing (and hostess wages are higher than waitress wages), and partly because they frequently do not have time to spare from taking orders and serving food to assume register duties. For both reasons, waitresses often ignore customers waiting to pay at the register. Some waitresses take cash only for their own customers and some only for those of their customers who are paying by credit card or have not yet left a tip. In these cases the waitress is motivated by the possibility that a customer who has to wait to pay may become annoyed and fail to add a tip to the credit charge, or neglect to return to the table with a gratuity before leaving the restaurant.

11. Table allocation can be complex, since stations expand and contract depending on the number and strength of servers on the floor. The flexibility of station borders is incompatible with the servers' territoriality, and much of the confusion — and tension — concerning the distribution of booths and tables arises during station shifts, when the arrival or departure of waitresses and call-outs necessitate the reapportionment of tables, or require certain waitresses to *move up* or *over* to a new station.

12. It is improbable that this waitress actually anticipated losing her job as a result of her actions. Following the episode she went into the office and told her manager what had occurred. He told her, "Don't worry about it," to which she responded, "I'm not worrying about it. I'm just letting you know in case she [the angry customer] writes a letter to the main office." Apparently, the waitress thought it more likely that her manager would be questioned about the incident by his superiors than that she would be questioned by him. It is possible, but doubtful, that she feared top-down repercussions. Complaints received by unit managers from higher-ups are fairly rare and are typically passed on to the concerned waitress (particularly if she is competent) in softened form and an apologetic tone. In this case at any rate, "nothing ever came about" concerning the incident.

13. Riesman differs from Mills and Hochschild in identifying the source and purpose of personality manipulation. In Riesman's conception, the worker engages in false personalization or forced friendliness, not because it is his job to do so, but because personalization has been deemed desirable by his peers. In personalizing his work relations, the individual secures the peer approval that Riesman perceives as the central motivating concern of the other-directed character type of the twentieth century.

## REFERENCES

Ardener, Shirley, ed. 1975. *Perceiving Women*. New York: John Wiley, Halsted Press.

Barron, Cheryll Aimee. 1989. "Getting Serious about Service." *New York Times Magazine*. June 11.

Burros, Marian. 1989. "Friendly Waiters and Other Annoyances." *New York Times*. May 24.

Federbush, Marsha. 1974. "The Sex Problems of School Math Books." In *And Jill Came Tumbling After: Sexism in American Education*. J. Stacey, S. Bereaud, and J. Daniels, eds. Pp. 178–84. New York: Dell.

Franzmeier, Stephen. 1987. "Guerrilla Tactics for Shoppers." *Star* (Lantana, Fla.). August 25.

Goffman, Erving. 1967. *Interaction Ritual: Essays on Face-to-Face Behavior*. New York: Pantheon Books.

Harris, Marvin. 1981. *America Now: The Anthropology of a Changing Culture*. New York: Simon & Schuster.

Hochschild, Arlie. 1983. *The Managed Heart: Commercialization of Human Feeling*. Berkeley: University of California Press.

Hollander, Stanley. 1985. "A Historical Perspective on the Service Encounter." In *The Service Encounter: Managing Employee/Customer Interaction in Service Businesses*. J. Czepiel, M. Solomon, and C. Suprenant, eds. Pp. 49–63. Lexington, Mass.: D.C. Heath, Lexington Books.

Jerome, Carl. N.d. "Tips on Tipping: Ten Commandments for All Food Servers." N.p. (from newspaper clipping posted on Route bulletin board).

Koepp, Stephen. 1987. "Pul-eeze! Will Somebody Help Me? Frustrated American Consumers Wonder Where the Service Went." *Time*. February 2.

Lanpher, Katherine. 1988. "Service with a Sneer." *Washington Post*. December 27.

Maister, David H. 1985. "The Psychology of Waiting Lines." In *The Service Encounter: Managing Employee/Customer Interaction in Service Businesses*. J. Czepiel, M. Solomon, and C. Suprenant, eds. Pp. 113–23. Lexington, Mass.: D.C. Heath, Lexington Books.

Mills, C. Wright. 1956. *White Collar: The American Middle Classes*. New York: Oxford University Press.

Molloy, John T. 1977. *The Woman's Dress for Success Book*. New York: Warner Books.

Powdermaker, Hortense. 1939. *After Freedom: A Cultural Study in the Deep South*. New York: Viking Press.

Riesman, David, with Nathan Glazer and Reuel Denney. 1953. *The Lonely Crowd: A Study of the Changing American Character*. Garden City, N.Y.: Doubleday.

Rothman, Robert A. 1987. "Direct-Service Work and Housework." In *Working: Sociological Perspectives*. Englewood Cliffs, N.J.: Prentice-Hall.

Scott, James C. 1985. *Weapons of the Weak: Everyday Forms of Peasant Resistance*. New Haven, Conn.: Yale University Press.

Simmel, Georg. 1950. "Types of Social Relationships by Degrees of Reciprocal Knowledge of Their Participants," and "Secrecy." In *The Sociology of Georg Simmel*. K. Wolff, ed. and trans. Pp. 317–44. New York: Free Press.

Sutherland, Daniel E. 1981. *Americans and Their Servants: Domestic Service in the United States from 1800 to 1920*. Baton Rouge: Louisiana State University Press.

Wessel, David. 1989. "Sure Ways to Annoy Consumers." *Wall Street Journal*. November 6.

Wolfson, Nessa, and Joan Manes. 1980. "Don't 'Dear' Me!" In *Women and Language in Literature and Society*. R. Borker, N. Furman, and S. McConnell-Ginet, eds. Pp. 79–92. New York: Praeger.

*Chapter 12*

# "The Customer Is Always Interesting": Unionized Harvard Clericals Renegotiate Work Relationships

• Susan C. Eaton

> As Harvard employees, we organized our Union around a single idea: that every employee should have the opportunity to participate in making the decisions that affect her or his working life.
> — Harvard Union of Clerical and Technical Workers (1993)

This essay paints a picture of clerical jobs in a gendered workplace and evaluates an innovative union's efforts to strengthen the participation of its mostly women members in decisions affecting their work. The Harvard Union of Clerical and Technical Workers (HUCTW), AFSCME, strives successfully to make clerical work more visible and less emotionally one-sided, and supports its members to renegotiate their work relationships with managers every day.[1] I argue the nature of clerical work organization shapes the unusual worker participation the union seeks. Yet ironically, HUCTW's very success at promoting "jointness" and "participation" in ways acceptable both to white-collar service workers and university managers may inhibit the union's ability to change the deeper inequities of power and control not explicitly challenged by its collaborative stance.

The union described here is unusually feminist and relational in its approach, and observers see in it a potential future model for the labor movement (Hoerr 1993; Hurd 1993). By "relational" I mean an approach to organizing and bargaining embedded in personal relationships and interactions that are mutually empowering, both within and across union-management lines.[2] HUCTW's success is based both in its responsiveness to its members' concerns and interests, and in its proactive strategy for organized involvement in work itself. HUCTW's novel approach to explicitly renegotiating relationships and participation in work organization holds important lessons for U.S. labor organizations and the women's movement as well as for managers and scholars of work organization.[3]

The paper begins by outlining the context for this study. In Part One, I argue that key features of clerical work from workers' perspectives include its basis in relationships and emotional labor, its frequent invisibility, and its gendered character. In Part Two, I profile HUCTW, AFSCME, and outline the institutional structures that define a university environment. I argue that this union's strategy to make its members' work more visible, more participatory, and less emotionally one-sided is based in its members' specific work experiences. As an example of participation in defining work, I explore the union's ongoing effort to promote an alternate language and practice for management's "customer service" initiative. In Part Three, I sketch three other case examples of labor-management interaction at Harvard to demonstrate the strengths and limits of participation as a strategy for worker empowerment and increased productivity. One shows how the union and health technicians handled a traditional speed-up problem. The second shows union leaders explicitly renegotiating interpersonal relationships with managers and the potential limits of participation without sufficient power to change work organization. The third case shows management permitting clerical union participation in certain decisions while withholding meaningful influence over key underlying choices. I evaluate these cases on their success at using negotiated joint forums to increase employee participation in their work. Throughout Part Three, I use a narrative discourse method, including interviews, stories, and observation.

I conclude in Part Four by assessing the potential of this innovative joint labor-management work in challenging the undervaluation and invisibility of clerical work and workers.[4] The union strategy empowers workers to renegotiate actual relationships between them and their managers through self-representation, and demands daily attention, visibility, and increased respect for the white-collar support work union members do. This union challenges the invisibility and devaluation of clerical work in a significantly different way than other feminist strategies, such as comparable worth (see Acker 1989; Blum 1991; Cobble 1993).[5] Members have experienced dramatic personal changes in their lives that are powerful and even life-changing, including developing leadership skills, confidence, and new insights. My focus here, however, is not principally on individuals and their changes but on the overall system of work relations.[6] The union's current limits in challenging systemic power inequality may arise from its very success at increasing joint participation and voice.

**Context for the Study:** More women work in clerical and administrative jobs than in any other kind of paid employment, including nearly 31 percent of paid women workers in 1992, part of a total of 14 million administrative workers.[7] Clerical work is classically gendered service-sector labor.[8] The work itself demands significant emotional labor, pays low wages, and often leaves the worker's role virtually invisible. Its work "products" are often jointly created interactions with others. Although scholars have chronicled the proletarianization of white-collar jobs (Braverman 1974), few document clericals actively influencing the organization of their work.[9] This essay is one effort to fill that gap.

While Harvard is an unusual employer in its public prominence and overall wealth, its 3,500 clerical and technical workers in 400 workplaces perform work typical of white-collar service sector jobs. The workers HUCTW represents include secretaries, faculty assistants, health care technicians, computer operators, data analysts, library clerks and specialists, and lab technicians (Hoerr 1993; Hurd 1993). Their experiences have important implications for other white-collar workers who experience unsatisfactory working conditions. Feminists' and unionists' efforts to change the way "women's work" is conceptualized could be more closely aligned than they are today, rather than assumed to be in opposition (as in Acker 1989: 213). The potential success of feminist unionism depends on the union, its members, and their interactions with the employer.[10]

## *Part One:*
## *Clerical Work — Gender, Relationships,*
## *Emotional Labor, and Invisibility*

Gender defines clerical workers' consciousness and culture. Rosabeth Moss Kanter's (1977) classic research on secretaries in a corporation describes secretaries as the "reserve of the human inside the bureaucratic" (p. 70), whose greatest amount of time was spent on the routine, but whose greatest rewards were garnered for the personal relationships they maintained. Her description of the rules governing clerical workers showed that their relationship to their work was patriarchal, not bureaucratic, and quite gendered. For instance, their pay and promotions were frequently tied to those of their bosses, not to their own skill development and job descriptions.[11] In extreme cases a marriage metaphor has been used to describe the secretary as functioning as the "office wife."[12]

While university clerical work may require fewer of these pressures than high-pressured corporate jobs, many of Kanter's insights hold for large non-profit corporations. Professors are just as likely as businessmen to manage women by flattery (Kanter 1977: 94), rather than by formal job descriptions and evaluations, and to tie their loyalty to them as individuals rather than to the university as a whole. This is reinforced by the decentralization of Harvard, where secretaries are employed directly by a particular school within the university. Clerical workers experience similar trade-offs, such as a direct relationship with their boss and some ability to negotiate better working conditions individually.

White women dominate clerical work today, although that has not always been the case (Goldin 1990: 100–110). More than 99 percent of all secretaries, 91 percent of all financial records processors, 88 percent of all information clerks, and 80 percent of all administrative support workers are women (U.S. Department of Labor 1993: 196–97). At Harvard, 78 percent of HUCTW members are women, as are 90 percent of secretaries and clerks. In contrast, nearly two-thirds of managers are men. In colleges and universities overall, 60 percent of faculty and 85 percent of tenured faculty are men. At Harvard, these figures are more skewed. Fully 80 percent of all faculty and 91.5 percent of all tenured faculty are men at Harvard, so the workplace is even more gendered than most.[13] Women of color make up about 10 percent of the HUCTW membership. While white women now hold a sizable portion of managerial jobs at lower and middle levels, the majority of clerical work takes place in both a gendered and class context, that is, a working-class or lower-middle-class woman working for an upper-middle-class or upper-class man.[14]

## Relational Work: The Power Context

Clerical work is embedded in personal relationships that define both worker identity and the day-to-day issues of service, production, and satisfaction. Production issues in the clerical workplace frequently center around interpersonal relations, communication, and understanding, usually occurring across a gender, class, and power divide. "Labor in general is a process whose determinate forms are shaped by the end result, the product," Harry Braverman (1974) wrote in *Labor and Monopoly Capital* (p. 316). Clerical workers produce documents, letters, reports, and other physical artifacts, but their essential product is relational: for instance, scheduling, buffering, and organizing their supervisor is often a critical part of their jobs. While administrators make efforts to quantify and control the production of clerical workers, their efforts are frequently stymied by the close relationships of clerical workers to their direct supervisors, often professionals with other primary concerns than getting a "fair day's work" out of their secretary (Kanter 1977). They may care more that "when they call in from Gdansk" on a consulting trip, as one administrator put it, that their secretary knows what they want done and how they want it done.[15]

These working relationships occur in a power context; they are more important to the clerical worker than to the faculty member, for example, since the worker is more dependent on their success for her livelihood. While Harvard workers, like most women union members, have more college education than typical union members or nonunion clerical workers, they usually do not possess the advanced degrees of the faculty they serve. Power between faculty supervisors and clericals is unequally distributed in economic, educational, and structural terms.

A fluid combination of factors determines how well the interactions that comprise service work are completed, according to all the parties involved.[16] Production in the service sector is evaluated by "customers" not only in measurable terms such as work load completed but also in terms of the quality of the relationship or interaction with the service provider. In health care, managers frequently seek to measure productivity quantitatively by patients per hour, revenues per bed, and the like. The first case described here arose from a management effort to increase productivity for dental hygienists, which the employees experienced as a speed-up.

Clerical workers are often pressed to perform more quantifiable "productive" work in less time. However, work organization issues in the clerical workplace are also relational issues, and participation in decisions frequently occurs in the context of particular ongoing personal work relationships.[17] Negotiated solutions to problems may be individualized and based on a particular understanding between as few as two parties, rather than generalized and based on quantitative variables, such as the line speed in an auto plant. For clerical workers, a simple increase in communication may lessen the stress they experience. Managers may avoid this process for their own reasons. For instance, one Harvard clerical complained that the professor who supervised her communicated with her only via voice mail and would not speak to her in person.[18] She felt this denied her the opportunity to create a good working relationship and to be recognized as human rather than machine.

## Emotional Labor: Put Your Feelings in a Trash Can

Closely tied to the relational nature of clerical work is the requirement that most workers perform "emotional labor." By this I mean that workers are required to manage their own emotions in the service of the job and to maintain a particular attitude toward their supervisor, client, or customer (Hochschild 1983). While "service with a smile" is not demanded as aggressively in a university context as in the airline Arlie Hochschild (1983) describes, clerical workers are routinely evaluated for their attitude and ability to get along with other people, especially their boss. One faculty assistant told me she was praised in her evaluation not for her computer skills and organization but for being so "cheerful."[19] Another said, "Making everybody happy is a major goal of our job."[20] To the clericals, having a faculty member "mad at you" is a very undesirable state of affairs. "The job should be livable, not just give, give, give. You can't sustain that without bitterness. We need to have different ways to think about work, not just as a tap dance to keep someone else happy," said one clerical worker.[21] At universities as in corporations, secretaries are expected to serve as a gatekeeper and buffer, weeding out undesirable calls and visits. When students cannot express anger to faculty because of his or her inaccessibility or their own lack of power, they are likely to express it to the secretary. The secretary is in a truly difficult situation, attempting to preserve relationships with strangers and still protect the professor's calendar.

Some university training seems to acknowledge the workers' emotional dilemma, but one such session has become legendary for its demeaning message to workers about controlling their emotional reaction to difficult clients. While addressing the highly stressed financial aid office staff, a trainer told workers who were upset by angry students' rebukes to "think of yourself as a trash can. Take everyone's little bits of anger all day, put it inside you, and at the end of the day, just pour it in the dumpster on your way out the door." Not surprisingly, workers found this advice "offensive and not helpful," says Carrie Normand, then a clerical worker and now a HUCTW organizer. "One of my friends tried to show how ridiculous it was. He said, 'Oh, it's just like being a toilet, and we should just flush everything, is that right?' And she didn't even get it. She said, 'Yes, that's it!' "[22]

These recommended techniques for dealing with hostile or angry clients recall Arlie Hochschild's (1983) description of flight attendant training. In both cases, trainers are effectively holding the service worker responsible for "handling" any unpleasantness from the client, and trying to get workers to ignore or suppress their predictable emotional responses of anger, distress, or revenge. Management does not endorse these images of workers, says Harvard's Assistant Director of Labor Relations Lianne Sullivan.[23] Nonetheless, this "trash can" story has made the rounds of Harvard clerical workers. It became part of the workers' culture, demonstrating the need for an organized union voice to demand more sensitive managers and fair treatment. For workers, thinking of oneself as a trash can is not a satisfactory solution to their concerns about dealing with unhappy students, faculty, or members of the public. To be effective, union strategy must provide an alternate option that empowers rather than humiliates workers dealing with emotional demands. The customer service training described below is such a strategy.

Deborah Kolb (1992) argues that behind-the-scenes conflict resolution is frequently performed by women in the workplace but not officially acknowledged. This special type of emotional work occurs not only among female professionals but among secretaries and technical workers. Dental hygienists at Harvard explained they have to "interpret" what the dentists say to patients, "because the doctors are so rushed . . . One doctor told a patient she had to have thirteen fillings and walked out. The patient burst into tears, and I had to stay there and console her and try to tell her it wasn't so bad. Often I have to explain what the doctor meant by what he said."[24] Clericals told similar stories of moderating and reinterpreting cryptic or rude faculty member comments to students and other workers. This is all part of "making everything smoother,"[25] which is not in any job description but still is essential work.

## Invisible Labor: Devalued Women's Work

Besides emotional labor demands, clerical workers often suffer from their work's lack of recognized value. Most of the work done by predominantly female clericals is literally invisible. The memos and reports they type have a faculty member's name on them. The course packets they put together, the materials they arrange for permission to photocopy, the syllabi they produce and reproduce, the letters they write—all are signed by their supervisor, not them. As support staff, their role is literally to "support" the person to whom they are assigned. Their work becomes incorporated into his or her work, in nearly all cases. Like so much predominantly female caretaking work, theirs is rarely publicly acknowledged or recognized, which makes it easy to devalue.

Another aspect of clerical invisibility is that the specific nature of the work is not well understood. Many faculty members, especially if they have never performed clerical work, think it is simpler than it actually is.[26] The myriad number of steps required to type, edit, correct, format, proof, print, duplicate, collate, staple, and distribute any single document, even with computer technology, are not often part of their consciousness. Often, workers report, their supervisors simultaneously want the clerical worker to be available to them and to do work that requires travel to other parts of the workplace. "They [faculty] always get upset with us if we're away from our desks, even if we're off doing their projects. . . . Then we get back and they're mad at us because we weren't there," said one faculty assistant.[27] Lack of understanding translates into an assumption of unimportance.

Joan Acker (1989) has documented the ways in which much emotional labor done by support staff remains invisible—to the extent that male evaluators in an Oregon pay equity study were reluctant to put it down on job evaluation forms.[28] "The types of knowledge perceived as natural to women have to do with caring, nurturing, mediating, organizing, facilitating, support- ing, and managing multiple demands simultaneously. In the Oregon study, women job evaluators had difficulty in making these job skills visible to the men" (Acker 1989: 213).

This type of work is performed daily at Harvard, and in virtually every other white-collar setting. One faculty secretary told me, "Besides keeping the faculty happy, I am working in the community, to make the whole thing smoother, to help other people when there is a crisis, to help the union, to bring in recycling for the school."[29] This kind of work is seldom recognized. The workers also help the divergent pieces of their university roles and assign- ments to fit together into a whole, without which real value is lost.

In their meetings with management, workers spend a lot of time explain- ing to their managers or faculty members what it is they do and what takes time. Much of what they do appears to be taken for granted. "They didn't understand how many steps it takes to get a project done," explained one faculty assistant.[30] The contract campaigns of the union exemplify the ongoing effort for literal and symbolic recognition of the value of HUCTW members' work. Even today, the union's desk stickers, plastered on copying machines and file drawers, read, "Harvard Works Because We Do." The union performs a great deal of interpretive and integrative work in helping workers understand their importance to the functioning of the university overall.[31]

In sum, much clerical work can be described as gendered, based in human relationships, requiring emotional labor, and frequently invisible. Efforts like HUCTW's and Harvard's to encourage worker participation in defining work must take account of these qualities. Next, I introduce the participation theme by outlining the institutional context of a university setting.

*Part Two:*
## *Clerical Work in a University Setting and Union Strategies*

Joint labor-management work or worker participation in any setting is shaped by the institutional power structure. In a university, complex relationships form between workers, managers, students, and faculty members. Ordinary complexities are heightened by the gender and class differences explored above. In a corporate office, clerical workers frequently have two lines of supervision (Kanter 1977). While their direct supervisor is often a professional worker or manager, they also have accountability to a human resources person or office manager/coordinator. A university context also highlights this tension, since human resources staff are indirect supervisors who hire, fire, and are responsible for overall efficiency.

## The Problem of Middle Managers

In the university setting, middle managers administer the support services required for assuring the quality education of future professionals and for conducting research. Yet managers are more limited in their ability to exercise power in a university than in a traditional private sector corporation. Their influence is leavened by the presence of a powerful interest group of faculty members, themselves deeply divided by discipline, rank, and tenure status but sharing certain interests. Often, the faculty, not the managers, directly supervise the clerical and secretarial staff.

Middle managers' lack of power is a problem endemic to the service sector and the university. The mid-level managers who do not have major decision-making authority but who are looked to by union and workers for relief of problems may find themselves in the uncomfortable position of having to defend policies they did not create, while at the same time being unable to exercise influence upwards effectively. At Harvard, most labor-management groups include middle managers but not top administrators.

Middle managers also have no protection if they challenge existing arrangements. When asked why they thought managers were resistant or nonresponsive to efforts to communicate through labor-management Joint Councils, one worker said, "They aren't like us in the union. They are afraid. They have no back-up. If they make a mistake, they're out the door."[32] Thus, he says, they have problems getting certain jointly agreed upon changes enacted.

## The Role of Faculty Members

Faculty have a different set of interests than managers. They have teaching, research, consulting, advising, and administrative work to do. In clerical matters, they want to have a good relationship with a qualified and reliable support person who will look out for their interests. They are usually not held accountable directly for cost, uniformity of practice, precedent, or overall organizational issues. While they often appear both more positive and more powerful to union members than administrators do, especially in joint labor-management settings, their behavior often reflects the different institutional and personal pressures on them. Faculty have less to lose than managers in being benevolent to staff (which does not mean that all of them are).[33] Faculty tend to develop their individual relationships with a secretary into one that will benefit them when they need help, irrespective of rules. Faculty create the daily context for emotional labor much more directly than administrators, and they may demand (or inspire) personal loyalty over institutional loyalty. Like all secretaries, Harvard clerical workers sometimes come to identify with and support their bosses, in part because their rewards and recognition come primarily through what Kanter (1977) calls "the patriarchal system." Invisibility is another problem endemic to the faculty–support staff relationship, since most faculty trained in an academic world attend more to the power of ideas than to the details of getting them in print. The value of their secretarial support is infrequently noted.

## The Role of Students

Students do not appear in most of the stories clerical workers or managers tell about their working relationships. They are often transient and thus relatively powerless in the work of the university, especially at Harvard, where demand for places far exceeds supply. A class gap also exists between workers and students; although many clerical workers attended college, most did not attend an Ivy League school or enjoy the many opportunities for their futures that young people at Harvard seem to have. One secretary said one summer student told a taxi driver to set his luggage in front of her desk and asked her how she would be getting it to his room for him.[34] Clericals serve as the administrative "connector" between students and the university. A modestly paid worker administering a policy she did not make can be "dumped on" by a student — who is now relatively junior in the hierarchy but will soon be quite privileged.

Students are a special segment of the public faced by public contact workers in financial aid, health care, and housing departments.[35] Students' apparent lack of importance is ironic since they are the largest constituency of the university (besides alumni). HUCTW is disadvantaged by the relative powerlessness of students since their interests, such as better facilities, higher staffing, and better training of support staff, potentially overlap. Their interests could also conflict in areas such as total cost of an education or worker health benefits. The case of the dental workers shows union members defending the rights of students to be treated well as patients instead of receiving shorter appointments and lower-quality care.

## Clerical Unions and HUCTW:
## Laying the Groundwork for Participation

Clerical workers are organized into unions at a relatively low rate in the United States, with 15.7 percent of all administrative workers represented by unions, mostly in the public sector (U.S. Department of Labor 1993: 239). An internal debate continues within some U.S. labor unions about the organizability of clerical workers and the adequacy of efforts to organize them. In other countries, many more clerical workers have organized into unions. In Canada, for instance, 32 percent of clerical workers belong to unions, although they are concentrated in the direct government and the broader public sector, such as health care (Eaton 1993c). Even more clericals are organized in industrialized European countries.

Many U.S. clerical workers and women have no personal history with unions and do not know much about them. One after another told me in interviews that before HUCTW they were unfamiliar with unions "not like the Teamsters with Jimmy Hoffa, unions that weren't threatening and scary."[36] Their initial reaction to unionization was based on conventional media images of male-dominated, corrupt, powerful, and distant organizations rather than on a home-grown or grass-roots, female-led organization advocating "kindness and respect" and seeking to create a "community at work" (Eaton 1992).[37] In many cases the Harvard union consciously dissociated itself from other unions, explaining that it was "different" than "those other unions" its members may have known.

The Harvard Union of Clerical and Technical Workers has developed an innovative and unique approach to labor-management jointness and participation in clerical work. Harvard workers voted for HUCTW as their union in 1988, after a fourteen-year organizing effort (Hoerr 1993). Management sponsored a strong anti-union campaign despite the union's decision not to run an anti-Harvard campaign.[38] Before negotiating the first contract, management and union members held joint sessions in which nearly one hundred mostly female clerical and technical workers talked about their work lives to managers who had never before been required to listen to them as equals. In the union leaders' understanding, this aspect of the prenegotiation period set a model for the new kind of participation and sharing of experience that they hoped would characterize the labor-management relationship.

HUCTW adds a new element to the traditional power-imbalanced, male-female scenario that Kanter (1977) describes. The union provides a voice, a legal entity, and an organized presence in the workplace in which clericals can participate, and through which they can renegotiate the terms and conditions of their employment.[39] HUCTW has chosen an unusual and explicitly gendered approach to its organizing work, emphasizing "kindness and respect" as its motto in the treatment of everyone. The union focuses on mutual "listening" rather than "demanding" as a negotiation strategy, and its leaders explicitly credit feminist research with reinforcing and expanding its founders' strategies.[40]

The union was founded and organized principally but not solely by women. As current HUCTW Director Bill Jaeger reports, "It [the union] definitely celebrates women's ways of learning and leading, but does that without malice toward men" (Hoerr 1993: 74). HUCTW's executive board consists of 71 percent women, and 75 percent of its principal officers are women. Many observers feel HUCTW represents an important, new "feminine model of organizing" (Eaton 1992; Hurd 1993; Oppenheim 1991–92).

HUCTW organizers consciously planned to appeal to the clerical work force, and their strategy evolved from the concerns of the workers they sought to represent. They specifically sought to address the issues of emotional labor, gendered workplaces, relational work, and invisibility of their members' efforts. Their goals include creating a "community at work," negotiating greater and genuine participation for members in the decisions that affect their work lives, and improving the daily conditions of members' lives through self-representation.

The collegial and self-governing environment of a university served as a reference point and validation for their aspirations.[41] "We are sure no Harvard administrator or professor would ever abdicate a right to participate in decision making, and we can no longer afford to give up that right ourselves," asserts HUCTW's 1988 statement of principles, "We Believe in Ourselves." In addition, organizers sought to create an alternate discourse about the meaning of work and the role of workers — one in which clerical and technical workers are recognized and respected for their invaluable contributions. The union's strategy has evolved from being very nonthreatening ("It's not anti-Harvard to be pro-union" was one early slogan) to being more assertive about members' roles. HUCTW's aspirations for reorganizing work are focused on a strategy of participation. The next sections illustrate the possibilities and limits of this goal.

The first clerical union contract at Harvard, in 1989, created an unusual model for the labor-management relationship, emphasizing decentralized decision-making and problem-solving focused at the local area and department level.[42] Most details of employment relations remained in the personnel manual, which had been "jointly rewritten" during bargaining. To promote ongoing clerical and technical worker input into the organization of work, the contract contained no management rights clause and no "inflexible work rules" (Hoerr 1993).

In the first contract article, the parties agreed to "build a framework for greater employee participation at Harvard," and to take up issues related to work organization or policy ("all workplace matters which have a significant impact on staff") in local bipartite bodies called "Joint Councils" (HUCTW and Harvard University 1989). This allowed them to consider both current policy and proposed changes affecting workplace and work-force arrangements. The Joint Councils were to "work in a spirit of trust and cooperation to reach consensus," and to make recommendations to deans or vice presidents, who would "seriously consider and respond promptly" to them. If no consensus was reached, matters could be referred to a university-wide Joint Council, which could proceed to mediation and then to arbitration. As of 1994, 42 Joint Councils met regularly around the university, with approximately 140 elected union representatives and the same number of appointed university managers.[43]

HUCTW leaders use the word "jointness" to describe what they are trying to achieve for their members. Union members say it means recognizing and including them in decisions that affect their working lives. Some managers seem to think this means "co-management," something that, as John Hoerr (1993: p. 8) points out, the union has never sought,[44] while others simply think it means increasing the union's *pro forma* consulting role. Neither correctly describes what the union has in mind. Contemporary labor-management relations research sheds light on the overall national context for this work, placing HUCTW somewhere between the co-managed Saturn–United Automobile Workers plant and less participatory, nonnegotiated forms of employee consultation (Applebaum and Batt 1993; Freeman and Rogers 1995; Kochan and Osterman 1994; Rubinstein, Bennett, and Kochan 1993).

Director Bill Jaeger describes one example of where "jointness would have made a difference to his members."

> Before the union, I remember seeing one of my co-workers who was extremely unhappy. Her manager had ordered new computers for the department, and she had a new work station with green characters on the screen. However, she had worked on computers before, and she knew that amber screens were easier on the eyes. Since the two colors cost the same, if they had asked her, she could have made a contribution at least for herself and maybe also for others by choosing the amber screen. But they never asked. That's when I knew we needed a way that workers could have a bigger voice in their jobs.[45]

While this is a simple example, Harvard workers give dozens more where they believe their participation can make work better for them and for the university.

The Joint Councils consist of union and university representatives from an entire school or administrative department, such as the Education School, the Medical School, or the Business School. Some have a small area covering one hundred or fewer employees, such as the University Health Services or the Design School. Others are vast, with more than five hundred employees covered. The contract encourages the creation of subcommittees and subcouncils, which have sprung up around the university to deal with specific issues. This pattern of setting up smaller or informal groups in addition to the formal Joint Councils has become so frequent that the union calls it "episodic jointness." In some cases, such as the public service training described below, the union has gone outside joint structures and created its own space from which to organize participation. The leaders believe this lays the basis for a more equal relationship.

### Promoting an Alternate Language in Public Service: "The Customer Is Always Interesting"

The union does not rely only on joint labor-management work to promote its vision of how workers can make a difference at work. In its new customer service training, the union creates its own alternate language and vision of worker responsibility, which is in direct contradiction to the university's paradigm. The union is performing interpretive work for members, attempting to challenge a dominant ideology that positions white-collar service workers as being always wrong if the customer is always right.

The concept that "the customer is always right," an overused slogan of the customer service model of the 1970s and 1980s, requires serious rethinking from the perspective of those who serve the customer. "If the customer is always right, we're always wrong," said one HUCTW member.[46] Unions representing service workers can make a valuable contribution to such rethinking. Even in nonprofit organizations, management consultants often focus on the customer as a way of talking about clients, patients, the public, or whoever is benefiting from the service provided by the nonprofit.

HUCTW has developed an alternative language and way of thinking about customer service. Union members agree that "we want to help people. Listening well to them, and trying to understand the concerns that they bring into any situation, is a way that people in jobs like ours can help people," as Bill Jaeger puts it.[47] But they object to what they call the "lack of balance" in the university's approaches.

The union leaders strongly object to the comparison to private sector models. "This isn't K-Mart," says Carrie Normand. "We have to be really careful about for-profit sector models and attitudes," says Jaeger. "We talk about 'public service' to resist efforts that are sometimes made to compare our work to commercial transactions. Different goals and ideas motivate the work that we do and the organizations we are in." The union calls the people whom their members serve "help-seekers" or "the public" if they are not students, faculty, or another defined constituency. Half the union's members work in support areas in the university that are not directly connected to teaching or research — such as Harvard Real Estate, University Health Services, or Financial Aid. Workers in these areas are more likely to have jobs that require them to deal with a "steady stream of help-seekers" and to have pressures put on them for increased "productivity," as do health care workers.[48] But even workers in academic departments face this issue.

A committee of union staff and activists designed a pilot training program for unionized clerical workers in the union's alternate model of public service, tentatively entitled "The Customer Is Always Interesting." This training was developed "out of the concerns and aspirations of the workers who do this kind of work . . . emphasizing the idea that one of the ingredients in healthy transactions is that kind of a dignified or self-respecting position for the service provider."[49]

The model for customer or client service, union members say, must provide not only for the satisfaction of the public but also for that of the worker. In nearly every job the union represents, workers have some set of challenges when members of the public come to them for service. "Why not start from the place that making the customer happy is not going to go well unless both people are happy and having their needs met in that transaction?" asks Jaeger.[50] Union members report that most training they have had from management ignores the interests of front-line workers, as in the now-famous "trash can" training described above. "Our jobs . . . are about the very complicated management of disagreements, basically, in a constant daily kind of way, in a very diverse community," says Jaeger.[51]

The training series is important because, along with the Joint Councils, work groups, and problem-solving teams, it represents a way for workers to articulate their perspective collectively, to share it with others, and to make their experience visible. The union becomes a place for framing the issues of how to deal with problems on the job and of how to think differently about ideas management is promoting. The training itself provides an alternative space for developing a language and vision respectful of worker concerns.[52] The training, besides teaching specific skills, will give workers an opportunity to tell stories to each other and to share solutions. "There's no sense [among management] of training each other here," says HUCTW's Normand, "even though it's a university. No sense that we're a community of learners. There's a sense that if you're only a staff assistant, you're not thinking."[53]

*Part Three:*
*Three Cases of "Jointness"—*
*Challenging Invisibility,*
*Renegotiating Relationships*

To understand what these workers gain in practice from workplace-based renegotiation of work and relationships, I chose three "stories," or "mini" case studies, from the Harvard experience. They occurred under the jurisdiction of three different Joint Councils. They demonstrate the power and success that the union has enjoyed in renegotiating work relationships on a day-to-day basis, but each one suggests a different limit to the union's collaborative participation approach. I chose these stories in part because they are widely known by members as examples of successes, so they have a value and influence beyond the individuals they directly affect; they are part of the workers' and union culture. At the same time, they demonstrate what is perhaps the union's most basic challenge: to change the unequal power relationships at the university through a strategy of jointness.

### Story 1: Shorter Dental Appointments—
### "Our Patients Will Suffer"

The first case exemplifies the union's role outside the formal Joint Council structure in supporting workers struggling with day-to-day problems of visibility and power. In this case, the union supported several technical workers in their collaborative and respectful but firm and ultimately successful opposition to a speed-up in their work schedules.[54]

At the University Health Services (UHS), HUCTW played an important role in helping technical workers make a case that a portion of their work was largely unrecognized in formal productivity measures. UHS provides medical and preventive care to Harvard students, affiliates, faculty, and employees. About 400 workers are employed in UHS, and 125 of them are represented by HUCTW. The three registered dental hygienists who complained to the union in 1993 are responsible for regular dental cleanings, patient education, infection control, and performing triage to decide which patients need to see a dentist. The three hygienists have a minimum of two years of technical training and varying levels of experience. One hygienist had been working at UHS for twenty-seven years, the other two for less than five years. None had been active in the union before this incident.

The dental hygienists are evaluated for their "production," meaning the number of patients they see in the time available. They are scheduled for ten forty-five-minute appointments a day, or fifty a week. But not every patient shows up, and some cannot be treated if they do show up because of illness. Some weeks, as a result, the hygienists' "production" is in the low to mid-forties. A clinic administrator told them she was going to change some of their appointments each day to thirty minutes to "bring their production up." The hygienists told me calmly: "We discussed it and we decided we didn't want to do it. We felt it was not fair to the patient, not to mention that it was not fair to us too, or the extra stress we would feel. But mostly we felt it was not fair to the patient."[55] They were worried they would not have time to do infection control procedures properly or to educate the patient about home care, especially new patients. Many of their patients have not had prior access to routine dental care, so cleanings are more difficult and lengthy. They also keep records and make reminder calls.

After some discussion with supervisors, they believed the idea had been dropped, and nothing changed for six months. Then one of the hygienists noticed on the computer that her next day's appointments had been shortened — without even a notice! This apparently unilateral action mobilized the hygienists, and one called the union. Union Director Bill Jaeger came and talked with them, and "helped us organize our ideas," according to one hygienist. He offered to meet with the clinic director with them, but they wanted first to try on their own.[56]

Each worker did research, one with the dental school on their appointment times, and one on the reasons for "low production." Hygienist Lisa Flanagan developed a computerized packet of information presenting the hygienists' case. Her headings included "Quality of Care," "Increased Failure Rate and Decreased Production," "Patient Perception and UHS Reputation," and a set of new procedures the hygienists felt should be implemented by others if this new schedule went into effect. Flanagan attached copies of UHS's own newsletter with articles about the quality of care, and highlighted notes about excellence, holding the employer accountable to its own standards. She attached a computerized chart and bar graph showing that the failure percentage (i.e., the number of patients who did not show up) was between 4 percent and 7 percent, not the 20 percent that had been rumored.

The dental hygienists worked hard to make their presentation professional and to stress their concern for patient care, especially infection control, record keeping, and patient relationships. One of their concerns was that patients not feel rushed. They predicted unforeseen side effects that might occur with the new schedule, since they would not have time to complete bite-wing x-rays, reminder calls, and the like. They even projected that the doctors' production levels might fall, since hygienists would have less time to refer patients to dentists.

Fortified with their extensive materials, the women set up a meeting with the clinic's chief dentist. They pointed out they were being "punished" for events beyond their control, like patient cancellations or no-shows, and they explained in minute detail the exact work they were doing in patient education and record keeping. The dentist said he had "forgotten" they were doing all those extra things. He did not want them to be unhappy. Before they completed their arguments, he agreed to return to the longer appointments.

Theoretically, this could have occurred without a union. However, the story would not have been the same. HUCTW was more than a back-up if their meeting with the dental manager had not gone well. Union staff validated the hygienists' concerns, helped them think through their approach in an integrative fashion, supported their desire to meet with the director as equals, and encouraged them to use their own knowledge of the job. Because of HUCTW, the technicians knew their jobs were not on the line for asserting their interests. The hygienists acknowledged the positive role of the union and also felt good about their own representation of their interests. They were a little surprised that the dentist did not want them to be so unhappy and that they had the power to resist the shortening of their patient appointments. Even though one of the hygienists had been there nearly thirty years, none of them had seemed sure that they could win this issue.

The victory the workers won involved more than keeping the forty-five-minute appointments. The hygienists had communicated directly with the head of the clinic. He admitted he did not know all the work they did, and he validated their account of their work. This level of increased communication, visibility, and respect seems as important to workers and the union staff as the actual victory, although the two are tied together. Hygienists also gained valuable recognition of their contribution, made their work visible, and gained experience and confidence at making a presentation to a doctor and supervisor. They actively redefined productivity and pointed out the costs of *not* doing the unrecognized integrative work they perform each day. Many of these gains would have existed even if they had lost their case.

The larger implications of this fight are less clear. Will it empower these workers to stand up for other issues involving patient care as well as their own working conditions? Will it change the relations of power and control at the clinic?[57] Or is this just a temporary reprieve? Finally, is this effort expressive of defensive craft unionism — or is it a successful effort to have a voice in decisions made about the work? I suggest this example represents both, where "defending" the status quo brought about an increase in visibility and respect between hygienists and their boss. If appointments had been shortened permanently, the results would likely have been worse for everyone: patients, doctors, and technical workers.

## Story 2: The Faculty–Faculty Assistant Joint Council— Influence or Authority?

The second case demonstrates the importance to workers of renegotiating personal relationships with faculty members, and the union's role in insuring that workers are treated respectfully and with equality. Because of the power imbalance in university clerical jobs, any effort at jointness that increases direct communication with supervisors and forces recognition of the work of clerical workers' jobs is highly valued by union members. At Harvard's Kennedy School of Government (KSG), creating a Faculty–Faculty Assistant Joint Council was the way HUCTW leaders helped turn a bad proposal (from the assistants' perspective) into an opportunity for increasing participation and communication. They thus transformed a potential win/lose confrontation into a win/win one, at least from their viewpoint. The faculty co-chair agrees but is more reserved, saying, "We've done a reasonable job. . . . Personally and professionally we've learned a bit more."[59]

Shari Levinson, an energetic, articulate faculty assistant at the Kennedy School of Government, became union co-chair of the Joint Council because of both relational and work load concerns:

> The [administration] had an idea to restructure the faculty assistants in "clusters." . . . There would be four or five faculty assistants working for a group of faculty, and they would share work loads, but somehow keep the primary relationship with their faculty person. It sounded like a secretarial pool to us. It seemed it would add a layer of supervision in the pool to dole out the work. We thought we would have twenty faculty descending on us, and one huge in-box and out-box. We thought it would depersonalize the work, and increase the work load, and reduce our ratio. . . . Now we have two senior or three junior faculty. It sounded like in this system we would have four or five apiece. We hated it.[59]

While the cluster idea was ultimately abandoned by administrators, Levinson says that the proposal raised other issues about how faculty assistants were not consulted about decisions affecting their work. "We wanted to be there and tell what it's like from our point of view," she explained. "So the union and the faculty assistants decided to take the Joint Council model and apply it to a smaller group. We proposed a committee made up of faculty and faculty assistants themselves. We had a lot to say!"

The resulting Faculty–Faculty Assistant Joint Council increased both communication and understanding about secretarial work. For six months, three faculty and three faculty assistants worked through their perceptions of what the others' jobs consisted of. All the members were somewhat surprised to learn what their counterparts did with their time. Levinson recalled:

> We thought their primary job was to teach! Boy, were we off base! We are the connection between the faculty and school . . . so teaching is a primary focus for us. But they told us about their research, and their consulting, and their administrative duties, and their projects. . . . For their part, they didn't realize what we were juggling. They didn't understand what it takes to get anything done.

Gender played a role in the Joint Council's slow progress. Levinson recalled that, at first, the power dynamic between the male professors and female faculty assistants was "a little overwhelming" to the women. She said, "They speak differently. They want to analyze and measure everything. We can do that, but we don't think that way about our jobs. They kept wanting to ask, 'What problem are we here to solve?'" The faculty assistants, however, felt that coming to understand each other's jobs was really part of the problem they were trying to solve. KSG Professor and Joint Council faculty co-chair Herman "Dutch" Leonard agreed with the union view that "we are not a complaint center. We are trying to examine the nature of the work, the relationship."[60] He saw the Joint Council as a place for reflecting on and renegotiating the workplace experience and relationships.

Council members tried to expand their newly acquired mutual understandings to a larger constituency, effectively raising the visibility of clerical jobs to a new level. A year into its existence, the Council sponsored an orientation program for new faculty members and new faculty assistants. It included a skit featuring role reversals where a dean played a faculty assistant and vice versa, as well as a "desert survival" (NASA version) game designed to get staff to work together as equals at least during that exercise. "It seemed revolutionary," said one assistant. "The hierarchy here is so separate. But it's still rare. The only complaint was from one faculty member who didn't do well."[61] Both the invisibility and devaluing of clerical work were challenged by this event, with support from the faculty Council members in their willingness to play clerical roles.

Ironically, the desert island exercise may also demonstrate the current limits of participation. The Council's successful orientation session was followed by a failure to achieve a change in the system of assigning faculty and assistants in a school that has a 30 percent turnover of assistants and many new or visiting faculty each year. The current system, organized by administrators, takes factors such as space, proximity, remodeling, and the staff-to-faculty ratio into account in making assignments. Neither faculty nor assistant preferences are specifically considered. For six months, the Joint Council discussed ways to incorporate both faculty needs and skills (such as computer use, transcriptions, and typing) and assistant preferences and skills (such as budgeting, report producing, and conferences) into the system. However, even with three faculty members (one of whom was a dean) on their committee, the Council apparently could not persuade administrative managers to incorporate their concerns into the process. "It was hard," said Levinson. "It did not happen. But we'll keep working on it."[62] The faculty manager, however, has a different view; Dutch Leonard says the administration is "trying to match people better, but . . . we don't want the committee to be participating in the administrative process."[63] Still, if the group cannot influence the administrative process, what is its participation supposed to be accomplishing?

The Faculty–Faculty Assistant Joint Council demonstrates both strengths and weaknesses of the union's efforts to achieve voice or participation. From many clerical workers' perspectives, positive, interdependent personal relationships with faculty supervisors are a key part of autonomous and dignified work environments. While it is difficult to negotiate these in a joint committee, workers want to preserve the space to make these relationships as best they can. This includes resisting clusters, typing pools, and other administrative controls on their direct personal relationships with faculty. A second lesson is that working relationships and productivity can be improved by genuine contributions from everyone. For instance, the orientation session assisted both faculty and assistants in working together better, and a new assignment system could dramatically improve satisfaction with the matching of skill and interest on all sides. Third, "jointness" means grappling with issues of gender as well as economic and political power. The assistants have to learn to deal with their faculty counterparts' overpowering styles, more constrained schedules, and different approaches to problems.

Members appear satisfied with the union's work here, however. "It had a magnitude and an impact," one said of the Council.[64] Efforts at jointness that increase direct communication are highly valued by clerical workers and secretaries, even if they do not overtly challenge underlying inequalities. At least in a university environment, clericals expect that increased understanding will lead directly to improved working conditions for them. For instance, if their supervisors understand why the assistants are away from their desks, the faculty will not be angry when they return, and the assistants' day-to-day lives will improve. This case lends support to Richard Hurd's (19993) argument that "the desire of clericals to seek justice while preserving harmony in the workplace" (p. 344) is made possible through the contractual Joint Council structure. Carol Gilligan (1982) might see here women workers' desires to "preserve connection" at work while not giving up the right to their own voice. In a more practical vein, I see workers striving to maintain control of a key power relationship with faculty rather than being assigned to a typing pool.[65]

Yet a genuine desire to preserve harmony or connection leads to certain harsh realities. It seems likely the faculty members could have more successfully influenced the assignment process if they strongly desired to do so. A management person says the Council "has a reasonable degree of influence, but no authority,"[66] thus articulating a management view of how things should work — which union members cannot contest effectively at this point. All Joint Councils require a majority vote to make recommendations to deans, who make the decisions. The unionists view jointness as a process of negotiating and increased understanding, not explicitly as a power play. Yet, HUCTW members do want the Joint Councils to exert authority and make effective change after processing the issues from all sides. This inevitably raises issues of power and decision-making at the university. Eighteen months after its formation, management is minimizing the formal influence of the Joint Council, while the union members are still hoping that they will be able to make significant administrative change over time. The key question is how power relationships will be changed. How can the Joint Council have real influence if it has no authority? HUCTW President Donene Williams says the union has to fight for change and has to stay well organized to have power it needs.[67]

This case also highlights the impossibility of separating relational issues from work concerns for white-collar service workers like clericals. The relationships seem more important to the clerical workers than to their supervisors, perhaps because the clericals have more stake in the particular relations with faculty than vice versa. Further, clericals are willing to give this process time and attention, while faculty have other demands and "less time," according to one faculty member.[68]

## Story 3: The Office Facilitator— "Should This Job Exist?"

The third case example shows clericals resisting administrative microsupervision of secretarial work in response to a management effort to increase efficiency. As a result, union members became involved in hiring their own new administrative coordinator. The union strategy was to empower a small group to organize worker participation in defining a proposed new coordinating job that managers wanted to create, again raising the visibility of clerical work. In this case, management allowed union participation at one level — the development of a job description and the hiring of a candidate — while prohibiting participation in the key decision that the contested new position was necessary. This case shows the value of participation but also its current limits when it does not include a voice in basic choices about work.

At the Harvard Business School (HBS), elevators are paneled with polished granite and desks are covered in a beautiful dark cherry wood. The contrast with anywhere else on campus, even at wealthy Harvard, is dramatic. HBS employs 190 faculty and 75 faculty secretaries. In the most famous management training school in the country, tension between administrators' goals, faculty needs, and secretarial concerns gave rise to a joint working group that has met with mixed success.

Kathy Randel is an HBS faculty secretary with four priority boxes behind her desk, labeled, "As soon as possible," "Today or tomorrow," "Sometime this week," and "When I have time." One of her professor-bosses calls the fourth box "Sometime this century." His comment reflects the high level of workplace stress at HBS. Randel had not been active in the union before this case began, but she decided, "For the union to work, everyone needs to participate in some way."[69] So she got involved.

In this situation as in the other two cases, management action led to union proposals of a joint working group. An administrator announced the creation of an "office facilitator" position, whose occupant would be responsible for coordinating the work flow generated by the faculty. This task had previously been performed by the faculty secretaries themselves, in their view — and by no one, in the management's view. Some secretaries were very upset and felt they did not need anyone else "looking over their shoulder." The level of distress was high enough that a Joint Council union member says he suggested the creation of a "working group," and invited Randel, one of the concerned secretaries, to join it.[70]

In another case of management and union differences in perception, the Harvard manager involved told the story somewhat differently. "We were thinking through the entire faculty services," he said. "We realized we were wasting resources all over the place, and that secretaries were a tremendous information resource. For instance, there was no budget for software programs, but each secretary ordered their own." Peter Capodilupo, Chief Human Resources (HR) Officer at HBS, said the new job was proposed to help both secretaries and faculty deal with larger "thematic" issues, including more efficient service provision and secretarial career development. He said he personally realized the job needed an "open airing, so I started calling key staff people and put together a group." He noted that the Joint Council at the school was interested when he consulted its members, and that they sent representatives to the new "work group."[71]

So both the secretaries (through their union) and managers (through their administrator) believed they were responsible for creating the group. Perhaps this is true ownership by both sides, but most likely it represents a management decision to create the job and a union reaction to the decision in the form of requesting participation. While the manager takes credit for convening the group, it was the union's presence that ensured its existence and the bargaining unit members' participation.

This working group's members reported continuing tension over its mission and the levels of participation it tolerated. Members first convened a meeting of all the secretaries "to hear their concerns," according to a secretary. About two-thirds of the secretaries attended. Randel felt that her co-workers reinforced what the union representatives on the work group had said — that the job was not necessary. However, managers refused to negotiate the issue of whether a facilitator was really needed. The HR officer described the meeting as "mostly me presenting history, and then we talked it out. I felt like a pin cushion." Tension persisted, partly over what the right question was. The union saw the meeting as a chance for secretaries to participate, with the hope their objections would be seriously attended to, while managers saw it as a chance to explain the rationale for the proposed job. This is classic "cross-talk."

As in the previous case, the secretaries wished to preserve their individual personal relationships with faculty. "Some were worried they would be told how to do their work in some way, or this person would get in between the relationship between the faculty and the secretary," said one.[72] The manager agreed that secretaries liked "the direct interaction with faculty members" best about their jobs. Several HBS faculty declined the invitation to participate in the work group, which could suggest they placed less importance than clericals on these relationships — or more importance on other demands on their time.

The committee created a feeling of genuine participation in the job definition and hiring, according to Randel. "We worked a lot on the wording of the job description," she said. "We processed this thing to death," said the HR manager. "It was a great process."[73] The resulting job description emphasized that the new facilitator would serve more as a "resource" or a "consultant" to the secretaries than as a supervisor. However, managers determined unilaterally that the position was "exempt" and therefore out of the bargaining unit.ᵇy the working group, according to HR chief Capodilupo. The committee members, including three union members, screened résumés and interviewed candidates for the job. Perhaps surprisingly, everyone agreed on the best candidate for the newly negotiated job description. In the end, the person hired was a respected member of the bargaining unit, so most people were satisfied. The position generated some conflict post-implementation, but much less than would have occurred without the involvement of the secretaries, according to union and management observers.

Manager Capodilupo feels positively about employee and union involvement. He believes that the union generally "has meant a change for the better," and that it "has led to people thinking more creatively about workplace issues," partly because management can better hear the voices of workers "through the focal point of the union."[75] He clearly believes that employee involvement strengthens the acceptance of any change, whether a building move or a new job. "I have every right to post this job, but I can't make this work all by myself," he says. Yet he also says that people in the working group only "tweaked" the job description. Despite the extensive process of participation and consultation, it seems that few substantive changes could have been made in the basic idea of creating this job. It was already decided by management.[76]

Some union members are uneasy about the depth of participation they have been "allowed" to have. One faculty secretary says: "Well, I think if the union or the workers are to be included in management discussions, I'd like to see them included in the *whole* discussion. Otherwise, it feels more like lip service. It looks good, but the underlying issues are not addressed. Our effectiveness was limited once we were just looking at how to define the position."

The future is unclear. One secretary states: "The trust is shaky. I still don't trust that we will not end up with a secretarial pool and three supervisors sometime in the future."[77] The manager involved says management does not want a typing pool but wants to "enhance the relationship" with faculty.[78] A lesson of the last two stories is that the direct faculty-secretary relationship is a source of power and influence for clericals, one they will fight to defend.

This case raises the question of whether the union is challenging management and faculty prerogatives sufficiently through joint committees and working groups. Some workers strongly felt that management had the right to create the job and that the joint working group was the best means of addressing their concerns. But in a contract without a management rights clause, should the union workers have questioned the basis for this job more persistently? The legal framework of labor-management relations does not encourage this.[79] Or, since it was defined as an exempt position, are they powerless to prevent its creation and limited to playing as large a role in its execution as possible? Members are divided on this question, but it raises the limits of participation as a strategy when management chooses not to allow participation in basic decisions.

*Part Four:*
*Assessing Participation as a Strategy*
*for Clerical Workers*

> Participation by employees concerning workplace issues which af-
> fect them is desirable for the university community. There should
> be employee participation within each school or administrative
> department.
> — Harvard University–HUCTW Contract (1993)

Officially, both sides say that Joint Councils work well, that they provide a place
for employee input and involvement. "They are useful structures. They keep
the lines of communication open at the local supervisor and union level," says
Lianne Sullivan, Assistant Director of Labor Relations at Harvard.[80] Union
leaders note that the number of Councils has proliferated, by mutual agreement, from twenty-two at the time of the first contract to forty-two in 1994. In
some areas, the union considers genuine joint work and participation to be
underway — often in smaller subgroups or Councils. In other places, little is
happening, to the great frustration of union leaders and members. "Harvard
doesn't know what jointness is. Some managers still think the union wants to
consult on the color of the chairs," says HUCTW organizer Kris Rondeau.
"Others have built real relationships. . . . The Joint Councils with faculty on
them work, and those with only administrators do not work. The faculty bring
a different view, they are more curious and unafraid, and they can strengthen
the administrators, who most often want to do nothing."[81] A Harvard labor
relations representative disagrees: "You have to look at each case. It's the people
involved, the title is not as important. They need to be good listeners, open and
interested in hearing other points of view."[82]

Faculty can make a positive difference to workers not because they are
necessarily better listeners, but because they are structurally positioned to
make different contributions and decisions, especially those that affect the
relational and invisible work of many clericals. Some administrators can work
well with workers, but they appear to have different constraints than faculty,
and as a group are not focused on transforming participation to jointness.

The examples reported above are unique in their details, their specific
players, and their institutional settings within Harvard. While they cannot
begin to represent all the joint decision-making that occurs between Harvard
managers and clerical workers, they represent specific realities of this unusual
collective bargaining agreement. What limits the effectiveness of Joint Councils? Should more independent union action, like the public service training
sessions, be expected? Will adversarial unionism replace collaboration if man-

agers persist in limiting participation? The following section outlines constraints and opportunities to achieve greater clerical participation, visibility, and equality.

One constraint — and opportunity — is the university's structure, including the lack of an effective universitywide coordinating body. Each school and major department has its own Human Resource program. Sharing successes and suggestions for joint action is far more difficult for the university than for the union, which regularly schedules universitywide meetings of activists and keeps information flowing across what unionists see as administrative "Berlin Walls." "The union is incredible, the networks they have," says one manager who wished to remain anonymous.[83] "The only universitywide approach we have as a university is the contract, and that's set up to be about local issues." Assistant Director of Labor Relations Sullivan asserts that the university does have a unified approach, but says that it is decentralized so schools will have flexibility: "Every six months or so the university pulls together the management Joint Council chairs, to connect them. They themselves asked for it."[84]

The union also feels the university leadership has sent mixed signals. While President Neil Rudenstine endorsed the Joint Councils in principle as part of the "innovative and unique" relationship with the union, each school determines its own program and level of commitment to jointness. The union perceives there has been no strong, high-level advocate of joint labor-management cooperation on the university side since Professor Emeritus John Dunlop resigned as chief negotiator several years ago.[85] Sullivan disagrees; she says she still "believes in problem-solving, not positional bargaining."[86]

Harvard managers also have little experience with anything approaching HUCTW's assertive insistence on partnership and participation. Harvard's seven other smaller, blue-collar culinary and police unions are more traditional in their approach. Harvard has never seen anything like HUCTW, which creates its agenda as it goes along in an inclusive and participatory spirit quite different from Harvard's hierarchical culture. Speaking of Harvard management, mediator James Healy said, "I don't think they have enough awareness of what goes on in the world to realize what an extraordinary value they have in a relationship like this" (quoted in Hoerr 1993: 82).

Finally, the university may have no single agenda for its clerical workers that everyone supports — ironically, perhaps because of the very invisibility and devaluing of their work. Some administrators are most interested in more efficient and productive work settings, while others are trying to detach faculty secretaries and assistants from their personal relationships with faculty members. The university has at least two managerial faces — one professorial and one administrative — and the interests of the various internal players on each side are not the same. Over time, professors develop individual relationships with their support staff and come to depend on their specific knowledge of the professors' work. Taking away a personal assistant and assigning a pool of clerical workers to a faculty member would likely encounter some internal faculty resistance.

The union, too, confronts institutional barriers to making the Joint Councils work well to meet its goals. Most fundamental is the need to "raise member expectations. . . . Remember, these are not people who are accustomed to having a lot of power in their lives," said Bill Jaeger. "Sometimes we have to help them see what they are entitled to."[87] Carrie Normand, the former Harvard secretary and Joint Council member now working for HUCTW, points to the gender dynamic as a basic organizing challenge: "You have to believe your experience is legitimate, like when you need help, or when a policy needs changing because the same problems keep occurring. A lot of people, especially women, have no sense that they can do that. We call it self-representation."[88]

Union organizers' work includes helping people take their own concerns about work seriously and pointing out organizational issues that need to be addressed. Many employees do not make the direct connection between working conditions and the quality of work they produce. For example, "when dental hygienists noted that shorter appointments were unfair to patients and also to themselves, they began to link patient care and working conditions, but did not complete the link."[89]

The union's own limited resources may serve as another constraint on its participation, paralleling the power difference between managers and secretaries meeting in a Joint Council. Women clerical workers usually have less status, education, and even time (given family responsibilities and an average salary of $24,000) to engage in joint work than managers. Managers have the responsibility to make administrative relationships work; union members have the job of keeping their supervisors happy and getting assigned work done. If they are away from work on joint meetings too frequently, they cannot keep up with their jobs. With forty-two Joint Councils to support as well as internal and external organizing, problem-solving, and other responsibilities, union staff are not able to devote as much time to the Councils as they might like. Organizer Kris Rondeau admits that it is difficult to keep joint work on the "front burner," but they try:

> Each Joint Council has a staff assigned, and team leader meetings, and Joint Council meetings, and special trainings, and trainings for new people. The hardest job is team leader. . . . The union can't give too much attention to the Joint Councils, but they are going on, living by their values. The members help each other. The union provides opportunities for them to do that.[90]

According to one faculty assistant, who relied on the union to support her work in a Joint Council, the union was doing a lot: "The union never leaves you stranded. It gives us guidance. It trains you [in] how to run a meeting, what to do when things are going wrong, how to persist if it's difficult, how to work as a group. Every meeting has a preparation meeting."[91]

The union's support of the value of decentralization at Harvard increases union members' ability to take a flexible attitude in different settings and to encourage innovation.[92] But it makes it harder to share ideas and experiences across a wide variety of independently managed work sites. Support for decentralized management may also limit the union's ability to demand greater participation and power-sharing across many workplaces in the future.

The union is developing an increasingly clear philosophy of work and of the role of the worker in its active interpretive role.[93] At varying levels, union members are pushing for a conception of work as belonging to both the worker and the employer, not just to the employer. In contrast, Assistant Labor Relations Director Sullivan says: "Jobs are created because you need to get a particular function done. If you can still get the job done by showing sensitivity to the needs of the people doing the job, it's just good management to do it."[94] One activist who had been involved in the negotiating team for the first contract describes "what we think the workplace should look like" by comparing himself to some managers he knows. "It's just something they [the managers] hadn't thought about," says Bob Mendelson, a science technician. "It's not that they were dumb. It's just something that, like myself, pre-union, they'd just go to work, get paid, and go home." Since his own union activism began, Mendelson has developed an entirely different idea about the importance of work in everyone's life, which he articulates clearly:

> It's what we call job ownership, that's really shared. The employee brings something to the job, the employer brings something to the job, and . . . it's up to the employee to sort of bend their skills to fit the job, but also the job can be molded to sort of fit the particular employee. . . . This is the way it ought to be. It's certainly not the way it is here.[95]

He described a wonderful moment in his union organizing life when a management counterpart listened to this, then said, "I think it's something I've felt all along, but I haven't allowed myself to think about that for years."

Union members frequently push each other to think more creatively and expansively about work, and to try to engage in a moral as well as political dialogue with managers. They are motivated strongly by their jointly developed beliefs about what a community at work should be and are reengaging in what James McGregor Burns (1976) might call "transformational leadership," trying to close the gap between values and reality. Further, they are seeking partnership across highly charged lines of gender, class, and authority. The university context makes possible what would be far more difficult in a corporate context, but it is still an extraordinary endeavor. Union activists are trying to "give every worker the chance to participate in decisions made about her or his work life," as the 1993 union letter to new members states, and are attempting to create real-life examples of this to show how it improves life not just for the worker but for the employer and customer as well.

Some Joint Councils are working well; some are not. Creative problem-solving at the local level requires trust and hard work on both sides. Clearly, Joint Councils provide a meaningful form of participation to some workers. "It's not an official decision-making process, but it still affects things. Human beings listening to other human beings has an effect," said one secretary. "It's slow, long-term work. It takes persistence. It's better than having things happen to us. Even if it may be several years before it [a desired change] is implemented, it wouldn't happen at all otherwise."[96] Without a union, workers would have no guaranteed participation and no way to get necessary training and support. The focus on local initiatives gives Councils flexibility. Still, the process is painfully slow, subject to doubts on both sides about intent, seriousness, commitment, and usefulness. Workers find that encouraging signs are often followed by doubtful ones. Power imbalances create frustration in some settings. Personal qualities matter too. Some managers are "dull, angry, and hostile. Others are shining lights," HUCTW's Rondeau says.[97] The lack of consistency creates problems for everyone.

## Conclusion: Participation versus Control

I began this study of service work from an industrial relations paradigm, asking questions about the union's role in helping clerical workers gain control of their work. I concluded early on that HUCTW and the joint processes described here had made important but limited progress in enabling workers to wrest control of their jobs from their managers. During my two-year study, I realized that the union, in its training and organizing and in its contract with Harvard, emphasizes exclusively participation and jointness, not control.[98] The union activists continually advocate listening respectfully and persistently to the views of others, and encourage their members to engage in self-representation of what is important to them. Director Bill Jaeger says he has never been obsessed with "control," because it seems like "something which someone 'has' and which is 'taken' by someone else; it's a very male concept, it can't be shared. . . . Yes, members want more influence, and power, and recognition . . . but we don't want to cut managers out. We don't have it in us to stop listening. That is a built-in, permanent starting place."[99]

While much social science and industrial relations literature is concerned with control of work, especially in manufacturing settings, I had to consider the possibility that "control" was not the primary issue for these workers — or for their union at this point. Communication, respect, and a genuine commitment to their serious inclusion and meaningful participation describe far more clearly what they are seeking, at least at Harvard. "Control" may be too simplistic a category of analysis in the clerical context. After all, the product of much of their work is a relational interaction, not a commodity. Certainly a goal of inclusion raises questions like: How much inclusion? Who includes whom, and when? What if there is no consensus? By any standard of measurement, Harvard clerical and technical workers are far more "included" in the process of making decisions that affect their work lives today than they were eight years ago, before their first labor agreement. Just as clearly, they have a long way to go to achieve what the union calls "jointness," or "co-ownership" of jobs, or even to become a full partner in making decisions that will advance the university and its workers. These case studies suggest the need to push the metaphor of participation further, to ask the harder questions, and to raise the issues of power and decision making. The union's customer/public service training is beginning to do just that.

The union's strategy is clearer than the university's, and HUCTW addresses issues of clerical invisibility, emotional labor, and disempowerment consistently and clearly, although in different terms. As Jaeger says:

> Employee involvement is the defining aspiration of our local union. . . .
> Relieving the economic burden, while it is very important, doesn't
> ever give a member of the union the feeling of progress in her soul and
> real improvement in her life, of having really gained something, in the
> same way that a rich, interesting successful participation in some sort
> of process does where power is shared in a new way.[100]

The union's role is especially important in a clerical or service setting because workers on their own may not have the experience, the shared knowledge, or the support they need to challenge their exclusion, as Jaeger points out:

> Almost every working person has the impulse that more participation
> is good. It feels better to be involved in planning and creative work
> and redesigning or defining work systems than to have it happen to

you. It feels bad to have people tell you how things should be where you are the expert. People have the impulse, yes, . . . but the idea that we can act on it, and the confidence that it's worth it to jump into it, have to be organized around and developed in people. We have to show them good examples. We have to prepare extensively, encourage people, and build meaningful personal connections. A lot of working people have the impulse but have enough fear and nervousness not to act on it, ever.[101]

In sum, many kinds and levels of worker control over and participation in work are possible, ranging from simple resistance to formal sharing or ceding of decisions between management and employees (Applebaum and Batt 1994; Kochan and Osterman 1994). Clerical workers, like all workers, have some power over how they perform their work, but much of their power lies in their ability to affect and negotiate the relationships that are the daily currency of their work. The efforts of the union and some managers have helped Joint Councils function with episodic jointness, providing valuable contributions to running the university. "The secretaries are a tremendous information resource," said one manager.[102] The effort needed to achieve small agreements may seem large in proportion to the issues resolved, but I argue in these cases that mutual understanding and respect have increased in ways that are difficult to measure precisely. However, without strong, coherent leadership from top managers at each of Harvard's schools, the opportunities for joint work can become frustrating experiences that alienate rather than engage workers.

The potential for gain is high, but the risk of doing little or nothing is great, for the union is developing a cohesive philosophy of work that is not currently matched by management's efforts. The next years will tell whether the larger and deeper questions can begin to be addressed through Joint Councils and their spin-offs — and whether all union members will prove to be as patient, constructive, and optimistic as some described here. Whatever else it is or is not, jointness is a dialectical relationship; both managers and workers change and develop through the process of listening to each other and renegotiating their relationships.

Harvard management could make better use of this union's initiative and interest. As John Dunlop said, "The union permits a conscientious management to get things done faster and more effectively than it could on its own" (quoted in Hoerr 1993: 79). Some managers have the leeway to seek union or worker involvement, and choose to do so.[103] Innovative managers could develop measures of performance that incorporate worker perspectives on the services being provided. When managers do not take joint efforts seriously, they can do more harm than good, generating anger, cynicism, and eventually poor service.

Unions that renegotiate relationships, not just wages and benefits, have great potential to address issues of concern to women and clerical workers. The U.S. labor movement's future could change if unions organized the 13 million unorganized private sector clerical workers (Eaton 1993c; Hurd 1993). To succeed at this task, unions can become advocates of issues raised by members themselves, as HUCTW has done successfully by renegotiating relationships at work. The emotional labor performed by most clerical and technical workers is largely unrecognized and invisible, and generally is not valued highly or explicitly by employers. But it is frequently impossible to keep everyone happy, and trying to do so can create unbearable stress on workers. Unions can play an invaluable role in helping workers set boundaries around their abilities to satisfy everyone, thereby creating a more equitable and mutually honest relationship with employers, supervisors, and "help-seekers." Much of the "hidden conflict in organizations" (Kolb and Bartunek 1992) could be engaged constructively through more effective self-representation of clerical workers; this conflict should not be the workers' burden to carry.

The future experience will tell if Bill Jaeger is correct when he suggests that "the potential is unlimited. We haven't found a case yet where there is too much participation. Every added increment of employee involvement is a good thing, and — we haven't found the limit yet."[104] Although participation is often an unsatisfactory description of workers' relations with managers, scholars need to analyze what participation means in each case. If everyone enjoys the "desert island" exercise in the joint orientation, but nothing changes back at the office, the union could take this promising strategy and push it further, with both members and the employers. One could start by asking clerical and other service sector workers if they have the chance to participate as much as they would like, and how they would do things differently if they were managing their own work. Without more sustained, creative representation efforts of this kind, workers' full potential will not be developed, and "women's work" in clerical, technical, and administrative jobs will continue to be devalued.

## NOTES

*Acknowledgments:* I appreciate the assistance of members and leaders of HUCTW, AFSMCE, and Harvard managers, especially those 30 or more individuals whom I interviewed, many of whom are not identified by name to preserve confidentiality. Bill Jaeger, Carrie Normand, Shari Levinson, and Kathy Randel kindly read and commented on earlier drafts. Other colleagues who read this chapter and made valuable suggestions on earlier drafts include Deborah Kolb, Renee Kazinski, Cameron Macdonald, Grey Osterud, Marshall Ganz, John Hoerr, Robert McKersie, Carmen Sirianni, and two anonymous reviewers. Support for this research came in part from the Schlesinger Library at

Radcliffe College through a Visiting Scholar appointment, Radcliffe's Bunting Institute, and a Harman Fellowship at the Center for Science and International Affairs, Kennedy School of Government, Harvard University. The conclusions and any errors remain my responsibility.

1. The union is affiliated with the American Federation of State, County, and Municipal Employees, or AFSCME, as Local 3650, AFL-CIO.

2. The terms "relational" and "relational practice" as I use them here emerge from recent feminist psychological and organizational literature as well as from my participation on a research team funded by the Ford Foundation consisting of Lotte Bailyn, Joyce Fletcher, Maureen Harvey, Robin Johnson, Deborah Kolb, Leslie Perlow, Rhona Rapoport, and myself. The "relational" literature is extensive but includes as key contributions Adamson, Briskin, and McPhail (1988); Belenky, Clinchy, Goldberger, and Tarule (1986); Fletcher (1994a,b); Gilligan (1982); Jordan et al. (1991); and Miller (1986).

3. The women's movement in the United States has not fully embraced unionization as a strategy for women's social and economic equality, with some exceptions. The opportunity to study the phenomenon of a predominantly women's union is relatively rare, since at present less than 11% of private-sector service workers are organized, while more than 30% of public-sector service workers are unionized. This study is not intended to serve as a survey of clerical worker unionization, but to explore closely the experience of one clerical workers' union to understand the nature of workplace participation and control issues in its organizing. Rather than pursuing a traditional union strategy of "shop-floor control," HUCTW has developed a strategy of jointness and participation that specifically suits its clerical and technical members.

4. While the union represents both clerical and technical workers, and one of my three case studies includes technical workers (dental hygienists), the essay concentrates on the situation of clerical workers who make up two-thirds of the union's membership and are more numerous in the economy than technical workers.

5. Of course the two strategies are not always in opposition, and some unions frequently negotiate comparable-worth agreements. However, some feminists have also found unions to be barriers to comparable-worth benefits. Comparable-worth advocates have sought to value clerical work more highly, but they have not achieved great success (Acker 1989). Unlike the legal and job-evaluation strategy of comparable worth, organizing a union relies on an empowerment strategy for workers.

6. Many related stories of interest emerged from my series of interviews over a 2-year period with members of HUCTW, union leaders, and Harvard managers. For instance, those who participated in union activities developed leadership skills, confidence, and new understandings. The union successfully created an inclusive, developmental, and relational organizing culture in the group (see Eaton 1992, 1993a, 1993c; Hoerr 1993; Hurd 1993; Oppenheim 1991–92). My focus here, however, is specifically on the meaning of "jointness" as experienced by the worker participants, and on the union's role in challenging the dominant discourse (common even in the nonprofit sector) of customer service and in promoting an alternate vision of positive public service that incorporates the dignified participation and concerns of service providers.

7. Gutek (1988); U.S. Department of Labor (1993). A full 31% of women workers and 7% of men workers (a total of 14 million) are in the job category of administrative support and clerical work (U.S. Department of Labor 1993: Table 56). In 1980, 32.2% of white women and 25.8% of nonwhite women held clerical jobs, making this

the largest occupation for white women, while service jobs (with 29.3% of nonwhite women and 16.3% of white women) formed the largest occupational group for non-white women (Goldin 1990: 74).

8. This paper focuses on the clerical rather than the technical workers at Harvard, in part because they are the large majority of union members (about two-thirds). The dental hygienists described here are technical workers; the rest of the cases concern clerical workers.

9. See Braverman (1974); for an important analysis of the proletarianization of white-collar work, see Garson (1988) for examples, Costello (1991) for someone who does look at unionized clericals, and Gutek (1988) for a recent summary of the literature. Of course, clerical workers' organizations like Nine to Five have published accounts of clerical worker activism, but these are not widely known in the academic world. See Cassedy and Nussbaum (1983) for one example.

10. Sixteen percent of clerical workers are represented by unions, primarily in the public sector.

11. Secretarial jobs are the only jobs frequently still paid according to the level of the boss, according to a compensation survey reported in the *9 to 5 Newsline* (January–February 1994), p. 4.

12. I am not endorsing such a metaphor, especially with the increasing consciousness of sexual harassment at the workplace. It does not shed much light on either the marital or the office relationship to confuse the two just because women have traditionally been asked to provide caring services for men in both.

13. Harvard figures from Harvard University (1992); Union statistics from an interview with HUCTW Director Bill Jaeger, November 24, 1993.

14. For women of color, clerical work mirrors the racial hierarchy in U.S. society, as women of color most often work for men (and sometimes women) who are white. African American and Latina women are moving into white-collar jobs, but they are more concentrated in the private-service sector and manufacturing than European American women, who perform more than 80% of administrative and clerical work. While 32.2% of white women were clerical workers in 1980, only 25.4% of nonwhite women were. For women of color, service work is a more common occupation (29%) than clerical work (Golden 1990: 74). Far more research needs to be conducted to analyze the specific situation of women of color in the clerical work force, including their concentration by industry and occupation, their different experiences in various ethnic groups, etc. Women of color are overrepresented in government and nonprofit clerical jobs compared to private industry. Harvard is an exception: more than 85% of its clerical and technical workers are European American, and more than 78% are female. Due to space limitations, I cannot address this question further here, but I hope to do so in future research.

15. I am indebted for the example of Gdansk to Peter Capodilupo, Chief Human Resources Officer at the Harvard Business School.

16. See Barzelay (1992). See also U.S. Congress, Office of Technology Assessment (1995) and Herzenberg, Alic, and Wial (forthcoming).

17. This struggle appears differently in many industrial workplaces governed by Taylorist principles. I do not mean to suggest that shop-floor struggles never centered around relationships with foremen, forewomen, or managers; they did and continue to do so. However, the work itself was not relational but related to particular tools and materials of production; this changes the nature of the stress experienced.

18. Reported in interview, October 28, 1993.
19. Interview, October 15, 1993.
20. Interview with Kathy Randel, October 27, 1993.
21. Interview with Carrie Normand, October 28, 1993.
22. Interview with Carrie Normand, October 27, 1993.
23. Interview with Lianne Sullivan, November 24, 1993.
24. Interview with Lisa Flanagan, Ann Cagos, and Bonnie Bigelow, October 25, 1993.
25. Interview with Randel, October 27, 1993.
26. To some extent this mirrors housework, also traditionally performed by women.
27. Interview, October 28, 1993.
28. "Tasks and associated skills . . . such as mediating office relationships or caring for mentally retarded 'students' were rendered invisible in the job evaluation instrument and in the evaluation process" (Acker 1989: 213).
29. Interview with Randel, October 27, 1993.
30. Interview, October 28, 1993.
31. Carmen Sirianni helped me see this pattern of integrative work.
32. Reported in interview with Bob Mendelson, November 2, 1992.
33. I appreciate Cameron Macdonald's insight on this point.
34. Reported in interview, October 27, 1993.
35. The issue of whether students are customers is a contested one, at least at Harvard. Some faculty and administrators, such as Herman "Dutch" Leonard of the Kennedy School of Government, reject this assertion. In 1993, Leonard explicitly denied that students are "customers" of the institution; rather, he believed they are "partners in learning." In 1992–93, this was contested by a group of mid-career students, who saw themselves very much as customers of a very expensive education (tuition and fees alone amounted to $18,000 that year) which often they (with an average age of 37) were financing. They objected to illegible reading lists, abrupt schedule changes, nonexistent office hours, and repeated trips to the bookstore or copy center to get materials. Secretaries were once again often caught in the middle. See Mid-Career Working Group (1993).
36. Interview with Sylvia Marks, November 30, 1992.
37. These are common phrases used by HUCTW organizers and leaders to summarize their philosophy and values.
38. See Hoerr (1993) for a fuller accounting of the internal dynamics of both union and university thinking as well as the campaign details; see also Hurd (1993). Union members sometimes say the organizing drive took 17 years, perhaps counting the first contract in 1989. In January 1987, HUCTW made an agreement to affiliate with AFSCME, which offered to support the organizing drive but agreed to stay out of internal affairs of the union. "We want to do it ourselves," the committee told AFSCME (interview with HUCTW President Donene Williams, January 3, 1992).
39. The contract was signed in 1990, retroactive to 1989. It provided for substantial economic benefits, including pension improvements and wage scale upgrades, as well as across-the-board raises, tuition reductions, and other gains for workers. Hurd (1993) quotes the union as saying the contract represented an average 32.3% wage increase over 3 years for HUCTW members.
40. Among the authors who influenced and broadened her thinking, lead organizer Kris Rondeau credits psychologists Jean Baker Miller, Carol Gilligan, and affiliates of the Stone Center at Wellesley, especially Judith Jordan (see Jordan et al. 1991). See also Oppenheim (1991–92).

41. I owe this insight to Carmen Sirianni.

42. Rather than filing individual grievances, union members were encouraged to resolve problems with supervisors, representing themselves with the support of a union co-worker. If they could not be resolved at that level, a local problem-solving committee was convened. Mediation was emphasized, although there was arbitration. For more details, see Hoerr (1993). For a description of an unusual and somewhat parallel labor-management agreement, see Rubinstein et al. (1993) on the Saturn-UAW agreement.

43. From the management perspective, the entire Joint Council structure was designed to reflect the university's desire for a decentralized implementation of the new agreement, to match the historic governing philosophy of "every tub on its own bottom," and to enable local members and managers to craft solutions appropriate to their workplaces. From the union perspective, it was the only way to ensure local participation and leadership development, and to attain truly joint decision-making. Yet its effectiveness rests on a foundation of trust and mutual willingness to work together to solve problems which cannot be mandated by either side.

44. See personal correspondence from John Hoerr, March 1994.

45. Interview with Jaeger, September 18, 1993.

46. Interview with Jaeger, November 24, 1993.

47. Ibid.

48. Interviews with Jaeger, September 28, 1993, and Normand, October 28, 1993.

49. Interviews with Jaeger, September 28, 1993.

50. Interview with Jaeger, September 28, 1993. Committee member Carrie Normand regretfully says this training will not be joint, "because management is not ready yet. They haven't really got the hang of listening to us, and letting the people who are to be trained have a part in identifying what it is they need" (interview October 28, 1993).

51. Interviews with Jaeger, September 28 and November 24, 1993. Examples include the financial aid worker dealing with a student who needs a loan or grant but has not been told of changes in regulations that exclude him or her, or a clerk assisting a scholar who wants to do research not permitted by regulation, law, or university rule.

    The union has its own motives besides challenging the university ideology of "service"; its leaders expect that HUCTW will be able to involve people who have not been active in formal joint activities or who have a particular problem but are suffering stress and pressure on their jobs without getting the support they need in order to provide support to their "customers." "We will teach basic negotiating skills that help, . . . like taking a break if the conversation is going badly, like asking for help, like framing something differently in a way that doesn't involve you. People need to learn to defuse situations, and to acknowledge that saying no is really hard," says Normand. "There are smaller things they can do when someone is upset or angry, even if they can't solve the problem" (interview, October 28, 1993).

52. The union is also planning a training for "group leaders," who are basically working supervisors, because they think the university trainings for this group of 150 or so members have been inadequate.

53. Interview with Normand, October 28, 1993.

54. In contrast to this case, consider a blue-collar union faced with a unilateral 33% cut in time allotted for an existing job. While meeting with a supervisor might have been the union's initial strategy, the union might have also initiated grievances, slow-downs, leaflets, news conferences, pickets, or other more confrontational approaches to resolv-

ing the problem. And the issues of invisible work, gender power relations, and rela-tional work likely would not have been in the forefront in a blue-collar setting.

55. Interview with Flanagan, Cagos, and Bigelow, October 25, 1993.

56. MIT Industrial Relations Professor Bob McKersie accurately points out that this is typical of professional and technical workers who often prefer to deal with manage-ment on their own, but I believe that the entire story of this example suggests that the union's role was instrumental nonetheless, despite not formally representing people at the meeting. That role is one that HUCTW discourages its activists from adopting in favor of promoting self-representation.

57. The role of the dentist here parallels the faculty role; his concern about patient care presumably outweighs his concern about increased production per day, perhaps be-cause he is a doctor before he is an administrator — yet he also did not have a complete idea of what constituted actual quality patient care before the worker presentation.

58. Interview, November 30, 1993.

59. Interview, October 28, 1993. Quotations from Levinson in the following paragraphs are from the same interview.

60. Interview, November 30, 1993.

61. Interview, October 28, 1993.

62. Interview with Levinson, October 28, 1993.

63. Interview, November 30, 1993.

64. Interview, October 28, 1993.

65. Upon reading a draft of this chapter, Jaeger told me that preserving connection was important, but was not the only goal of members. "We primarily want to make change, and we desperately want to do it in a way that preserves connection," he said (interview, November 24, 1994).

66. Interview with Leonard, November 30, 1993.

67. Personal communication, December 2, 1993. The local union has an elected president and executive board and an appointed AFSCME staff including Kris Rondeau and Bill Jaeger.

68. Interview with Leonard, November 30, 1993.

69. Interview with Randel, October 27, 1993.

70. Interview, October 28, 1993.

71. Interview with Peter Capodilupo, December 9, 1993.

72. Reported in interview with Randel, October 27, 1993.

73. Interview with Capodilupo, December 9, 1993.

74. Bill Jaeger points out that there are between 1,000 and 2,000 employees at Harvard who are exempt from the bargaining unit but who could arguably be included in it; the union and management have an ongoing committee meeting to discuss the appropriate composition of the unit. This position is one example of a nonsupervisory, exempt employee whom the union feels should be in the bargaining unit but whom manage-ment has excluded.

75. Interview, December 9, 1993.

76. At least some of the underlying conflict and issues remain unresolved. When it came time to hire a second office facilitator, the union members of the committee expected to reconvene for a similar procedure. "We were not supposed to disband," says Randel. But Capodilupo posted the second job anyway. He says that he notified members first and that the posting was just a formality to get through the required posting period of 3 weeks. Committee members say he refused to return phone calls from work group

members over a 6-week period. This rift seems to have somewhat undermined the good feeling created through the working group. A worker Joint Council representative in the group feels that "this is not a good example of jointness." Management has a different view: "It's less than tension, maybe a misunderstanding," Capodilupo says of the lack of meetings on the second position. "By nature the second isn't the same process. . . . It appeared abrupt."

77. Interview, November 24, 1993.
78. Interview, December 9, 1993. It is possible that the primary goal of the coordinator is to deal with faculty, more than secretaries, although clericals see their lives impacted more immediately.
79. See U.S. Department of Labor and U.S. Department of Commerce (1994) and Eaton (1993b) for a summary of labor law changes recommended to increase the ability of workers to influence their workplace without violating labor laws.
80. Interview, November 24, 1993.
81. Interview with Rondeau, October 18, 1993.
82. Interview with Sullivan, November 24, 1993.
83. Interview, October 15, 1993.
84. Interview with Sullivan, November 24, 1993.
85. Dunlop's departure was widely seen in the Harvard-Radcliffe community as a victory for the more anti-union forces, especially the deans of the larger, wealthier schools, who some view as unenthusiastic about Rudenstine's plans to centralize and coordinate more universitywide functions such as fundraising and presumably labor negotiations. Some sources suggest that retiring President Derek Bok requested Dunlop's resignation, but neither has confirmed this. See Hoerr (1993).
86. Interview, November 24, 1993.
87. Interview with Jaeger, November 24, 1993.
88. Interview, October 27, 1993.
89. Interview with Flanagan, Capos, and Bigelow, October 25, 1993.
90. Interview with Rondeau, October 18, 1993.
91. Interview with Shari Levinson, October 28, 1993.
92. I am indebted to John Hoerr for pointing out that the union's support for decentralization, documented in the third paragraph of the preamble to the contract, is often used by hostile administrators to fight the union's agenda for more consistent and centralized treatment. Personal correspondence, March 1994.
93. This is made more difficult since in a university context, faculty are presumed to be the legitimate interpreters of much of the world and what goes on in it; secretaries are not assumed to play that role, as Carmen Sirianni notes.
94. Interview, November 24, 1993.
95. Interview, November 2, 1992.
96. Interview, October 28, 1993.
97. Interview, October 18, 1993.
98. I was also aided by Carmen Sirianni, who asked me why I kept asking about "control" when that was not the language I reported the union was using. Sometimes the paradigms we hold from our own training and experience are hard to release!
99. Interview, November 24, 1993.
100. Interview, November 24, 1993.
101. Ibid.
102. Interview with Sullivan, November 24, 1993.

103. In the Shad Hall Steering Committee at the Business School, union Joint Council member Cliff Moreland reported, "The managers really wanted input. They wanted to make the facility the best." So they created a committee of managers, students, workers, and faculty, both users and nonusers of the facility, and asked for their help. A number of jointly approved programs were created and improvements made (interview, October 28, 1993).

104. Interview, November 24, 1993.

## REFERENCES

Acker, Joan. 1989. *Doing Comparable Worth*. Philadelphia: Temple University Press.

Adamson, Nancy, Linda Briskin, and Margaret McPhail. 1988. *Feminist Organizing for Change*. Toronto: Oxford University Press.

Applebaum, Eileen, and Rosemary Batt. 1994. *The New American Workplace*. Ithaca: Cornell University Press.

Barzelay, Michael, with the collaboration of Barbak J. Armanji. 1992. *Breaking through Bureaucracy: A New Vision for Managing in Government*. Berkeley: University of California Press.

Belenky, Mary Field, Blythe McVicker Clinchy, Nancy Rule Goldberger, and Jill Mattuck Tarule. 1986. *Women's Ways of Knowing*. New York: Basic Books.

Blum, Linda M. 1991. *Between Feminism and Labor: The Significance of the Comparable Worth Movement*. Berkeley: University of California Press.

Braverman, Harry. 1974. *Labor and Monopoly Capital: The Degradation of Work in the Twentieth Century*. New York: Monthly Review Press.

Briskin, Linda, and Patricia McDermott, eds. 1993. *Women Challenging Unions: Feminism, Democracy, and Militancy*. Toronto: University of Toronto Press.

Burawoy, Michael. 1979. *Manufacturing Consent: Changes in the Labor Process under Monopoly Capitalism*. Chicago: University of Chicago Press.

Burns, James McGregor. 1976. *Leadership*. New York: Harper.

Cassedy, Ellen, and Karen Nussbaum. 1983. *Nine to Five: The Working Woman's Guide to Office Survival*. New York: Penguin.

Cobble, Dorothy Sue, ed. 1993. *Women and Unions: Forging a Partnership*. Ithaca: Cornell University, ILR Press.

Costello, Cynthia. 1991. *We're Worth It! Women and Collective Action in the Insurance Workplace*. Urbana: University of Illinois Press.

Eaton, Susan C. 1995. "Union Leadership Development in the 1990s and Beyond." *Workplace Topics* 4(2). Washington, DC: AFL-CIO.

——. 1993a. "Stories Make Things Real: A Reflection on Union Activism and Personal Change for Five Activists." Unpublished paper. Harvard University, Graduate School of Education, Cambridge, MA.

——. 1993b. "Women and Labor Management Relations: Lessons from Canada." Unpublished paper. U.S. Department of Labor, Women's Bureau, Washington, DC.

——. 1993c. "Women Workers, Unions, and Industrial Sectors in North America." Unpublished paper. International Labor Organization, Interdepartmental Project on Equality of Women in Employment, Geneva.

——. 1992. "Union Leadership Development in the 1990s and Beyond: A Report with Recommendations." Working Paper 92-05. John F. Kennedy School of Government,

Center for Science and International Affairs, June. Harvard University, Cambridge, MA.

Fletcher, Joyce K. 1994a. "Castrating the Female Advantage: Feminist Standpoint Research and Management Science." *Journal of Management Inquiry* 3(1).

——. 1994b. "Toward a Theory of Relational Practice in Organizations: A Feminist Reconstruction of 'Real' Work." Ph.D. dissertation. Boston University.

Freeman, Richard, and Joel Rogers. 1995. "Worker Representation and Participation Survey: First Report of Finding." Paper delivered at 47th annual meeting of the Industrial Relations Research Association, Washington, DC, January.

Garson, Barbara. 1988. *The Electronic Sweatshop: How Computers Are Transforming the Office of the Future into the Factory of the Past*. New York: Simon and Schuster.

Gilligan, Carol. 1982. *In a Different Voice*. Cambridge, MA: Harvard University Press.

Goldin, Claudia. 1990. *Understanding the Gender Gap: An Economic History of American Women*. New York: Oxford University Press.

Gutek, Barbara A. 1988. "Women in Clerical Work." In Ann Stromberg and Shirley Harkness, eds., *Women Working: Theories and Facts in Perspective* (pp. 225–40). Mountain View, CA: Mayfield Publishing Company.

Harvard Union of Clerical and Technical Workers. 1993. "Letter to New Members." Mimeographed.

——. 1988. "We Believe in Ourselves." Mimeographed.

Harvard Union of Clerical and Technical Workers, AFSCME Local 3650, AFL-CIO, and Harvard University, 1993. "Agreement: July 1, 1992–June 30, 1995."

——. 1989. "Agreement: July 1, 1989–June 30, 1992."

Harvard University. 1993. *The President's Report: 1991–1993*. Cambridge, MA: Harvard University.

——. 1992. *Affirmative Action Report*. Cambridge, MA: Harvard University.

Heckscher, Charles. 1988. *The New Unionism: Employee Involvement in the Changing Corporation*. New York: Basic Books.

Herzenberg, Stephen, John Alic, and Howard Wial. Forthcoming. *Better Jobs for More People: A New Deal for the Service Economy*. A Twentieth Century Fund book.

Hochschild, Arlie Russell. 1983. *The Managed Heart: Commercialization of Human Feeling*. Berkeley: University of California Press.

Hoerr, John. 1993. "Solidaritas at Harvard." *The American Prospect* 14(Summer): 67–82.

Hurd, Richard. 1993. "Organizing and Representing Clerical Workers: The Harvard Model." In Dorothy Sue Cobble, ed., *Women and Unions: Forging a Partnership* (pp. 316–36). Ithaca: Cornell University ILR Press.

Joffe, Carol. 1986. *The Regulation of Sexuality: Experiences of Family Planning Workers*. Philadelphia: Temple University Press.

Jordan, Judith V., Alexandra G. Kaplan, Jean Baker Miller, Irene P. Stiver, and Janet L. Surrey. 1991. *Women's Growth in Connection: Writings from the Stone Center*. New York: Guilford Press.

Kanter, Rosabeth Moss. 1977. *Men and Women of the Corporation*. New York: Basic Books.

Kochan, Thomas A., and Paul Osterman. 1994. *The Mutual Gains Enterprise: Forging a Winning Partnership among Labor, Management, and Government*. Boston: Harvard Business School Press.

Kolb, Deborah. 1992. "Women's Work: Peacemaking in Organizations." In Deborah Kolb and Jean Bartunek, eds., *Hidden Conflict in Organizations* (pp. 63–91). Newbury Park, CA: Sage Publications.

Kolb, Deborah, and Jean Bartunek, eds. 1992. *Hidden Conflict in Organizations*. Newbury Park, CA: Sage Publications.

Kumar, Pradeep. 1993. "Collective Bargaining and Women's Workplace Concerns." In Linda Briskin and Patricia McDermott, eds., *Women Challenging Unions: Feminism, Democracy, and Militancy* (pp. 207–30). Toronto: University of Toronto Press.

Mid-Career Working Group. 1993. Unpublished materials of the Mid-Career Working Group for Program, Policy, and Academic Excellence, in the possession of Sue Williamson at the Kennedy School of Government, Harvard University.

Midwest Center for Labor Research. 1988. "Feminizing Unions." *Labor Research Review 11* 7(1): 1–95.

Milkman, Ruth. 1985. "Women Workers, Feminism, and the Labor Movement since the 1960s." In Ruth Milkman, ed., *Women, Work, and Protest: A Century of U.S. Women's Labor History* (pp. 300–22). Boston: Routledge & Kegan Paul.

Miller, Jean Baker. 1986. *Toward a New Psychology of Women*. 2nd ed. Boston: Beacon Press.

Nine to Five, National Association of Working Women. 1994. *9 to 5 Newsline*. Cleveland, OH.

Oppenheim, Lisa. 1991–92. "Women's Ways of Organizing: A Conversation with AFSCME Organizers Kris Rondeau and Gladys McKenzie." *Labor Research Review* 18 (Fall/Winter): 45–60.

Rankin, Tom. 1990. *New Forms of Work Organization: The Challenge for North American Unions*. Toronto: University of Toronto Press.

Rubinstein, Saul, Michael Bennett, and Thomas Kochan. 1993. "Reinventing the Local Union: The Partnership between Saturn and UAW Local 1853." In Bruce Kaufman and Morris Kleiner, eds., *Employee Representation: Alternatives and Future Directions* (pp. 339–70). Madison, WI: Industrial Relations Research Association.

Sirianni, Carmen. 1991. "The Self-Management of Time in Postindustrial Society." In Karl Hinrichs, William Roche, and Carmen Sirianni, eds., *Working Time in Transition: The Political Economy of Working Hours in Industrial Nations* (pp. 231–74). Philadelphia: Temple University Press.

Tannen, Deborah. 1990. *You Just Don't Understand: Men and Women in Conversation*. New York: William Morrow and Company.

U.S. Congress, Office of Technology Assessment. 1995. "Productivity, Technology, and Employment in the Service Sector." Unpublished draft report in the author's possession.

U.S. Department of Labor, Bureau of Labor Statistics. 1993, January. *Employment and Earnings*. Washington, DC: U.S. Government Printing Office.

U.S. Department of Labor and U.S. Department of Commerce. 1994, December. *Report and Recommendations: Commission on the Future of Worker-Management Relations*. Washington, DC: U.S. Government Printing Office.

Weiler, Paul. 1990. *Governing the Workplace*. Cambridge, MA: Harvard University Press.

*Chapter 13*

# The Prospects for Unionism in a Service Society

• Dorothy Sue Cobble

idway through teaching one of my first undergraduate courses at Douglass College—a 1990 honors seminar on "The Future of Work" for first-year women—the question of the relevancy of unions surfaced. "So, how many of you have ever belonged to a union?" I queried, knowing that many of them had extensive work histories and that close to a quarter of the New Jersey work force was still unionized (Johnson 1995). The class giggled at such a far-fetched notion. "What? Unions for baby-sitters?" someone finally said as I looked at them quizzically, unable to interpret their laughter. The rest of the class was now emboldened. "Yeah, that's ridiculous." "Of course, we haven't belonged to a union. There aren't any unions for waitresses or salesclerks or file clerks." "Part-timers can't join unions. Can they?" "And what exactly do unions do for people who don't work in factories anyway?" The objections and skeptical questioning continued at a torrential pace for the rest of the session.

About a month later, we moved into the policy section of the course and returned once more to unions. But this time the discussion was shockingly different. "We've looked at legal and legislative remedies," I began, "and the reforms initiated by employers. But what about the need for employee organizations—you know, groups like unions that are organized independently of the employer and whose representatives meet with employers to discuss problems, resolve grievances, and make suggestions for workplace reform?" The response was swift and pointed. "Why, of course, employees need a collective and independent voice. We don't want to have to beg," one student asserted indignantly. To a woman, their heads nodded in militant agreement.

These two class sessions, I later came to understand, laid out in a simple yet powerful way the challenges unions must face if they are to represent the twenty-first-century work force. Women comprise 39 percent of all union members, and manufacturing employees represent less than a third of the unionized work force (Johnson 1995; Spalter-Roth, Hartmann, and Collins 1994b; U.S. Department of Labor 1994), but many still perceive unions as organizations whose primary and even sole constituency is the blue-collar male worker. Of equal importance, although slightly less than half of American workers would vote for a union at their workplace, 60 percent approve of unions and 90 percent approve of "employee organizations" (Freeman and Rogers 1993: 33). In other words, although many workers perceive today's union institutions as not meeting their needs, the central premise of union-ism — the notion that collective representation is necessary for the protection and advancement of the interests of employees — is still widely accepted. The new work force does not reject *unionism* per se; it rejects the *particular form* of unionism that is dominant today.

This chapter is in part what I would have liked to have said to my students. It is also a continuation of my ongoing research on the transformations in the world of work and the implications of those changes for employee representa-tion. I will look first at the relationship between unions and women, focusing in particular on women service workers. The labor movement, historically and in the present, has been quite diverse — both in terms of who it has represented and the forms it has taken. Baby-sitters may not have organized, but wait-resses, flight attendants, nurses, teachers, and even Playboy bunnies did. In the past, unions successfully represented women and service workers — two major components of today's new work force[1] — and they are still doing so today, despite the increased power of capital and the outmoded public policy govern-ing labor-management relations.

Nevertheless, if the labor movement is to organize the vast numbers of women and service workers now outside its ranks, it must reform not only its agenda but its institutional practice. The old-style factory unionism of the 1930s is no longer appropriate for many sectors of today's work force.[2] The second part of this chapter will analyze this mismatch between the current work force and the inherited models of unionism. How does the new work force differ from the work force of the 1930s? What are the implications of these changes for employee representation? I will conclude by describing some of the new models of unionism that are struggling to be born and the changes in public policy that would nurture their progress.

## *The Feminization of Unions?*

Women's share of union membership grew steadily in the decades following World War II as the feminization of the work force picked up speed. For the first time, women made up a sizable if not majority constituency in a number of unions. Women employed primarily as telephone operators and clericals comprised 40 percent or more of the Communication Workers of America (CWA), for example. Waitresses, maids, and women working in a variety of other hospitality occupations claimed close to a majority in the Hotel Employees and Restaurant Employees Union (HERE).[3]

In the 1960s and 1970s an even more dramatic change in the gender balance of organized labor occurred as unionism spread into female-dominated sectors of the economy such as education; federal, state, and municipal government; and, to a more limited degree, health care. In 1954, women comprised 17 percent of organized workers; by the early 1980s, the figure had almost doubled (Milkman 1985). Many of the most powerful and vocal internationals within the labor movement—the American Federation of State, County, and Municipal Employees (AFSCME), the Service Employees International Union (SEIU), and the teacher unions—now had large female constituencies (Cobble 1993).

In the 1980s, these unions provided national leadership on a wide range of women's concerns, from pay equity to parental leave (Blum 1991; Cobble 1993). They also pioneered more democratic, participatory approaches to organizing and representation (Eaton, Chapter 12; Hoerr 1993; Hurd 1993). Their sensitivity toward and successful advocacy of women's issues have helped undermine the longstanding feminist critique of unions as bastions of male power and privilege.[4]

In part because of the increased power of women in certain sectors of the labor movement, women (as compared to men) are now reaping enhanced economic dividends from unions. Union membership has always offered both women and men higher earnings.[5] But in the public sector and in white-collar jobs, where women have achieved the most power within their unions, the union premium (or the amount unionization raises wages) is now much higher for women than for men (Freeman and Leonard 1987). Indeed, over all, unions not only raise wages but reduce income inequality between men and women as well as between white workers and workers of color (Spalter-Roth et al. 1994a: 39; 1994b: 202–3). Unions, of course, also continue to provide women other benefits, such as a greater voice in decisions that affect their working conditions, increased job security, due process rights through grievance and arbitration procedures, and health and other fringe benefits (Cobble 1993; Spalter-Roth et al. 1994a).

But problems remain. Women have been feminizing an institution in rapid decline. Union density in the United States has fallen continuously since the early 1950s, making U.S. unionization rates among the lowest of any industrialized country. In 1991, 17 percent of the U.S. work force was organized, contrasting sharply with the rates of Sweden (85 percent), Denmark (73 percent), the United Kingdom (42 percent), Germany (34 percent), and even Japan (27 percent) (Freeman and Rogers 1993: 15). And, of equal importance, in part because of their declining membership, unions have less power to deliver enhanced earnings, job security, and other workplace benefits either through collective bargaining or legislative initiative. Much of this decline can be traced to factors largely beyond the control of union institutions: structural shifts in the economy away from heavily organized sectors, the globalization and deregulation of markets, technological disruption and deskilling, and an increasingly unsympathetic political and legal establishment.

Yet, ironically, labor could do much to reverse its decline if it were willing to feminize even more. The changes that have occurred — the increase in the proportion of union members who are women and the new awareness of the gender-specific needs of women currently represented by unions — are necessary but insufficient. To move beyond its shrinking base and organize the 87 percent of working women outside its ranks (Johnson 1995), labor must be willing to recognize itself as a gendered institution whose very structures and institutional forms must be feminized. The labor movement as we know it today was created to meet the needs of a male, factory work force. If it is to appeal to women and in particular to the majority of women who work in service occupations, it must rethink its fundamental assumptions about organizing and representation. Labor as an institution must be transformed to meet the needs of a transformed work force: those outside the factory gates in the restaurants, hotels, hospitals, and offices that dominate the landscape of the service society.

But some would argue that labor has been acting rationally. A movement with limited resources, it focused its effort on organizing those workers where it perceived the return to be the greatest. For the labor movement of the 1930s and 1940s, that meant targeting male workers in large industrial work sites. And, in the 1960s, as opportunities opened outside of manufacturing, labor shifted its priorities. Organizing successes in such female-dominated settings as education and public-sector clerical employment helped dispel long-held beliefs that women were "unorganizable." Academic writings helped undermine remaining prejudice. Surveys revealed that women favored unions more than men and that this sympathy translated into more frequent union election victories (Bronfenbrenner n.d.; Kochan 1979).[6]

A new myth, however, has replaced the old. The old idea that women were unorganizable has now been superseded by the unsubstantiated notion that certain kinds of jobs (almost all of which are female-dominated) are unorganizable. The reasoning here is circular. The sectors of the work force that are the least organized have certain identifiable characteristics, particularly in the private sector. The service industries — for example, business services, retail trade, and personal services — are disproportionately nonunion when compared to the goods sector: 12 percent as opposed to 34 percent. Only 7 percent of part-time workers belonged unions in 1993; full-timers enjoyed 18 percent organization (U.S. Department of Labor 1994: 248). The figures contrasting all nonstandard employees (those working on a part-time, part-year, contracted, temporary, or at-home basis) with standard employees (those working as full-time, full-year, on-site, regular "hires") would be even more dramatic were they available. Similarly, large work sites tend to be more unionized than small. Workers in firms with more than one hundred employees constitute by far the largest share of union members, over 80 percent for both men and women (Brown, Hamilton, and Medoff 1990; Spalter-Roth et al. 1994b: 199).

Yet these statistics really tell us more about who has *not* been organized than about who *can*. Although large numbers of those working in service-sector jobs, at small work sites, or on a part-time, part-year, or contingent basis remain unorganized, that does not mean these jobs are unorganizable. Instead, I would argue that organization lags among these groups of workers because they require different models of organization and representation. Until the distinctive characteristics of these jobs are recognized and the implications of these differences for employee representation are explored, these groups of workers, the heart of the service society, will indeed remain ipso facto "unorganizable."

## How the New Service Work Force Differs from the Old

But what is so different about the work lives of the new, so-called postindustrial work force?[7] Aren't the problems plaguing them largely the same ones that have always troubled workers? Hasn't the proposition that the postindustrial work force would be a radical departure from the old — that it would mean the disappearance of the working class and the emergence of a bright new work world comprised of white-collar technicians and professionals (Bell 1973) — been thoroughly discredited? Well, yes and no.

Currently, the fastest growing occupations are not the highly skilled and well-paid knowledge jobs but those such as food server, janitor, and retail

salesperson—jobs that are low-paid, lack promotion opportunities and benefit coverage, and exhibit high turnover (Nussbaum and Sweeney 1989; Silvestri and Lukasiewicz 1985). Given this new working poor, the wisdom has
been that the primary implications for unions of the rise of the service sector
are obvious. Workers need the basics unions have always provided: wages,
benefits, improved working conditions, and job security. I agree. These issues
will remain central for the new work force just as they were for the old. Yet
there are discontinuities as well as continuities that warrant attention.

At least four fundamental transformations are reshaping the world of
work. First of all, 90 percent of all new jobs in the last decade have been
created in the service sector. These new service jobs (as well as the "old" service
jobs) differ in significant ways from the blue-collar factory jobs that for so long
have dominated conceptions of work and the work environment. Many of
these jobs—both low-level and professional—involve personal service or interaction with a client, customer, or patient. The employment relationship is
not the classic one described by Marx nor even the conventional adversarial
one. A new third party, the customer, complicates and transforms the old
dyad. Many service workers may perceive this third party as *more* important in
determining their wages and working conditions than the employer (Cobble
1991a: 44–48; Hochschild 1983: 174–84). This attitude may prevail regardless of whether the worker's income is derived wholly from the customer (the
professional in private practice or the self-employed home cleaner), only partially so (the waiter, bartender, or cab driver), or not at all (the nurse or
teacher).

Many of these service jobs also differ from the typical manufacturing job in
that the line between employee and employer is more indistinct than in the
traditional blue-collar, mass production factory. Service-sector workers (with
the exception of government services) tend to be found not only in smaller establishments (restaurants, dental offices, retail shops) but in situations of close
personal contact with their immediate boss (for example, clerical).[8] Employee-
employer relations may be personal and collaborative rather than adversarial,
formalized, and highly bureaucratic.

Of equal importance, many nonfactory workers have always engaged in
certain "managerial" functions such as making decisions affecting the quality
and delivery of service. Since genuinely friendly service and attentive caring
cannot best be extracted through authoritarian and close supervision, many
service workers enjoy more autonomy from management. Especially in the
direct service environment, employees may work in semiautonomous, self-
managing teams where the senior member takes responsibility for organizing
the flow of work, supervising less skilled co-workers, and maintaining work
quality. This blurring of managerial and worker roles contrasts sharply with

the Taylorist model of factory relations in which efficient production was to be achieved through strict separation of managerial and worker functions, detailed work rules, narrow job classifications, and a hierarchical decision-making structure (for examples, see Armstrong 1993; Benson 1986; Cobble 1991a).

Second, in addition to the rise of service work, the new postindustrial work world appears to be increasingly characterized by the growth of what many term "nonstandard" or "atypical" employment (Cordova 1986). The dominant employment arrangement (at least since World War II) consisted of on-site employees who worked full-time, full-year, with the expectation of long-term tenure, benefits, and promotion opportunities. This traditional relationship—with its defined boundaries and its deepening mutual obligations as employees increased in seniority, pension contributions, and presumably skills and productivity—is eroding. Roughly one-quarter or more of all workers in the United States now fall outside this "standard" work arrangement: they are part-time, part-year, temporary, leased, on-call, subcontracted, off-site workers. Few put in a nine-to-five work week at the office, shop, or factory, and fewer still have long-term continuous relations with a single employer (Christensen and Murphree 1988; Plewes 1988). This "casualized" work force may not see the employer as either friend or enemy: their relationship with individual employers is brief, distant, and often mediated by a subcontractor or temporary agency.

Third, work sites themselves are changing. Economic restructuring and the growth of service work have meant the proliferation of smaller work sites and the decentralization of production. Even industrial workplaces have followed this pattern (Nussbaum and Sweeney 1989). Home-based workers—the seamstresses, legal transcribers, or business consultants toiling alone in home work sites scattered across the decentralized residential landscape—represent one aspect of this deconcentration of the work force (Boris and Daniels 1989). The "virtual office"—"not a place but a nonplace" (Patton 1993: 1) where a mobile, plugged-in corps of insurance sales agents or other technologically sophisticated professionals can "converse" periodically—is yet another indication of decentralization. In this instance, the workplace has not only shrunk but has almost disappeared as a spatially rooted entity.

Fourth, the longstanding separation between home and work is being challenged. With the phenomenal entry of women into the waged sphere beyond the home, the dissolution of the traditional family, and the aging of the work force, the problems of household production and human reproduction have become business concerns. Those juggling work and family—primarily women but some men as well—are demanding family support services such as child care and family leave. But they are also calling for a "new work ethic" and asking that the workplace adjust to family needs rather than vice versa. Why, for example, should waged work be structured along the traditional male model of a nine-to-five, five-day (or more) week? Why should intermittent, noncontinuous, and part-time work be penalized? Why should productivity gains be taken in the form of higher wages rather than shorter hours? Why should leisure or retirement years all be taken in one's sixties — a time when many women are still quite healthy and are free of child-care responsibilities? Why not, as Swedish economist Gosta Rehn suggests, provide paid time off from wage work in one's early and middle years when household responsibilities are the greatest? (AFL-CIO 1990; Hochschild 1989; Howe 1977; Schor 1991; for Rehn's ideas see Ratner 1979: 427–28). When the *New York Times* can report that 59 percent of women and 32 percent of men would give up a day's pay for a day of free time (Kerr 1991), what Carmen Sirianni (1988) has called "the politics of time" must be given more attention.

## Reconceiving Collective Representation

But in what ways is factory unionism, based as it is on the male-dominated, blue-collar industrial plant, a poor "fit" for today's work force? For one, with the advent of a female-dominated work force and the changed relation between home and work, the bargaining agenda of the labor movement must shift to incorporate the needs of these workers. Demands for child care and paid parental leaves must be joined to those that question the male model of work with its presumption of continuous, full-time work made possible by a stay-at-home, supportive spouse (for examples, see Briskin and McDermott 1993 or Cobble 1993).

Of equal importance is the need to rethink the very assumptions embedded in the institutional practices of a unionism centered on the factory workplace. Under the New Deal/post–New Deal framework of labor relations, both labor and management accepted certain Taylorist principles of work organization. These premises were inscribed in governmental labor policy and incorporated into numerous contracts governing the behavior of employers and employees. Yet Taylorist notions of strict and clear demarcations between employee and employer and of a single, one-dimensional adversarial relation between worker and boss are inappropriate to the service and white-collar work world with its heightened personalism, its blurring of employer-employee roles, and its concern with the service encounter as much as the boss-employee relation. Union campaigns based merely on an antiboss message may have little appeal, for example.

Similarly, the factory model of labor relations in which management retains full authority over the design and organization of work and employees are denied any control over quality, work organization, or standards for worker competency may not be attractive to the new work force. The service worker is on the front lines of the feedback loop. Of necessity, poor service is as much their concern as it is management's. Indeed, for many service workers, the quality of service they provide and the amount of control they exert over the service interaction is as central to their financial security as to their dignity and job satisfaction. Preserving the intrinsic rewards of the service encounter — seeing the patient's health improve, humoring a group of hungry, irritable diners, calming a distraught three-year-old — must be seen as a critical aspect of employee representation. Improving the quality of the service relationship may be as important to lessening service worker exploitation and alienation as transforming their relationship to management.

The unionism of the 1930s also assumed a long-term, continuous, on-site, and full-time commitment to a single employer — what I have termed its fundamentally "work-site" orientation (Cobble 1991a). The long, drawn-out elections required for union recognition; the small, site-based bargaining units of full-time employees certified by the National Labor Relations Board (NLRB); and the tying of union benefits to long-term tenure with a single employer — all these aspects of unionism fit poorly if at all with the changed employment structures of the new work world. Organizing and representing workers on a site-by-site basis, for example, is problematic not only for those who are mobile or contingent, but for those employed at small work sites or who lack work sites at all. A representational system based on employee ties to an individual work site when work sites are mobile or nonexistent is doomed to fail.

## Signs of Change:
### The Emergence of New Models

A number of unions have begun rethinking traditional models. By devising new agendas and representational models that are suited to those long thought unorganizable, these unions are calling into question the notion that unionism is outmoded in a service society. In the following section, I will describe the emergence of this new-style unionism by looking at innovative union campaigns among a range of service workers — clericals, nurses, waitresses, flight attendants, janitors, and home health-care workers. I will conclude by discussing the kinds of changes in public policy that would facilitate the emergence of these new and other alternative models.

The Harvard Union of Clerical and Technical Workers (HUCTW) is one of the best examples of a union that is attuned to the particular needs of the workers it seeks to represent (see Eaton, Chapter 12). The union reflects its female-dominated, service-worker constituency not only in its bargaining agenda but in the actual institutional structures it has built. Kris Rondeau, one of the lead organizers of HUCTW, proclaims the approach "a feminine style of organizing" (Hoerr 1993). It is also a "style of organizing" that reflects the occupational work culture and concerns of clerical employees.

As epitomized in their slogan "You don't have to be anti-Harvard to be pro-union," the Harvard organizers eschewed an antiboss, antiemployer campaign. They assumed that clerical workers cared about the enterprise in which they worked and about the quality of the service they delivered. Part of the role of the union would be improve the services clericals offered and to enhance the reputation of the university (Hurd 1993).

Harvard clerical workers also rejected Taylorist principles of top-down, bureaucratic decision-making and of strict demarcation between labor and management. They created an inclusive, democratic unionism that offered workers an opportunity for participating in decisions affecting them. Their grass-roots, bottom-up approach to union organizing relied upon personal, face-to-face contact rather than mimeos, leaflets, and letters. The union was about creating relationships among workers, not convincing them of a particular message. Indeed, the organizers consciously avoided developing specific goals or demands for the organization before the majority of workers belonged. Instead, they emphasized open-ended concerns such as dignity, recognition of the value of clerical services, and democratic decision-making in the workplace. In Rondeau's words, "we didn't organize against the employer. Our position was that the employer was irrelevant. It didn't matter how the employer acted, what our working conditions were like, or what our pay or benefits were. Our goals were simply self-representation, power, and participation" (Green 1988: 5; Oppenheim 1991–92).

Similarly, once HUCTW secured recognition in 1988 and began negotiations with Harvard, the union insisted on a nontraditional approach to collective bargaining and workplace governance. Collective bargaining sessions took place in the style of the Polish Solidarity negotiations, with large numbers of small teams grouped around tables, working out compromises on specific issues. Collective bargaining also involved, according to Rondeau, "many initial days where our people simply told their life stories. You see, management needed to know the realities of our lives and to know that our lives were as important as theirs" (Rondeau 1991). The distinctions between work and family, between the personal and technical, between labor and management, were being dissolved.

The first round of negotiations produced significant wage gains for clericals, new child-care and family-leave policies, and a decidedly nontraditional form of workplace governance. Instead of the older industrial model of problem-solving in which management takes responsibility for productivity, quality, and discipline, the HUCTW-Harvard agreement called for an elaborate system of joint committees. These committees would resolve disputes between workers and supervisors and recommend improvements in service delivery and working conditions (Hoerr 1993; Hurd 1993).

Some academic and union commentators view the involvement of unions in these kinds of participatory cooperative structures as a sign of declining militance and union weakness. The Harvard model suggests otherwise. It demonstrates that militance and employee solidarity need not be based on unwavering opposition to management. The union combined adversarial and cooperative approaches (Hurd 1993). Their collective bargaining agreement, based on "principle rather than rules," points to how worker rights can be protected and enhanced without rigid rules and strict boundaries between labor and management, boss and worker (Hoerr 1993). In short, their more flexible, open-ended, and "cooperative" structures enhanced their power vis-à-vis management. By creating structures that encouraged clerical worker involvement, the union forged an organization in which commitment and creativity flourished. Their faith in the power, competency, and skill of the membership paid off. Within a short time after contract implementation, front-line supervisors wanted a return to the traditional, rules-bound contract. With it, they felt they had some protection from vocal, opinionated, and persuasive employees who in many cases had better ideas about how to run the university than management.

The unions and associations that represent female-dominated professions such as nurses, teachers, and social workers also have eschewed certain aspects of the factory model of unionism. Before the spread of collective bargaining in the 1960s, the professional associations in this sector focused on what they defined as "professional concerns": status, control over workplace decisions affecting the worker-client relation, ability to set standards for competence, and the overall health of the enterprise or sector. Gradually, these organizations shifted their emphasis to more traditional union matters: salaries, benefits, seniority rights, and job protection. They also dropped their opposition to such confrontational union tactics as strikes and collective bargaining (Brooks 1971; Murphy 1990).

Yet, as Charles Kerchner and Douglas Mitchell (1988) observe for teacher unions, many are now moving toward a "third stage of unionism" in which they are as concerned with the welfare of the overall educational system and with meeting the needs of their clients as with protecting their own interests as employees. Indeed, the strongest organizations for female professionals may be those who extract the best of both the professional association and collective bargaining traditions and meld them into a new amalgam that will fit the particular needs of women service professionals.

In her work on nurses, for example, Pat Armstrong (1993) argues that, taken separately, neither the male model of professionalism nor traditional collective bargaining unionism "neatly fits" the needs of nurses. The male model of medical professionalism preached a "scientific paradigm with a considerable amount of specialization, organized in a hierarchical fashion with doctors on the top, and focused on treatment rather than care." Nursing was based on "alternative principles" (Armstrong 1993: 309). Similarly, the unionism that many nurses embraced by the 1970s offered them advantages, but it also excluded "management" nurses, ignored the regulation of professional conduct, and tended toward adversarial, hierarchical bargaining structures. Armstrong (1993) maintains that nurses care about "retaining the particular character of nursing work, about ethics, and about a commitment to care" (p. 311). In her view, a reconceived nurses organization would concern itself with preserving the "ethic of care" as well as the status of the occupation. It would build on the best of the professional traditions — its concern for "collegial participation, individual rights, and for influencing public policy," without abandoning the union emphasis on "equity, collective rights, and improving conditions of work and pay" (Armstrong 1993: 320).

## Waitresses and Occupational Unionism

Nonprofessional, or "blue-collar," service workers also have relied upon models of unionism quite unlike the industrial or factory model.[9] From the turn of the century to the 1960s, for example, waitresses practiced a surprisingly effective form of unionism that I have termed "occupational unionism." Beginning in 1900 with the founding of the Seattle waitresses local, waitresses established all-female unions and joined mixed culinary locals of waiters, cooks, and bartenders in numerous communities across the country. Affiliated almost exclusively with the Hotel Employees and Restaurant Employees (HERE), these food service locals survived the pre–New Deal period intact and experienced unprecedented growth in the 1930s and 1940s. By the end of the 1940s, union waitresses had expanded their ranks to nearly a fourth of the trade nationally, and in union strongholds such as San Francisco, New York, and Detroit, a majority of food servers worked under union contract (Cobble 1991a; 1991b).

For waitresses, craft or occupational identity was one of the prime elements of their work culture and overall world view. (Armstrong [1993] has noted a similar orientation for nurses, terming it their "vocational commitment" [p. 312]). The unions built by waitresses reflected this emphasis on protecting and advancing the interests of the occupation. They sought not only to enhance wages, provide job security, and other economic benefits but to improve the image and standing of the occupation. Although society at large and their culinary union "brothers" thought otherwise, waitresses argued that their work required skill and was worthy of being considered, in the words of Chicago waitress leader Elizabeth Maloney, "a real trade by which any girl might be proud to earn her living" (Franklin 1913: 36).

Like professional associations, waitress unions devised entrance standards for their trade, oversaw training, developed guidelines for acceptable work performance, and took responsibility for enforcing those standards at the workplace. The union controlled the selection of supervisors (they had to be union members), and union members could be brought up before their peers when infractions of work rules occurred. Wayward members might be fined and in some cases removed from their jobs. Waitresses themselves policed these standards and meted out the appropriate discipline (Cobble 1991a; 1991b).

Locals held trials in which members accused by employers of inattention to duty were brought before their sister waitresses. One such trial, held before the executive board of the San Francisco local in 1951, for example, involved "the trouble at Jeanettes with a customer." The waitress, appearing in her own defense, said she had been "very busy working her station . . . and [only] threw her tray at the customer . . . after he called her a slob." As it was her first offense, the waitress escaped with a warning and a lecture on handling offensive customers (Hotel Employees and Restaurant Employees 1951).

This concern for what I have termed "peer management" makes the occupational unionism of the past a potentially useful model for organizing and representing service workers today, both of the nonprofessional as well as the professional and technical rank. A unionism that emphasized occupational identity and shouldered responsibility for upgrading and monitoring occupational standards would appeal to some so-called blue-collar service workers as well as to teachers and nurses. Many blue-collar service workers, like their better-paid counterparts, want an organization that assists them in improving the image of their occupation, in achieving professional recognition, and in performing their work to the best of their abilities. Organizing campaigns among restaurant workers in the high-priced, high-profit sector of food service—the traditional bastion of restaurant unionism—have suffered from a widely held view among food servers that unionization would lower performance standards and that inept, "overprotected" employees would drive away customers, hence reducing tip income (Cobble 1991b; Cobble and Merrill 1994). In an ironic reversal of its status fifty years ago, HERE membership now connotes *inferior* skill and competence.

HERE could take some steps to recover its lost traditions of peer management. It could invest more in training, for example, and initiate more participatory or joint decision-making labor relations structures. But the current legal framework severely hampers the ability of unions to set entrance requirements for the trade, to oversee job performance, and to punish recalcitrant members. Almost by necessity, HERE has had to adopt a more factorylike model of employee representation.

Where HERE has continued to innovate, however, has been in responding to the particular needs of a "sexualized" service work force. Many service jobs involve not only nurturing or what Arlie Hochschild (1983) has called "emotional labor" but also the selling of one's sexual self — from flight attendants to TV news reporters to Playboy bunnies. With the backing of HERE International Vice-President Myra Wolfgang, Detroit Playboy bunnies organized into HERE in the early 1960s, and eventually HERE negotiated a national contract covering Playboy Clubs across the country. Wolfgang mounted an astute public relations campaign, attacking the Playboy philosophy as "a gross perpetuation of the idea that women should be obscene and not heard" and praising the Playboy bunnies who had guts enough to "bite back." After winning their first contract with the Detroit club in 1964 and ending the employer's "no wage" policy — the bunnies had been expected to live solely on tip income — attention turned to issues of female sexuality and attractiveness (Cobble 1991a: 128–30).

Disputes ranged from who would define "attractiveness" and its relation to competency to who would control when and in what way bunnies could "sell" their sexuality. When management fired bunnies in New York, Detroit, and other cities, claiming "loss of bunny image," the women contested the firings using the various state commissions on human rights, the EEOC, and the union grievance procedures. Although the Playboy Club publicly defined "bunny image" as having "a trim youthful figure . . . [and] a vibrant and charming look," bunnies claimed that defects cited in the Playboy literature included "crinkling eyelids, sagging breasts, varicose veins, stretch marks, crepey necks, and drooping derrieres." Not all of the fired bunnies regained their jobs, but in Detroit and other cities, the arbitrator ruled in the union's favor and reinstated the "defective" bunnies. Hugh Hefner had finally been "displaced as the sole qualified beholder of bunny beauty," quipped Wolfgang (Cobble 1991a: 128–29).

What servers would wear at work was another contested issue. In national negotiations during the 1970s, HERE and the Playboy Clubs International debated just how much of the server's body would be revealed by the bunny costume. In other less publicized negotiations in the 1970s involving cocktail waitresses and "barmaids," HERE restricted employer choice of uniform, arguing in one case that the employers provide "uniforms that fit— [some employers refused to buy uniforms over a size 12] — and adequately covered all parts of the body normally covered by personal clothing" (Cobble 1991a: 131).

The issue remains very much alive today. The HERE local in Atlantic City, New Jersey, recently threatened a "pantyhose arbitration" over the sheerness of the pantyhose management required casino waitresses to wear. The waitresses preferred thicker, less sheer pantyhose because they experienced less harassment. Heavier "support" hose also were more comfortable, helped tired legs, and covered varicose veins (Cobble and Merrill 1994).

The history of flight attendant unionism is rife with similar kinds of controversies over who would define "attractiveness" and who would determine when to "use" it. Courts helped the struggling airline food servers in the 1960s and 1970s by ruling illegal certain airline practices: the bans on married women and on women over thirty. But less blatantly discriminatory policies remained in place. Since the 1950s, flight attendant unions have complained about management's control over their weight, clothing, hair style, and make-up. They also pressed for more leeway in customer-client interaction and disputed management's continuing allegiance to the notion that the customer is always right, whether belligerent, sexually overbearing, or abusive. In one recent showdown, American Airline flight attendants struck successfully for higher wages, more control over their schedules, and an end to management practices such as sending attendants home who report to work with pimples and firing workers who return incivility in kind. A mandatory "Commitment to Courtesy" class in which instructors divided flight attendants into small groups and assigned them to draw pictures on flip charts showing "attendants being nice" particularly galled the women, one activist explained. "People got livid" (Ciotta 1994; Kilborn 1993; Lewin 1994; Neilsen 1982; Rapport 1986).

Clearly, curtailing the abusive server-customer relationship should be an integral part of any successful service unionism. Sexual service workers have received the most attention in recent decades, in part because of the shifting legal climate defining sexual harassment in the workplace as illegal and holding employers and unions accountable. Yet service workers, from retail clerks to social service professionals, suffer not just emotional and sexual abuse but physical violence from customers, clients, and the general public. One-third of emergency room nurses, for example, are assaulted on the job each year. Indeed, the leading cause of death on the job for women is not faulty or dangerous equipment or hazardous chemicals but homicide. Forty percent of women who die on the job are murder victims, due partially to the concentration of women in retail trade and other interactive service occupations (Rosier 1994a; U.S. Department of Labor 1993).[10]

## Organizing the Contingent, Nonstandard Work Force

Aspects of occupational unionism hold promise for organizing and representing the proliferating contingent work force. Unlike the factory unionism that came to dominate in the 1930s, occupational unionism was not a work-site-oriented unionism. Occupational unionism focused on fostering ties between workers within a given occupation rather than uniting all those employed at a particular site. Occupational unionists recruited and gained union recognition on an occupational–local market basis. Once organized, they stressed employment security rather than job rights at an individual work site; they also offered portable rights and benefits. Benefits and union privileges came by virtue of membership in the occupation and were retained as workers changed employers or moved from site to site (Cobble 1991b).

An alternative to site-based unionism is essential if today's more mobile and contingent work force is to be organized. A mobile work force, whether full- or part-time, does not stay with one employer long enough to utilize the conventional election procedures and card-signing associated with NLRB-style site-based organizing. Part-time, at-home, and contracted workers are often ineligible to vote because of their more tenuous relation to the work site and to a single employer. Employees at small, individual work sites have minimum economic leverage against a multinational corporate employer or a chain-style enterprise.

Based largely on their occupational and professional ties, some groups of contingent workers have organized themselves into guilds or associations.[11] For example, home-based clericals, a group deemed inhospitable to u.    , by many, are organizing across work sites. Their associations provide critical services to their members: information about job referrals, data on the reliability of prospective employers, and training opportunities. They also function to set minimum occupational standards by making wages and working conditions a group rather than an individual decision (Christensen 1993). Although these organizations do not bargain formally with employers, they, like unions, exist to advance the interests of a group of employees. Indeed, they offer many of the same services that occupational unions provided historically.

Other nonstandard workers, notably janitors and home health-care aides, have built successful union organizations in the last decade, relying by and large on non-site-based organizing approaches. SEIU (Service Employees International Union), for example, launched its "Justice for Janitors" campaign in the early 1980s and in ten years organized thousands of cleaning workers. Currently a fifth of all janitors now belong to unions, some two hundred thousand workers (Ybarra 1994). The strategic key to their organizing victory, according to Stephen Lerner (1991), director of the Building Service Division of SEIU, was a rejection of site-by-site NLRB organizing and the substitution of a geographically based or regionwide approach. Rather than organize the individual subcontractors or cleaning vendors who hire and supervise a janitorial work force scattered across hundreds of cleaning sites in downtown office buildings, they targeted the entire industry in a particular city or region. They used civil disobedience, political pressure, community boycotts, and "shaming" publicity, going after the subcontractor's employer — mainly commercial landlords — and their tenants (Howley 1990).

Home health-care aides relied upon a similar array of nontraditional approaches. Currently the fastest growing occupational group in percentage terms, home health-care workers offer an alternative to institutionalized care, assisting the elderly and the disabled in their own homes (Kilborn 1994). Steeped in the community-based organizing approaches of the National Welfare Rights Organization, the United Farm Workers, and the Association of Community Organizations for Reform Now (ACORN), many of the leaders of the home health-care organizations brought these strategies into their labor organizing in the early 1980s. They orchestrated campaigns that embraced all home health-care aides within a particular locale and that drew upon local institutions and community leaders for support (Kelleher 1986, 1994; Mitchell 1991; Walker 1994). Some home health-care groups reached out to the clients as well, making the case that raising wages for aides would help clients maintain quality service. Since social service agencies often pay the wages of home-care aides from Medicaid and other public funds (although clients may hire and supervise their aides), clients frequently supported wage increases for their "employees." Clients did express fear, however, that unionization might lessen their control over aides (Walker 1994). By 1995, some 45,000 home health-care workers had organized in California alone, securing improved wages and benefits. Flourishing locals also exist in Chicago, New York, New Orleans, and other cities, bringing the total unionized to over 70,000 ("Homecare Workers Join SEIU" 1994; Kilborn 1995; Rosier 1994b; SEIU 1994).

Many of today's successful organizing drives among mobile, contingent workers combine this communitywide grass-roots approach with "top-down" organizing, that is, they pressure employers for voluntary recognition instead of securing recognition by winning an NLRB-conducted election of employees.[12] The work force must be solidly organized, however, since it is the workers themselves who hold demonstrations, picket, and generally make life unpleasant for nonunion employers. In the case of janitors and home health-care aides, ethnic and racial bonds as well as occupational ties helped forge and sustain solidarity. In Los Angeles, for example, where the "Justice for Janitors" campaign secured its initial critical breakthrough, four-fifths of cleaners are Hispanic, with many recent immigrants from Mexico (Pastreich 1994). Similarly, home health-care workers are overwhelmingly African American and Latina women (Kilborn 1994).

Present-day unions are turning to another technique relied upon historically by occupational unions: the use of union employment exchanges, hiring halls, or job registries. In the early 1900s, for example, waitresses in Butte, Montana, organized against the "vampire system" of high-fee employment agencies. For the next half-century, no waitress worked in Butte unless she was dispatched from the union hiring hall. The Los Angeles waitress local, founded in the 1920s, had a thriving hiring hall as late as 1967, where, according to the *Los Angeles Times*, 350 "extras" were sent out on a typical weekend (Cobble 1991a; 1991b). The local's secretary likened the hiring hall to Travelers Aid, where transient and impoverished waitresses came in search of help. "Some of them come to town with children in the car, no money, and somebody here comes up with money for a hotel room and a job" (Cobble 1991a: 138). These worker-run employment agencies bound workers together and created a structure for ongoing and positive contact with the union. Hiring halls also facilitated organizing because they offered the employer a valuable service: a steady source of trained, reliable labor.

Union-run employment agencies would appeal to today's mobile work force. Many workers desire mobility between employers and a variety of work experiences (Olesen and Katsuranis 1978: 316–38). In particular, those balancing work and family are concerned with shortened work time and flexible scheduling. Well-run agencies could provide such variety and flexibility. They could also offer high-quality benefits that would not penalize work-force intermittence, and, presumably, pay higher wages than an agency run for profit.

A number of settings appear ripe for union-run agencies. In addition to the cleaning and food service sectors mentioned, the health-care industry offers a potential site for union-run agencies. The use of temporaries in the health-care industry has burgeoned. On the one hand, this restructuring is a form of employer cost-cutting; on the other, at least among nurses, the workers have demanded more flexible schedules. The increased reliance on nurse registries has been one solution. In response, unions have negotiated protections involving the use of these commercial registries; they have also experimented with providing the employer with a unionized pool of temporary or short-term workers (Engberg 1993). In other words, through the union the nurses themselves have taken over the function of the commercial agencies.

## Reshaping Public Policy to Encourage Postindustrial Unionism(s)

The new models of unionism emerging among service workers will only be sustained at great cost and are unlikely to expand to broad sectors of the work force unless the public policy governing labor relations is reformulated. Factory unionism has been dominant in the United States since the 1930s in large part because court and legislative decisions made it difficult for other kinds of unionism to function effectively. Ironically, the industrial paradigm spread in the postwar era even as the number of workers for whom it was appropriate declined. Exceptions under the law for construction trades, garment workers, and other nonfactory unions were deleted; court and National Labor Relations Board rulings were made with the factory shop-floor foremost in mind (Cobble 1991a; 1994a). Space precludes offering a full discussion of the labor law reforms that would be necessary for the realities of women's work and of the new service economy to be recognized. A number of concerns, however, do appear paramount.

The exclusion of broad sectors of the work force from coverage under the current labor law is a crucial issue. By my conservative estimates, a third of the private-sector work force (some 32 million workers) are now explicitly exempted from exercising collective bargaining rights under the National Labor Relations Act (Cobble 1994a). Domestic and agricultural workers, the self-employed, and others were originally excluded under the Wagner Act in 1935. Later legislation and legal rulings rescinded the bargaining rights of supervisors, managers, professional employees deemed "managerial," and "confidential" employees. These workers are not defined as "employees" in part because they do not resemble blue-collar industrial workers: their work world is not "industrial," nor are they behind the Taylorist curtain, removed from all "managerial" knowledge and responsibility. The law needs to be amended to open up eligibility to this growing sector of nonfactory workers.

In addition, many workers are effectively barred from collective representation because they have nonstandard employment relations. As has been discussed, the traditional site-by-site organizing and representational system creates innumerable barriers to their participation. Although some unions have cleared these hurdles and organized janitors and home health-care workers, their continuing success and the success of subsequent groups (many without access to the resources of a national union) are tenuous without legal reform.

In particular, if a mobile, decentralized service work force is to have representational rights, unions must once again have the ability to exert many of the economic pressures on employers that were once legal. The millions of nonfactory workers — teamsters, longshoremen, waitresses, cooks, musicians, and others — who successfully organized before the 1950s relied on mass picketing, recognitional picketing (prolonged picketing with the explicit goal of gaining union recognition), secondary boycotts (putting pressure on one employer to cease doing business with another), "hot cargo" agreements (assurances from one employer that "he" will not handle or use the products of another nonunion or substandard employer), and prehire agreements (contracts covering *future* as well as current employees), all tactics now illegal under current labor law. Making them legal again would facilitate the organizing of workers from home-based legal transcribers and domestic cleaners to the millions of fast-food workers toiling for minimum wages. McDonald's, for example, is unionized in Denmark, Finland, Mexico, Australia, and other countries in large part because of the legality of secondary boycotts and other kinds of economic pressures. Unionized employees at milkshake supply centers, truckers, and printers all helped bring McDonald's to the bargaining table by refusing to produce and deliver goods to the chain (Cobble 1991a; Cobble and Merrill 1994).

Yet even when employer recognition is achieved, the small bargaining units typically decreed by the NLRB make meaningful bargaining difficult. Decentralized, firm-based bargaining fuels employer resistance by heightening the economic burdens on the few unionized employers.[13] It also demands an inordinate degree of union staff and resources. The Hotel Employees and Restaurant Employees, for example, cannot negotiate individual contracts with the thousands of independent and family-owned eating establishments that exist in even one metropolitan area.

Changes in the law would help remedy this situation. Employers who withdraw from voluntarily constituted multiemployer agreements could be penalized. Legislation could encourage the extension of collectively bargained standards to other employers on an industry, occupational, or geographical basis, as is true in Canada and many European countries.[14] Removing the restrictions on the economic weapons allowed to labor also would encourage multiemployer and marketwide bargaining. Increasing the power of unions historically often has meant that employers — especially small employers in highly competitive markets — voluntarily sought multiemployer bargaining (for example, see Feinsinger 1949).

These fairly specific recommendations would do much to facilitate new forms of employee representation. On the most fundamental level, however, the framework of our current labor relations system is in need of wholesale reconceptualization. Fully integrating the realities of women's work and of service work into labor relations theory and policy would cause a reevaluation of the most basic premises upon which our labor law and institutional practice rely. The male worker and the factory shop floor must be dislodged as the basis upon which generalizations are made. The work lives and work needs of the new majority must be seen not as deviant or as belonging to a special interest group but as the norm, as expressive of the dominant reality.

History tells us that diversity is not new. People have long done many different kinds of work, and the environment in which that work has taken place has also been diverse. Over its century and a half of existence, the American labor movement has accommodated that diversity, as the variable practices of representation among waitresses, teachers, janitors, construction workers, and others attest. The labor movement must once again think in terms of multiple and competing forms of unionism. The test of unionism in the twenty-first-century service society will be whether it can recover and extend that tradition of multiple unionism.

## NOTES

1. The most frequently noted aspect of the new work force is its multiethnic, multiracial, and female character. Minorities will comprise close to a fourth of the work force by the year 2000, with the greatest increases posted by Hispanics and Asians. Women currently make up 46% of waged workers and may be half by the end of the century (AFL-CIO 1990). Yet, as I argue herein, the new work force also is defined by the nature of the jobs they do.

2. A number of commentators have called for models of unionism that move beyond the industrial or factory model of the 1930s. See Armstrong (1993), Heckscher (1988), O'Grady (1992), and my own work on occupational unionism (Cobble 1991a; 1991b; 1994a). Although no agreement has emerged on which alternative models hold the greatest promise, a consensus of sorts has been reached: the issue is no longer whether new models are needed but what form these new models should take.

3. See Cobble (1994b) for a fuller discussion of the postwar feminization of unions and for documentation on the gender-conscious activities of women trade unionists in this period.

4. Although earlier feminist literature on the relation between women and unions judged unions harshly (Hartmann 1976; Kessler-Harris 1975), more recent evaluations see unions as more flexible institutions and judge their impact on women workers as beneficial (Milkman 1993; Spalter-Roth, Hartmann, and Collins 1994b).

5. In 1994, for example, women union members earned $130 a week more than nonunion women ($504 versus $374) and union men earned $118 more than nonunion men ($608 versus $490). Unionization also raises the wages of African American and Hispanic women and men more than those of whites (Oravec 1994).

6. Kochan's 1979 findings that 40 percent of women would vote for a union if given the

chance (as compared to only 33 percent for all nonunion workers) has been confirmed by other, more recent research (Kruse and Schur 1992). Bronfenbrenner's (n.d.) analysis of AFL-CIO organizing data revealed that unions won 59% of elections in units with "a substantial majority of women" and 33% where women comprised less than half of the unit.

7. The following section draws heavily upon Cobble (1993: 13–16).

8. According to Wial's (1993) calculations, the average service-producing establishment has about 13 workers; the average manufacturing about 51. In the private sector, women are much more likely than men to work for small firms and at work sites with fewer people (Brown et al. 1990: 1–15).

9. The first three paragraphs of this section draw on Cobble (1991b).

10. In response to increasing workplace violence, some unions petitioned for a federal standard on workplace violence under the Occupational Safety and Health Act; others have pushed for laws requiring retail stores to improve lighting, install surveillance cameras, and provide immediate 911 access (Rosier 1994).

11. Despite high job turnover, the new service work force often demonstrates a strong occupational stability, moving from employer to employer yet remaining in the occupation for a long time (Butler and Skipper 1983). Many carry job skills from site to site, encouraging an investment and identity with their occupation although not with an individual employer.

12. Although the law restricts union activities in this regard, some locals won a form of "prehire" agreement (termed "Recognition Process Agreements") from individual vendors in which the vendors promised organizers access to work sites, neutrality throughout the union campaign, and recognition of the union once a majority of workers signed cards. These campaigns have sometimes lasted upwards of five years or more, draining the limited resources of these fledgling locals (Gallagher 1994; Kelleher 1986).

13. Employers in the United States, as Jacoby (1991) observes, are "exceptional" in their resistance to unionism. In part, their antagonism is based on strongly held cultural notions of "management rights" that presumably flow from property ownership. But additionally, the anti-unionism of U.S. employers is fueled by the higher economic costs of being unionized in the United States. The wage gap between unionized and non-unionized employers is higher in the United States than in many other countries, for example, and the unionized sector in the United States is small and often competes with a large number of nonunionized firms.

14. For the Canadian system of sectoral bargaining as it exists and is being proposed, see Fudge (1993). The extension of prevailing wage legislation to sectors other than the construction industry would establish a floor below which wages and benefits could not fall and lower the union premium for unionized employers. Prevailing wage legislation requires that all employers in an area pay a rate equal to that prevailing in the area among similar employers. For the first time in 1994, AFSCME, working with a church-based community organization in Baltimore, succeeded in passing a prevailing wage law in Baltimore that required "a living wage" for all workers employed on service contracts by the city (Bureau of National Affairs 1995).

## REFERENCES

AFL-CIO, Department of Economic Research. 1990. *American Workers in the 1990s: Who We Are . . . How Our Jobs Will Change*. Washington, DC: AFL-CIO.

Armstrong, Patricia. 1993. "Professions, Unions, or What?: Learning from Nurses." In Linda Briskin and Patricia McDermott, eds., *Women Challenging Unions* (pp. 304–21). Toronto: University of Toronto Press.

Bell, Daniel. 1973. *The Coming of Post-Industrial Society.* New York: Basic Books.

Benson, Susan Porter. 1986. *Counter Cultures: Saleswomen, Managers, and Customers in American Department Stores, 1890–1940.* Urbana: University of Illinois Press.

Blum, Linda M. 1991. *Between Feminism and Labor: The Significance of the Comparable Worth Movement.* Berkeley: University of California Press.

Boris, Eileen, and Cynthia Daniels. 1989. *Homework: Historical and Contemporary Perspectives on Paid Labor at Home.* Urbana: University of Illinois Press.

Briskin, Linda, and Patricia McDermott, eds., 1993. *Women Challenging Unions: Feminism, Democracy, and Militancy.* Toronto: University of Toronto Press.

Bronfenbrenner, Kate. n.d. "Successful Union Strategies for Winning Certification Elections and First Contracts: Report to Union Participants, Part 1: Organizing Survey Results." Unpublished paper.

Brooks, Thomas R. 1971. *Toil and Trouble: A History of American Labor.* New York: Delacorte Press.

Brown, Charles, James Hamilton, and James Medoff. 1990. *Employers Large and Small.* Cambridge, MA: Harvard University Press.

Bureau of National Affairs. 1995. "Special Report: Low-Wage Workers—AFSCME, Church Group Sponsor Workers' Organization in Baltimore." *Daily Labor Report 1* (January 3).

Butler, Suellen, and James Skipper. 1983. "Working the Circuit: An Explanation of Employee Turnover in the Restaurant Industry." *Sociological Spectrum* 3: 19–33.

Christensen, Kathleen E. 1993. "Reevaluating Union Policy toward White-Collar Home-Based Work." In Dorothy Sue Cobble, ed., *Women and Unions: Forging a Partnership* (pp. 246–59). Ithaca: Cornell University ILR Press.

Christensen, Kathleen E., and Mary Murphree. 1988. "Introduction." In Kathleen E. Christensen and Mary Murphree, eds., *Flexible Workstyles: A Look at Contingent Labor* (Conference Summary) (pp. 1–4). Washington, DC: U.S. Department of Labor, Women's Bureau.

Ciotta, Rose. 1994. "A Perfect Strike: A Women's Union Flexes Its Muscle." *MS* (March/April): 88–90.

Cobble, Dorothy Sue. 1994a. "Making Postindustrial Unionism Possible." In Sheldon Friedman et al., eds., *Restoring the Promise of American Labor Law* (pp. 285–302). Ithaca: Cornell University ILR Press.

———. 1994b. "Recapturing Working-Class Feminism: Union Women in the Postwar Era." In Joanne Meyerowitz, ed., *Not June Cleaver* (pp. 57–83). Philadelphia: Temple University Press.

———. 1993. "Remaking Unions for the New Majority." In Dorothy Sue Cobble, ed., *Women and Unions: Forging a Partnership* (pp. 3–23). Ithaca: Cornell University ILR Press.

———. 1991a. *Dishing It Out: Waitresses and Their Unions in the Twentieth Century.* Urbana: University of Illinois Press.

———. 1991b. "Organizing the Postindustrial Work Force: Lessons from the History of Waitress Unionism." *Industrial and Labor Relations Review* 44(3): 419–36.

Cobble, Dorothy Sue, and Michael Merrill. 1994. "Collective Bargaining in the Hospitality Industry in the 1980s." In Paula Voos, ed., *Contemporary Collective Bargaining in the Private Sector* (pp. 447–89). Ithaca: Cornell University ILR Press.

Cordova, Efren. 1986. "From Full-Time Wage Employment to Atypical Employment: A Major Shift in the Evolution of Labour Relations?" *International Labour Review* 125(6): 641–57.

Cowell, Susan. 1993. "Family Policy: A Union Approach." In Dorothy Sue Cobble, ed., *Women and Unions: Forging a Partnership* (pp. 115–28). Ithaca: Cornell University ILR Press.

Engberg, Elizabeth. 1993. "Union Responses to the Contingent Work Force." In Dorothy Sue Cobble, ed., *Women and Unions: Forging a Partnership* (pp. 163–75). Ithaca: Cornell University ILR Press.

Feinsinger, Nathan. 1949. *Collective Bargaining in the Trucking Industry*. Philadelphia: University of Pennsylvania Press.

Franklin, S. M. 1913. "Elizabeth Maloney and the High Calling of the Waitress." *Life and Labor* 3(February): 36–40.

Freeman, Richard B., and Jonathan S. Leonard. 1987. "Union Maids: Unions and the Female Work Force." In Clair Brown and Joseph Pechman, eds., *Gender in the Workplace* (pp. 189–212). Washington, DC: Brookings Institution.

Freeman, Richard B., and Joel Rogers. 1993. "Who Speaks for Us? Employee Representation in a Non-Union Labor Market." In Bruce K. Kaufman and Morris E. Kleiner, eds., *Employee Representation: Alternatives and Future Directions* (pp. 13–79). Madison, WI: Industrial Relations Research Association.

Fudge, Judy. 1993. "The Gendered Dimension of Labour Law: Why Women Need Inclusive Unionism and Broader-Based Bargaining." In Linda Briskin and Patricia McDermott, eds., *Women Challenging Unions* (pp. 231–48). Toronto: University of Toronto Press.

Gallagher, Michael. 1994. Telephone interview with the Campaign Director, SEIU Local 509, Cambridge, Massachusetts, conducted by Jeanine Nagrod, October 17.

Green, James. 1988. "Union Victory: An Interview with Kristine Rondeau." *Democratic Left* (September–October): 4–6.

Hartmann, Heidi. 1976. "Capitalism, Patriarchy, and Job Segregation by Sex." *Signs* 1(3): 137–69.

Heckscher, Charles. 1988. *The New Unionism: Employee Involvement in the Changing Corporation*. New York: Basic Books.

Hochschild, Arlie. 1989. *The Second Shift: Working Parents and the Revolution at Home*. New York: Avon.

——. 1983. *The Managed Heart: Commercialization of Human Feeling*. Berkeley: University of California Press.

Hoerr, John. 1993. "Solidaritas at Harvard." *The American Prospect* 14(Summer): 67–82.

"Homecare Workers Join SEIU." 1994. *California AFL-CIO News* 37(November 11): 2.

Hotel Employees and Restaurant Employees. 1951. "Local 48 Executive Board Minutes," February 13. Local 2 Files, San Francisco.

Howe, Louise. 1977. *Pink-Collar Workers: Inside the World of Women's Work*. New York: G. P. Putnam's Sons.

Howley, John. 1990. "Justice for Janitors: The Challenge of Organizing in Contract Services." *Labor Research Review* 15(Spring): 61–72.

Hurd, Richard. 1993. "Organizing and Representing Clerical Workers: The Harvard Model." In Dorothy Sue Cobble, ed., *Women and Unions: Forging a Relationship* (pp. 316–36). Ithaca: Cornell University ILR Press.

Jacoby, Sanford M. 1991. "American Exceptionalism Revisited: The Importance of Management." In Sanford M. Jacoby, ed., *Master to Managers: Historical and Comparative Perspectives on American Employers* (pp. 173–200). New York: Columbia University Press.

Johnson, Candice. 1995. "Changing Face of Labor Reflects New Horizons for Organizing." *AFL-CIO News*, January 9, p. 1.

Kelleher, Keith. 1994. Telephone interview with the Head Organizer, SEIU Local 880, Chicago, conducted by Jeanine Nagrod, October 17.

———. 1986. "ACORN Organizing and Chicago Homecare Workers." *Labor Research Review* 8 (Spring): 33–45.

Kerchner, Charles Taylor, and Douglas E. Mitchell. 1988. *The Changing Idea of a Teachers' Union*. New York: The Falmer Press.

Kerr, Peter. 1991. "Tempus Fugit, But You Can Buy It." *The New York Times*, October 10, pp. D8–D10.

Kessler-Harris, Alice. 1975. "Where Are the Organized Women Workers?" *Feminist Studies* 3: 92–110.

Kilborn, Peter T. 1995. "Union Gets the Lowly to Sign Up: Home Care Aides Are Fresh Target." *The New York Times*, November 21, p. A10.

———. 1994. "Home Health Care Is Gaining Appeal." *The New York Times*, August 30, p. A14.

———. 1993. "Strikers at American Airlines Say the Objective Is Respect." *The New York Times*, November 22, p. A12.

Kochan, Thomas. 1979. "How American Workers View Labor Unions." *Monthly Labor Review* 102: 25.

Kruse, Douglas L., and Lisa A. Schur. 1992. "Gender Differences in Attitudes toward Unions." *Industrial and Labor Relations Review* 46 (October): 89–102.

Lerner, Stephen. 1991. "Let's Get Moving: Labor's Survival Depends on Organizing Industry-Wide for Justice and Power." *Labor Research Review* 18 (2): 1–16.

Lewin, Tamar. 1994. "USAir Agrees to Lift Rules on the Weight of Attendants." *The New York Times*, April 8, p. A14.

Milkman, Ruth. 1993. "Union Responses to Work Force Feminization in the U.S." In Jane Jenson and Rianne Mahon, eds., *The Challenge of Restructuring: North American Labor Movements Respond* (pp. 226–50). Philadelphia: Temple University Press.

Milkman, Ruth, ed. 1985. *Women, Work, and Protest: A Century of U.S. Labor History*. Boston: Routledge & Kegan Paul.

Mitchell, Marsha. 1991. "Jackson Rallies with LA's Home Care Workers." *Los Angeles Sentinel*, October 24, sec. A, pp. 1–2.

Murphy, Majorie. 1990. *Blackboard Unions: The AFT and the NEA, 1900–1980*. Ithaca: Cornell University Press.

Neilsen, Georgia Painter. 1982. *From Sky Girl to Flight Attendant: Women and the Making of a Union*. Ithaca: Cornell University ILR Press.

Nussbaum, Karen, and John Sweeney. 1989. *Solutions for the New Work Force*. Cabin John, MD: Seven Locals Press.

O'Grady, John. 1992. "Beyond the Wagner Act, What Then?" In Daniel Drache, ed., *Getting on Track: Social Democratic Strategies for Ontario* (pp. 153–69). Montreal: McGill-Queen's University.

Olesen, Virginia, and Frances Katsuranis. 1978. "Urban Nomads: Women in Temporary Clerical Services." In Ann Stromberg and Shirley Harkess, eds., *Women Working: Theories and Facts in Perspective* (pp. 316–38). Mountain View, CA: Mayfield Press.

Oppenheim, Lisa. 1991–92. "Women's Ways of Organizing: A Conversation with AFSCME Organizers Kris Rondeau and Gladys McKenzie." *Labor Research Review* 18(Fall–Winter): 45–60.

Oravec, John R. 1994. "Membership and Union Advantage Moving Ahead." *AFL-CIO News* 39(February 21): 1–2.

Pastreich, Manny. 1994. Telephone interview conducted by Jeanine Nagrod, September 29 and October 4.

Patton, Phil. 1993. "The Virtual Office Becomes Reality." *The New York Times*, October 28, sec. C, pp. 1, 4.

Plewes, Thomas. 1988. "Understanding the Data on Part-Time and Temporary Employment." In *Flexible Workstyles: A Look at Contingent Labor* (Conference Summary) (pp. 9–13). Washington, DC: U.S. Department of Labor, Women's Bureau.

Rapport, Sara. 1986. "'I'm Cheryl—Fly Me to Court': Flight Attendants vs. the Airlines, 1960–1976." Unpublished seminar paper. Rutgers University History Department.

Ratner, Ronnie, ed. 1979. *Equal Employment Policy for Women*. Philadelphia: Temple University Press.

Rondeau, Kris. 1991. "Organizing Harvard Workers." Lecture given at the University College Labor Education Association Annual Conference, Miami, April.

Rosier, Sharolyn A. 1994a. "Assaults at the Workplace." *AFL-CIO News*, December 12, p. 5.

———. 1994b. "Home Health Care Workers Look to Unions." *AFL-CIO News* 39(October 17): 2.

Schor, Julie. 1991. *The Overworked American: The Unexpected Decline of Leisure*. New York: Basic Books.

Service Employees International Union (SEIU). 1994. "Memo on Home Health-Care Locals." Unpublished data.

Silvestri, George, and John Lukasiewicz. 1985. "Occupational Employment Projections: The 1985–1995 Outlook." *Monthly Labor Review* 108(November): 42–57.

Sirianni, Carmen. 1988. "Self-Management of Time: A Democratic Alternative." *Socialist Review* (October–December): 5–56.

Spalter-Roth, Roberta, Heidi Hartmann, and Nancy Collins. 1994a. "What Do Unions Do for Women?" Lecture given at the Conference on Women and Labor Law Reform sponsored by the Women's Bureau, U.S. Department of Labor, Washington, DC, October.

Spalter-Roth, Roberta, Heidi Hartmann, and Nancy Collins. 1994b. "What Do Unions Do for Women?" In Sheldon Friedman et al., eds., *Restoring the Promise of American Labor Law* (pp. 193–206). Ithaca: Cornell University ILR Press.

U.S. Department of Labor, Bureau of Labor Statistics. 1994, January. *Employment and Earnings*. Washington, DC: U.S. Government Printing Office.

———. 1993. *First National Census of Fatal Occupational Injuries Reported by BLS*. Washington, DC: U.S. Government Printing Office.

Walker, Harold. 1994. Telephone interview with the Lead Organizer, Home Care Division, SEIU Local 250, San Francisco, conducted by Jeanine Nagrod, November 3.

Wial, Howard. 1993. "The Emerging Organizational Structure of Unionism in Low-Wage Services." *Rutgers Law Review* 45(Summer): 671–738.

Ybarra, Michael. 1994. "Janitor's Union Uses Pressure and Theatrics to Expand Its Ranks." *Wall Street Journal*, March 21, pp. A1–A6.

# Contributors

**Nicole Woolsey Biggart** is Professor of Management and Sociology at the University of California, Davis, where her research concerns issues in economic and organizational sociology. Her book *Charismatic Capitalism: Direct Selling Organizations in America* (Chicago: Chicago University Press, 1989) analyzes the economic uses of social relations in the direct selling industry. She has written about economy and society in the context of business networks in Asia, examining the relation between Asian social structures and economic activity. Her next project, which will focus on rotating savings and credit associations in developing and migrant communities, will examine how people use their social collateral to build financial institutions.

**Dorothy Sue Cobble** is Associate Professor at Rutgers University, where she teaches labor studies, history, and women's studies. Her books include *Dishing It Out: Waitresses and Their Unions in the Twentieth Century* (1991), which won the 1992 Herbert A. Gutman Award, and an edited anthology *Women and Unions: Forging a Partnership* (1993). Her essays have appeared in *Dissent, Feminist Studies, Industrial and Labor Relations Review, Labor History*, and other journals.

**Susan C. Eaton** is a writer and researcher affiliated with Radcliffe College's Public Policy Institute, and is also pursuing doctoral studies at Sloan School of Management, Massachusetts Institute of Technology. She holds a Master's in Public Administration (MPA) from the Kennedy School of Government. Eaton worked for twelve years as a union organizer, negotiator, trainer, and manager for the Service Employees International Union (SEIU), AFL-CIO,

CLC. She researches service-sector work, union innovation, nursing home work organization, work-family balance, and clerical work. Her previous publications include the 1993 International Labor Organization *Report on Women Workers, Unions, and Industrial Sectors in North America* and "Women in Trade Union Leadership" in G. Adler and D. Suarez, eds., *Union Voices* (Albany: State University of New York Press, 1993).

**Greta Foff Paules** is a cultural anthropologist who holds a doctorate from Princeton University. Her first book, *Dishing It Out: Power and Resistance among Waitresses in a New Jersey Restaurant* (Philadelphia: Temple University Press, 1991), is an ethnographic analysis of resistance strategies among waitresses.

**Linda Fuller** teaches sociology at the University of Oregon. Some of her research on the organization and control of paid work has appeared in her *Work and Democracy in Socialist Cuba* (Philadelphia: Temple University Press, 1992) and in "The Socialist Labor Process and the GDR Revolution" (forthcoming in *International Journal of Labor and Working Class History*). She has recently completed a manuscript on paid work, class, and workers' politics during the 1989–90 revolution in the German Democratic Republic.

**Evelyn Nakano Glenn** is Professor of Women's Studies and Ethnic Studies at the University of California, Berkeley. She has written extensively on the intersection of race and gender and on work-technology issues. She is the author of *Issei, Nisei, War Bride* (Philadelphia: Temple University Press, 1986), and editor (with Grace Chang and Linda Forcey) of *Mothering: Ideology, Experience, and Agency*. Her current research centers on the race-gender construction of labor and citizenship.

**Robin Leidner** is Associate Professor of Sociology at the University of Pennsylvania. Her research on interactive service work is reported more fully in *Fast Food, Fast Talk: Service Work and the Routinization of Everyday Life* (Berkeley: University of California Press, 1993). She has also published work on democracy in feminist organizations, and she is currently researching how parents find and respond to information and advice about child rearing.

**Steven H. Lopez** is a graduate student in sociology at the University of California, Berkeley. In addition to writing about potato chips, he has studied migrant farm worker organizing in the Midwest, and he has just completed (with Harley Shaiken and Isaac Mankita, under the auspices of the National Center for the Workplace) a study of new ways of organizing work in the auto industry. Currently he is beginning work on a dissertation that will compare industrial restructuring efforts in the steel industries of western Pennsylvania and the Ruhr area of Germany during the 1980s and early 1990s.

**Cameron Lynne Macdonald** is a doctoral candidate in sociology at Brandeis University. Her dissertation research examines the division of mothering labor between working mothers and their child-care providers. Her interest in the effects on U.S. workers of the shift to a service-based economy, as well as her nine years of experience working in the hotel and restaurant industries, prompted her to collaborate in the creation of this book — a collection which touches on most, but not all, of her former occupations. She teaches social theory and research methods in the program in Social Studies at Harvard University.

**Jennifer L. Pierce** is Assistant Professor of Sociology and an affiliate of the Center for Advanced Feminist Studies (CAFS) at the University of Minnesota. She is a former associate editor of *Signs: Journal of Women in Culture and Society.* Her book *Gender Trials: Emotional Lives in Contemporary Law Firms* (Berkeley: University of California Press, 1995) examines the gendered division of emotional labor in law offices by considering the experiences of paralegals and trial lawyers. She is currently co-editing, with the CAFS editorial collective, an anthology titled *Social Justice, Feminism and the Politics of Location.* She has also published articles in *American Sociological Review*, *Signs*, *Berkeley Journal of Sociology*, and *Explorations in Ethnic Studies.*

**Judith Rollins** is Professor of Africana Studies and Sociology at Wellesley College. Her book excerpted for this volume, *Between Women: Domestics and Their Employers* (Philadelphia: Temple University Press, 1985), received the Jessie Bernard Award of the American Sociological Association for its contribution to women's studies. Author of articles on the civil rights movement, domestic service, the social psychology of domination, and the American women's movement, Rollins recently published her second book, an oral history of an elderly African-American activist, *All Is Never Said: The Narrative of Odette Harper Hines* (Philadelphia: Temple University Press, 1995).

**Carmen Sirianni** teaches in Sociology and the Heller School at Brandeis University. He is Editor-in-Chief of the Civic Practices Network, an online journal that brings together innovators and educators from diverse fields to share best cases and best practices of community and workplace empowerment and civic renewal. In 1994 he served as research director of the Reinventing Citizenship Project, funded by the Ford Foundation and convened in conjunction with the Domestic Policy Council at the White House. He has been a member of the Institute for Advanced Study in Princeton and co-chair of the Labor and Industry Group at the Minda de Gunzburg Center for European Studies at Harvard. He is currently completing a book with Lewis Friedland entitled *Participatory Democracy and Civic Innovation in America*, to be published by Cambridge University Press. He has also been a visiting professor in Social Studies at Harvard, where he received the Hoopes Prize for Excellence in Teaching. He is co-editor of the Labor and Social Change series for Temple University Press.

**Vicki Smith** is Associate Professor of Sociology at the University of California, Davis. She teaches and does research in the areas of contemporary work organization, corporate restructuring, employee participation programs, and gender and race in the workplace. Her book *Managing in the Corporate Interest* (Berkeley: University of California Press, 1990) examines the effects of corporate restructuring on the labor process and on the social relations of middle managers. She has published various pieces on these topics, and currently is conducting research on flexible production and staffing practices in diverse work settings.

**Amy S. Wharton** is Associate Professor of Sociology at Washington State University. Her recent publications include "The Consequences of Caring: Exploring the Links between Women's Job and Family Emotion Work," *The Sociological Quarterly* (1995), and "Women, Work and Emotion: Managing Jobs and Family Life," in *Women, Work and Family in the United States, Europe and the Former Soviet Union*, edited by Kaisa Kauppinen-Toropainen (London: Avebury Press, 1995). Wharton's current projects include studies of gender, work, and family in the service sector and research on the construction and consequences of "difference" in workgroups.